Penguin Books
Zelda Fitzgerald

D0545722

Nancy Milford is a graduate of the University of
Michigan and received her M.A. from Columbia
University. She was a President's Fellow at
Columbia from 1967 to 1968 and taught English
there from 1968 to 1969. She now lives in
Manhattan with her husband and two children.

Nancy Milford

Zelda Fitzgerald

Penguin Books

Penguin Books Ltd, Harmondsworth,
Middlesex, England
Penguin Books Australia Ltd, Ringwood,
Victoria, Australia

First published in the U.S.A. as
Zelda: A Biography 1970
Published in Great Britain by The Bodley Head 1970
Published in Penguin Books 1974

Copyright © Nancy Winston Milford, 1970

Made and printed in Great Britain by
Hazell Watson & Viney Ltd, Aylesbury, Bucks
Set in Linotype Times

For Kenneth,
with love and thanks.

For Matthew and Jessica Kate

CONTENTS

ACKNOWLEDGEMENTS

There were many people and many sources of information that were of great help to me during the six years of research and writing of this biography. Some of them I can and will thank on these pages. But for various reasons I am not able to directly express my gratitude to others who were just as helpful. I was fortunate enough to have had certain rare privileges of research extended to me which enabled me to draw on materials previously unavailable.

If it had not been for the early encouragement and backing of Lewis Leary when I was a graduate student at Columbia University I might never have begun. I cannot thank him enough. Let me also thank Joseph V. Ridgely for his sound counsel and friendship. And William York Tindall, who, one spring when I needed it, gave me his office to work in; and John Unterecker, who read an early and somewhat informal draft of part of this manuscript.

Of the more than one hundred people I interviewed and corresponded with, I am especially indebted to Mrs Harold Ober, the late Dr John Neustadt, Mrs Sara Murphy and her husband, the late Gerald Murphy, Arthur Mizener, Judge and Mrs John Biggs, Jr, Paul McLendon, H. Dan Piper, the late Dorothy Parker, Mrs Laura Guthrie Hearne, Georges Poull, Sheilah Graham, C. Lawton Campbell, Dr Oscar Forel, Mrs Eleanor Browder Addison, the late Carl Van Vechten, and to Robert Taft for the loan of and permission to quote from Alexander McKaig's diary.

I am also grateful to people who were kind enough to share with me their impressions of the Fitzgeralds, among them: Admiral Edouard Jozan, the late Andrew Turnbull, Dame Rebecca West, Edmund Wilson, Zack Waters, Sir Shane Leslie, Mrs Bayard Turnbull, John Dos Passos, Mrs Lois Moran Young, Gilbert Seldes, Princess Lubov Troubetskoy-Egorova, Mrs Isabel Owens, Mrs Robert S. Carroll, Mrs Mary Porter, Landon Ray, Mrs Livye Hart

Ridgeway, Mrs May Steiner Coleman, Mrs H. L. Weatherby, Malcolm Cowley, Mr and Mrs Clifford Durr, Mrs C. O. Kalman, Gwinn Owens, Miss Sara Mayfield, Miss Lucy Goldthwaite, the late Leon Ruth, Fred Ball, Louis Whitfield, Mrs Isabel Amorous Palmer, Mrs John Hume Taylor, Calvin Tomkins, Mrs Paul Scott Mowrer, Mrs Helen F. Blackshear, Mme Claude Amiel, Charles Angoff, and Mr and Mrs Archibald MacLeish.

The New York Public Library has generously granted me the privilege of working in the Frederick Lewis Allen Room, and to the boys in that excellent back room, Peter Burchard, Bill Fisher, Jim Flexner, David Hawke, and Frank Lundberg, I can only say that my education was deepened and whatever art I have was sharpened by your good talk and company. I am also indebted to the Princeton University Library for extending all sorts of privileges to me during five summers of work. My thanks to Alexander P. Clark and Mrs Wanda Randall for giving so freely of their knowledge and assistance.

To Vesta Svenson who first suggested that I read Fitzgerald, to Mrs Toni Milford who offered intelligent advice, to Judith Gustafson who typed for more years than we like to recall and to Nancy Wechsler for her counsel in my behalf, my best thanks. A final note of gratitude to my editor Genevieve Young for her constant belief and her clear head.

And to the only person who was behind me the whole way, who lived with me as I lived with and tried to shape the materials of this book, *Ich bin din . . .*

Grateful acknowledgement is hereby made to the following publishers and individuals for permission to reprint the material specified:

Mrs Helen Thurber, for quotations from 'Scott in Thorns' in *Credos and Curios*, by James Thurber, published by Hamish Hamilton Ltd.

Malcolm Cowley and the *Saturday Review* for excerpts from 'A Ghost Story of the Jazz Age', 25 January 1964. Copyright 1964 by Saturday Review, Inc.

Jonathan Cape Ltd, for excerpts from *Save Me the Waltz*, by Zelda Fitzgerald.

Mrs Julie Hayden Nathan for excerpts from George Jean Nathan's unpublished letters.

Harold Matson Company, Inc., for the use of material from *That Summer in Paris*, by Morley Callaghan.

W. C. C. Publishing Company for extracts from Zelda Fitzgerald's review of *The Beautiful and Damned*, originally published in the New York *Herald Tribune*, 2 April 1922.

Charles Angoff for an excerpt from *H. L. Mencken: A Portrait from Memory*, published by Thomas Yoseloff, Inc., New York, 1956.

Charles Scribner's Sons for excerpts from: *Editor to Author: The Letters of Maxwell E. Perkins*, edited by John Hall Wheelock, and for the use of two excerpts from previously unpublished letters written by Maxwell Perkins.

PROLOGUE

Biography is the falsest of the arts.

F. SCOTT FITZGERALD, General notes to *The Last Tycoon*

When I was young in the midwest and had dreams of my own, it seemed to me a fine thing to live as the Fitzgeralds had, where every gesture had a special flair that marked it as one's own. Together they personified the immense lure of the East, of young fame, of dissolution and early death – their sepia-tinted photographs in rotogravure sections across the country: Scott, in an immaculate Norfolk jacket, gesturing nervously with a cigarette, Zelda brightly at his side, her clean wild hair brushed back from her face. But it was not her beauty that was arresting. It was her style, a sort of insolence toward life, her total lack of caution, her fearless and abundant pride. If the Fitzgeralds were ghostly figures out of an era that was gone, they had nevertheless made an impact on the American imagination that reverberated into my own generation. I wanted to know why.

In the spring of 1963, when I had just turned twenty-five, I began to gather reminiscences from people who had known the Fitzgeralds well. People who had shared a summer house, or a childhood. I remember Gerald Murphy turning to me once and saying suddenly, 'Zelda was an American value!' He said it almost in fury, as if she had eluded him until that very moment. For she was an elusive woman. She was also vulnerable and wilful and in deep hiding. Sara Murphy caught something of it in her letter to Scott written after Zelda's first breakdown, 'I think of her face so often, & so wish it had been *drawn*.... It is rather like a young Indian's face, except for the smouldering eyes. At night, I remember, if she was excited, they turned black – & impenetrable – but always full of impatience – at *something*, the world I think. She wasn't of it anyhow.... She had an inward life & feelings that I don't suppose anyone ever touched – not even you – She probably thought terribly dangerous secret thoughts ...'

What was Zelda to Scott that she haunted his fiction? What was it like to come to New York City in the spring of 1920, fresh out of Alabama, before your twentieth birthday? And marry Scott Fitzgerald, who was going to name the new decade the Jazz Age and make you the first American Flapper? I remember talking to two old men in Montgomery, Alabama, at the fiftieth reunion of Zelda's high-school graduation, about the time she had ridden down Dexter Avenue in the centre of town in a one-piece flesh-coloured knit bathing suit with her legs draped nonchalantly over the back of the rumble seat of somebody's electric. A group of boys, who were called Jelly Beans, hollered at her as she went by, and, seeing them, she stood up in the car, laughing, stretched out her arms wide and called, '*All my Jellies!*' One of the men said, 'You see, you've got to remember, to us Zelda was a ... a Kingmaker.'

Was it Zelda, then, shooting craps like Nancy Lamar in 'The Jelly Bean', tippling with the boys at Princeton and later at the Ritz Bar in Paris? How curious that the same woman who kissed men on fire escapes because she liked the shapes of their noses or the cut of their dinner jackets would also spend hours drawing Scott pictures of Gatsby, drawing him again and again until her fingers ached and until Scott could see him. Certainly we knew more about Gloria and Sally Carrol and Nicole Diver than we did about Zelda Fitzgerald.

In the summer of 1963 my husband and I travelled more than a thousand miles from New York to Baltimore and Washington, into the Smoky Mountains of Asheville, and then down deeper through the heat and pines of Georgia to Montgomery, Alabama, in search of Zelda. It was on that first trip into the Deep South that, piecemeal, I began to read the documents that are the backbone of this book. The hundreds of letters, the albums of clippings, scrapbooks, the dark-red Moroccan leather book with its wonderful array of addresses – from 'Charlie McA's bootlegger' in Manhattan and 'trick corsets' on the rue d'Alger in Paris to the peripatetic 'Ernest Hemminway, 113 Rue Notre Dame des Champs', 'Ernest Hemminway, Hotel Taube Schruns, Vorarlberg, Austria', until she finally corrects the spelling of his name and settles his address firmly: 'c/o Guaranty Trust Co.'.

Sitting up late at night in Henderson, North Carolina, in a small tourist home reading Zelda's letters to her husband moved me in a way I had never been moved before, touched something in me that before those letters had been untouched. We were not pursuing a nostalgic past, nor did the Fitzgeralds represent it to us. Rather we read those letters out loud to each other as if they had just arrived, not knowing from what terrain of their lives they had been written or what the next one would say. They were hopelessly mixed up and undated, without, in most cases, envelopes to give them dates. All the clues were internal, and were to be pieced together on other days and nights during the ensuing years. A note from Gertrude Stein would fall out thanking the Fitzgeralds for their visit – but what visit, and where? A snapshot taken in North Africa of Scott and Zelda riding camels might come next or a gold lock of Zelda's hair tied in a pink ribbon. I had somewhat innocently – if a passionate curiosity about another's life is ever innocent – entered into something I neither could nor would put down for six years, and in that quest the direction of my life was changed. Ahead of me were encounters in this country, in London, Paris, and Switzerland I could never have dreamed of, never invented.

In Montgomery, at the end of her life, disfigured by years of fighting against a recurring mental illness, Zelda would often walk out to a large ante-bellum home when the sun was strong. She had been invited to paint in the gardens whenever she liked. It was a spacious house, encircled by a fine white portico and by lush and fragrant growths of flowers. There was a cutting garden, a formal garden, and a rambling one carefully cultivated to appear wild. In the summertime the grand pieces of richly carved dark furniture were draped in white cloth, and wooden-bladed fans gently stirred the heavy air. There, in the gardens by the house, Zelda would put up her easel and paint until the sun went down. The bold southern flowers now fascinated her more than the subtle violet or the complex rose; she liked the waxy, almost artificial-looking tropical flowers, the calla lily and the large blossoms of the japonica. Once Zelda asked the lady whose gardens they were, what a *datura* meant to her. The puzzled woman replied, 'Well, it's just a pretty flower, that's all.' Zelda said nothing and continued to paint. The *datura* is also known as Angel's Trumpet because of its shapely long white flaring blossom. It is not only beautiful but highly poisonous. Years later, sitting on the portico of that house as the summer light grew dim, the woman leaned toward me and asked quietly, 'Where was she that she could not come back? Where did she go? Where?'

Writing about Montgomery, but calling it Jeffersonville, Zelda had said, 'Every place has its hours ... So in Jeffersonville there existed then, and I suppose now, a time and quality that appertains to nowhere else.' The time is of our past. The landscape is by Rousseau and something savage lurks in the extravagantly green gardens. Zelda would come full circle to her origin. She was the American girl living the American dream, and she became mad within it.

New York City   NANCY MILFORD
February, 1970

Of Lovers ruine some sad Tragedie:
I am not I, pitie the tale of me.

SIR PHILIP SIDNEY, *Astrophel and Stella*, 45

1. Southern Girl

1

If there was a Confederate establishment in the Deep South, Zelda Sayre came from the heart of it. Willis B. Machen, Zelda's maternal grandfather, was an energetic entrepreneur tough enough to endure several careers and robust enough to outlive two of his three wives. He came to Kentucky from South Carolina as a boy when the new state was still a frontier. Young Machen began his career refining iron with a partner in Lyon County; soon he was successful enough to open his own business. It failed, and he was nearly ruined; but he managed to repay his debts and begin again. He built turnpikes until a severe injury forced him to turn in a completely fresh direction, the law. He never failed again. Soon he had built up a large clientele in the south-western part of the state, and he became a member of the convention that framed the constitution of Kentucky.

He served as a state senator until the outbreak of the Civil War, at which time Kentucky, a border state, was violently embroiled in choosing sides. Although the state formally declared its allegiance to the Union, the secessionists, Machen prominent among them, set up a provisional state government. He was elected to the Confederate Congress by residents of his district and by the soldiers in the field. At the close of the war, fearing reprisals, he fled to Canada. His third wife and their young daughter Minnie joined him shortly afterward.

Machen was pardoned and returned to Kentucky. He was urged to accept the nomination for governor of the state but declined because of some confusion about his eligibility. In 1872 he was appointed to the United States Senate, in which he served for four months. At the Democratic National Convention in Baltimore in July of the same year his name was presented by the delegation from Kentucky for the Vice-Presidential nomination. It was a distinction he did not achieve.

By 1880 Machen was a powerful member of the Kentucky railroad commission and his patronage was eagerly sought. He chose to retire to his fine red-brick manor house, Mineral Mount, near Eddyville, Kentucky; it stood on three thousand acres in the fertile valley of the Cumberland River, and there he raised tobacco. The pastoral elegance of Machen's splendid home must have been somewhat diminished by the running of the Chesapeake & Ohio railroad line past the foot of the hill upon which Mineral Mount was built. Still, Machen had achieved the pinnacle of Southern society, for as both planter and lawyer he belonged to the ruling class. And it was in that atmosphere of privilege that young Minnie grew up.

In a scrapbook which Zelda kept during her girlhood there is a photograph of her mother taken when Minnie Machen was nineteen. Her curling hair is caught up in a braided bun behind her pierced ears, from which fall small jewelled earrings in the shape of flowers. It is a pretty face, which with maturity would become handsome, for it is well-boned and definite. Her nose is straight, her square chin determined-looking, and only the thinness of her lips mars a face that would otherwise have been called beautiful. Beneath the photograph is the inscription 'The Wild Lily of the Cumberland'.

Minnie was the artistic member of her family and her poems and short sketches were frequently published in local Kentucky newspapers. She was an ardent reader of fiction and poetry, and when she ran out of books to read she turned to the encyclopedia. But her dreams centred upon the stage. She had a small clear soprano voice and she played the piano nicely. Her father sent her for 'finishing' to Miss Chilton's School in Montgomery, Alabama. His good friend Senator John Tyler Morgan lived in Montgomery, and it was at a New Year's Eve ball given by the Morgans that Minnie met a nephew of Senator Morgan's, the quiet and courtly young lawyer Anthony Dickinson Sayre, whom she would eventually marry.

She was not, however, so smitten by Mr Sayre that she would relinquish a trip to Philadelphia which she had persuaded her father to allow her. She spent the winter season in Philadelphia with friends of her family, and while there she pursued her secret ambition by studying elocution. When Georgia Drew, the head of the famous Drew-Barrymore theatrical family, held a try-out for one of her plays, Minnie read for her and was offered a role in the company. Machen learned of his daughter's adventure and was outraged. He ordered her home at once, telling her that he would rather see her dead than on the stage. Minnie returned to Kentucky immediately, but she had suffered a disappointment she never forgot. Years later, with her family grown and out of her home, she shifted the story slightly, remarking to a neighbour that if she hadn't married Judge Sayre she would have had a career in the opera or on the stage; she reconciled herself by singing in the choir of the Church of the Holy Comforter, which she attended without her husband.

Anthony Sayre's family took pride in having been among the early settlers of Long Island, and they eventually came to Alabama, via New Jersey and Ohio, after the territory achieved statehood in 1819. By the time of the Ciivil War, some forty years later, their sentiments were entirely Southern.

Anthony's father founded and edited a newspaper in the rural town of Tuskegee and later moved to Montgomery, where he was editor of the *Post*. Sayre Street, which ran through the most fashionable section of Montgomery, was named in honour of Anthony's uncle, who had built the White House of the Confederacy for Jefferson Davis and who was a founder of the First Presbyterian Church. Anthony's mother, Musidora Morgan, was the sister of Senator John Tyler Morgan, who served in the United States Senate for thirty-one years.

Anthony Sayre was a brilliant student in mathematics at Roanoke College in Virginia; he graduated at nineteen and began teaching at Vanderbilt College. But he did not feel cut out to be a teacher and soon came back to Alabama, having decided to read law in Montgomery. It was two years later, in 1882, that he began to court Minnie Machen. It must have been an attraction of opposites, for Minnie was known for her gaiety and vivacious charm, while the grave A.D., as she called him, possessed an air of sober dignity that set him apart from other young men.

It was after Minnie's abortive trip to Philadelphia and her return to Kentucky that Sayre won her hand; they were married in January 1884, at Mineral Mount. Minnie was twenty-three, and no longer considered young. The war had taken its toll of eligible men and there was a surfeit of women of marriageable age in the South. Anthony Sayre had no source of private income when he married, and although he may not have married above himself socially, economically he probably had. But there was a sureness about him, a sense of authority matched by his complete dedication to the law, which must have been attractive. Clearly, he was a man who would not be easily checked by the uncertainties of life, or in the pursuit of his career. At the time of their marriage he was clerk of the city court in Montgomery.

The first years of the Sayres' marriage were happy ones and they soon had a baby daughter, Marjorie. But the little girl was fretful and sickly from infancy. A beautiful, healthy son was born to them the following year, but when he was eighteen months old he died without warning of spinal meningitis. Mrs Sayre shut herself away in her room and refused to see anyone or to eat. For a while her family humoured her, hoping that she would recover her equilibrium. But she did not until their family doctor forced his way into her room and, taking her by her shoulders, told her that she had a little girl downstairs who needed her; she had to live for the living. It was prophetic advice and Mrs Sayre would have occasion to remember it often during her long and full life.

Two more daughters were born to them, Rosalind and Clothilde, and a son, Anthony D. Sayre, Jr. Minnie was frequently ill during her pregnancies and it was all she could do to manage her large family. At one time a Louisville publisher asked her to write a novel for him, but she found less and less time to devote to her literary ambitions. Her younger sister, Marjorie, had come to live with them, as had Mr Sayre's bachelor brother, Reid, and the elderly Mrs Sayre. The young children remembered their grandmother as a peculiar and strong-willed old woman who wove endless stories about bloodthirsty Yankees with horns and constantly reminded them of their Morgan heritage. Some people in Montgomery still remember old Mrs Sayre sitting on the front porch in her bonnet and grey wrapper, watching the people who passed by. She was known to have 'a whipping tongue'. There were two Mrs Bells in Montgomery, and one day the wealthier of them was walking by the Sayres' house and greeted the old lady. Mrs Sayre replied, 'Are you the nice Mrs Bell, or are you the wealthy, ordinary, and very common Mrs Bell?'

The family moved frequently as it grew in size. They usually rented homes, for Mr Sayre refused to be in debt, even to the extent of taking on a mortgage. He worried constantly over their finances, for there were now nine members in his household, and he insisted that expenses be held to a minimum. He worked relentlessly and well, becoming in his thirties a member of the Alabama House of Representatives; after four years he was elected to the state Senate, governing it as president during his final year in office. By 1897 he was elected judge of the city court in Montgomery. He is remembered from this period as an increasingly remote and reserved figure in Montgomery and, one suspects, within his own family. It was remarked that the only place one saw Judge Sayre (as he would thereafter be called by everyone, including his wife) was waiting at the streetcar either on his way to work or on his way home.

On 24 July 1900, the Sayres' sixth child, a daughter, was born at home on South Street. Minnie was nearly forty and Judge Sayre was forty-two. Minnie was still an avid reader and she named her baby after a gypsy queen in a novel: Zelda. Marjorie was fourteen at Zelda's birth, Rosalind not quite eleven, Clothilde nine, and Tony seven. From the beginning she was her mother's darling and her pet. She was the only one who took after the Machen side of the family, for Zelda was as fair, golden, and blue-eyed as the other children were dark. Treasuring the baby who would undoubtedly be her last, Mrs Sayre nursed Zelda until she was four years old. She showered her with attention and praise; her faults were quickly excused.

Zelda was like a rush of fresh air into the Sayre household, lively and irrepressibly gay and wayward. Her sisters and brother were too old to be true playmates and they remember her only in motion: running with a dog, flying on a swing hung from a magnolia tree in their back yard, racing on roller skates as soon as she could stand well enough to navigate on them, swimming and diving fearlessly. And dancing. Showing off new steps and imitating dances she had seen.

When Zelda was asked later in her life to describe herself as a child, she said she was 'independent – courageous – without thought for anyone else'. But she also remembered herself as 'dreamy – a sensualist', who was bright and loved sports, especially imaginative, active, competitive games. 'I was a very active child and never tired, always running with no hat or coat even in the Negro district and far from my house. I liked houses under construction and often I walked on the open roofs; I liked to jump from high places. . . . I liked to dive and climb in the tops of trees – I liked taking long walks far from town, sometimes going to a country churchyard where I went very often all by myself.' In summary she said: 'When I was a little girl I had great confidence in myself, even to the extent of walking by myself against life as it was then. I did not have a single feeling of inferiority, or shyness, or doubt, and no moral principles.'

People in Montgomery still remember Zelda as being 'smart as a whip' and 'quick as a steel trap', and recall seeing her pulling a red wagon with her rag doll Patsy in it and her little dog running behind. Once she arrived late at a birthday party carrying a big pot of pink geraniums. It seemed to be such an unusual gift that after the party the mother of the girl for whom the party had been given called Mrs Sayre. After hearing the story, Mrs Sayre said, 'So that's what became of my geranium!'

Mrs Sayre indulged Zelda completely and was charmed by

her. What direction or discipline Zelda (who was to be called Baby by both her mother and her father all her life) required was left to the Judge. There was a disarming vagueness and pleasant permissiveness about Mrs Sayre. One of the Sayre children has said, 'We were all independent characters, especially for Montgomery. Mother didn't supervise us very much – I don't know why; it was just the way our family was.'

Minnie Sayre was not thought to be 'socially minded' by her neighbours, and people weren't quite sure how to take her. There is a story that Zelda's sisters used to bath on their back porch. One day a group of respectable ladies felt they had to tell Mrs Sayre about the young men who were watching the girls. They suggested that the girls bath elsewhere. Mrs Sayre is reputed to have replied, 'Why should they? God gave them beautiful bodies.' The women quickly retreated. Mrs Sayre was undoubtedly aware that such advice would not be repeated if she met it head on. If her neighbours found her a little odd, or 'artistic', as some of them chose to express it, perhaps she found them dull and provincial. To the end of her long life, when she had become known by everyone as Mama Sayre, she would insist that there were certain things she did not know about Montgomery, because she was not a native (although she was to live there for seventy-five years).

In Zelda's scrapbook there is a snapshot of her mother and father and herself when she was about five. Her father's face is entirely in the shadow cast by the brim of his white straw hat, his dark suit shines as though it were made of black silk, and he is leaning gently upon a furled black umbrella. Minnie, with stray wisps of hair curling out from beneath her hat, stands looking full face into the camera, solid and matronly in a white blouse with a high, snug collar. Zelda stands close to her mother, holding Patsy's face pressed next to her own; her fair hair, cut in a Dutch bob, is very straight. None of them are touching or smiling.

Zelda started school in 1906, but didn't like it, came home, and refused to return. Her mother waited another year, until she was seven, and sent her again. This time she stuck. At about the same period in her life, the family moved from the house on South Street, which had become too small for them, to another on Morgan Avenue. They were to move twice again before settling at 6 Pleasant Avenue, where Zelda lived until she married.

The Pleasant Avenue house was a roomy white frame building with five bedrooms and a large brick front porch. Zelda's room was upstairs at the front of the house, above the tin roof of the porch, and overlooked gardens which were all that remained of the old Wilson plantation. It was painted white, with light cotton curtains and a plain white bed in the corner. A friend of hers said it looked like a hospital room in its spartan simplicity. All her life Zelda remembered the fragrance of the pear trees across the street that filled her room at night. She awoke in those soft, suffocatingly warm Southern mornings to the cries of black women taking their wares to market at the foot of Court Street.

The Sayres always lived in what was the silk-hat district of Montgomery, on 'The Hill', but never in one of the more elegant residences of the area. About forty thousand people lived in Montgomery at that time, and it retained all the charm as well as the many restrictions on privacy of a small town. Certainly most of the families in the Sayres' neighbourhood knew each other. They tacitly considered themselves the 'thoroughbreds' of the genteel South, although it would have been considered a breach of decorum to mention it. Behind their backs in the surrounding blocks the residents of The Hill were called 'The Elite and Sanitary', with a measure of amusement and more of envy. For in Montgomery it was never simply wealth that counted socially, but family. There were very definite lines of social distinction; one was not invited to parties on The Hill if one was in trade, or Catholic, or Italian, or Shanty Irish. World War I would do a little to change the social rigidity, but for the time being it persisted. The young ladies of these families were expected to behave themselves, to be decorative and charming. One was taught to sit without letting one's back touch the chair, to cross one's ankles, but not one's legs. White gloves were buttoned before one left the house and remained immaculate in the warmest weather. Zelda must have chafed under these restrictions. She was too full of life and deviltry to follow the rules for long, or to be throttled by them.

A younger friend of hers, Sara Mayfield, who was also the daughter of a judge, remembered one of Zelda's shows of spirit. The Mayfields had invited her for a ride in their new brougham, which was their mother's pride. It was equipped with the latest fixtures, glass windows, and tufted red leather seats. As soon as Zelda laid eyes on it she said, 'If I had a pumpkin, I'll bet I could make me one!' And then quickly, before anyone realized what she was up to, she climbed into the driver's seat and gave the matched bays a hard slap. The carriage shot forward, careering wildly toward the street. Within seconds, just as the horses cleared the gate, the hub of a rear wheel caught and brought the carriage to an abrupt stop. The family ran up to it, and Zelda calmly stepped out of the brougham and ran to play with her friend. It was that special combination of nerve and defiance which thrilled Miss Mayfield. She said that from that moment she adored Zelda.

For her part, even as a child Zelda was not unaware of the effect she created. She possessed early a certain command over others, making them do what she wanted them to. She also had a knack of drawing attention to herself. Stories about her escapades abound in Montgomery. There is one about when Zelda, having nothing better to do on a fine summery day, called up the fire department and told them that a child was caught on a roof and couldn't get down. Then Zelda got a ladder, climbed up to the roof of her own house, pushed the ladder away and waited. The fire engine came clanging its bell and the neighbours rushed out to see where the fire was. There Zelda sat marooned, and delighted by the commotion. The Judge had no sympathy whatsoever for such pranks.

In 1909 Zelda's father was appointed an associate justice of the Supreme Court of Alabama. His salary was $5,000. Her oldest sister, Marjorie, who had been teaching in the public schools, married that year, and Zelda began ballet lessons. As it later turned out they were to make a lasting impression upon her.

With sisters so much older than she and a brother to whom she apparently never felt close, Zelda was left to her own devices. Later in her life she said that she had no memories of a youth shared with any of them. She thought her sisters rather pretty (Clothilde was by reputation the prettiest after Zelda, and it was Clothilde with whom she quarrelled most), but they were largely indifferent to each other. Rosalind would one day comment that Zelda was the most vigorous and healthy of all the Sayre children and that her one great attachment was for their mother.

There were summers spent in the cool mountains of North Carolina during the adjournment of the Supreme Court; from the time Zelda was ten she usually went with her parents while a relative from Kentucky stayed with the older Sayre children in Montgomery. They stayed at a hilltop inn in Saluda, where it was quiet and the food was delicious. There was nothing to do but sit on the veranda and look at the mountains or take walks to the post office in the tiny village below, or perhaps pick blackberries before the sun got hot. Sometimes the whole family would go to Mountain Creek in Alabama for the summer, with the Judge coming up on weekends. When he arrived his pockets would be filled with penny candies and he would take Zelda for walks by the railroad tracks to get handfuls of beautifully coloured clay and would mould tiny animals for her. One of Zelda's sisters remembers, 'When we were children he was wonderful to us, but once we were grown I guess he just figured we were on our own. I know he must have loved us, though.'

In 1914 Zelda entered the new Sidney Lanier High School. Her teachers found her mischievous, but an apt pupil. In her first year she maintained a high B average, was rarely absent, and consistently did well in English and mathematics.

Her schoolmates noticed that Zelda had much more freedom after school than they did, and often instead of going directly home Zelda could be found at the local ice-cream parlour having a double banana split or a dope, which was a concoction of Coca-Cola spiked with aromatic spirits of ammonia to give it a slight kick. Some of the girls envied her for not having to call home first to report where she was going. She rarely did her homework at home but instead raced through it during class.

Once the class had been told to write a poem as homework. Zelda jotted hers down in class the next day, then waved her hand to be called first. The poem was not quite what her teacher had in mind, but it delighted her classmates:

> I do love my Charlie so.
> It nearly drives me wild.
> I'm so glad that he's my beau
> And I'm his baby child!

It was a typical prank of Zelda's. She did not quite risk becoming a troublemaker but she was quickly establishing a reputation for cheekiness. To her teachers Zelda seemed increasingly impatient, restless, and undisciplined. They had the impression that she could have done much better had she cared enough to work – and had she been more closely supervised at home. Zelda was to offer a similar explanation later in her life. She said her studies simply had no value for her. She read whatever she found at home, 'popular tales for boys, novels that my sisters had left on a table, books chosen by accident in my father's library: a life of John Paul Jones, lives written by Plutarch, The Decline and Fall of the Roman Empire by Gibbons, and fairy tales a lot'. She read Wilde and Galsworthy and Kipling, 'and all I found about the civil war. . . . The fairy tales were my favourite.'

It was becoming clear that Zelda was just marking time at school. Her lack of interest was evident in small details like her clothing. She wore the ordinary middy blouses and pleated skirts of the day, but hers were always worn carelessly. Her skirts, which were rolled at the waist to shorten them, were uneven, and her slip usually showed. There was a puzzling drabness, even dowdiness, about all of Zelda's daytime garb. Her sister Rosalind, as well as several of her school chums, have said repeatedly that Zelda had no sense of style. But that lack of style must have been something she shared with her mother, for Mrs Sayre rather than a seamstress made all her clothes.

Whether she was stylish or not, at night Zelda shone in her mother's creations. Eleanor Browder, one of Zelda's friends from school, remembers that 'Mrs Sayre had an unerring sense of what would make her beautiful daughter glamorous and could turn out dresses of tulle and organdie that turned Zelda into a fairy princess.'

At fifteen Zelda was striking, her skin flawless and creamy and her hair as golden as a child's. Other girls began secretly to use blondine on their hair, but Zelda didn't need to. She borrowed rouge and lipstick from her older sisters to heighten her colouring and her powder was the whitest she could find. Eleanor remembers that Zelda wore mascara before any of the others did. Zelda was on the verge of becoming the most spectacular belle Montgomery would ever know; Mrs Sayre's party dresses were the first tributes paid to her daughter's beauty.

2

High in a white palace the king's daughter, the golden girl . . .
F. SCOTT FITZGERALD, *The Great Gatsby*

In the spring of 1916 a ballet recital was held in the old City
Auditorium in Montgomery. It was an exceptionally hot night
and somewhat surprisingly the auditorium was filled. There
was to be ballroom dancing afterward and perhaps that was why
so many young men had come. Zelda Sayre, who was not yet
sixteen, danced a solo. She wore a stiff pink organdie dress
made by her mother, with fresh flowers at her waist, and as she
began to dance the audience grew quiet. Her hair was long like
a child's, and she wore it in ringlets with lovelocks at her temples. She moved gracefully and seemed completely self-assured.
After her dance the young men swarmed about her. Everyone
wanted to know who she was. Zelda accepted the surge of admirers as if they were her due, and that night marked her trans-
formation into a belle. It was as complete as the happy ending
of a fairy tale.

Mrs Sayre watched her daughter with pride. Before the programme began she hadn't been sure how Zelda, who was still
considered a tomboy at home, would react to the ballroom
dancing. To make sure that all went smoothly she'd requested
a friend of Zelda's, Leon Ruth, to ask her for the first dance.
Then, in an odd gesture of complicity, Mrs Sayre took the
young man aside and showed him a large, chunky bracelet she'd
bought for Zelda. She wanted him to offer it to her when he
asked her to dance. He was puzzled and said he could get his
own presents, but Mrs Sayre insisted, and not wanting to be
impolite he did give it to Zelda. He remembered. 'We danced
for no more than a few turns and then all the other boys came
around and I didn't have a chance to take Zelda's hand again

all evening. But we did walk home together down Monroe
Street to Pleasant Avenue. It was dark walking there and I felt
happy to be next to such a pretty girl in her pink ballet skirt
who all the boys would now be after.'

That summer a story appeared on the society page of the
Advertiser beneath the silhouette of Zelda wearing a tam.

You may keep an eye open for the possessor of this classic profile
about a year from now when she advances just a little further beyond
the sweet-sixteen stage. Already she is in the crowd at the Country
Club every Saturday night and at the script dances every other
night of the week.

She has the straightest nose, the most determined little chin and
the bluest eyes in Montgomery. She might dance like Pavlova if
her nimble feet were not so busy keeping up with the pace a string
of young but ardent admirers set for her.

The 'script' (short for subscription) dances were held out of
doors at Oak Park, where there was a large old dance pavilion
with a hardwood floor. A group of young men, usually college
boys, hired a dance band and then they posted a list of girls'
names on the door at Harry's. Harry's was an ice-cream parlour
where the boys, who were called 'Jelly Beans', or 'Jellies', loafed
and hung out with their girls. A young man then signed his
name next to the name of the girl he wanted to take; it was first
come first served, with the prettiest, most popular girls signed
for first. The only hitch from the girls' point of view was that
they had almost no say about who signed for them, and their
only out was refusing to go.

There were chaperones at the dances, but Zelda completely
ignored them. She danced cheek to cheek, which was considered
improper, and it took very little persuasion to get her to sneak
out during intermission to the cars which were parked just out
of sight. She 'boodled' (which was local slang for necking in
cars at a place called Boodler's Bend), she smoked, and she
drank gin, if there was any, or corn liquor cut with Coke, if
there wasn't.

Zelda did not have the knack for forming close friendships

with girls her own age; she didn't belong to any of their clubs, and she was not invited to their overnight parties. She didn't indulge in the trading of confidences and gossip; she neither asked for advice nor gave it. It was the attention of the boys that she clearly preferred and got. She stopped taking ballet lessons because she was too busy going out; she had dates every night of the week. One of her beaux remembers her as 'a restless person with lots of energy. She was in for anything. Let's do something for the hell of it. I remember once at a dance that summer it got hot and Zelda slipped out of her petticoat and asked me to put it in my pocket for her until we got home. And I did. She was like none of the others.' He would pick her up for a dance and on the way she'd ask him to stop the car so she could go wading, and he'd join her, both of them all dressed up, splashing in the water, laughing. Maybe they wouldn't make the dance at all and it didn't seem to make a bit of difference to Zelda. 'She lived on the cream at the top of the bottle.'

She looked fragile and fresh, but there was nothing demure in her appetite for life. Perhaps it was her *brio* and lack of inhibition that many of the girls found unmanageable. Zelda was equally impatient with their more conventional behaviour. One evening, while double-dating at an outdoor play being given at Miss Margaret Booth's School for Girls, Zelda suggested to her date and the other couple that they leave. It was a dull performance, but the other girl attended the school and could have been expelled if she had been caught walking out. She hesitated. Zelda watched her for a moment and drawled sharply, 'Oh, get some guts about you!' and left. Miserably the other girl followed.

Zelda said of herself that she cared for two things: boys and swimming. There is a snapshot of her standing next to a boy beside a swimming pool, their arms draped jauntily around each other's waists. Zelda is standing straight as a grenadier, her other hand on her hip, and she is laughing into the camera. Beneath the snapshot is the inscription 'What the Hell – Zelda Sayre!' The man who was with her then says: 'Zelda just wasn't afraid of anything, of boys, of being talked about; she was absolutely fearless. There was this board rigged up at the swimming pool and, well, almost nobody ever dived from the top. But Zelda did, and I was hard put to match her. I really didn't want to. She swam and dived as well as any of the boys and better than most of us. She had no more worries than a puppy would have, or a kitten. ... But she did have a bad reputation. ... There were two kinds of girls, those who would ride with you in your automobile at night and the nice girls who wouldn't. But Zelda didn't seem to give a damn.'

She wore a one-piece flesh-coloured silk jersey swimming suit that summer. There were stories that she swam in the nude, which she laughed at but did not deny. She was sharply aware of the criticism that was being levelled against her. Later in her life she wrote about Alabama Beggs, the heroine of her intensely autobiographical novel *Save Me the Waltz*:

'She's the wildest one of the Beggs, but she's a thoroughbred,' people said.

Alabama knew everything they said about her – there were so many boys who wanted to 'protect' her that she couldn't escape knowing. ... 'Thoroughbred!' she thought, 'meaning that I never let them down on the dramatic possibilities of a scene – I give a damned good show.'

Rumours about her behaviour flew around Montgomery that summer; it was said that when Judge Sayre forbade her to go out at night she climbed out her bedroom window and went anyway – sometimes with the help of her mother. Outwardly Zelda flouted the Judge's standards. She called him 'old Dick' behind his back, and her waywardness was an open challenge to his authority.

Judge Sayre was a model of respectability and conservatism. His full head of hair had turned completely white; he wore striped diplomatic trousers with a black jacket, which were made for him by a tailor in Atlanta who came once a year for fittings; and he carried a walking stick. Colleagues called him 'The Brains of the Bench', and his conservative opinions were articulately written. His life seemed perfectly ordered. He kept a chessboard permanently set up in his office, at which he and Judge Mayfield played daily, resuming their game where they had left off the day before. When he came home in the evening he ate a sandwich and retired for the night promptly at eight o'clock. Entirely devoted to his work, he had very little time for Minnie and the children. He was not thought to be unkind, only remote. Minnie, on the other hand, loved to have people about, and the Judge called the odd collection of people who assembled at their house 'Minnie's Menagerie'. There was an old poet who smelled bad, and a Mormon who tried to convert Minnie. (One member of the family commented that Mrs Sayre 'loved to listen, but she never, never changed her mind'. She did, however, toy with the idea of becoming a theosophist.) She had more time now that her family was nearly grown; she gardened, and wrote occasional poems which were printed in the *Advertiser*.

With the gentility of the Sayres behind her Zelda was in an important sense immune to criticism. Her stunts and escapades would be commented upon in private to be sure, but as the daughter of Judge Sayre she was granted a sort of social deference. She could rely upon the knowledge that her father's position and reputation would protect her. That immunity had, however, another and potentially damaging aspect, one which Zelda did not grasp fully at seventeen, but understood all too clearly later in her life. For even as her father's position protected her, it also 'absolved his children from the early social efforts necessary in life to construct strongholds for themselves'. In this respect they were 'crippled' (Zelda's word for it) by that insulation of family position. It was not only Zelda who was affected. Tony Sayre had a reputation for being dissolute, and he left Auburn after a mixed career without earning his degree. A fraternity brother of his remembers his spending more of his time at cards than books, and said that Tony was fonder of hazing the freshmen than his ΣΑΕ brothers thought acceptable. He told his family that he would like to paint more than anything else in the world, but he never did.

As for the other Sayre children, Rosalind was intelligent, energetic, and perhaps most like Zelda in her spunk. She was one of the first young ladies from a good family to go to work in Montgomery. She wrote a column for the society page on her uncle's newspaper, and she loved it. Clothilde and Marjorie were temperamentally alike, quiet and serious. Clothilde was dark-haired with flawless skin, dead white like the magnolia. Marjorie was never well. She taught school (which prior to Rosalind's adventure was the only acceptable form of work for maiden ladies), married, and had one daughter, who was also named Marjorie. The Sayres were close-mouthed about her illnesses, and when Marjorie's little daughter came to live with them she was told her mother was away on a 'visit'. There was hushed talk of a nervous breakdown. The Sayres' Victorian refusal to name her illness for what it was, not unusual in Montgomery or elsewhere at that time, was part of the essential make-up of their family. When Mrs Sayre's own mother died a suicide the children were never told directly about it, but were left to overhear what they could from more talkative relatives. Everyone *knew*, but covertly, for it was never openly discussed.

Zelda chafed against the emotional restraint of her family and she felt herself being suffocated in the small arena that both her family and Montgomery offered her. Zelda's release from that world was suddenly within reach, for with the United States entry into World War I in the summer of 1917 Montgomery altered profoundly. Thousands of soldiers and aviators poured into the city to train at Camps Sheridan and Taylor, which were just outside of town. New shops, restaurants, and hotels opened to accommodate them; the country club became almost an auxiliary officers' club, and unfamiliar faces from Ohio and New York and Pennsylvania were seen in the streets. There was token resistance to the quartering of Yankee soldiers just outside Montgomery, and one recalcitrant old Confederate even tried to form a club to rekindle the local youngsters' hatred of Sherman and his dread troops. But it was no good; the young didn't want to remember the past, and besides, as one lady remembers, the Yankees were such good dancers. Jolted from its somnolence, Montgomery became more festive, more alive, than it had been since the days when it was the headquarters to the Confederacy. Mrs Sayre remembered, 'There was a lot of excitement in the air, a lot of people here in Montgomery that we had never seen before, and I had three very good-looking daughters.' The men came from every imaginable economic and social level of American life, 'men who were better dressed in their uniforms than ever before in their lives', as Zelda wrote later, 'and men from Princeton and Yale who smelled of Russian Leather and seemed very used to being alive . . .' The larger world that Zelda dreamed of was at her doorstep and accessible.

In September 1917 Zelda began her senior year in a flurry of dances and parties. The Sayres' front porch looked like a barracks, and in a glove box she began to collect the colourful insignia officers gave her from their uniforms, as tokens of their affection. Soon the little box was filled with gold and silver bars, castles and flags and curled serpents. The Judge disapproved of Zelda's behaviour and the hours she kept, but Mrs Sayre came to her defence and was amused by Zelda's pretty trinkets.

Zelda's girlish imagination was fired by the idea that the droves of young soldiers who courted her were being trained to fight the Hun in Europe, and faced death in the trenches. In a burst of patriotic sentiment she wrote a poem about them for the school paper which won a prize and was published in the newspaper as well. (Mrs Sayre probably had a hand in its composition, for when Zelda pasted it in her scrapbook she wrote across the face of the poem, 'Not only is "*Necessity* the *Mother* of *Invention*", but a "*Mother* of *Invention*" is a necessity! !') She called it 'Over the Top with Pershing'.

> The night was dark, the rain came down,
> The boys stepped off with never a frown.
> Into the trench all mud and slime,
> And thousands of miles from their native clime,
> They took their places in face of death,
> And waited their turn with bated breath,
>   'Til the order came to open fire,
>   They screwed their courage higher and higher.
>
> *
>
> Over the top they go to fight
> For suffering friends and human right,
>   Over the top they see their way
>   To a clearer aim and a freer day,
> Over the top, O God of Might,
> Help our laddies to win the fight.

But it was not only the soldiers who pursued Zelda; during the Christmas holidays she attended balls and dances and fraternity parties in Anniston, Marion, Auburn, and Birmingham, all college towns in Alabama. She led the grand march at the Alpha Tau Omega ball at the Exchange Hotel in Montgomery and the newspapers reported that she looked exquisite in her gown of rose velvet, a bouquet of pink roses in her arms. During the intermission of that dance Zelda and a group of her friends left the hotel for refreshments at a nearby café. On their way they passed a photographer's shop with a large framed picture of one of Zelda's beaux in the display case and paused to admire it. One of the crowd teased Zelda about the boy's being in the shop window rather than with her. In an instant Zelda kicked in the glass and took the photograph. Her friends were frightened by what she had done and tried to hurry her away, but Zelda laughed at them and gaily walked into the café with the photograph openly clasped under her arm.

One of Zelda's attractions was that she was utterly herself; she did what she pleased when she pleased. It would be a mistake, however, to assume that she was unaware of the traditional attitude towards Southern women even when she ran contrary to it. In January 1918, for example, she was invited to the house party and dance given by the Key-Ice Club at the University of Alabama. At the dance the boys sported hip flasks of whisky, which they tried to persuade their brightly painted girls to share after they strutted to the new ragtime. Key-Ice had as its central ritual a ceremony which its young men performed during the intermission of their dances. The lights were lowered in the ballroom and the men marched in solemnly, carrying flaming torches, while at the rear of the procession four of them walked beside a long cake of ice drawn on a cart. One lifted a glass of water to his lips and began a toast: 'To woman, lovely woman of the Southland, as pure and chaste as this sparkling water, as cold as this gleaming ice, we lift this cup, and we pledge our hearts and our lives to the protection of her virtue and chastity.'

This extravagant and somewhat sinister homage to Southern womanhood has the social context in which Zelda grew up, and against which she was reacting. Her family was firmly fixed in it, and if many of its tenets were more literary than practical it made little difference, for their acceptance in the Deep South was almost complete. Women were expected to be submissive, if not passive. The Southern belle had certain prerogatives that her more ordinary sisters were not granted, but she had won these by her beauty, her spirited veneer, and her ability to manage men without seeming to do so. The art of dissembling perforce became a valuable social asset for a girl. (In this respect the white Southern woman's position was remarkably similar to the Negro's.) The tensions inherent in that charade of Southern womanhood were to drive Zelda one day to write: '... it's very difficult to be two simple people at once, one who wants to have a law to itself and the other who wants to keep all the nice old things and be loved and safe protected'. It was not only difficult; it called upon contradicting definitions of herself. The ideal was perverse, but she had not yet realized its ability to damage.

School wasn't going well and Zelda, who always started out at the top of her class, nearly flunked history and second-year French. She was absent frequently and her conduct report sank to 'unsatisfactory' in the marking period before graduation. She remarked later: 'I did not study a lot by then. I left my studies in school and as there were a lot of soldiers in town I passed my time going to dances – always in love with somebody, dancing all night, and carrying on my school work just with [the] idea of finishing.' Every Friday night she was at the vaudeville show, where she would take careful note of the dance routines in order to imitate them herself at the Saturday-night dances at the country club.

On April Fool's Day the entire senior class played hookey and Zelda was one of the ringleaders. They pooled their money, and Zelda and Eleanor Browder cajoled the ticket taker at the Empire Theatre into letting them all into the movies for ninety cents. Afterwards they posed for a snapshot in front of the movie house, the boys in their soft-billed caps and high laced black shoes, sitting on the kerb with their arms thrown around each other's shoulders, the girls clowning in the back row. Then they went on a picnic. On 2 April they were all expelled. The president of their class, a handsome boy named Irby Jones, talked the principal into letting them return, and the penalties for having gone skylarking ended up being mild: there was to be no more stopping or talking in the halls, and the class was to attend school on Saturday to make up for the day they had cut.

Zelda was voted The Prettiest and The Most Attractive girl in her class, and in the composite picture of the ideal senior girl Zelda was chosen for her mouth. Her graduation picture shows her wearing a middy blouse, while all the other girls are pictured in their best dresses. Beneath her photograph are these lines:

> Why should all life be work, when we all can borrow.
> Let's only think of today, and not worry about tomorrow.

Graduation was held at the Grand Theatre the evening of 31 May. There had been a lot of discussion about what the girls should wear, some wanting expensive dresses and no flowers, while others thought that dresses for which the materials were not more than five dollars would be best, with each girl carrying red roses, which were plentiful and cheap. One of Zelda's classmates, Lucy Goldthwaite, said, 'None of us had too much money in those days in the South, and our vote was finally for the five-dollar dresses with flowers.' A few of the girls were disappointed but in an era when store-bought clothes were scarce everyone set about getting their Negro seamstresses to make the prettiest dresses possible within the five-dollar limit. That evening as they gathered behind the stage for the procession, Zelda turned up in a magnificent white silk dress with a tunic of chiffon floating over it, and a large-brimmed hat with long streamers down her back. 'You can't imagine how lovely she was', Lucy said, 'but of course we were all shocked and some of us were resentful. I mean, it wasn't fair.' No one knows why Zelda ignored the five-dollar limit, or whether she had told her mother, who had undoubtedly made the costume, about it, but everyone agreed that it was just like her. One of the girls said rather cattily that maybe the Sayres couldn't afford to give Zelda both a graduation dress and a dress for the parties and country club dances she went to every Saturday night, and so Zelda had chosen a dress that would be used more than once. At the last moment Zelda sat in the audience rather than on the stage with the other members of her class, and afterward told Irby Jones that she didn't care much for ceremonies anyway and had come just to hear him speak. He swore she was laughing at them all.

3

In July 1918, a little more than a month after her graduation, Zelda met Scott Fitzgerald at the country club. It was a hot Saturday night and she had almost not gone, but she had been asked to do a dance, and finally she relented and performed the 'Dance of the Hours'. Scott, a first lieutenant in the 67th Infantry, which had moved into Camp Sheridan in the middle of June, was standing at the edge of the dance floor watching her and quickly he asked if anyone knew her. Someone told him that she was a local high-school girl and too young for him. But the vivid girl with the long golden hair was the most beautiful girl he'd ever seen and he asked to be introduced to her. Later in her life Zelda remembered that when they danced, 'There seemed to be some heavenly support beneath his shoulder blades that lifted his feet from the ground in ecstatic suspension, as if he secretly enjoyed the ability to fly but was walking as a compromise to convention.' Once having met they were irrevocably drawn toward each other, for if ever there was a pair whose fantasies matched, as Edmund Wilson was later to remark, it was Zelda Sayre and Scott Fitzgerald. They shared a beauty and youth which seemed to ally them against the more sober world before them. They even looked alike.

Scott was strikingly handsome, his features classically regular, almost delicate, with a high, wide brow and a straight nose. His eyes were perhaps his best feature, heavily lashed and a clear ice green that changed colour with his moods, and his mouth was his worst, thin-lipped and tensely held. He was not tall, about five feet seven, but he cut a smart figure in his officer's tunic, impeccably tailored by Brooks Brothers in New York.

He chose to wear dashing yellow boots and spurs (other officers wore the puttees issued to them). It was his freshness, a clean, new look about him, that people immediately noticed.

Francis Scott Key Fitzgerald was Irish, a Roman Catholic, and a Midwesterner. He was born in September 1896 in St Paul, Minnesota. When he was two his family moved to Buffalo, where they remained (except for a brief stint in Syracuse) for his boyhood. In 1908 his father, Edward Fitzgerald, was fired from his job with Procter & Gamble and the family returned to St Paul. It was a frightened young son who, upon learning of his father's dismissal, prayed that they would not all go to the poorhouse. His father's career continued to founder, and he apparently never fully regained his self-respect. In St Paul he fell back upon the cushion of his wife's wealthy relatives and began to drink just a little too much.

Scott once wrote, 'Almost everything worth while I may have in the way of brains or energy comes from mother's side, where I am Irish.' Yet it was neither his money nor his prosperous Irish relatives (who had made their money in the wholesale grocery business) whom Scott Fitzgerald admired. His mother had spoiled him badly and he resented her and the coddling. On his father's side he was descended from old and aristocratic Maryland families, the Scotts and the Keys. 'He . . . came from another America', Scott wrote at his father's death. 'I loved my father – always deep in my subconscious I have referred judgements back to him, what he would have thought, or done. . . . I was born several months after the sudden death of my two older sisters & he felt what the effect of this would be on my mother, that he would be my only moral guide.' Edward Fitzgerald instilled in his son not only beautiful manners, but a sense of honour, an almost eighteenth-century code of decorum that Scott Fitzgerald prized. He also inadvertently gave him a model of masculine failure. 'When I was a little older I did not understand at all why men that I knew were vulgar and not gentlemen made him stand up or give the better chair on our verandah. But I know now. There was new peasant stock coming up every ten years & he was of the generation of the colonies and the revolution.' And it was from his father that he 'acquired an extended and showy, if very superficial, knowledge of the Civil War (with an intense southern bias. . . .)'. It is not surprising, then, to discover that his son saw in that conflict the 'broken link in the continuity of American life'.

The Fitzgeralds lived always on the edge of the best neighbourhood in St Paul, but never at its centre. They settled finally and firmly at the end of the finest street in the area, Summit Avenue. As Scott's biographer Arthur Mizener has said, 'The symbolism is almost too neat, and Fitzgerald was acutely aware of it.' Scott also exaggerated it. For however uncertain Scott Fitzgerald felt socially, the wealth of his mother's family assured him entrée into St Paul society; if anything held him back for a time, it was his own self-consciousness and conceit. He once wrote his daughter, with the disarming honesty that was an essential part of his make-up, 'I didn't know till 15 that there was anyone in the world except me, and it cost me *plenty*.'

When he was fourteen he began keeping a diary which he called his *Thoughtbook*. It is a curiously candid little book for a boy his age to have kept, for it records in great detail his ups and downs in the scale of popularity, and those of his friends. It was also an early manifestation of Fitzgerald's lifelong habit of keeping a record of his experiences. He not only cared deeply about what others thought of him – 'Jack Mitchell said that Violets opinean of my character was that I was polite and had a nice disposition and that I thought I was the whole push' – he also analysed what he thought of others: 'For a long time I was Pauls ardent admirer Cecil and I went with him all the time and we thought him a hero. Physically he is the strongest boy I have ever seen. . . . He was awfully funny, strong as an ox, cool in the face of danger polite and at times very interesting. Now I dont dislike him. I have simply out grown him.' *

He began at the same time to write stories for his school's magazine, and at the end of the summer of 1911 he wrote a

---

* The spelling and punctuation used by both Fitzgeralds has been reproduced exactly; no error, no matter how glaring, has been corrected. What they wrote stands as they wrote it whenever the original sources were available to me. I do not use the pedantic *sic*.

play which he directed and in which he starred. But he was not a good student, and his family decided to send him to Newman, a Catholic prep school in Hackensack, New Jersey, in the hope that some learning might be drilled into him. His first year was a miserable one; he was considered fresh, yellow at football, and his grades were poor. His only really happy times were when he escaped to New York to go to the theatre; it provided the balm for his wounded self-esteem. 'I saw a musical comedy called The Quaker Girl, and from that day forth my desk bulged with Gilbert & Sullivan librettos and dozens of note-books containing the germs of dozens of musical comedies.' In the spring of his second year he found a musical score lying on top of a piano. It was for a show called *His Honor the Sultan,* put on by the Triangle Club of Princeton University. That settled it; he decided to go to Princeton, the Southerner's Northern university.

During the summer he wrote and produced a Civil War melodrama called *The Coward,* and began to drink something stiffer than the sherry of his boyhood. Mizener observes that 'twice during the year Fitzgerald was drunk enough to remember the occasions as special ones. He began to be known around St Paul as "a man who drank", a reputation which gave him a certain romantic interest which he undoubtedly enjoyed.' In September 1914, barely managing to pass his entrance exams, he enrolled at Princeton.

He decided to become one of the 'gods of the class', but the quickest path to that position was closed to him when he wrenched his knee at football practice, badly enough to keep him from playing for the rest of the season. If he was to make his mark, time was short and the pressure great, for the eating clubs which lined Prospect Avenue elected new members during their sophomore year. Where you fell as a sophomore was where you stayed at Princeton; there were no reprieves in this tight system. Scott was a Catholic boy from a little-known Catholic prep school, competing with boys from St Paul's, Groton, Hill, and Lawrenceville. With football out of the question, the Triangle Club was his next best route to achieving distinction.

While Scott Fitzgerald schemed to excel socially, there were men at Princeton whom Fitzgerald would come to know and know well who were of an entirely different bent. They were perhaps mavericks, but not obviously so. As a classmate of Scott's said, with perfect Princetonian aplomb, 'they dressed as everyone else did. [It was] just that they were literary, which was not something to be at Princeton.' Among these men were John Peale Bishop and Edmund Wilson, Alexander McKaig, Townsend Martin, and John Biggs, Jr. It was from the first two that Scott Fitzgerald acquired his first taste of the literary life. Bishop, older than the other undergraduates, austere and somewhat affected in his dress, was already something more than a fledgling poet. Edmund Wilson, whose extraordinary intelligence and taste had already begun to emerge at Hill, would serve as Fitzgerald's 'intellectual conscience' for the rest of his life. Wilson was rather scornful of Scott's social ambitiousness, preferring to remain aloof from the undergraduate scene. However, both Bishop and Wilson were members of Triangle.

It was in this overlapping of the intellectual and social worlds at Princeton that Scott's own talents began to take shape. Eagerly he plunged into the arena. He wrote the lyrics for *Fie! Fie! Fi-Fi!*, the Triangle show which, as he said later, 'blooms in a dozen cities every Christmastide', and only his academic ineligibility prevented him from appearing in it. He returned to St Paul for the holidays and basked in the celebrity that *Fie! Fie! Fi-Fi!* brought him. At home he was beginning to be known as a man who had made it at Princeton. He met and fell in love with Ginevra King, a rich and wildly popular visitor from Chicago, who at sixteen had the social ease of a young duchess. A beauty with dark curling hair and large brown romantic eyes, she had an air of daring and innocent allure. To Fitzgerald, Ginevra King was the embodiment of a dream, and he was immediately and completely captivated. He later wrote that he would never forget 'one night when she made luminous the Ritz Roof' at the Frolic in New York. For her part, Ginevra for a time considered Scott to be the 'top man' among her many beaux.

At Princeton he made Cottage Club, the pinnacle of social

success (and at the section party passed out from drinking for the first time in his life). In short order he was elected secretary of Triangle and to the editorial board of *The Tiger*; his stories and poems began to appear in the *Nassau Lit*.

Then at the beginning of his junior year his world fell in. The young man who would write of the hero of his autobiographical first novel, 'It was always the becoming he dreamed of, never the being', flunked examinations in Latin and chemistry and was again made ineligible for the prizes he had won through such single-minded pursuit. In November 1916 he left Princeton because he was ill. He wrote later: 'But I had lost certain offices, the chief one was the presidency of the Triangle Club. . . . To me college would never be the same. There were to be no badges of pride, no medals, after all. . . . I had lost every single thing I wanted – and that night was the first time that I hunted down the spectre of womanhood that, for a little while, makes everything else seem unimportant.'

Although he returned to Princeton the following fall grimly determined to make a fresh start, he had been badly hurt. As he wrote later, 'A man does not recover from such jolts – he becomes a different person and, eventually, the new person finds new things to care about.' In January, in a final *coup de grâce*, he lost Ginevra King, and that too he took hard. As he tried to recover from his losses he did find something new to care about; he read more widely than ever before: Shaw, Tarkington, Wells, Swinburne, Compton Mackenzie. And he decided to become a writer. By the end of that academic year he had written and published nine poems, five reviews, and eight stories in the *Nassau Lit*.

There is no doubt that his reverses, including the loss of Ginevra King, marked his new fiction. But even before he met Miss King, Fitzgerald had begun to form the kind of heroine he would make famous, the romantic teenage fatal woman. In 'A Luckless Santa Claus', written while Scott was at the Newman School, Christmas 1912, Fitzgerald wrote: 'Miss Harmon was responsible for the whole thing. If it had not been for her foolish whim, Talbot would not have made a fool of himself. . . .' Her challenge to Talbot that he could not even give away

$25 on Christmas Eve brings about his humiliation, for he tries and cannot and is beaten for his attempt. Five years later in a one-act play called *The Debutante,* his heroine has come into fuller bloom. Her name is Helen, she smokes, carries a silver flask, and as the scene opens she stands practising expressions before a pier glass. She says of herself, 'I like to run things, but it gets monotonous to always know that I am the key to the situation.' Selfish, exceedingly pretty, she belongs to herself, 'or rather to the crowd', rather than to any single suitor. In a reversal of the accepted sexual roles, it is not the female who is the prey. Helen says: 'I like the feeling of going after them, I like the thrill when you meet them and notice that they've got black hair that's wavey. . . . Then I like the way they begin to follow you with their eyes. . . . Then I begin to place him. Try to get his type . . . right then the romance begins to lessen for me and increase for him.' As the music begins downstairs for her party, she kisses the reflection of herself in the mirror and runs from her room.

In 'Babes in the Woods', also written in 1917, Fitzgerald has his young models perfectly paired. Of Isabelle and Kenneth he says: 'They had both started with good looks and excitable temperaments and the rest was the result of certain accesable popular novels, and dressing room conversation culled from a slightly older set. . . . He waited for the mask to drop off, but at the same time he did not question her right to wear it.' It is this final sentence that will reverberate in Fitzgerald's adult fiction, as well as in his life. He grants his girls, for all their potential ability to promote ruin among their men, their right to do it. And, more than that, he admires their destructive high-handedness, for it is that female quality which attracts him.

His last undergraduate story, 'The Pierian Springs and the Last Straw', was his most ambitious and his best, for in it the reader comes to understand more about the nature of the woman who is able to reduce her men to pathetic figures. She demands that they be heroes while challenging them in such a way that they fail utterly. Then she rejects them. She has 'beauty and the most direct, unprincipled personality I've ever come in contact with'. Fitzgerald then tells his reader something about the fatal flaw in his men that attracts them to their women:

> All the time I was idealizing her to the last possibility, I was perfectly conscious that she was about the faultiest girl I'd ever met. She was selfish, conceited and uncontrolled and since these were my own faults I was doubly aware of them. Yet I never wanted to change her. Each fault was knit up with a sort of passionate energy that transcended it. Her selfishness made her play the game harder, her lack of control put me rather in awe of her and her conceit was punctuated by such delicious moments of remorse and self-denunciation that it was almost – almost dear to me.... She had the strongest effect on me. She made me want to do something for her, to get something to show her. Every honor in college took on the semblance of a presentable trophy.

If his men idealize, or romanticize, his women do not. Their allure is apparently in their total self-centredness and overwhelming instinct for conquest; it is matched only by their extraordinary spirit. When inevitably the man in the story loses his girl, he described his reaction:

> I wandered around ... like a wild man trying to get a word with her and when I did I finished the job. I begged, pled, almost wept. She had no use for me from that hour. At two o'clock I walked out of that school a beaten man.
> Why the rest – it's a long nightmare – letters with all the nerve gone out of them, wild imploring letters; long silences hoping she'd care; rumors of her other affairs.

But for all the young author's talk of the enticing loveliness of his girls, only one is made love to (in 'Sentiment – and the Use of Rouge'), and even then Fitzgerald presents the lovemaking ambiguously. 'He knew what was wrong, but he knew also that he wanted this woman, this warm creature of silk and life who crept so close to him. There were reasons why he oughtn't to have her, but he had suddenly seen how love was a big word like Life and Death. . . . Still they sat without moving for a long while and watched the fire.' Perhaps these girls were not meant to be possessed, but always lost, for the

other girls are not even kissed, much less touched. The fault
seems to lie in the puritanical restraint of Scott Fitzgerald's
boys rather than in his girls. Never evenly matched, the boys
forfeit what might have been their upper hand to the girls'
imperious selfishness. By failing them again and again the
boys, perhaps unwittingly, trap the girls into permanent performance of their game. Both sexes seem to survive on the
nervous edge of the sexual manoeuvre while never achieving
anything more than the retreat of the male and the end of the
story. From the girls' point of view it must have been a desperately unsatisfying sport they provoked; they are the creatures
of a young man's puritanical conscience, which is fascinated by
the preliminary sexual game, the tease, but would prefer to lose
it rather than enjoy the woman herself.

Fitzgerald spent the summer of 1917 in St Paul and wrote to
Edmund Wilson, who was already in the army, that he had taken
his examinations for the regular army and had 'given up the
summer to drinking (gin) and philosophy (James and Schopen-
hauer and Bergson)'. He returned to Princeton for his senior
year really only waiting until his commission came through. In
November he left for Officer's Training Camp at Fort Leavenworth, Kansas. He had also begun a novel which he called *The
Romantic Egotist,* about himself, Princeton, and his generation, 'and really', he wrote Wilson, 'if Scribners takes it I know
I'll wake some morning and find that the debutantes have made
me famous overnight. I really believe that no one else could
have written so searchingly the story of the youth of our generation . . .'

Zelda Sayre was not like any of the girls Scott had known
before. Zelda's beauty and vivacity equalled Ginevra King's,
but her assurance stemmed entirely from confidence in her own
good looks and drawing power. While Ginevra had moved in a
larger world than Scott had known – a world of Eastern finishing schools, of wealth and social position taken for granted –
Zelda's was even more restricted than his own. To Zelda, Scott
was a dazzling visitor from a place where life was lived on a
grand scale.

Scott was a romancer who, never overly popular with men, was on the other hand completely at ease with girls. He was talkative, merry, imaginative, and filled by his own dreams of success and wealth and fame. His novel, which he had completed at breakneck speed on weekends at Fort Leavenworth, was still in Scribner's hands. Shane Leslie, an Irish novelist and critic whom Scott had known from his days at Newman, and to whom he had sent the manuscript of *The Romantic Egotist,* gave this summary of its possibilities when he forwarded it to Scribner's, his own publisher. 'I marvel at its crudity and its cleverness. . . . About a third of the book could be omitted. . . . Though Scott Fitzgerald is still alive it has a literary value. Of course when he is killed it will also have a commercial value.' For he was certain that Fitzgerald would die on active service as had Rupert Brooke. So was Scott, and his novel had an even greater value for him than it would have had under normal circumstances. By comparison his military career seemed to him a waste of time. To a fellow officer in his division who had been with him since Fort Leavenworth, Scott seemed pleasant enough, but immature and irresponsible.

In August 1918 his novel was rejected by Scribner's, but praised by an editor there named Maxwell Perkins. Scott sent a chapter of it to Zelda with a note saying:

Here is the mentioned chapter . . . . . a document in youthful melancholy. . . . .

However . . . . . the heroine does resemble you in more ways than four. . . . .

Needlessly I may add that the chapter and the sending of it are events for your knowledge alone. . . . . Show it not to man woman or child.

I am frightfully bored today –

> Desirously,
> F Scott Fit—

If his attitude of amorous nonchalance seemed a little stilted, nevertheless his note with its delicious secrecy intrigued Zelda and she carefully kept it with her momentos. Scott had appealed to something in Zelda which no one before him had perceived:

a romantic sense of self-importance which was kindred to his own.

Whenever he was free Scott came into Montgomery on the great rattletrap bus that brought all the soldiers into town, and from there he took a taxi to 6 Pleasant Avenue. He telephoned every day, and when he couldn't come he called twice. As the lazy summer passed, he too lost his insignia to Zelda's little glove box. But Scott was not the only man who courted her; a moustached aviator amused her for a while, until he proposed and she flatly turned him down. Astonished at having been refused, he asked her why she had kissed him, and she replied that she'd never kissed a man with a moustache before.

Her honour was fought over so frequently behind the Baptist Church that it became known as a sort of personal battlefield. The aviation officers used to perform fancy stunts in their aeroplanes over the Sayre house until the gallant exhibitions were forbidden by the commanding officer of Taylor Field. But not before two officers had crashed on the nearby Speedway, one of them a desperate beau of Zelda's – the moustached gentleman whom she had enjoyed kissing. In a spirit of rivalry, an inspired infantry officer performed the manual of arms for the infantry before her door.

Scott never forgot his first invitation to dinner at the Sayres' late that summer. Zelda teased her father into such a rage that, grabbing up the carving knife, he chased her around the dining table. Everyone else ignored them and after a few moments they both sat down. It was never mentioned again to Scott, but it was a harrowing introduction to the Sayre family.

They began to see more and more of each other. Scott carved their names in the doorpost of the country club to commemorate their first meeting, and it irritated her a little when he told her again and again how famous he would be, for he neglected to include Zelda in his enthusiastic prevision, or to compliment her on her own considerable local fame. Describing her attraction to him, she wrote: 'Dancing with [him], he smelled like new goods. Being close to him with her face in the space between his ear and his stiff army collar was like being initiated into the subterranean reserves of a fine fabric store exuding the delicacy of cambrics and linen and luxury bound in bales.' When she saw him leave with another girl she was suddenly jealous, not only of the girl but of him; of the aloofness which he could summon and which held him apart from her. She wanted it to be herself alone with whom he shared that pale detachment. With the summer nearly gone Scott carefully noted in his Ledger that on 7 September he had fallen in love with Zelda.* He had many competitors, and she encouraged them, but that provoked his desire for her even further. Shrewdly, she understood that quite clearly. Many years later she wrote: 'He was almost certainly falling in love which was acceptable to him. He had planned his life for story anyway. [She] told him about how poor she was and how he wouldn't have wanted her had he seen her somewhere else. This displeased [him]; he could weave his own romance and was well able to do so with what there was at hand: [she] was wonderful despite, and partly because of, her rhapsodic disavowals of any appropriateness whatsoever. . . . [He] was proud of the way the boys danced with her and she was so much admired. The glamour of public premium . . . gave [her] a desirability which became, indeed, indispensable to [him].'

They spent afternoons together talking about poetry, sitting in the swing on the Sayres' front porch and sipping long drinks filled with fruit and crushed ice. Playfully Scott told her that according to both Browning and Keats he should marry her. They discussed love and seduction while they walked in the pine groves and fields at the edge of town. She teased him and said he was an 'educational feature; an overture to romance which *no* young lady should be without'. When she treated him casually, or made fun of him, he was hurt and sulky, and, certain that he was to be sent overseas at any moment, he tried to press her for a commitment. But she was apparently wary of limiting herself to him alone. It was not only Scott himself, but the uncertainty of his future in those

*This Ledger contains, among other records, his 'Outline Chart of My Life', an astonishingly accurate personal monthly account of his life, which he began in 1922 and continued into the middle of the 1930s.

months prior to the end of the war, which were behind her reluctance. It did nothing to help his cause that the Judge disapproved of him because he drank too much. Surrounded by so many young men, she was impervious to Scott's pleas.

In October, Fitzgerald at last received his orders to go North and from there presumably to France; he left Montgomery on the 26th. Once in New York, however, his orders were altered and he was sent to Camp Mills on Long Island. While he was waiting there, the Armistice ending the war was signed. In Montgomery it was celebrated with flowers and confetti dropped from the aeroplanes of the aviators stationed at Taylor Field. Fitzgerald returned to Montgomery to await discharge from the army. Once back, he and Zelda quarrelled bitterly. He wrote a letter to an old friend in whom he had confided when he was East: 'My affair still drifts – But my mind is firmly made up that I will not, shall not, can not, should not, must not marry – Still, she *is* remarkable – I'm trying desperately *exire armis* –' There is only this one piece of evidence that he ever seriously intended to break off with Zelda, and by December, after he had been back in Montgomery less than two weeks, he entered the single word 'Love' in his Ledger. He had not tried very hard to disentangle himself from Zelda and it was during this interim period of his life that he again fell deeply and entirely in love with her. He was to call it 'The most important year of my life. Every emotion and my life work decided. Miserable and exstatic but a great success.'

Soon they were alone together whenever he could borrow a car; they drank gin and kissed in the back rows of the Grand Theatre during the vaudeville shows; and Zelda showed him a diary she kept which Scott found so extraordinary that he was to use portions of it in his fiction, in *This Side of Paradise, The Beautiful and Damned,* and 'The Jelly Bean'. They spent Christmas together happily before the fire at the Sayre home, and they began to move, enchanted by each other, into a more passionate attachment. This time Zelda was more willing to commit herself. Cautious as she had been in the late autumn about pledging herself to Scott, her behaviour was now incautious enough to earn his description of it, although he wrote it many years later, as 'sexual recklessness', for Zelda shared none of Scott's Irish Catholic contrition.

Bewilderingly, she continued to go out with other men. She may have done so as a challenge to him, or to keep intact her private vision of herself as a belle; or she may have used her dates as a front for Montgomery. Whatever her motives, she felt her behaviour did nothing to diminish her love for Scott, while it drove him into a frenzy of jealousy. It was at the very least a sign of her inability to place herself in his position, a sign of her refusal to feel the hurt she was capable of inflicting on Scott. Zelda did, as she always had in the past, as she pleased, and Scott, who admired her fearlessness in their affair to the point of awe, was unable to make her his alone. They quarrelled when she went out, Scott drank in retaliation, but she managed to soothe his feelings and continued to see other men when she wanted to. He took pride in the fact that she was invited to the inaugural ball of the Governor of Alabama that January 1919, and later in their lives he would tell people they had met there. All of the dances on Zelda's card were taken, but Scott's name was not on it.

From Zelda's point of view Scott was a new breed of man. Unathletic, imaginative, and sensitive, he represented a world she did not know and could not hope to enter, much less possess, without him. Beguiled by his palaver and sharing with him the view that anything done moderately was better left undone, she decided that she loved him. They were both eager to conquer New York, and their entire future rested upon Scott's success there. He decided to try journalism to support himself until his stories began to sell. He was not willing to have Zelda come North until he could show her the style of life he so wholeheartedly wanted them to share. Zelda was both astonished and delighted by the fervour of Scott's dreams for glory, and there is no doubt she shared them. 'She, she told herself, would move brightly along high places and stop to trespass and admire...'

On 14 February 1919 Scott's discharge from the army came through and on the 18th he left Montgomery for the East. In a gesture of consummate confidence he wired Zelda from New

York that the world was a game: '. . . WHILE I FEEL SURE OF
YOUR LOVE EVERYTHING IS POSSIBLE I AM IN THE LAND
OF AMBITION AND SUCCESS AND MY ONLY HOPE AND
FAITH IS THAT MY DARLING HEART WILL BE WITH ME
SOON.'

4

Throughout the spring of 1919 their letters crossed, written in that first flush of romance and absence keenly felt. Eagerly each awaited the other's reply, and the letters were in turn amorous and promising, filled with the news of what they did, wanted to do, and might yet accomplish. Unfortunately, Scott's letters have not survived, except for several wires, which Zelda pasted in her scrapbook, and his calling card sent with a special present. But Scott did keep Zelda's, and just as he had carefully noted in his Ledger when he had fallen in love, because there was 'something in his mind that catalogued and classified', so it was his instinct to preserve her love letters to him. She wrote in pencil usually, quickly and carelessly, not bothering to date her letters, nor to punctuate them, except for the characteristic schoolgirlish dash that separated each thought, or the occasional word underlined for emphasis. Her hand was large and round and upright; she called it her 'sun-burned, open-air looking script'.

These letters form the only record we have of her side of the affair. In them are the clues, in her own words rather than through Scott's interpretation, of what she was at eighteen. The only other written record that Zelda had kept up to this point in her life was her diary. And that apparently was lost or destroyed a long time ago. Scott had taken it with him to New York and showed it to at least one friend of his that spring, who said that it was 'a very human document, but somehow I cannot altogether understand it'.

Zelda's letters provide a key to her side of their romance. She had a striking ability with words that had nothing to do

with formal education; her thoughts drifted, swerved, and
tumbled in peculiarly swift transitions all her own; they teetered
sometimes on the edge of that special guile she could wield
toward Scott. But in these letters she could also be utterly open
with him; they are like conversations held in the dark between
lovers when they chart the small manoeuvres and upheavals
of their love.

Once in New York, Scott told his parents about his love for
Zelda and asked his mother to write a letter of welcome. At the
end of February Zelda told him: 'I s'pose you knew your
Mother's anxiously anticipated epistle at last arrived – I really
am so glad she wrote – Just a nice little note – untranslatable,
but she called me "Zelda"–'

Scott knew that a few days after he left for New York Zelda
was invited to Auburn for the week of 22 February. Her date
was Auburn's football hero Francis Stubbs, one of the most
skilful and attractive players the champions of the Southern
League possessed. No two men could have differed more than
Stubbs and Fitzgerald and no man could have seemed a more
formidable suitor in Scott's eyes than the dashing and superbly
confident Stubbs. For her scrapbook, Zelda clipped a photograph of him standing indolently with the great letter 'A' upon
his jersey, his soft leather helmet hanging loosely from his
hand. At the bottom of his invitation to Auburn he had written:
'Have a date with you Saturday P.M. Look out.' Today he remembers Zelda as 'a very popular and beautiful young lady and
she was not what is known as wild . . . but she was very much
full of life and pep'. He had not fallen in love with her, but
his room-mate had and kept a life-size photograph of her in his
room and 'thought he was going to marry her right up to the
time she married Scott Fitzgerald'. In Zelda's honour a special
society was formed at Auburn, known waggishly as Zeta Sigma;
its initiation rites included pilgrimages to 6 Pleasant Avenue
in Montgomery, and its members, five football players, were,
according to a newspaper clipping in her scrapbook, 'noted for
their almost rabid devotion to the principles of their fraternity'.
Understandably, Scott was worried, but Zelda rather blithely

reassured him: 'Sweetheart, please don't worry about me – I want to always be a help – You know I am all yours and love you with all my heart.'

Still, her trip had disconcerted him, for while he was trying to break into journalism in New York his girl was not exactly cooling her heels at home. He had arrived in the city and presented his calling card 'to the office boys of seven city editors asking to be taken on as a reporter. I had just turned twenty-two, the war was over, and I was going to trail murderers by day and do short stories by night. But the newspapers didn't need me.' So he settled on writing advertising copy for ninety dollars a month and was not happy with his compromise. (He came up with the only one snappy jingle, for a steam laundry in Iowa.) He wrote during every bit of spare time that he had and began a collection of rejection slips, which he carefully pinned on the walls of his rented room in the cheap and unfashionable Upper West Side. Zelda had promised to write every day.

Darling, I've nearly sat it off on the Strand to-day and all because W. E. Lawrence of the Movies is your physical counter-part. So I was informed by half a dozen girls before I could slam on a hat and see for myself – He made me so homesick – I thought at first waiting must grow easier later – but every day I want you more ... I am acquiring myriad wrinkles pondering over a reply to your Mother's note – I'm so dreadfully afraid of appearing fresh or presuming or casual – Most of my correspondents have always been boys, so I am at a loss – now in my hour of need – I really believe this is my first letter to a lady – ... An old flame from the Stone Ages is calling to-night – He'll probably leave in disgust because I just must talk about you – I love you so, and I'm *so* lonesome –

Her sister Clothilde was leaving for New York the following day to rejoin her husband, who had returned from service. The whole Sayre family got up before dawn to see Clothilde off.

It's the first time I've really seen early morning in a terribly long time – The sun all yellow and red, like a huge luminous peach hanging on a black shadow-tree – just visible thru the mist – and the family all sleepy-eyed and sad. Cold toes and tangled hair – I don't think I'll forget this morning. It's so much nicer to wake up early – I've felt so clean and wholesome all day because I saw the sun rise –

She took her first swim in the icy spring waters, and she reminded Scott:

Remember last summer how hard we tried to get a swim together? Tilde [Clothilde's nickname] informed me that I'd certainly do all my swimming in a bath-tub in New York – So please have a huge one, big enough for us both –

Darling, your love is so wonderful – I even believe you do as much as I do – Cource I will come – as soon as you're ready for me – There's nothing on earth I want like you – and you know I am yours – forever –

Then she told him about a prize fight she'd gone to, her first, and how exciting she found it, and about the loan a boy had made her of his motorcycle:

... it's most exhilirating – and I love flying thru the sand on the road where we walked once – and fussed about the woods –

March came and Scott sent her a glorious pair of pyjamas, which she said made her feel like a *Vogue* cover: '. . . I feel sure I'll never be able to keep off the street in 'em'; and he told her he adored short hair.

You really mustn't say short hair thrills you – Just after I've lived in Vaseline, thereby turning mine dark, to make it long like you wanted it – But anyway, it didn't grow, so I really am glad you're becoming reconciled to the ways of convenience – I still think how nice the back of my neck *would* feel –

More seriously she told him:

Darling, I guess – I know – Mamma knows that we are going to be married *some* day – But she keeps leaving stories of young authors, turned out on a dark and stormy night, on my pillow – I wonder if you hadn't better write to my Daddy – just before I leave – I wish I were detached – sorter without relatives. I'm not exactly *scared* of 'em, but they *could* be so unpleasant about what I'm going to do –

adding a little cryptically:

But you know we will, my Sweetheart – when you're ready – ... I don't see how you can carry around as much love as I've given you –

But Scott's life in New York was not going as smoothly as he had expected; his work bored and irritated him and, although there were parties and pleasant suppers in the evening with old friends from Princeton, he was no closer to having Zelda with him than when he left Montgomery. He was melancholy over his lack of funds and his inability to sell any of his stories, and his letters to Zelda reflected his unhappiness. Was she willing to wait for him and for how long could he count on her? Weren't her letters less frequent than before? Zelda tried to reassure him, and if she too was worried by his uneasiness, she concealed it as best she could.

Sweetheart

Please, please don't be so depressed – We'll be married soon, and then these lonesome nights will be over forever – and until we are, I am loving, loving every tiny minute of the day and night – Maybe you won't understand this, but sometimes when I miss you most, it's hardest to write – and you always know when I make myself – Just the ache of it all – and I CAN'T tell you. If we were together, you'd feel how strong it is – you're so sweet when you're melancholy. I love your sad tenderness – when I've hurt you – That's one of the reasons I could never be sorry for our quarrels – and they bothered you so – Those dear, dear little fusses, when I always tried so hard to make you kiss and forget –

Scott – there's nothing in all the world I want but you – and your precious love – All the material things are nothing. I'd just hate to live a sordid, colorless existence – because you'd soon love me less – and less – and I'd do anything – anything – to keep your heart for my own – I don't want to live – I want to love first, and live incidentally – Why don't you feel that I'm waiting – I'll come to you, Lover, when you're ready – Don't – don't ever think of the things you can't give me – You've trusted me with the dearest heart of all – and it's so damn much more than anybody else in all the world has ever had –

How can you think deliberately of life without me – If you should die – O Darling – darling Scot – It'd be like going blind. I know I would, too, – I'd have no purpose in life – just a pretty – decoration. Don't you think I was made for you? I feel like you had me ordered – and I was delivered to you – to be worn – I want you to wear me, like a watch – charm or a button hole bouquet – to the world. And then, when we're alone, I want to help – to know that you can't do *anything* without me.

I'm glad you wrote Mamma.* It was such a nice sincere letter – and mine to St Paul was very evasive and rambling. I've never, in all my life, been able to say anything to people older than me – Somehow I just instinctively avoid personal things with them – even my family. Kids are so much nicer.

It was an extraordinary letter, for it revealed Zelda's perception of Scott in relation to herself and to money; they were inextricably bound together. That she seems to have understood something of that link was remarkable. Scott was far more aware of the power of money than Zelda; he wanted it badly. Once he had it he would treat it with indifference, but its possession, as well as the people who possessed it, would become major elements of his fiction. Zelda's letter reassures Scott that while money, or 'All the material things', didn't matter to her, she knew that they did to him, and that because they did so deeply he would love her less were she not embellished by them. The extravagant language of Zelda's letter also expressed her feeling that without Scott she was nothing. It was through him, through private possession of him ('to know that you can't do *anything* without me'), that she spoke of their love. It was unfortunate that she thought of herself as having been 'ordered . . . to be worn' by Scott. She would accept being his creation, his fictional girl; she would match his ideal to the letter, if she could.

Buoyed by her letter, Scott offered Zelda an engagement ring which had been his mother's. On 22 March he wired her: 'DARLING . . . THE RING ARRIVED TONIGHT AND I AM SENDING IT MONDAY I LOVE YOU AND I THOUGHT I WOULD TELL YOU HOW MUCH ON THIS SATURDAY NIGHT WHEN WE OUGHT TO BE TOGETHER DONT LET YOUR FAMILY BE SHOCKED AT MY PRESENT.' When the small package arrived Rosalind inadvertently opened it. Enclosed along with the ring was Scott's calling card with this note written across it: 'Darling

---

*Scott had written to Mrs Sayre telling her he loved Zelda, something she undoubtedly already knew.

– I am sending this just the way it came – I hope it fits and I wish I were there to put it on. I love you so much, much, much that it just hurts every minute I'm without you – Do write every day because I love your letters so – Goodbye, My own Wife.' Scott had also written a letter to Judge Sayre, which he rather inappropriately intended Zelda to deliver for him. She read it and wrote Scott: 'I like your letter to A. D. and I'm slowly mustering courage to deliver it – He's so blind, it'll probably be a terrible shock to him, but it seems the only straight-forward thing to do.' Scott again wired her: '. . . BETTER GIVE LETTER TO YOUR FATHER IM SORRY YOURE NERVOUS DONT WRITE UNLESS YOU WANT TO I LOVE YOU DEAR EVERYTHING WILL BE MIGHTY FINE ALL MY LOVE.'

Zelda was delighted with the ring and told Scott it was beautiful. 'Every time I see it on my finger I am rather startled – I've never worn a ring before, they've always seemed so inappropriate – but I love to see this shining there so nice and white like our love – And it sorter says "Soon" to me all the time – Just sings it all day long.' That Saturday night she wore it to a dance at the country club to everyone's astonishment. 'You can't imagine what havoc the ring wrought,' she reported. 'A whole dance was completely upset last night – . . . I am so proud to be your girl – to have everybody know we are in love – It's so good to know you're always loving me – and that before long we'll be together for all our lives –'

Opinion in Montgomery was, however, by no means as simple as Zelda expressed it to Scott. Privately more than one swain wondered just how long their long-distance romance would endure. Zelda was not known for the longevity of her amours and Scott had already been gone for more than a month. The Sayres did not consider Zelda seriously engaged to Scott, and among themselves hoped that she wouldn't be. Although Mrs Sayre genuinely liked Fitzgerald, her notes to Zelda about impoverished writers unable to make their way took the effect they were intended to. Fitzgerald was a charming and attractive but uncertain young man; he had not graduated from Princeton, he was Irish, he had no career to speak of, he drank too much, and he was a Catholic.

Still, their correspondence flourished. Zelda wrote Scott that she hoped his mother would like her. 'I'll be as nice as possible and try to make her – but I am afraid I'm losing all pretense of femininity, and I imagine she will demand it –' Then, because he wanted to know exactly what she did with her time, she told him about a 'syndicate' she and Eleanor Browder had formed: '. . . we're "best friends" to more college boys than Solomon had wives – Just sorter buddying with 'em and I really am enjoying it – as much as I could anything without you – I have always been inclined toward masculinity. It's such a cheery atmosphere boys radiate – And we do such unique things –' The day before, a good friend of hers from the University of Alabama, John Sellers, was short of his return train fare. Zelda helped him collect what he needed by dressing up in long skirts, with a floppy old hat pulled low over her eyes, and carrying a tin cup at the railroad station while they begged for alms. She was having a grand time 'acquiring a bad name', as she put it, and thrived on the sensation she created.

As though to pacify any reaction to her cutting up, she added in one letter: '. . . every night I get very loud and coarse, and then I always wish for you so – so I wouldn't be such a kid –' But this did little to assuage his feelings about her adventures, and wild letters again crossed between New York and Montgomery. Zelda was obviously having fun, and even as she assured him of her love she was also writing him: 'The Ohio troops have started a wild and heated correspondence with Montgomery damsels. . . . I guess the butterflies will flitter a trifle more – It seems dreadfully peculiar not to be worried over the prospects of the return of at least three or four fiancées. My brain is stagnating owing to the lack of scrapes – I haven't had to exercise it in so long –' And in her fashion she added: 'Sweetheart, I love you most of all the earth – and I want to be married soon – soon – Lover – Don't say I'm not enthusiastic – You ought to know –' But Scott was beginning to wonder; April began and he visited Clothilde in New York in order to search for a suitable apartment for himself and Zelda.

Meanwhile Zelda was growing impatient in Montgomery; she was tired of waiting for Scott to make his fortune, and her petulance began to show in her letters. Writing about a woman she knew, she told Scott that all women 'love to fancy themselves suffering – they're nearly all moral and mental hypocrondiacs – If they'd just awake to the fact that their excuse and explanation is the necessity for a disturbing element among men – they'd be much happier, and the men much more miserable – which is exactly what they need for the improvement of things in general.' It was a nearly perfect summary of Zelda's own attitude toward men and Scott did not miss it. He put her letter almost verbatim into his novel *This Side of Paradise* as a pertinent description of 'Rosalind', who was partly patterned upon Zelda: 'Women she detested. They represented qualities that she felt and despised in herself – incipient meanness, conceit, cowardice, and petty dishonesty. She once told a roomful of her mother's friends that the only excuse for women was the necessity for a disturbing element among men.'

By the next letter Zelda's mood had again shifted; she told him all about a wild drive to Auburn 'with ten boys to liven things up' and an escapade down on Commerce Street near the river in the worst part of Montgomery, where she had donned men's clothes and gone to the movies with a gang of boys. Fitzgerald was furious. Rather coolly she assured him:

Scott, you're really awfully silly – In the first place, I haven't kissed anybody good-bye, and in the second place, nobody's left in the first place – You know, darling, that I love you too much to want to. If I did have an honest – or dishonest – desire to kiss just one or two people, I *might* – but I couldn't ever want to – my mouth is yours.

Maddeningly, she went on:

But s'pose I did – Don't you know it'd just be absolutely *nothing* – Why can't you understand that nothing means anything except your darling self and your love – I wish we'd hurry and I'd be yours so you'd *know* – Sometimes I almost despair of making you feel sure – so sure that nothing could ever make you doubt like I do –

It was definitely not the sort of letter that would reassure

Scott and, afraid that other men were seeing Zelda often, too often, on April he took a few days' holiday and went to Montgomery. After the trip he wrote in his Ledger: 'Failure. I used to wonder why they locked princesses in towers.'

But, if Scott considered the trip a failure, Zelda did not seem to.

Scott my darling lover –
everything seems so smooth and restful, like this yellow dusk. Knowing that I'll always be yours – that you really own me – that nothing can keep us apart – is such a relief after the strain and nervous excitement of the last month. I'm so glad you came – like Summer, just when I needed you most – and took me, back with you. Waiting doesn't seem so hard now. The vague despondency has gone – I love you Sweetheart.

He'd apparently brought some gin when he came, the 'best at the Exchange', and Zelda told him, 'I'd rather have had 10c. a quart variety – I wanted it just to know you loved the sweetness – To breathe and know you loved the smell –' Then, abruptly, the transition being perhaps the aroma of the gin, she added:

I think I like breathing twilit gardens and moths more than beautiful pictures or good books – It seems the most sensual of all the senses – Something in me vibrates to a dusky, dreamy spell – a smell of dying moons and shadows –

I've spent to-day in the grave-yard – It really isn't a cemetery, you know, trying to unlock a rusty iron vault built in the side of the hill. It's all washed and covered with weepy, watery blue flowers that might have grown from dead eyes – sticky to touch with a sickening odor – The boys wanted to get in to test my nerve to-night – I wanted to *feel* 'William Wreford, 1864'. Why should graves make people feel in vain? I've heard that *so* much, and Grey is *so* convincing, but somehow I can't find anything hopeless in having lived – All the broken columnes and clasped hands and doves and angels mean romances – and in an hundred years I think I shall like having young people speculate on whether my eyes were brown or blue – of cource, they are neither – I hope my grave has an air of many, many years ago about it – Isn't it funny how, out of a row of Confederate soldiers, two or three will make you think of dead lovers and dead loves – when they're exactly like the others, even to the yellowish moss? Old death is so beautiful – so very beautiful – We will die together – I know –

> Sweetheart –

Touched by the beauty of her letter, he sent her a marvellous flamingo-coloured feather fan. It was the perfect gift for Zelda, frivolous and entirely beautiful; she was delighted by it.

Those feathers – those wonderful, wonderful feathers are the most beautiful things on earth – so soft like little chickens, and rosy like firelight. I feel so rich and pompous waving them around in the air and covering up myself with 'em. . . .

I love you most of everything on earth, and somehow you [your] visit made things so much saner, and I *do* believe in you – Just the wild rush and knowing what you did was distasteful to you – made me afraid – I'd die rather than see you miserable. . . . I want to go to Italy – with you, Darling – It seems so yellow – dull, mellow yellow – and that's your color –

Each year a secret society called *Les Mysteriéuses*, which was composed of sixty socially prominent young matrons and girls, gave a ball. That April it was a 'Folly Ball', and Mrs Sayre and Rosalind wrote the playlet that preceded it. The auditorium in which it was presented was covered with a canopy of yellow and black ribbons intertwined and baskets of yellow roses. The part of Folly was played by Zelda, who, dressed in a costume of black-and-gold malines trimmed with tiny bells, danced upon her toes, 'using numbers of small balloons as she went through the mazes of the dance'. Zelda had Kodak snapshots taken of herself for Scott, as she posed in her costumes among her mother's roses in their back yard. Her face had taken on a haunting prettiness; she was slimmer than she had ever been before (she said in a letter to Scott that she wanted to be '5 ft. 4 in. x 2 in.'), and with her piercing eyes, high cheekbones and straight nose she looked very much (as John Peale Bishop was later to describe her) the 'barbarian princess'.

Zelda continued to cut up and just for the fun of it she and Eleanor Browder talked a streetcar conductor into letting them drive his trolley, and before the poor man realized what he'd done the girls had run it off the track, or so Zelda wrote to Scott.

Then we got fired – but we were tired, anyway! Mothers of our associates just stood by and gasped – much to our glee, of cource – Things like the preceeding incident are our only amusement –

Darling heart, I love you – truly.... I must leave or my date (awful boob) will come before I can escape –

Good Night, Lover

She closed her letter with a pencil drawing of the outline of her lips; 'This is the biggest kiss of any on earth – because I love you.'

Some of the fun was not so innocent, however:

Look at this communication from Mamma – all on account of a wine-stained dress – Darling heart – I won't drink *any* if you object – Sometimes I get so bored – and sick for you – It helps then – and afterwards, I'm just more bored and sicker for you – and ashamed –

When are you going to marry me – I don't want to repeat those two months – but I've just got to have you – When you can – because I love you, my husband –

                                                                Zelda

The enclosed note read:

Zelda:

If you have added whiskey to your tobacco you can substract your Mother.... If you prefer the habits of a prostitute don't try to mix them with gentility. Oil and water do not mix.

In May the 4th Alabama regiment arrived in Montgomery from France, and the town turned itself into a colourful Mardi Gras to welcome them. There were large booths built along the streets, decorated with flags and confetti and streamers, and all the houses including the Governor's were opened to welcome the returning heroes. Old costumes and masks were taken out of chests and dusted off and refurbished for the celebration. Rosalind's husband's company was going to march with the ranks unfilled; twenty-three of his men had been lost. Zelda wrote: 'It almost makes me cry – I would if I weren't expending all my energy on gum.

'I've started a continuous chew again – Your disapproval used to put me on the wagon, but now I've got the habit again –'

Scott had written her that he wanted to come to Montgomery again the middle of the month, and she replied, 'Darling Sweetheart, I'll be *so* glad to see you again –' But she didn't leave it at that; she told him that if he waited until June he could accompany her as far as Atlanta, where she was to attend the commencement at Georgia Tech. 'I'm going to ... try my hand in new fields', she added with a stunning insensitivity to his feelings. Ruthlessly she stimulated his already intense sense of competition for her.

In a rather pathetic attempt to keep her home, Scott had sent her Compton Mackenzie's book *Plasher's Mead* to read. But she didn't like it: 'Nothing annoys me more than having the most trivial action analyzed and explained.' She said the heroine was 'ATROCIOUSLY uninteresting' and maybe she'd save the book and try to read it again in rainy weather. But she also tipped her hand more than she may have intended, for in the same letter she told him, 'People seldom interest me except in their relations to things, and I like men to be just incidents in books so I can imagine their characters –' Everything, it seemed, had to revolve around her, her perceptions, her games, or she was not interested and refused to play. Certainly that letter carried a note of warning about herself, if Fitzgerald had been in any condition to receive it. But he was not. He knew the terms, they were remarkably like his own, and that exquisite egotism drew him even more completely to her.

But what he did not fully perceive, perhaps because Zelda did not, was the uncertainty within his girl. For, as worldly as she loved to seem to be, as reckless and ebullient as she was, Zelda knew nothing first hand of any world other than the protected Southern one of provincial towns and families who knew one another and were kin. For all her banter, New York, chic and fabulous, must have seemed as remote to her as the Orient.

Scott had sent Zelda a map of Manhattan, which she said might just as well have been China. 'All I saw was the dot where we would live – I couldn't help wondering over the fact that two rooms and bath took up the same space as Washington Square and Statue of Liberty.' In a last-ditch effort to arouse Zelda's jealousy, Scott told her a story about an attractive girl he had met in New York, an actress, but it backfired when Zelda replied quite seriously, 'Anyway, if she's good-looking, and you want to one bit – I know you could and love me just the same.' That was not the reaction he had bargained for, and he was left without a rebuttal. If she was faking, she cleverly made it sound as if she meant what she said – and, if she approved such behaviour for him, might she not intend to do the same herself?

Zelda had said she wanted him to come South again; he replied that he still preferred to make the trip in May. He arranged to come for a few days and they had fun together, but he returned to New York with nothing settled; he promised her he'd come again in three weeks. Feeling more and more disheartened by his dreary lack of fortune in New York, Scott began to take it out on his friends there. He threatened to jump from the window of his club and the rest of the young men, weary of his moping, encouraged him; abashedly he climbed back down. There was one piece of luck. His story 'Babes in the Woods' (which he had written while at Princeton) was bought by *The Smart Set* for $30. It wasn't much, but it was a beginning. With the money he bought himself a pair of smart white flannels and sent Zelda a sweater. She wrote that it was 'perfectly delicious – and I'm going to save it till you come in June so you can tell me how nice I look – It's funny, but I like being "pink and helpless" – When I know I seem that way, I feel terribly competent – and superior.' Adding, with that touch of self-perception she summoned for Scott alone: 'I keep thinking, "Now those men think I'm purely decorative, and they're just fools for not knowing better" – and I love being rather unfathomable. You are the only person on earth, Lover, who has ever known and loved all of me. Men love me cause I'm pretty – and they're always afraid of mental wickedness – and men love me cause I'm clever, and they're always afraid of my prettiness – One or two have even loved me cause I'm lovable, and then, of cource, I was acting.'

Zelda told him she was just beginning to realize the seriousness of their attachment, just beginning to believe in a future that would hold them together. 'I can't think of anything but nights with you – I want them warm and silvery – when we can be to-gether all our lives – . . . I don't want you to see me growing old and ugly. I know you'll be a beautiful old man – romantic and dreamy – and I'll probably be most prosaic and wrinkled. We will just *have* to die when we're thirty. I wish your name were Paul, or Jacquelyn. I'm going to name all our children that – and Peter – yours and mine – because we love each other –' That letter must have calmed him considerably.

But by the end of May the dances and parties at the colleges had begun in earnest and Zelda did not languish at home. She would soon be nineteen; her sisters were married; Clothilde and Rosalind were already in New York. Zelda was alone with her parents, and definitely not eager to stay there for long.

After one particularly gay weekend away from Montgomery she wrote Scott: '. . . I'll never feel grown. I absolutely despair of it. . . . And still I'm so mighty happy – It's just sort of a "thankful" feeling – that I'm alive and that people are glad I am.' Her letters to him, however, had begun to be less frequent; she said he'd been sweet about writing '– but I'm so damned tired of being told that you "used to wonder why they kept princesses in towers" – you've written that, verbatim, in your last *six* letters! It's dreadfully hard to write so very much – and so many of your letters sound forced – I know you love me, Darling, and I love you more than anything in the world, but if its going to be so much longer, we just *can't* keep up this frantic writing. It's like the last week we were to-gether –' Evasively, she said she wanted to feel that he knew she was thinking of him always. 'I hate writing when I haven't time, and I just have to scribble a few lines – I'm saying all this so you'll understand – Hectic affairs of any kind are rather trying, so *please* let's write calmly and whenever you feel like it.'

She had a nervous habit of biting the skin on her lips, which irritated Scott and which she had tried hard to break. But it began again, she said, as she 'relapsed into a nervous stupor. It feels like going crazy knowing everything you do and being utterly powerless not to do it –' She wrote that she felt like screaming. With what must have been a painful and supreme exercise of will power, he did not write to her for one week. When at last he did, Zelda said she appreciated his letter: 'It must have been a desperate struggle to write it, but your efforts were not wasted on an unreceptive audience.' Then, in a typical aboutface, she chided him. 'Just the same, the only thing that carried me through a muddy, rainy, boring Auburn Commencement was the knowledge that I'd have a note, at least, from you when I got home – but I didn't. ... Not that letters make so much difference, and if you don't want to write we'll stop, but I love you so – and I hate being disappointed day after day.'

Scott's next letter must have sounded hysterical, for that was a word he was using frequently in his Ledger to describe these months. Zelda's reply was hardly soothing.

There's nothing to say – you know everything about me, and that's mostly what I think about. I seem always curiously interested in myself, and it's so much fun to stand off and look at me –
But this:
I know you've worried – and enjoyed doing it thoroughly, and I didn't want you to *because* something always makes things the way they ought to be – even this time – AND ITS ALL RIGHT – Somehow, I rather hate to tell you that – I know its depriving you of an idea that horrifies and fascinates – you're so morbidly exaggerative – Your mind dwells on things that don't make people happy – I can't explain, but its rather kin to the way kids 13 feel when everybody goes off and leaves them at home – if they aren't scary, of cource. Sort of deliberately experimental and wiggly –

Two of his letters were not delivered because he had forgotten to put stamps on them. Zelda said it looked to her 'like wild nights and headachy mornings', and told Scott that because she had not heard from him she had sought consolation with a young man from Georgia Tech who was in Montgomery for the golf tournament at the country club. 'I'll be in Atlanta till Wednesday, and I hope – I want you to so much – you'll come down soon as I get back.' But she was definitely set on going to Georgia Tech. She had said she was going to try her hand in the new fields and she did. The society columns and rotogravure sections in both Atlanta and Montgomery newspapers burst with pictures and stories of her exploits in their Sunday sections: 'Pretty Montgomery Girl Creates Stir Among Atlanta Youths';

they called her 'One of Montgomery's most popular girls, and bewitchingly pretty . . .'

Zelda left Montgomery wearing a fluffy light dress, and her Leghorn hat with streamers down the back. When she arrived in Atlanta there were four young men waiting to meet her at the train station. Each thought he was her date, for she had separately agreed to be the date of each of the gentlemen. This was just the beginning of the stir she raised in Georgia that weekend. At one point it was rumoured that she was going to swim in the nude at a private pool, but it was simply her flesh-coloured bathing suit again. One of the young ladies who was with Zelda that weekend remembered coming back late one night to the fraternity house where they were both guests to find Zelda and her date, drunk as lords, playfully smashing Victrola records over each other's heads – an event that was not reported in the newspapers. When Zelda returned to Montgomery she was pinned to the young golfer she had met during the golf tournament.

Once home and sober, Zelda thought better about being pinned while being engaged to Scott and returned the Georgian's fraternity pin with a sentimental note. Carelessly – for she was to insist that it was an accident – Zelda put the letter intended for the young golfer into an envelope that she sent to Scott. Furious, he asked her never to write to him again. Nevertheless, Zelda did try to explain, but it was an awkward situation for which there really was no explanation.

Scott wired her desperately that he would be in Montgomery on the next train. The precarious balance of their affair had tipped downward; neither of them could bear the strain of the past few months any longer. Edgy and fatigued, knowing full well, as he was to write, 'I was in love with a whirlwind and I must spin a net big enough to catch it', Scott decided that Zelda had to marry him immediately. They sat together in the the familiar front room of the Sayres' house and Scott asked her to marry him now. Zelda refused. Both cried, and Scott stormed and tried to force her into marrying him with wild kisses and frantic arguments. He began to beseech Zelda, which was not at all the right tactic, for it demeaned him in her eyes, and she more resolutely than ever shied from accepting his proposal. He became self-pitying and would not leave the house.

Scott had expected her to be certain of him when he was most uncertain of himself. When everything in New York had failed him, his career and his writing, he turned to Zelda with a proposal of immediate marriage made as much out of desperation as of love. It was an effort on Scott's part to redeem at least a fraction of his dreams for success and happiness, but Zelda must have felt it to be founded in failure and she could not accept marriage on that basis. Scott said that he had to have her with him in order to succeed, but perhaps Zelda sensed that if she did marry him and he was still unsuccessful the onus of his failure would rest squarely on her shoulders. For Zelda marriage was the only means of altering the scope of her life. Scott would never forget her refusal; he would in time explain it away by saying that she was afraid to risk a life with him until he was a moneymaker. But that was unfair; it was only as his own faith in himself waned that hers became increasingly unsure. Finally Zelda told him to leave. He boarded the next train for New York, with his mother's ring in his pocket, certain that he had lost his girl forever. But even as he left a part of him admired Zelda's unwillingness to give up the bright and irrevocable dreams that possessed her. He believed, as he would soon write, 'the girl really worth having won't wait for anybody'.

However shaken Zelda was by her broken engagement, she did not confide her feelings to any of her friends, nor did she give her family a word of explanation. If there was a sense of relief from the strain of their affair, that too she kept to herself. With Scott gone, that summer in Montgomery drifted by as every one before it had for Zelda; the heat and the inertia caused by it slowed the tempo of the city into its usual lull. There were dances and swimming parties. On one particular summer afternoon Zelda went swimming with a group of girls at a pool which was built behind the local chemical plant to be used in case of fire. It had a diving board and Zelda eagerly climbed the ladder and got into position for a swan dive. As she moved her arms forward the straps on her swimming suit caught uncomfortably across her arms, and swiftly she released the straps and stepped out of the suit. She stood poised for an instant like a water nymph, rose upon her toes and leaped from the board. The others were held spellbound by her audacity and beauty; they were also terrified that she would be seen or that their mothers would hear about it.

In a story Zelda wrote later, she said there existed in Montgomery then 'a time and quality that appertains to nowhere else. It began about half past six on an early summer night, with the flicker and sputter of the corner street lights going on, and it lasted until the great incandescent globes were black inside with moths and beetles and the children were called in to bed from the dusty streets.' Lawns were drenched with arcs of water thrown from hoses, and everything, even time, seemed to stand still before the onslaught of the heat. 'The drug stores are bright at night with the organdie balloons of girls' dresses under the big electric fans. Automobiles stand along the curbs in front of open frame houses at dusk, and sounds of supper being prepared drift through the soft splotches of darkness to the young world that moves every evening out of doors. Telephones ring, and the lacy blackness under the trees disgorges young girls in white and pink, leaping over the squares of warm light toward the tinkling sound with an expectancy that people have only in places where any event is a pleasant one. Nothing seems ever to happen ...'

Scott had returned to New York just long enough to quit his job and indulge in a spectacular bender that lasted until Prohibition closed the bars three weeks later. On Independence Day, with Hugh Walpole's novel *Fortitude* under his arm, he took the train home to St Paul. He had decided to rewrite his novel; it was, he wrote, 'my ace in the hole'. If it was good enough he could recoup all his losses, and if it wasn't he was no worse off than when he began. For the rest of July and all of August he worked on the novel, which he had decided to call either *The Education of a Personage*, *The Romantic Egotist*, or *This Side of Paradise*. He wrote Edmund Wilson in August that since he had last seen him 'I've tried to get married and then tried to drink myself to death but foiled, as have been so many good men, by the sex and the state I have returned to literature'. By September his novel was again at Scribner's in the hands of Maxwell Perkins, who had read his earlier drafts. Within two weeks Scott was sent a contract for the publication of *This Side of Paradise*. As soon as he received word of its acceptance he wrote Perkins pressing for immediate publication. 'I have so many things dependent on its success – including of course a girl – not that I expect it to make me a fortune but it will have a psychological effect on me and all my surroundings. . . .' Zelda could not then have known anything about it, for Scott had not corresponded with her since their break in June. It was Fitzgerald, and not she, who connected the success of *This Side of Paradise* with a willingness on her part to marry him. But so far its only success was that Scribner's was going to publish it.

In a section of the novel called 'The Débutante', Scott had come to terms with his loss of Zelda. He called her Rosalind and used portions of Zelda's letters and diary to help create the atmosphere of her charm. ('The Débutante' had been written while Scott was at Princeton and still under the spell of Ginevra King, on whom he modelled the character of Helen. But in rewriting this section for his novel Helen became Rosalind, just as his impressions of Ginevra melded into those of Zelda.) 'Rosalind,' he wrote, 'is – utterly Rosalind. She is one of those girls who need never make the slightest effort to have men fall in love with them. Two types of men seldom do: dull men are usually afraid of her cleverness and intellectual men are usually afraid of her beauty. All others are hers by natural prerogative.' That was taken almost word for word from a letter Zelda had written him in the spring. Several paragraphs later he added: 'She danced exceptionally well, drew cleverly but hastily, and had a startling facility with words, which she used only in love-letters. ... She was perhaps the delicious, inexpressible, once-in-a-century blend.'

Scott had not been able to put Zelda out of his mind and in October he wrote to her, telling of his success and asking whether he might come South to see her once again. She replied:

I'm mighty glad you're coming – I've been wanting to see you (which you probably knew) but I *couldn't* ask you – ... It's fine, and I'm tickled to death.

And another thing:

I'm just recovering from a wholesome amour with Auburn's 'startling quarter-back' so my disposition is excellent as well as my heath [health]. Mentally, you'll find me dreadfully detiorated – but you never seemed to know when I was stupid and when I wasn't, anyway –

Please bring me a quart of gin – I haven't had a drink all summer, and you're already *ruined* along alcoholic lines with Mrs. Sayre – After you left, every corner ... was occupied by a bottle (or bottles). ...

'S funny, Scott, I don't feel a bit shaky and 'do-don't'ish like I used to when you came – I really want to see you – that's all –

After he heard from Zelda, he wrote to Ludlow Fowler, in

whom he had confided about his affair: 'Hope you've guarded well the great secret. God! Lud I'll never get over it as long as I live. There's still a faint chance. Thank fortune.' It was less than five months since he and Zelda had last seen each other, and Scott went to Montgomery that November in 1919 to see if he wanted her as badly as he once had. Before he left he again wrote Fowler: '... not even the family knows I'm going to Montgomery so keep it dark. ... God knows tho', Lud, I may be a wreck by the time I see you. I'm going to try to settle it definitely one way or the other.'

Certainly Scott was returning to Zelda triumphantly, but as they sat in the front room of the Sayres' house everything looked smaller than he remembered it. In a story called 'The Sensible Thing' Scott described how he felt that afternoon as he realized that for himself the first fresh exhilaration of love was a perishable sensation: 'Well, let it pass, he thought. ... There are all kinds of love in the world, but never the same love twice.' He had fought for his rare girl; his novel, he could now tell her, would be published; but he wanted to force the scene of their reconciliation into a greater intensity than it could yield. He had had five months in which to let his imagination play over this meeting and the reality of it could not match his expectations. Nonetheless, before he left her for New York they had renewed their engagement; they decided to marry as soon as his book was published.

Zelda understood him better than he thought, for after he left Montgomery she wrote to him that if he felt he had lost his feeling for her, if he'd be happier without their marrying, she would release him from whatever promises had once been made. And she added: 'Somehow "When love has turned to kindliness" doesn't horrify me like it used to – It has such a peaceful sound – like something to come back to and rest – and sometimes I'm glad we're not exactly like we used to be – and I can't help feeling that it would all come again.'

Whether the timing of their marriage date was Zelda's or Scott's idea is unknown. What is certain is that Zelda could not possibly have agreed to marry him, as he later thought, on the basis of his having made money. He had made very little by

November 1919. But what she did see quite clearly was that Fitzgerald was no longer unsure of himself or the direction of his career. The cheeky young man who wrote (to a girl he knew in St Paul),

> Mr Fate
> Can't berate
> Mr Scott.
> He is not
> Marking time : ...

on the news of the acceptance of his novel was as effervescent as the young lieutenant who had promised Zelda New York with 'all the iridescence of the beginning of the world'.

When he left Montgomery he gave Zelda a manuscript copy of *This Side of Paradise*. After she had read it she wrote him: 'Why can't I write? I'd like to tell you how fine I think the book is and how miserably and completely and – a little unexpectedly – I am thine.' In another letter, probably written a few days later, she added : 'I am very proud of you – I hate to say this, but I don't *think* I had much confidence in you at first. ... It's so nice to know that you really can do things – *anything* – And I love to feel that maybe I can help just a little – I want to so much – ... I'm so damn glad I love you – I wouldn't love any other man on earth – I believe if I had deliberately decided on a sweetheart, he'd have been you –'

Scott had already begun to make plans for where they would live and Zelda asked him not to 'accumulate a lot of furniture. Really, Scott, I'd just as soon live *anywhere* – and can't we find a bed ready-made? Someday, you know we'll want rugs and wicker furniture and a home – I'm terribly afraid it'll just be in the way now. I wish New York were a little tiny town – so I could imagine how it'd be. I haven't the remotest idea of what it's like, so I am afraid to make any suggestions.' But she did tell him that she imagined their apartment decorated with large orange and black fruits on the walls and bright yellow ceilings.

Her sister Rosalind sent her a programme from the *Follies* in New York, telling Zelda that she looked enough like Marilyn Miller to be her twin. Zelda wrote Scott that it 'upset me so I couldn't do anything *but* act and dance for a day or two –' But, despite the glimmer of ambition, she saw her own limitations with a good deal of perception. 'I hope I'll never get ambitious enough to try anything. It's so *much* nicer to be damned sure I *could* do it better than other people – and I might not could if I tried – that, of cource, would break my heart –'

Scott was not content to suppose that he could do anything better than the next man; he was out to prove that he was a writer of the first water. Stimulated by the sale of *This Side of Paradise*, he was working hard, old stories were refurbished and tightened, and he wove fresh material into fiction almost as soon as something happened to him. All of it began to sell. He had acquired an agent in New York, the young Harold Ober, who worked for the Reynolds Agency, and it was Ober who sold Scott's story 'Head and Shoulders' to the *Saturday Evening Post* for $400. The first sale to the *Post* was important to Scott, for he intended to make money, a lot of it, and he knew that the smaller magazines or the more literary ones, like *The Smart Set*, to which he had sold a few stories, couldn't be expected to pay as the *Post* would.

Each time a story was taken he wired Zelda of his success and he drank to celebrate it; he even acquired his own bootlegger, which was a bit of a novelty in those early days of Prohibition. Four pages of Zelda's scrapbook are filled with these wires, which with very few exceptions coupled an assurance to her of his love with the latest news of his literary sales. 'THE SATURDAY EVENING POST HAS JUST TAKEN TWO MORE STORIES PERIOD ALL MY LOVE.' 'I HAVE SOLD THE MOVIE RIGHTS OF HEAD AND SHOULDERS TO THE METRO COMPANY FOR TWENTY FIVE HUNDRED DOLLARS I LOVE YOU DEAREST GIRL.' At this point in their lives Zelda was already committed to him and these wires were sent more for Scott's satisfaction than hers. Perhaps he realized that Montgomery acquaintances were saying that of course it was *nice* that Scott was a writer and had sold things to the *Saturday Evening Post*, but it wasn't really a *position*. By January 1920 a combination of the emotional strain he put himself through in order to write and the drinking had worn him out, and he decided to go to

New Orleans to rest and to search for new story material. He would also be only a few hours from Zelda. In his Ledger he wrote that by 10 January he had made $1,700.

Although Zelda told Scott that it would break her heart to try to do something and find out that she could not, and that faced with that choice she would rather not try, she was nevertheless aware that Scott had drawn on some of her own writing in *This Side of Paradise*, and half seriously, she suggested maybe she would try to write, too. In a letter to Scott she revealed something of her own ambivalence about the effort involved, and something of her idea of herself:

Yesterday I almost wrote a book or story, I hadn't decided which, but after two pages on my heroine I discovered that I hadn't even started her, and, since I couldn't just write forever about a charmingly impossible creature, I began to despair. 'Vamping Romeo' was the name, and I guess a man would have had to appear somewhere before the end. But there wasn't any plot, so I thought I'd ask you how to decide what they're going to do. Mamma answered my S.O.S. with one of O. Henry's, verbatim, which I discarded because he never *created* people – just things to happen to the same old kind of folks and unexpected ends, and I like stories with all the ladies like Constance Talmadge and the men just sorter strong, silent characters or college boys – ... And so you see, Scott, I'll never be able to do anything because I'm much too lazy to care whether it's done or not – And I don't want to be famous and fêted – all I want is to be very young always and very irresponsible and to feel that my life is my own – to live and be happy and die in my own way to please myself –

She also added a remarkably sensible reply to Scott's anxiety about the lost intensity of their love. She said he was trying too hard to convince himself that they were like old people who had lost their most precious possession. 'We really haven't found it yet – And only weaklings ... who lack courage and the power to feel they're right when the whole world says they're wrong, ever lose –' If Scott was worried about losing the fire and sweetness of desire, Zelda was not. 'That first abandon couldn't last, but the things that went to make it are tremendously alive', and she asked him not to mourn for a memory when they had each other.

Scott made two trips to Montgomery during January, and after one of them he sent Zelda a lavish platinum-and-diamond wristwatch. He bought it with the $2,500 from the sale of 'Head and Shoulders' to the movies. Zelda, who adored any gift but especially one which was like none anyone else in Montgomery possessed, was delighted with it. She said, 'I've turned it over four hundred times to see "from Scott to Zelda"', which was inscribed on its back.

Mamma came in with the package, and I thought maybe it might interest her to know, so she sat on the edge of the bed while I told her we were going to marry each other pretty soon. She wants me to come to New York, because she says you'd like to do it in St. Patrick's. Now that she knows, everything seems mighty definite and nice, and I'm not a bit scared or shaky – What I dreaded most was telling her – Somehow I just didn't think I could – Both of us are very splashy, vivid pictures, those kind with the details left out, but I know our colors will blend, and I think we'll look very well hanging beside each other in the gallery of life.

She added in brackets that this was '*not* just another one of my "subterranean river" thoughts'. She even loved him enough, she reported, to read a novel by Frank Norris, *McTeague*, which Scott had recommended very highly to her.

It certainly makes a miserable start – . . . All authors who want to make things true to life make them *smell* bad – like McTeague's room – and that's my most sensitive sense. I do hope you'll never be a realist – one of those kind that thinks being ugly is being forceful –
When my wedding's going to be, write to me again – and if you'd rather have me come up there I will – I told Mamma I might just come and surprise you, but she said you mightn't like to be surprised about 'your own wedding' – I rather think it's MY wedding –

During Scott's trips up from New Orleans they resumed their affair. In February Scott left New Orleans for New York to await the publication of his novel. On 26 February, while staying at Cottage Club in Princeton, he wrote a friend of his who knew only that Scott and Zelda's engagement had been broken the previous June. This friend had recently written Scott to tell him that he had been right in breaking off the relationship. The timing of the letter was, of course, awkward. Scott replied that candour compelled him to admit that it was Zelda and not he who had broken their earlier engagement. He said that he realized his friends were unanimous in advising him against marriage to Zelda and that he was used to it.

No personality as strong as Zelda's could go without getting criticism.... I've always known that, any girl who gets stewed in public, who frankly enjoys and tells shocking stories, who smokes constantly and makes the remark that she has 'kissed thousands of men and intends to kiss thousands more', cannot be considered beyond reproach even if above it.... I fell in love with her courage, her sincerity and her flaming self respect and its these things I'd believe in even if the whole world indulged in wild suspicions that she wasn't all that she should be.... I love her and that's the beginning and end of everything. You're still a catholic but Zelda's the only God I have left now.

He then wired Zelda, who had sent him a photograph of herself: 'THE PICTURE IS LOVELY AND SO ARE YOU DARLING.'

Lawton Campbell, a tall, blond and rather elegant young gentleman from Montgomery, who had gone to Princeton with Scott, ran into him in New York while lunching at the Yale Club, where the Princeton Club had temporary quarters that March. As Campbell started up the stairs to the second floor Scott was coming down, beaming.

He had in his hand a color-illustrated jacket cover of a book. On seeing me, with almost childish glee and radiating good news he said, 'Look what I have here!'
He showed me the cover. I read '*This Side of Paradise*. F. Scott Fitzgerald. Charles Scribner and Sons.' ...
'It's all about Princeton,' Scott said in that breathless way he spoke when he was excited. 'You'll probably recognize some of your friends. You might even recognize something of yourself.'
Then he added, 'It'll be out before the end of the month.'
Zelda flashed across my mind. I told him I had seen her when I

was in Montgomery and had put in a good word for him. He thanked me and then looked at the jacket-cover. He knitted his brow a minute as if to indicate that the months of hard labor on the book would be rewarded in more ways than one. He smiled and said:

'I phoned her long distance last night. She's still on the fence and I may have to go to Montgomery to get her but I believe this will do the trick.'

By March, of course, the trick had already been turned, but perhaps Scott was no longer taking anything for granted. At this point the only thing Scott and Zelda were on the fence about was the exact date of their marriage.

The Sayres announced Zelda's engagement on 20 March, and Scott sent her a corsage of orchids, her first. Scott had moved to his club in Princeton to await Zelda's arrival and while there went to the prom and completed work on a story called 'May Day', Zelda wrote Scott one last letter before she came to him for good.

Darling Heart, our fairy tale is almost ended, and we're going to marry and live happily ever afterward just like the princess in her tower who worried you so much – and made me so very cross by her constant recurrence – I'm sorry for all the times I've been mean and hateful – for all the miserable minutes I've caused you when we could have been so happy. You deserve so much – so very much –

I think our life together will be like these last four days – and I *do* want to marry you – even if you do think I 'dread' it – I wish you hadn't said that – I'm not afraid of anything. To be afraid a person has either to be a coward or very great and big. I am neither. Besides, I know you can take much better care of me than I can, and I'll always be very, very happy with you – except sometimes when we engage in our weekly debates – and even then I rather enjoy myself. I like being very calm and masterful, while you become emotional and sulky.... I'm absolutely nothing without you – Just the doll that I should have been born – You're a necessity and a luxury and a darling, precious lover – and you're going to be a husband to your wife –

This Side of Paradise was published on 26 March. Scott took rooms at the Biltmore Hotel and waited for Zelda to arrive from Montgomery with her sister Marjorie; he was still not certain of the exact date of her arrival. At last they decided to marry on Saturday 3 April and Scott wired her on 30 March: '... WE WILL BE AWFULLY NERVOUS UNTIL IT IS OVER AND WOULD GET NO REST BY WAITING UNTIL MONDAY FIRST EDITION OF THE BOOK IS SOLD OUT.'

Zelda was giddy with excitement the night before she left Montgomery and stayed up until morning laughing and devising fantastic schemes with Eleanor Browder about what she would do as the wife of F. Scott Fitzgerald in Manhattan. Her plots ran to turning cartwheels in hotel lobbies and sliding down the banisters of the great hotels. Right up to the last moment one of her beaux thought she might reconsider his proposal and not marry Scott. When friends of her mother's saw her shopping for her trousseau and asked her if the lucky young man was indeed Scott Fitzgerald as they had heard, she winked at one of them and said, 'It might be and it might be Red Ruth.'

Her friends thought she had made a brilliant match, but her family was still anxious about her marriage. Neither the Judge nor Mrs Sayre went with Zelda to New York. Other members of the family thought that her parents would not have been happy about the prospect of a Catholic marriage in Montgomery.

The day before Easter Sunday, 3 April 1920, Scott and Zelda met in the rectory of St Patrick's Cathedral. The entire wedding party was to consist of eight people – Marjorie, Clothilde and John Palmer, Rosalind and Newman Smith, and Scott's best man, Ludlow Fowler. They were to be married at noon, but Scott grew fidgety before the appointed time and insisted that the ceremony begin immediately, before the Palmers had arrived. Zelda wore a suit of midnight blue with a matching hat trimmed with leather ribbons and buckles; she carried a bouquet of orchids and small white flowers. It was a brilliantly sunny day and when they stepped outside the cathedral Zelda looked for all the world like a young goddess of spring, with Scott at her side as consort.

2. The Twenties

6

So you see that old libel that we were cynics and skeptics was nonsense from the beginning. On the contrary we were the great believers.

F. SCOTT FITZGERALD, 'My Generation'

Zelda and Scott put their first wedding present, a Tiffany chocolate set, on the dresser in their Biltmore suite 2109, and beside it a wilting Easter lily, which remained in place throughout their honeymoon. One of the first things that Zelda did as the wife of F. Scott Fitzgerald was to go shopping with a friend of Scott's from St Paul, Marie Hersey. Zelda's trousseau had been put together in Montgomery with only the sketchiest notion of the fashionable requirements of cosmopolitan life. Somewhat painfully Scott saw Zelda for the first time against the background of the restrained chic of the East, and as he later wrote: '... no sooner does a man marry his reproachless ideal than he becomes intensely self-conscious about her'. Zelda had organdie dresses with great flounces and ruffles, and a glorious pair of velvet lounging pants, but very little that was appropriate for New York. Scott felt she needed the tactful guidance of Miss Hersey's taste, and together they bought her a smart Patou suit. Zelda said it felt strange to be charging things to Scott.

Zelda seemed to be amenable to the shopping lesson, but her resentment was simply hidden. She wrote later: 'It was the first garment bought after the marriage ceremony and again the moths have unsymmetrically eaten the nap off the seat of the skirt. This makes fifteen years it has been stored in trunks because of our principle of not throwing away things that have never been used. We are glad – oh, so relieved, to find it devastated at last.'

But in the spring of 1920 the Fitzgeralds were just beginning; they were young and happy, *This Side of Paradise* was becoming a brilliant success, and for the moment the angels were on their side. Zelda called Scott her 'King of the Roses', and themselves, 'The Goofos', and ordered fresh spinach and champagne for midnight snacks at the Biltmore. Those days in New York were gaudy ones, and Zelda caught the spirit of the city when she wrote about it later,

Vincent Youmans wrote the music for those twilights just after the war. They were wonderful. They hung above the city like an indigo wash.... Through the gloom, the whole world went to tea. Girls in short amorphous capes and long flowing skirts and hats like straw bathtubs waited for taxis in front of the Plaza Grill; girls in long satin coats and colored shoes and hats like straw manhole covers tapped the tune of a cataract on the dance floors of the Lorraine and the St. Regis. Under the sombre ironic parrots of the Biltmore a halo of golden bobs disintegrated into black lace and shoulder bouquets.... It was just a lot of youngness: Lillian Lorraine would be drunk as the cosmos on top of the New Amsterdam by midnight, and football teams breaking training would scare the waiters with drunkenness in the fall. The world was full of parents taking care of people.

But there were no overseeing parents in Scott and Zelda's world to protect them, and in 1920 they would have scoffed at the idea of needing any, for no young couple rode the crest of good fortune with more flair than they. Scott undressed at the *Scandals*, Zelda, completely sober, dived into the fountain at Union Square, and when they moved from the Biltmore to the Commodore they celebrated by spinning around in the revolving doors for half an hour. As she wrote in *Save Me the Waltz*, 'No power on earth could make her do anything, she thought frightened, any more, except herself.'

Dorothy Parker never forgot meeting Zelda for the first time – astride the hood of a taxi with Scott perched upon the roof. 'Robert Sherwood brought Scott and Zelda to me right after their marriage. I had met Scott before. He told me he was going to marry the most beautiful girl in Alabama *and* Georgia!' Mrs Parker thought that even then their behaviour was calculated to shock. 'But they did both look as though they had just stepped out of the sun; their youth was striking. *Everyone* wanted to meet him. *This Side of Paradise* may not seem like much now, but in 1920 it was considered an experimental novel; it cut new ground.' Within eight months the novel had sold 33,000 copies, but its sales alone were not what counted; it was reviewed and talked about everywhere. Scott was suddenly 'the arch type of what New York wanted'. He wrote later, 'I who knew less of New York than any reporter of six months' standing and less of its society than any hall-room boy in a Ritz stag line, was pushed into the position not only of spokesman for the time but of the typical product of that same moment.' And it was not Scott alone, but Zelda, too, who was caught up in the swirl of publicity, and not knowing what New York expected of them they 'found it rather confusing', Scott wrote. 'Within a few months after our embarkation on the Metropolitan venture we scarcely knew any more who we were and we hadn't a notion what we were.'

Scott was the first of his group of Princeton friends living in New York to marry. Edmund Wilson was a hard-working journalist and co-editor with John Peale Bishop of *Vanity Fair*. Each of these men had made fine starts in the literary world, with Scott having the most commercially successful career. They were all quite naturally curious about his bride. Alexander McKaig, who was another Princeton classmate and friend of Scott's, came to know the Fitzgeralds intimately during the first year of their marriage. He, Wilson, and Bishop, sometimes with Ludlow Fowler and Townsend Martin, met frequently for dinner parties and conversation. McKaig had a job in advertising and wrote on weekends and in the evening. Boyish looking with a snub nose and dark curling hair, he appeared more cherubic than he was. He kept a diary in which he made frequent entries concerning his life and the lives of his friends. Although it is a perceptive record, it is also an envious one. Nine days after Scott and Zelda's marriage McKaig made the following entry: 'Called on Scott Fitz and his bride. Latter temperamental small town, Southern Belle. Chews gum – shows knees. I do not think marriage can succeed. Both drinking heavily. Think they will be divorced in 3 years. Scott write something big – then die in a garret at 32.'

Dorothy Parker's impressions of Zelda were similar: 'I never thought she was beautiful. She was very blond with a candy box face and a little bow mouth, very much on a small scale and there was something petulant about her. If she didn't like something she sulked; I didn't find that an attractive trait.'

Lawton Campbell remembers being invited some time later to lunch with the Fitzgeralds; he was working and had only one hour to spare.

When I entered, the room was bedlam. Breakfast dishes were all about, the bed unmade, books and papers scattered here and there, trays filled with cigarette butts, liquor glasses from the night before. Everything was untidy and helter-skelter. Scott was dressing and Zelda was luxuriating in the bath-tub. With the door partly open, she carried on a steady flow of conversation.

'Scott,' she called out, 'tell Lawton 'bout ... tell Lawton what I said when ... Now ... tell Lawton what I did ...'

Before Scott could comply, she would proceed to tell me herself about last night's wild adventure. Scott would cue her and then laugh at her vivid description.... Going back to the kitchens at the old Waldorf. Dancing on the kitchen tables, wearing the chef's headgear. Finally, a crash and being escorted out by the house detectives. This badinage went on until Zelda appeared at the bathroom door, buttoning up her dress. I looked at my watch. It was five minutes of two. My lunch hour had gone.

When the Fitzgeralds moved into the Commodore, McKaig visited them there. Scott and Zelda were propped up on their bed, smoking. McKaig sat on a pillow on the floor eating sandwiches delivered from a delicatessen. They talked until dawn. Their conversation ran playfully to theories, as Zelda wrote in *Save Me the Waltz*,

that the Longacre Pharmacies carried the best gin in town; that anchovies sobered you up; that you could tell wood alcohol by the smell. Everybody knew where to find the blank verse in Cabell and how to get seats for the Yale game.... People met people they knew in hotel lobbies smelling of orchids and plush and detective stories, and asked each other where they'd been since last time.... 'We're having some people,' everybody said to everybody else, 'and we want you to join us,' and they said, 'We'll telephone.'

All over New York people telephoned. They telephoned from one hotel to another to people on other parties that they couldn't get there – that they were engaged. It was always tea-time or late at night. . . . New York is a good place to be on the up-grade.

To their own surprise and delight, Scott and Zelda discovered that they were being heralded as models in the cult of youth. Scott was asked to lecture before audiences that were ready to adore him as their spokesman. A literary gossip column reported. 'We watched him wave his cigarette at an audience one night not long ago, and capture them by nervous young ramblings, until he had the room (mostly "flappers") swaying with delight. Then the autograph hunters! This admiration embarrassed him much – but after we had escaped into the outer darkness he acknowledged, with a grin, that he rather liked it.' Still he and Zelda were safe, Scott thought, 'apart from all that', and if the city bewitched them by offering fresh roles for them, they played them because 'We felt like small children in a great bright unexplored barn'.

In May they decided to buy a car. Scott was not getting to his writing in the city, and they thought that if they took a house in the country for the summer the peace and quiet would be conducive to work. For a part of Scott was aware that the sense of tranquillity he had once observed in Edmund Wilson's New York apartment, where 'life was mellow and safe, a finer distillation of all that I had come to love at Princeton', would elude him forever if he did not soon make an effort to secure it for himself.

Swimming was a necessity for Zelda and as long as they found a place close to water she could be happy. A car would facilitate their search. Leon Ruth, an old Montgomery friend of Zelda's, was in New York studying at Columbia and it was his advice the Fitzgeralds sought when they went car hunting. Ruth recalled: 'Neither of them could drive much. Scott used to borrow my car in Montgomery when he was courting Zelda, so I knew fairly well the limits of his ability. As I remember it we went down to the Battery and it was a choice between a new sedan and a second-hand Marmon sports coupé. Of course,

they couldn't resist the Marmon. Well, we bought it and drove
them up to 125th Street. I showed Scott how to shift on the way
and both of them knew something about steering. Then they
put me out and struck off.'

Eventually, in Westport, Connecticut, a short distance from
the Sound, they found the Wakeman cottage, a grey-shingled
house surrounded by countryside. It seemed a perfect retreat
and they took it. Zelda wrote Ludlow Fowler:

> We have a house with a room for you and a ruined automobile
> because I drove it over a fire-plug and completely deintestined it ...
> and much health and fresh-air which is all very nice and picturesque,
> although I'm still partial to Coney Island – And as soon as we get
> a servant and some sheets from Mamma you really must come out
> and recuperate and try to enjoy the home you helped so much to
> get organized. Only, by the time you *do* come I'll probably have
> grown so fat like this [sketch of a circle with arms and legs and
> head] that you won't be able to recognize me. I s'pose I'll have to
> wear a [a measure of music with the words 'Red, red rose' written
> beneath it] to disclose my identity – or condition – At present, I
> *think* it's the home-cooking of Mrs. M——— but, of course, one
> never knows.... But it's a deep secret and you MUST keep very
> quiet and not laugh too hard and be VERY sympathetic –

As it turned out, she was not pregnant. Within a few weeks they
arranged with the Japanese Reliable Servant Agency to hire a
houseboy and began to invite their friends for weekend visits.
It was going to be a relaxed and productive summer with guests
coming out only on Saturday or Sunday. They joined one of the
quieter bathing clubs; Zelda was to spend her time swimming
and reading; Scott was fiddling with an idea for a new novel,
The Flight of the Rocket. It would be about Anthony Patch and
his wife, Gloria Gilbert: 'How he and his beautiful young wife
are wrecked on the shoals of dissipation ...'

After McKaig's first visit to Westport he wrote: 'Fitz &
Zelda fighting like mad – say themselves marriage can't succeed.' By the fourth of July their partying had become as time-
consuming in Westport as it had been in New York. McKaig
noted that Scott spent $43 for liquor in one day and then left
McKaig to pay for the food for dinner.

During one of their carnival nights in Westport, Zelda sounded the fire alarm. Within a few minutes three fire engines and a score of cars came into the Compo Beach area. There was no fire and no one could be found who knew anything about the alarm. Angrily the fire chief traced the call to the Wakeman house, but Scott and Zelda claimed they knew nothing about it. According to a newspaper report which Zelda clipped for her scrapbook, a member of the Fitzgerald family suggested to the chief that perhaps someone had come into their house during their absence and sent in an alarm. The article said that everyone was greatly worked up over the false alarm and that there was a statute which dealt with people who sent in false alarms for the fun of it. The Fitzgeralds were brought before court the following week, but because the evidence was only circumstantial no blame could be fastened to them. Scott gallantly said that he would bear the costs of the department's run.

George Jean Nathan, who with Mencken edited *The Smart Set*, which had first published Scott, began to visit them frequently during the summer. An urbane and witty bachelor, Nathan quickly took to Zelda and began a flirtation that consisted of teasing Scott and writing gay notes to Zelda facetiously signed 'Yours, for the Empire, A Prisoner of Zelda.' Zelda was delighted by the attention of a man whom Scott clearly admired and respected. Soon each of Nathan's letters to Westport was addressed to Zelda alone; they ran along the following lines:

Dear Blonde: Why call me a polygamist when my passion for you is at once so obvious and so single? Particularly when I am lit. Is it possible that Southern Gals are losing their old perspicacity?

I am very sorry to hear that your husband is neglectful of his duties to you in the way of chewing gum. That is the way husbands get after five months of marriage.

During one of his weekends in Westport he had discovered her diaries. 'They interested me so greatly that in my capacity as a magazine editor I later made her an offer for them. When I informed her husband, he said that he could not permit me to publish them since he had gained a lot of inspiration from them and wanted to use parts of them in his own novels and short stories, as for example "The Jelly Beans".' Zelda apparently offered no resistance to this rather high-handed refusal of Nathan's offer, and the diaries remained Scott's literary property rather than hers.

By the end of the summer the friendship between Nathan and the Fitzgeralds had cooled considerably and they did not see him for a while. Zelda was not always discreet in her show of affection and something had occurred to arouse Scott's jealousy. The balance in their marriage was undergoing a subtle shift. During their courtship Zelda had consistently held the upper hand, and held it somewhat imperiously. Now Scott found that he did not entirely trust Zelda and was vexed by her flirtatiousness; the rift with Nathan was not serious because neither Nathan nor Zelda was serious, but the flirtation had irritated Scott.

Their differences began to surface. Zelda discovered that Scott was a fearful man and that he invented stories to cover himself. As there was not a particle of fear within Zelda she found it hard to fathom Scott's sudden attacks of jitters. Zelda was finicky about her food and Scott was not. Scott could not fall asleep unless his bedroom was hermetically sealed; Zelda could not bear sleeping without a window open. Zelda did not have the vaguest notion about sewing on shirt buttons when they came off, or seeing that shirts went to the laundry. She simply let everything pile up in the recesses of a closet while Scott fumed about a lack of fresh laundry, for he was accustomed to changing twice a day if he felt like it. Minor though these differences were, they broke the spell of the honeymoon. What remained were the long talks throughout the night, those joint monologues like shared dreams which brought with them a closeness so binding that it was to last a lifetime.

By mid-July Zelda seemed both restless and homesick. The tug of the South soon became irresistible and impulsively Scott suggested that they take an automobile trip to Montgomery. He later wrote amusingly about the trials of their trip in a three-part article called 'The Cruise of the Rolling Junk'. A rolling junk was exactly what their Marmon turned out to be; it was, to put it gently, past its prime. The decision to travel was Scott's and he came about it quite casually – if one can believe the article.

Zelda was up. This was obvious, for in a moment she came into my room singing aloud. Now when Zelda sings soft I like to listen, but when she sings loud I sing loud too in self-protection. So we began to sing a song about biscuits. The song related how down in Alabama all the good people ate biscuits for breakfast, which made them very beautiful and pleasant and happy, while up in Connecticut all the people ate bacon and eggs and toast, which made them very cross and bored and miserable—especially if they happened to have been brought up on biscuits.

The song over, Zelda complained that even if there were biscuits in Connecticut there weren't any peaches to go with them. Overwhelmed by the logic of her complaint, Scott suggested that they drive to Alabama, where there were both biscuits and peaches. Two months earlier Zelda had received the following telegram from a group of her Southern beaux.

HURRY BACK TO MONTGOMERY AS TOWN IS SHOT TO PIECES SINCE YOU LEFT. NO PEP. NO FUN. NO ONE TO GIVE THE GOSSIPERS A SOURCE OF CONVERSATION. THE COUNTRY CLUB IS INTÉNDING FIRING THEIR CHAPERONE AS THERE IS NO FURTHER NEED FOR HER. KNITTING PARTIES PREVAIL. JAIL CONVERTED INTO SEWING ROOM. FOR THE SAKE OF SAVING DEAR OLD MONTGOMERY PEP UP AND HURRY BACK!

Now she would have a chance to show off her famous husband and to broadcast the things they had done together in New York. No one in Montgomery could match their exploits, and because she felt more at home in the South than she yet did in New York or Connecticut, it would be not only a triumphant return but a welcome respite.

The trip itself was a series of minor catastrophes: there were blowouts, lost wheels, and broken axles. Zelda, who was to navigate, had no idea how to read a map. Her white knickerbocker suit (which had been made to match Scott's) was considered shocking enough in Virginia almost to keep them out of a good hotel. The manager eventually relented and Zelda compromised at the next stop by putting a skirt on over the outfit. At last they reached Alabama. 'Suddenly Zelda was crying because things were the same and yet were not the same. It was for her faithlessness that she wept and for the faithlessness of time.'

They stayed for less than two weeks and returned by train, having sold their battered Marmon to the first susceptible buyer. When they left they had persuaded the Judge and Mrs Sayre to visit them in Westport.

The Sayres came North in the middle of August, and Scott and Zelda went to New York to meet them. When Zelda's mother was an old woman she recalled an episode from this time.

I remember sitting in the lobby of the Biltmore Hotel with Scott, waiting for Zelda to come down so we could all go out to dinner. (Zelda was always late for everything, and Scott was charming to be so patient with her. I always had an especially deep respect for that quality in him.)

As we were waiting, Scott said to me, 'I'll bet you don't know half what you should about Zelda', as though he was about to impart something shocking.

I said, 'Why, Scott, what a thing to say! I know all there is to know about Zelda; I'm her mother.'

Then Scott grinned and said, 'Well, you couldn't know possibly how beautiful she is, could you? You just watch that elevator, because Zelda will be down in a minute, and then watch all the men here in the lobby. . . . There must be 50 men here who will tell you exactly how beautiful Zelda is. Just watch them when Zelda gets off the elevator.'

Zelda appeared, and Scott stood there bursting with pride as she walked over to us, and I was amazed to see every man seem to watch her as she walked over to us. And Scott was right, she was a beautiful girl.

During the Sayres' visit Zelda wrote the following note to Ludlow Fowler:

We've been in Alabama for two weeks. . . . It's been a tremendously long time since our parties at the Biltmore and I'd like to show you how much improvement I've made along the party line during the summer.... The joys of motoring are more or less fictional, and, too, we had to leave the car in Alabama....

Please come out to see us – Scott's hot in the midst of a new novel and Westport is unendurably dull but you and I might be able to amuse ourselves – and both of us want to see you dreadfully.

Mamma and Daddy are here this week and I can't tell you how glad I was to see them – however I feel very festive and I guess its hardly conventional or according to Hoyle to take one's family on a celebration of the kind I feel in dire need of.

It's been a wild summer, thank God, and I have several anecdotes collected from the wreckage that I've been saving to tell you – At present, I'm hardly able to sit down owing to an injury sustained in the course of one of Nathan's parties in N.Y. I *cut* my *tail* on a broken bottle and can't possibly sit on the three stitches that are in it now – The bottle was bath salts – I was boiled – The place was a tub somewhere – none of us remembers the exact locality –

One can imagine the Judge's glacial attitude toward the life Scott and Zelda were leading. The Sayres' visit was not a success and they left a full week earlier than they had anticipated.

At the end of August Zelda and Scott reappear prominently in McKaig's diary:

Midnight. Fitz & Zelda blew in noisily and offensively drunk as usual. Fitz advised me to stick to advertising business plus literature. Said I ought to make half a million a year. Said that everybody was now laughing at me and booing me since I had begun to sell stuff just as they did at him. Practically every one of us did boo him but I never did ... Fitz again told me I would never be able to do anything worth while in literature.

August 31: Discussing with John [Bishop] the fact that of entire group of 8 or 10 only one man believes in another – Wilson in him. Springs from the fact they were friends in college, not because of similarity in literary tastes, ideals, beliefs.

September 4: Fitzgeralds came in, drunk. Scott says John Biggs sent him first four chapters of his novel and they are great ... Fitz having declared John Biggs has done something wonderful John Bishop declares he knew it all along (he never said a word about it).

We discussed what a boon for Princeton it would be if we all came through. In regard to passion and wisdom in American literature he said Amy Lowell was interested only in light and color and play of words; Frost had only weather wisdom of New England farmer; Masters a little superficial irony about the overtones of life but not nearly as much [in] his whole books as Masefield in one poem. Louis Untermeyer devoted part strength to jewelry and part to poetry so that both suffered – etc. Declared passion in literature impossible in American with its passion for business minutiae. I said it was impossible with England in its passion for conventions.

September 11: Dinner with Bunny Wilson. Read his 'Death of the Welfare Expert' for 'Undertakers Garland'. Great stuff . . . Then he read me the intro. – which I don't believe in at all. Says modern American civilization is death. I certainly will be glad when this book is finished. I'm sick of having unfinished portions read to me . . . Fitz second book out 'Flappers and Philo' . . . Bunny W and I at dinner bewailed the misconception of his character (the omission of his Byronic trait which he claims but no one else sees except Edna Millet)

Met Edna Millet for a minute at Bunny Wilson's, light dim. She seemed pleasant and better looking than I had been led to believe. Bunny evidently much in love with her. Not much chance to get impression from her myself though I think from her verse she must be a genius. Modern Sappho. 18 love affairs and now Bunny is thinking of marrying her.

September 15: In the evening Zelda – drunk – having decided to leave Fitz & having nearly been killed walking down R R track, blew in. Fitz came shortly after. He had caught same train with no money or ticket. They threatened to put him off but finally let him stay on – Zelda refusing to give him any money. They continued their fight while here . . . Fitz should let Zelda go & not run after her. Like all husbands he is afraid of what she may do in a moment of caprice. None of the men, however, she knows would take her for a mistress. Trouble is – Fitz absorbed in Zelda's personality – she is the stronger of the two. She has supplied him with all his copy for women. – Fitz argued about various things. Mind absolutely undisciplined but guesses right, – intuition marvelous. Knows me better than any of the rest. Senses the exact mood & drift of a situation so surely & quickly – much better at this than any of rest of us.

What Scott's friends did not see in Zelda was that part of her where she was not the stronger of the two. Shortly after the incident McKaig refers to, Zelda wrote Scott a letter, a fragment of which exists, in which she tried to express her dependence on him. (Scott was to work portions of her letter as well as the episode itself into *The Beautiful and Damned*.)

I look down the tracks and see you coming – and out of every haze & mist your darling rumpled trousers are hurrying to me – Without you, dearest dearest I couldn't see or hear or feel or think – or live – I love you so and I'm never in all our lives going to let us be apart another night. It's like begging for mercy of a storm or killing Beauty or growing old, without you. I want to kiss you so – and in the back where your dear hair starts and your chest – I love you – and I cant tell you how much – To think that I'll *die* without your knowing – Goofo, you've *got* to try [to] feel how much I do – how inanimate I am when you're gone – I can't even hate these damnable people – Nobodys got any right to live but us – and they're dirtying up our world and I can't hate them because I want you so – Come Quick – Come Quick to me – I could never do without you if you hated me and were covered with sores like a leper – if you ran away with another woman and starved me and beat me – I still would want you *I know* –

> Lover, Lover, Darling –
> Your Wife

Increasingly, their friends were Scott's friends, the pace of their life was being set by the demands of Scott's work and his success, and Zelda, who had established the tone of their courtship, must have felt their marriage slipping precariously into unknown regions in which she might become lost. The passion of her letter, the wild and intense description of her love for Scott, was an indication not only of her need for him but also of her uncertainty about herself within the life they were leading. The woman who realized that she wanted to be two simple people at once was finding the 'one who wants a law to itself' in ascendance in her marriage. Zelda was becoming entangled in the crosscurrents of a complex of opposing roles, making an effort to be both daring and loving, to not give a damn and to care deeply, to be proud of Scott's drawing on her for his fiction while resenting it.

In January 1921, when Scott was interviewed for a slick magazine called *Shadowland,* he drew a direct contrast between 'the sexless animals writers have been giving us', and his own wife. 'Girls, for instance, have found the accent shifted from chemical purity to breadth of viewpoint, intellectual charm and piquant cleverness . . . we find the young woman of 1920 flirting, kissing, viewing life lightly, saying damn without a blush, playing along the danger line in an immature way – a sort of mental baby vamp. . . . Personally, I prefer this sort of girl. Indeed, I married the heroine of my stories. I would not be interested in any other sort of woman.' That Zelda might find it a strain to be always this startling creature of Scott's fiction, much as she also relished the attention it brought her, or that it placed her under a burden of performance, did not seem seriously to trouble either of the Fitzgeralds.

The day after McKaig's entry about their quarrel and trip to New York he saw them again.

September 16: Zelda came in & woke me sleeping on couch at 7:15 for no reason. She has no sense of decencies of living . . . Fitz picture and an article to go in Vanity Fair. Autobiographical note about him in Metropolitan this month – got $900 for it and had unhappy ending! His vogue is tremendous.

September 17: Bunny Wilson and Edna Millet in intolerable situation. He wants her to marry him. She tempted because of her great poverty and the financial security he offers (he has private income). However, in addition to curse of Apollo she has curse of Venus. While her heart is still in the grave of one love affair she is making eyes at another man. It nearly kills her but she can't help it.

September 20: Bunnie has repeated to Edna . . . things John [Bishop] said about her . . . John is very distressed. I've come to think he's damn stupid – interested only in himself, poetry, & women, and loves most the sound of his own voice, & liquor, & adulation (when he can get it).

September 27: John spent weekend at Fitz – new novel sounds awful

– no seriousness of approach. Zelda interrupts him all the time – diverts in both senses. Discussed his success complex – artists desire for flattery & influence – member of financially decadent family ('Four Fists'). John says my success complex more healthy – striving – test of powers (that's wrong). Fitz bemoaning fact can never make more than hundred thousand a year – to do that have to become a Tarkington.

September 28: One of younger Millay girls told this anecdote of his [Wilson's] visit to them last summer – Offered coffee, Bunny declared he never drank coffee, a cigarette, Bunny said he never smoked – offered a drink, Bunny said he never drank. Other guest at dinner – a stranger – turned and said – 'Ah – he must write the minor poetry.' (Bunny has never told this anecdote about himself.)

October 7: Bunny came for evening – we discussed John's lack of ideas & borrowing them. Bunny, being under stress & strain, did parlor magic tricks. Says he does them for hours in front of glass to quiet his nerves, instead of smoking. We discussed unreality of college – reality of army & navy life. Bunny said he did not think himself badly off having to work at Vanity Fair. Regrets lack of will power lately to work nights – since meeting Edna. She certainly has played hell with him.

In the late fall the Fitzgeralds moved back into New York and took a tiny apartment on West Fifty-ninth Street, which was conveniently close to the Plaza Hotel. Scott summarized his impression of the year's progress in his Ledger: 'Work at the beginning but dangerous at the end. A slow year, dominated by Zelda & on the whole happy.' There were first nights at the theatre with Nathan (who had been forgiven), and they continued to see Alec McKaig. One evening Zelda and McKaig dropped in at Lawton Campbell's apartment: she had come, she told Campbell, so that 'Scott could write'.

'She would stretch out on the long sofa in my living room with her eyes to the ceiling and recount some fabulous experience of the night before or dream up some strange exploit that she thought would be a "cute idea". One day she came in with the queerest looking hat. My mother asked her where she had found it. Zelda replied quite casually, "Oh, I made it myself . . .

out of blotting paper." No one knew whether she actually had or whether she was pulling their legs. Campbell says, 'If her remarks were occasionally non sequitur one didn't notice it at the time. She passed very quickly from one topic to another and you didn't question her. It wouldn't occur to you to stop her and ask what she meant.'

McKaig continued to record the undercurrents of discontent he noticed between Scott and Zelda.

October 12: Went to Fitzgeralds. Usual problem there. What shall Zelda do? I think she might do a little housework – apartment looks like a pig sty. If she's there Fitz can't work – she bothers him – if she's not there he can't work – worried what she might do. Discussed her relations with other men. I told her she would have to make up her mind whether she wanted to go in movies or get in with young married set. To do that would require a little effort & Zelda will never make an effort. Moreover, she and Fitz like only aristocrats who don't give a damn what the world thinks or clever bohemians who don't give a damn what the world thinks. That narrows the field. Nathan came and then Ludlow. Nathan left. Lud and Zelda went to a delicatessen store & got a good cold dinner – ate it in apartment. Fitz read me his bookshop story. Damn good. And part of his novel – fair ... Walked home with Ludlow afterwards – great gross wonderfully human and sympathetic Ludlow. Fitzg makes a good criticism of himself – does not see more than lots of other people but is able to put down more of what he sees.

October 13: Fitz made another true remark about himself ... cannot depict how any one thinks except himself & possibly Zelda. Find that after he has written about a character a while it becomes just himself again.

October 17: Fitz has been on wagon 8 days, talks as if it were a century. Zelda increasingly restless – says frankly she simply wants to be amused and is only good for useless, pleasure-giving pursuits; great problem – what is she to do? Fitz has his writing of course – God knows where the two of them are going to end up.

October 18: Millay's response to F. Scott Fitzgerald's saying he wrote 'The Camels Back' between 8 p.m. and 2 a.m. 'Fitz affects all the attributes he believes a genius should have.'

October 20: Fitz is hard up now but Zelda is nagging him for a $750 fur coat & she can nag. Poor devil.

October 21: Went up to Fitzgeralds to spend evening. They just recovering from an awful party. Much taken with idea of having a baby. Have just planned a good baby and a bad baby – former has Scott's eyes, Zelda's nose, Scott's legs, Zelda's mouth etc. Latter has Zelda's legs, Scott's hair, etc. Scott hard up for money in spite of fact he has made $20,000 in past 12 months.

October 25: Follies with Scott & Zelda. Fitzg very cuckoo. Lost purse with $50.000 & then after every one in place hunted for it, found it. He did not have enough money to pay check of course. Home 3 a.m.

November 7: Evening at Fitzgeralds. Tremendous argument – men of thought v. men of action. To decide, took characteristics of good minds – memory, attention, clarity (intelligence), imagination, curiousity and influence. Then selected 6 men of action and 6 men of thought and graded them. Results 26 to 27 favor men of thought ... A very interesting talk. We both bawled out Bishop for his unassimilated literary patter. Damned interesting. Fitz admitted he had no 'attention'.

November 13: Spent evening at Fitzgeralds. Scott told me how he had cried over two of his stories.

November 27: Fitz making ... speeches before select audiences. I spent evening shaving Zelda's neck to make her bobbed hair look better. She is lovely – wonderful hair – eyes and mouth.

November 28: Suggested to Scott and Zelda they save – they laughed at me. Scott said – to go through the terrible toil of writing man must have belief his writings will be eagerly bought forever. Terrific party with two Fitz ...

December 4: Lunch at Gotham. T. [Towsend Martin?] Zelda, Scott & I. Then took Zelda to cocktail party at John Coles and then tea in Biltmore. In taxi Zelda asked me to kiss her but I couldnt. I couldnt forget Scott – he's so damn pitiful. Went to see 'Enter Madame'. Zelda fell off seat – actors complained of our behaviour. Zelda got mad and left followed by Scott. I stayed. When I got home found telephone message from Scott to call him up. I did so. He said most awful thing had happened, just come up immediately – it would be a test of friendship. I rushed up expecting to find a death or serious accident. When I got there he was talking to Bernard. He said hello casually & went on talking. I asked him in Christs name what the matter was – it seemed they had a quarrel. Zelda went into the bathroom, turned on the water to hide noise of footsteps & walked out the door. Instead of trying to find her himself he sat in the middle of floor & telephoned all his friends. Finally Zelda called up & I went for her – she having had many adventures.

December 11: Evening at Fitz. Fitz and I argued with Zelda about notoriety they are getting through being so publicly and spectacularly drunk. Zelda wants to live life of an 'extravagant'. No thought of what world will think or of future. I told them they were headed for catastrophe if they kept up at present rate.

December 18: John read me 'Death of God'. Great stuff. Stupendous. Best thing he's done . . . We discussed glamor of Fitz phrases. I mentioned his intuition. Also his dissipation all aimed to hand down Fitzgerald legend. His claiming now to be great grandson of Frances Scott Key is part of it. Never claimed that till recently – now it is being press-agented. I think he is really a grand nephew.

January 17 [*1921*]*:* Saw Fitz. He is drunk every night, but mentally is expanding and maturing rapidly.

February 6: Zelda, Fitz & I out for dinner. Very heated discussion about reality: if a girl has a crooked nose but sufficient charm to give her face an appearance of beauty, which is truthful, a photograph showing the girl ugly with her crooked nose or a painting showing her beautiful because of her charm. Fitz & I said painting – Zelda said photo.

April 17: Fitz confessed this evening at dinner that Zelda's ideas entirely responsible for 'Jelly Bean' & 'Ice Palace'. Her ideas largely in this new novel. Had a long talk with her this evening about way fool women can rout intelligent women with men. She is without doubt the most brilliant & most beautiful young woman I've ever known.

Zelda and Scott had spent a lonely Christmas together in New York and as Scott later wrote, 'Finding no nucleus to which we could cling, we became a small nucleus ourselves and gradually fitted our disruptive personalities into the contemporary scene of New York'. On Valentine's Day Zelda discovered she was pregnant and took a trip to Montgomery to visit her parents. While she was in Montgomery she was asked to take part in the annual *Les Mysteriéuses* ball, which she did. This time a Hawaiian pageant was put on with the stage banked in palms and tropical plants. As it happened Lawton Campbell, who was also in Montgomery visiting his relatives, had been invited to attend the ball. He remembers Zelda's part in it:

> During this number, the audience began to notice that one masker was doing her dance more daring than the others. All eyes were concentrated on her. Finally the dancer in question turned her back to the audience, lifted her grass skirt over her head for a quick view of her pantied posterior and gave it an extra wiggle for good measure. A murmur went over the auditorium in a wave of excitement and everybody was whispering 'That's Zelda'! It was Zelda and no mistake! She wanted it known beyond a doubt and she was happy with the recognition.

By the end of April Scott had nearly completed *The Beautiful and Damned*. It was the story of a ruined marriage, and it was not, Scott insisted, autobiographical. Serial rights were bought by the *Metropolitan Magazine*. With Zelda only two months pregnant, they decided to take a trip to Europe before the baby was born. During their courtship Zelda had wanted to go to Italy with Scott; now they would visit England and France as well, and stay perhaps until early fall.

Before their departure they accidentally ran into Lawton Campbell at the Jungle Club, a fashionable speakeasy with an elegant bar, dancing floor, and head waiters in white tie and tails. It also had a formidable bouncer. Campbell remembers:

> I was sitting one evening at a table with three friends, when I spied Scott at the door of the bar. He was obviously under the influence and rather uncertain on his feet. I noticed that he was having words with the bouncer. Apparently the bouncer thought Scott had more

than his share and would not permit him to go back into the bar.
Fearing a scrap, I immediately went up to Scott and persuaded him
to join me. He acquiesced and mumbled something about the
bouncer, which was far from complimentary. In a few minutes,
Zelda appeared at the door of the bar, looking around for Scott. I
went over to her and escorted her to our table but she refused to sit
down, because as she said, Scott had walked out on her. I told her
that Scott had had a slight altercation with the bouncer and tried to
divert her with a dance. No, thank you, she was going back to the
bar and Scott was coming with her. She took Scott by the arm and
demanded that he accompany her on grounds of desertion and said
to us at the table.

'No so-and-so bouncer can prevent Scott from going anywhere he
pleases.'

Despite my entreaties, Scott and Zelda with heads high and with
the grim determination of young Davids, went to the door of the
bar. The bouncer let Zelda by but refused admittance to Scott.
Zelda turned in the doorway and spoke to Scott wherewith he took
a feeble punch at his opponent, which missed its mark. A few other
phantom attempts were made and finally the bouncer lost his
patience and gave Scott a shove that sent him half-way across the
room, crashing into a table.

I ran over to Scott, lifted him to his feet and finally persuaded
him to leave with me and my friends. As we were leaving, I looked
around for Zelda but she had disappeared. I decided to get Scott
down to a taxi and come back for Zelda. Downstairs we collected
our coats and found a cab. Just as Scott was getting into the
cab, Zelda dashed onto the sidewalk, hatless and wrapless and
yelled

'Scott, you're not going to let that so and so get away with that.'

She pulled him out of the taxi and led him unsteady as he was
back into the Jungle Club.

The incident ended predictably with Scott being beaten by the
bouncer. Zelda had not only egged Scott on, she had witnessed
his defeat and could not understand it. She fully expected him
to perform manfully in a situation where he was placed against
considerable odds. Still, Scott understood Zelda's reaction far
better than anyone else could have and was willing to be manipulated by her. He had written in the manuscript of his new
novel: 'Herself almost completely without physical fear, she

was unable to understand, and so she made the most of what she felt to be his fear's redeeming feature, which was that though he was a coward under a shock and a coward under a strain – when his imagination was given play – he had yet a sort of dashing recklessness that moved her on its brief occasions almost to admiration, and a pride that usually steadied him when he thought he was observed.'

They sailed for Europe on 3 May, and on arrival in England went first to London. Maxwell Perkins had arranged an introduction to John Galsworthy, who invited them to dine with St John Ervine, the dramatist and novelist, and Lennox Robinson, the Irish playwright. They saw Lady Randolph Spencer Churchill and her son Winston, who was reportedly charmed by an hour's dinner conversation with Zelda. But the most exciting event of their visit was a walking tour with Shane Leslie around the waterfronts of London. Scott, Shane Leslie later wrote, 'wanted to see the real Dockland Stepney Limehouse Wapping where there was no taxis no police – We wore tweed caps and slacks. We had to be ready to carry Zelda – but she was light and enjoyed the adventure.' With Zelda dressed in men's clothes and with no money or jewellery, they prowled the haunts of Jack the Ripper. From London they travelled to Windsor and Cambridge and Grantchester, where they took snapshots of each other: Scott standing in a garden path in three-piece suit, soft Knox hat, and silver-headed cane. Zelda wrote beneath Scott's picture a line from Rupert Brooke, 'The men observe the rules of thought', and beneath her own, 'And is there honey yet for tea?' Back to London, then, off to Paris for a few disappointing days – an evening at the Folies, a day at Versailles and Malmaison – and on to Italy. Venice. Florence. Rome and back to England. By July they had returned to the United States. Scott wrote Edmund Wilson, who had been telling them the glories of the continent: 'God damn the continent of Europe. It is of merely antiquarian interest. . . . You may have spoken in jest about New York as the capital of culture but in 25 years it will be just as London is now. Culture follows money and all the refinements of aestheticism can't stave off its change of seat (Christ! what a metaphor). We will be the Romans in the next generation as the English are now.'

After much discussion about where their baby should be born they settled on Montgomery; '– it seemed inappropriate to bring a baby into all that glamour and loneliness', Scott wrote, explaining why they had rejected staying in New York. But Montgomery proved to be a poor choice. It was hot and Zelda, who at six months looked as if she might be having twins, donned a tank suit and went swimming at one of the local pools. In 1921 women in Montgomery were still only rarely seen in the streets when they were in her condition, and she was asked to leave the pool. At the end of August, after only a month in Montgomery, they 'played safe and went home to St Paul'.

Zelda gained a great deal of weight during the final term of her pregnancy and did nothing to hide the fact when she wore a red jersey maternity dress to greet Scott's friends. She did not make a good impression and made only one friend among the women, Xandra Kalman, who not only found the Fitzgeralds a summer house on White Bear Lake but also purchased all of the baby things the Fitzgeralds would soon require. Zelda seemed unaware of what would be needed and left the decisions up to Mrs Kalman.

In his Ledger Scott described the year as a bad one. 'No work. Slow deteriorating repression with outbreak around the corner.' In September he recorded that Zelda was all but helpless because of her weight. Zelda wrote: 'In the fall we got to the Commodore in St Paul, and while leaves blew up the streets we waited for our child to be born.' Finally on 26 October 1921, their baby was born. Zelda's labour was long and difficult. Scott, as nervous as a cat, was not too unnerved by the waiting to miss recording Zelda's groggy comment as she came out from under the anaesthesia: 'Oh, God, goofo I'm drunk. Mark Twain. Isn't she smart – she has the hiccups. I hope its beautiful and a fool – a beautiful little fool.' She would never quite forgive him his detachment. He would later use the experience in describing Daisy Buchanan's reaction to the birth of her daughter in *The Great Gatsby*.

They named their daughter Patricia, and then changed it almost immediately to Frances Scott Fitzgerald (although as late as 1926 Zelda would refer to her as 'Pat'). Scottie, as she was nicknamed, was baptized a Catholic. As soon as Zelda was on her feet again she regained enough of her sass to write Ludlow Fowler: 'We are both simply mad to get back to New York. This damn place is 18 below zero and I go around thanking God that, anatomically + proverbially speaking, I am safe from the awful fate of the monkey.' Adding later in the same letter, 'Anyway, you are an excellent person to write me about my baby. She is *awfully* cute and I am very devoted to her but quite disappointed over the sex –'

7

'We had run through a lot, though we had retained an almost
theatrical innocence by preferring the role of the observed to that
of the observer.'

F. Scott Fitzgerald, 'My Lost City'

Becoming a mother did not have a noticeably quieting effect
on Zelda. Scottie's care was left primarily to her nurse while
Zelda fretted about being overweight. When the first photographs were taken of mother and baby for the society section
of the St Paul papers Zelda clipped them for her scrapbook
and carefully shaded her nose, cheeks, and chin with a pencil
in an effort to slim her face. As the winter season came into
full swing Scott and Zelda moved from their hotel into a house
in the middle of the town. In January, on Friday the 13th, a
Bad Luck Ball was given at the University Club, which was
swathed in black crepe and decorated with undertakers' advertisements. During the course of the evening a newspaper called
The Daily Dirge was distributed, to be sold for the price of a
'sweet kiss'. The Fitzgeralds were behind the spoof and together they wrote a gossip column as well as advertisements
for themselves: 'Mrs F. Scott Fitzgerald had always wanted
eyelashes. She had used every preparation, including stove-
polish and blackberry wine with no result. She went into a
store and bought a set of *Pigman's Portable Eyelashes* and
now she is not ashamed to go anywhere.'

There were weekly hops at the clubs, where the toddle was
not yet passé and where rye flowed as though it were an elixir.
The Fitzgeralds began to give parties; Zelda was a conspicu-
ously uneager hostess, for she said the noise woke the baby and
made her cry.

During the day, when Scott was not working at the office he
had rented downtown, he and Zelda discussed last-minute
changes in *The Beautiful and Damned*. He was not satisfied

with the serialized version which was running in the *Metropolitan Magazine* prior to the book's publication in March 1922 by Scribner's. But the changes he did make were not substantial ones and the novel remained seriously flawed; in December he was writing Perkins: '. . . I am almost, but not quite, satisfied with the book'. Then, with his usual burst of confidence he added: 'I prophesy that it will go about 60,000 copies the first year – that is, assuming that Paradise went about 40,000 the first year. Thank God I'm thru with it.' The jacket sketch irritated him because he thought the drawing of the man on the cover was 'a sort of debauched edition of me', and Zelda drew her own version. It was a nude kneeling in a champagne goblet, her blonde bobbed hair flying, her apricot colouring remarkably similar to Zelda's – a childlike mermaid sloshing happily in a cocktail. But it was not used.

At the end of January Scott wrote Edmund Wilson that he was bored with St Paul, and said he and Zelda would probably come East in March. 'The baby is well – we dazzle her exquisite eyes with gold pieces in the hopes that she'll marry a millionaire.' By February Scott noted in his Ledger that they had been sick and were drinking heavily. They longed for a change; Scott was restless and Zelda loathed the harshness of winter in Minnesota. A snapshot taken of her that winter shows her sitting on a sleigh surrounded by drifts of snow; she is clutching her sides with mittened hands and there are snowflakes on her hat and shoulders. When Scott's novel was published on 3 March it gave them the excuse they were looking for to take a trip East. The New York holiday turned out to be a continual round of parties, with neither of them drawing a sober breath until they returned exhausted and irritable to St Paul two weeks later.

There was something else which made them edgy. In late January (or early February) Zelda discovered that she was again pregnant. They apparently decided that they did not want another child so soon after the birth of Scottie. In Scott's Ledger during March he cryptically entered 'Zelda & her abortionist', and it is not clear whether the abortion was performed in New York or in St Paul.

In a section of his manuscript of *The Beautiful and Damned* Fitzgerald used a similar episode between Anthony and Gloria. In the first draft Gloria is with child and finds the situation intolerable. Anthony asks her if she can't ' "talk to some woman and find out what's best to be done. Most of them fix it some way" '. Gloria asks if he wants her to have the child and he says he is indifferent, but he does want to be a sport about it and not go to pieces. The situation is resolved almost offhand-edly a few pages later when the reader finds out that Gloria is not pregnant. This ending was kept in the published version, but there were significant alterations in the material leading up to it. In rewriting the scene Scott reduced the pregnancy to only a probability, but, believing herself pregnant, Gloria's role in the episode is essentially the same. It is Anthony's that under-goes change. His comments about 'fixing it' are cut and the decision to abort (although, delicately, the word is never used) the imagined baby is entirely Gloria's.

As Scott weakened the scene the emphasis changed subtly and Gloria became unremittingly self-centred; a baby would ruin her figure and distort her idea of herself. Since Zelda's second pregnancy and abortion occurred just before the pub-lication of *The Beautiful and Damned,* it could not have pro-vided the raw material for this scene. But the Fitzgeralds had thought that Zelda was pregnant on an earlier occasion; the letter Zelda wrote to Ludlow Fowler hinting at this (although it turned out to be a false alarm) was written at the time Scott was working on the first draft of his manuscript.

Gloria mirrored something of Scott's understanding of Zelda. In January, Scott had written Edmund Wilson a letter concern-ing the important influences upon his life and writings, for Wilson was writing what Scott considered to be one of the first important critical essays on his fiction; it would be pub-lished in the *Bookman.* In it Wilson underlined what he thought were three significant influences upon Scott. These were the Midwest (specifically the society of St Paul and country clubs), his Irishness, and liquor. At Scott's request mention of the last influence was cut from the article. Even then Scott commented: '. . . your catalogue is not complete . . . the most enormous influence on me in the four and a half years since I met her has been the complete, fine and full-hearted selfishness and chill-mindedness of Zelda'.

While the Fitzgeralds were in New York at the Plaza, Burton Rascoe wrote to Zelda asking her to review *The Beautiful and Damned*. He had just begun a book department for the New York *Tribune* and wanted to include pieces that would add sparkle to his new venture. 'I think if you could view it, or pretend to view it, objectively and get in a rub here and there it would cause a great deal of comment.' It would also help the sales of the book, he thought. Zelda accepted his challenge and wrote the review under her maiden name. It was her first published piece since high school.

The tone of the review was self-conscious as Zelda indulged in light mockery: she asked the reader to buy Scott's book for a number of 'aesthetic' reasons, which included her own desire for a dress in cloth of gold and a platinum ring. She humourously evoked a vision of herself as the author's greedy and self-centred wife, and she saw the book as a manual of contemporary etiquette, an indispensable guide to interior decorating – and in Gloria's adventures an example of how not to behave. About Anthony she said nothing at all; it was Gloria who dominated her attention. Zelda did not try to conceal the parallels between Gloria and herself:

It also seems to me that on one page I recognized a portion of an old diary of mine which mysteriously disappeared shortly after my marriage, and also scraps of letters, which, though considerably edited, sound to me vaguely familiar. In fact, Mr Fitzgerald – I believe that is how he spells his name – seems to believe that plagiarism begins at home.

We cannot know to what extent Scott used Zelda's diary but we have her word for it (as well as George Jean Nathan's) that he did. One such portion from the novel, called 'The Diary', reads:

April 24th – I want to marry Anthony, because husbands are so often 'husbands' and I must marry a lover . . .

What grubworms women are to crawl on their bellies through colorless marriages! Marriage was created not to be a background but to need one. Mine is going to be outstanding. It can't, shan't be the setting – it's going to be the performance, the live, lovely, glamorous performance, and the world shall be the scenery. I refuse to dedicate my life to posterity. Surely one owes as much to the current generation as to one's unwanted children. What a fate – to grow rotund and unseemly, to lose my self-love ...

Scott's portrayal of Gloria was hardly a flattering one, and by the close of Zelda's review she had dropped her bantering tone:

I think the heroine is most amusing. I have an intense distaste for the melancholy aroused in the masculine mind by such characters as Jenny Gerhardt, Antonia and Tess (of the D'Urbervilles). Their tragedies, redolent of the soil, leave me unmoved. If they were capable of dramatizing themselves they would no longer be symbolic, and if they weren't – and they aren't – they would be dull, stupid and boring, as they inevitably are in life.

It becomes evident in the review that Zelda was defending that part of herself within the portrait of Gloria. Zelda had been wounded by the characterization, but she did not express that directly and instead tried to cover herself by flippancy – as in the opening of the review. Gloria, it would seem, though not entirely Zelda, was representative of something Zelda felt it necessary to stand up for.

John Peale Bishop was keenly aware of the connection between Fitzgerald's fiction and his life. Bishop wrote that *The Beautiful and Damned*

concerns the disintegration of a young man who, at the age of twenty-six, has put away all illusions but one; this last illusion is a Fitzgerald flapper of the now famous type – hair honey-colored and bobbed, mouth rose-colored and profane.

He continued pointedly:

But, as with *This Side of Paradise*, the most interesting thing about Mr Fitzgerald's book is Mr Fitzgerald. He has already created about himself a legend ... The true stories about Fitzgerald are always published under his own name. He has the rare faculty of being able to experience romantic and ingenuous emotions and a half hour later regard them with satiric detachment. He has an amazing grasp of the superficialities of the men and women about him, but he has not yet a profound understanding of their motives, either intellectual or passionate.

Bishop cheated a little in his review; he knew very well, for Scott had admitted it to him in McKaig's presence, that drawing on himself and Zelda was a problem in his writing. Bishop's review included a sentence that Zelda clipped for her scrapbook, placing it beneath a photograph of herself.

Even with his famous flapper, he has as yet failed to show that hard intelligence, that intricate emotional equipment upon which her charm depends, so that Gloria, the beautiful and damned lady of his imaginings, remains a little inexplicable, a pretty, vulgar shadow of her prototype.

Either as a result of the favourable reaction to her review of *The Beautiful and Damned* or through Rascoe's efforts Zelda was asked by *McCall's* magazine for a 2,500-word article on the modern flapper, and they offered her ten cents a word. In October they sent her $300 for an article called 'Where Do Flappers Go?' but they did not publish the piece. In June the *Metropolitan Magazine* did publish her 'Eulogy on the Flapper' Above the article was a sketch of Zelda done by Gordon Bryant. It is an astonishing likeness, which caught in profile the curiously savage intensity of her look. The caption beneath it again emphasized the connection between the real Zelda and the fictional one, stating that she had been put in both of Fitzgerald's novels, and adding rather inanely, 'Everything Zelda Fitzgerald says and does stands out.' Zelda wrote that the flapper was dead and that she grieved the passing of so original a model, for she saw in the flapper a code for living well. Not too surprisingly, Zelda had taken the flapper quite seriously and saw in her someone who experimented with life, who was self-aware and did the things she did consciously for their effect and to create herself anew.

How can a girl say again, 'I do not want to be respectable because respectable girls are not attractive', and how can she again so wisely arrive at the knowledge that 'boys *do* dance most with the girls they kiss most', and that 'men *will* marry the girls they could kiss before they had asked papa?' Perceiving these things, the Flapper awoke from her lethargy of sub-deb-ism, bobbed her hair, put on her choicest pair of earrings and a great deal of ·audacity and rouge and went into the battle. She flirted because it was fun to flirt and wore a one-piece bathing suit because she had a good figure, she covered her face with powder and paint because she didn't need it and she refused to be bored chiefly because she wasn't boring. She was conscious that the things she did were the things she had always wanted to do. Mothers disapproved of their sons taking the Flapper to dances, to teas, to swim and most of all to heart. She had mostly masculine friends, but youth does not need friends – it needs only crowds ...

There were rights that only youth could give:

I refer to the right to experiment with herself as a transient, poignant figure who will be dead tomorrow. Women, despite the fact that nine out of ten of them go through life with a death-bed air either of snatching-the-last-moment or with martyr-resignation, do not die tomorrow – or the next day. They have to live on to any one of many bitter ends ...

By the conclusion of her essay Zelda had fallen into the familiar position of the spirited young feminist who dislikes most women. 'Flapperdom' was a curative against the ills of society and Zelda insisted that it made young women intelligent by 'teaching them to capitalize their natural resources and get their money's worth. They are merely applying business methods to being young.'

At twenty-one Zelda had formulated a sort of philosophy of life; it was remarkably like Gloria's. It was an application of business acumen to femininity: you created yourself as a product and you showed yourself with all the flair of a good advertising campaign. Women were to dramatize themselves in their youth, to experiment and be gay; in their old age (in their forties) they would be magically content. What Zelda intended to avoid at all costs was her vision of the legion of unhappy women, saddled with domesticity, weary and yet resigned to it. She was perceptive enough to understand that in their apparent resignation they thought of themselves as martyrs, and that was a position she abhorred for its dishonesty. What she wrote was a protest, but it was also a defence of her own code of existence. That this code was potentially destructive and that it would demand its own continual and wearying performance she did not take into account.

In the summer-time of 1922 the Fitzgeralds and Scottie's nurse moved out of St Paul to the Yacht Club on White Bear Lake; they lived there until, as one of their friends said, they 'made such an unholy rumpus day and night that they were asked to move out'. They found a house nearby and the summer continued with Zelda swimming and golfing, and Scott working on a play, called first *Gabriel's Trombone* and later *The Vegetable*. Mrs Kalman, who had helped them settle in St Paul the year before, played golf with Zelda every day. 'She was very athletic and wanted to be out doing something. Zelda was rather a good golfer, or at any rate, far better than Scott. She was not at all interested in going out with the girls, and when Scott wanted to remain at home, Zelda stayed with him. Certainly she enjoyed being different and was definitely not our idea of a Southern belle – there just wasn't a bit of the clinging vine about her. She and Scott were always thinking up perfectly killing things to do. You know, entertaining stunts which were so gay that one wanted to be in on them. Zelda didn't seem so awfully different then. She was a natural person, who didn't give a damn about clothes. But there weren't many people whom she liked. I won't say she was rude, but she made it quite clear. If she didn't like someone or if she disapproved of them, then she set out to be as impossible as she could be.'

By September they had exhausted whatever interest St Paul had held for them and decided to return East. Leaving Scottie with her nurse, they went to New York to hunt for a house. It was in New York, while they were temporarily living at the Plaza, that they first met Ring Lardner and John Dos Passos. Dos Passos had recently published *Three Soldiers* (1921) and had established his own literary reputation with that novel. It was natural that he should meet Fitzgerald, and he remembers:

'I met them together for the first time at the Plaza. . . . Wilson had introduced us, I believe. Scott called and asked me if I would care to join him for lunch; Sherwood Anderson would be there, and it might be fun if I came along. I did. That was when I first met Zelda. She was very beautiful, [she possessed] a sort of grace – a handsome girl, good looking hair – everything about her was very original and amusing. But there was also this little strange streak.'

After they had finished lunch someone suggested that they all go house hunting with the Fitzgeralds. Dos Passos continues: 'This was just before they moved into their house on Great Neck – so off we went. We wound up seeing Ring. Lardner was a very drunk and mournful man. Somehow, perhaps to cheer ourselves, we all decided to go to a carnival that was nearby. It was quite late by this time. At the carnival I remember thinking – Zelda and I had gone off together for a Ferris wheel ride – can you imagine that? Well, there we were up in the Ferris wheel when she said something to me. I don t remember what it was, but I thought to myself, suddenly, this woman is mad. Whatever she had said was so completely off track; it was like peering into a dark abyss – something forbidding between us. She didn't pause as I recall, but went right on. I was stunned. I can honestly say that from that first time I sensed that there was something peculiar about her.' Not being able to recall a specific instance of what he meant, he added simply: 'She would veer off; she wouldn't exactly get mad. . . . [Scott] would try to stop her if she went too far, you know, try to get her off the track.

'Sometimes she'd tell me how badly I danced; that sort of thing. We all used to go dancing together. I was never much for that kind of thing, but I'd go in those days. Zelda did have a manner of becoming personal that wasn't really very amusing. You see, there was a lot of banter between all of us; it was the period of the great wisecrack. Her humor was good about minor things, but she'd go off into regions that weren't funny anymore.

'There were also things about which one didn't tease her, and you found them rather suddenly. Sometimes she would go on, but there was always a non sequitur in it. It stunned one for a moment. She seemed in such complete self-possession.'

At the time *The Beautiful and Damned* was published Scott was $5,600 in debt to Scribner's. Although that was not much for Scribner's to have advanced to such a popular author, the debt was nevertheless an indication of the Fitzgeralds' inability to keep their expenses anywhere near in line with their income. His novel had been rather gently received by the critics and its sales were just over 40,000 copies for the first year – a little short of the sales of *This Side of Paradise*. Scott published a selection of short stories in September 1922, called *Tales of the Jazz Age,* which would be bought, he predicted to Perkins, 'by *my own personal public* – that is, by the countless flappers and college kids who think I am a sort of oracle'. And he was right; it sold 12,829 copies its first year, a good sale for a collection of stories. But still their expenditures far outran their income, and Scott borrowed frequently from both Scribner's and his agent, Harold Ober, to keep abreast of his debts. As Zelda was to write, '[They] were proud of themselves and the baby, consciously affecting a vague *bouffant* casualness about the fifty thousand dollars they spent on two years' worth of polish for life's baroque façade. In reality, there is no materialist like the artist, asking back from life the double and the wastage and the cost on what he puts out in emotional usury.'

In October the Fitzgeralds found the house in Great Neck, which they rented for $300 a month (Zelda called it 'our nifty little Babbit-home'), hired a nurse for Scottie at $90 a month, a couple to take care of the house for $160, and a laundress who came twice a week for another $36; they also bought a swank, although secondhand, Rolls coupé. Thus equipped they began the life of what Scott ironically called the newly rich: 'That is to say, five years ago we had no money at all, and what we now do away with would have seemed like inestimable riches to us then. I have at times suspected that we are the only newly rich people in America, that in fact we are the very couple at whom all the articles about the newly rich were aimed.'

Frank Crowninshield, the editor of *Vanity Fair,* had introduced Scott to Ring Lardner earlier that fall. Now they discovered they were neighbours in Great Neck. The two men had liked each other immediately and begun a friendship which was important to both of them. Lardner too was a Midwesterner, and at thirty-seven (eleven years older than Scott), he was writing a syndicated weekly column out of New York. He was not only a successful sports writer, but also the author of satirical sketches and stories, poems and comic burlesques. At Scott's suggestion, Lardner brought together a collection of his short stories, which Scott helped him select and which Scribner's published under the title Fitzgerald had thought up, *How to Write Short Stories.* It did very well and brought Lardner his first taste of critical recognition as a serious observer of the American scene. Lardner and Fitzgerald also shared a liking for the bottle and quickly became drinking companions. They would sit up all night talking about writing and planning pranks they sometimes pulled off, such as the time they danced somewhat noisily around the Long Island estate where Joseph Conrad was staying in order to attract his attention. Instead, the caretaker threw them out

Lardner enjoyed teasing Scott about Zelda, of whom he was equally fond. He made the Fitzgeralds Cinderella and the Prince in one of his burlesques: 'Well, the guy's own daughter was a pip, so both her stepmother and the two stepsisters hated her and made her sleep in the ash can. Her name was Zelda, but they called her Cinderella on account of how the ashes and clinkers clung to her when she got up noons.' At one of the Fitzgeralds' dinner parties Zelda made Lardner a place card in the form of a winking red-headed nude wearing a grey fedora, kicking toward his name with one bright red-heeled slipper. At Christmas Lardner sent her a poem in an envelope with his photograph on the front, cut into the shape of a tear; he called it 'A Christmas Wish – and What Came of It.'

Of all the girls for whom I care,
And there are quite a number,
None can compare with Zelda Sayre,
Now wedded to a plumber.

*

I read the World, I read the Sun,
The Tribune and the Herald,
But of all the papers, there is none
Like Mrs Scott Fitzgerald.

God rest thee, merry gentlemen!
God shrew thee, greasy maiden!
God love that pure American
Who married Mr Braden.

When Scott came to make his summary of 1922 for his Ledger, he wrote that it was a 'comfortable but dangerous and deteriorating' time, 'No ground under our feet'.

Although both Scott and Zelda had felt the urge for privacy when they returned to New York that autumn, and had taken their house in Great Neck to avoid the constant havoc of Manhattan, they were irresistibly drawn into the life of the city. Newspapers relished tidbits of gossip from the Fitzgerald household. In the Sunday section of the *Morning Telegraph* their slightest whims were reported: 'F. Scott Fitzgerald prefers piquant hors d'oeuvres to a hearty meal. He is also fond of Charlie Chaplin, Booth Tarkington, real Scotch, old-fashioned hansom cab riding in Central Park and the "Ziegfeld Follies". He admires Mencken and Nathan, Park & Tilford, Lord & Taylor, Lea & Perrins, the Smith Brothers, and Mrs Gibson, the pig lady, and her Jenny mule.' A clipping found in Zelda's scrapbook read: 'We are accustomed enough to this kind of rumor in regard to stage stars, but it is fairly new in relation to authors. The great drinking bouts, the petting may be what the public expects of Fitzgerald whose books told so much of this kind of life.' When Reginald Marsh did an Overture curtain for *The Greenwich Village Follies*, he crowded his scene of

Village life with portraits of the newly famous artists. In a truck tearing across Seventh Avenue were Edmund Wilson, Bishop, Dos Passos, Gilbert Seldes, and Scott. At the centre of the curtain, diving into the fountain at Washington Square, was the dazzling Zelda.

There were parties where the Fitzgeralds did not arrive until midnight and Scott would wheel in performing card tricks he said he had learned from Edmund Wilson, and relate the plot of 'the great American novel', which he told everyone he was writing. Mencken was at one such party and insisted on calling Scott Mr Fitzheimer. Scott brought the party to an end that evening by singing a sad ballad he had written, called 'Dog, Dog, Dog'.

Gilbert Seldes, who was then editor of *The Dial*, met Scott and Zelda for the first time that winter in New York. There was what he calls 'a long long party' at Townsend Martin's, and Seldes had eventually and somewhat groggily lain down on Martin's bed to recover. The room itself was lavishly decorated with painted screens and resplendent silk pillows thrown upon the bed into which Seldes sank. 'Suddenly, as though in a dream, this apparition, this double apparition, approached me. The two most beautiful people in the world were floating toward me, smiling. It was as if they were angelic visitors. I thought to myself, "If there is anything I can do to keep them as beautifull as they are, I will do it." ' The heavenly pair turned out to be the Fitzgeralds. That was how they struck people. There have been dozens of memoirs written wherein one catches glimpses of Scott and Zelda sleeping like children in each other's arms at a party; Zelda necking with young men because she liked the shapes of their noses or the cut of their dinner jackets; Scott drinking and radiating his sunny charm. Everyone wanted to meet them, to have them for dinner guests, to attend their parties, and to invite them to their openings. The youthful handsomeness of the Fitzgeralds, their incandescent vitality were qualities they possessed jointly and effortlessly. *Hearst's International* ran a full-page photograph of Scott and Zelda that was picked up by newspapers and magazines throughout the country. They were the apotheosis of the twenties: *The F.*

Scott Fitzgeralds: Scott sitting behind Zelda, leaning slightly forward, his right hand casually holding her fingers, both of them pouting a little, dramatically; Zelda in a dress trimmed with white fur, wearing a long strand of pearls, with her hair parted uncharacteristically in the middle and falling back from her brow in deeply marcelled waves. Zelda, who rarely photographed well, and did not wear jewellery, not even her wedding ring, was always to refer to this portrait as her 'Elizabeth Arden Face'.

Even the bearish H. L. Mencken was not immune to the aura of success that clung to them like gold dust, but he also noticed the signs of flaw. 'Fitzgerald blew into New York last week. He has written a play, and Nathan says that it has very good chances. But it seems to me that his wife talks too much about money. His danger lies in trying to get it too rapidly. A very amiable pair, innocent and charming.' Zelda did talk too much about money, and Scott seemed in more of a hurry to get somewhere than to know his destination. There began to be a touch of the vaudeville team about their performances in public, and their privacy was almost non-existent.

Scott's drinking was also becoming a problem. In his Ledger at the beginning of 1923 he mentioned battling insomnia, and he wrote of 'My dream of the baseball player, football player and general to put me to sleep', and in February he noted, 'still drunk'. By their third anniversary he said he was on the wagon, but then they fought and he became 'Tearing drunk'. There were two- and three-day binges in New York from which he returned shaken, not remembering where he had been or with whom. What he had written in *The Beautiful and Damned* had been an exaggerated view of themselves, but now they were drifting dangerously close to it: 'The magnificent attitude of not giving a damn altered overnight; from being a mere tenet of Gloria's it became the entire solace and justification of what they chose to do and what consequence it brought. Not to be sorry, not to loose one cry of regret, to live according to a clear code of honour toward each other, and to seek the moment's happiness as fervently and persistently as possible.'

Carl Van Vechten (whom Zelda immediately chose to call

'Carlos') met the Fitzgeralds during one of their trips into New York City. After a successful career as a leading music and drama critic in New York, he was enjoying a certain vogue as a novelist. 'You know, I was famous in my forties before I had even heard of F. Scott Fitzgerald', he once remarked quietly. One of the things which Van Vechten noticed early in his friendship with them was Scott's inability to hold his liquor. 'He could take two or three drinks at the most and be completely drunk. It was incredible. He was nasty when he was drunk, but sober he was a charming man, very good looking, you know, beautiful, almost. But they both drank a lot – we all did, but they were excessive.'

Zelda had intrigued Van Vechten from the first time he met her. He just liked her. 'She was an original. Scott was not a wisecracker like Zelda. Why, she tore up the pavements with sly remarks. She taunted bell boys and waiters – just, maybe, to see what would happen. She didn't actually write them down, Scott did, but she said them.' There is nothing quite so perishable as a wisecrack and Van Vechten had a hard time remembering specific remarks of Zelda's: 'She said something like this to me, "Why do you always use in your books the perfume I used last year?" And then she would look up at me with that little half smile.'

Rebecca West's impressions of the Fitzgeralds were entirely different: 'My relations with Mrs Fitzgerald were few and fragmentary. I don't know if you'll find anybody to confirm my impression that she was very plain. I had been told that she was very beautiful, but when I went to a party and saw her I had quite a shock. She was standing with her back to me, and her hair was quite lovely, it glistened like a child's. I am sure this was natural. Then she turned round and she startled me, I would almost go so far as to say that her face had a certain craggy homeliness. There was a curious unevenness about it, such as one sees in Géricault's pictures of the insane. Her profile seemed on two different planes. Everybody told me how lovely she was, but that is and always has been my impression.

'We got on quite well, though our relationship was interrupted by Scott Fitzgerald's anger at me because I did not come to a party . . . the trouble was that nobody had told me where the party was. Recently someone reminded me . . . that we had both been at a party where she had talked to us about her dancing. And there came back to me a very unpleasant memory. She had flapped her arms and looked very uncouth as she talked about her ballet ambitions. The odd thing to me always was that Scott Fitzgerald, who might have been expected from his writings to like someone sleek like Mrs Vernon Castle, should have liked someone who was so inelegant. But she was not at all unlikable. There was something very appealing about her. But frightening. Not that one was frightened from one's own point of view, only from hers.'

Zelda's sister Rosalind spent some time with the Fitzgeralds during July and August of 1923, but it was not a comfortable visit. She remembers being taken to a party at a Long Island estate that lasted all night and into the morning; Scott would not leave and insisted on trying to drop an entire orange peel down his throat in front of an admiring audience that had gathered about him. In exasperation Zelda left without him. It was the only time that Rosalind could recall Zelda's being in any way critical of Scott in front of her. When they left, Zelda said quietly, 'I never did want to marry Scott'.

When the drinking got out of hand at their own home visitors would receive apologetic notes from Zelda the following day. 'I am running wild in sack cloth and ashes because Scott and I acted like two such drunks the other night – Aside from the fact that you were horribly bored, I am sorry because we saw nothing of you. It's been years since we three spent a satisfactory evening to-gether – so won't you please come back Saturday or Sunday or whenever you will so we can astound you with our brilliant conversation and splendid example of what is known as tee-totalers?' That Zelda was straining to create an effect of gay abandon did not seem to occur to anyone. The appearance had not given way.

Although Scott was often the subject of newspaper articles, that autumn Zelda was also interviewed by a reporter from the

Baltimore *Sun*. The public, he had told her, wanted to know if she was the heroine of Scott's books. When the reporter arrived he found Zelda sitting far back in the plastic over-stuffed chair in the living room of their Great Neck house. She told him this was her first interview and then called out to Scott to come help her. The reporter described Scott as he came into the room as tall, blond, and broad-shouldered, towering over his petite wife. They began to speak about three short stories Zelda was writing. She said there were no typewriters in their house, for they both wrote their first drafts in long-hand. 'I like to write. Do you know, I thought my husband should write a perfectly good ending to one of the tales, and he wouldn't! He called them "lop-sided", too! Said that they began at the end.' Then she interrupted herself to talk about Scott's writing; her favourite short story was his 'The Offshore Pirate'. 'I love Scott's books and heroines. I like the ones that are like me! That's why I love Rosalind in *This Side of Paradise*. You see, I always read everything he writes. It spoils the fun, the surprise, I mean, a bit. . . . But Rosalind! I like girls like that. . . . I like their courage, their recklessness and spendthriftness. Rosalind was the original American flapper.'

At this point in the interview Scott explained that Zelda's youth was spent going to proms and living in Montgomery. 'That's a mighty long way from New York', he added. The reporter asked him to describe his wife. 'She is the most charming person in the world.' And, after receiving Zelda's thanks, he continued: 'That's all. I refuse to amplify. Excepting – she's perfect.'

Zelda said, 'But you don't think that. . . . You think I'm a lazy woman.'

'No, I like it. I think you're perfect. You're always ready to listen to my manuscript, at any hour of the day or night. You're charming – beautiful. You do, I believe, clean the ice-box once a week.'

Then Scott fired off several direct questions to Zelda: 'Whom do you consider the most interesting character in fiction?'

Zelda's answer was Becky Sharp of Thackeray's *Vanity Fair*.

'Only I do wish she'd been pretty', Zelda added somewhat wistfully.

'What would your ideal day constitute?'

She answered: 'Peaches for breakfast. ... Then golf. Then a swim. Then just being lazy. Not eating or reading, but being quiet and hearing pleasant sounds – rather a total vacuity. The evening? A large, brilliant gathering, I believe.'

Asked if she was ambitious, she replied, 'Not especially, but I've plenty of hope. I don't want to belong to clubs. No committees. I'm not a "joiner". Just be myself and enjoy living.'

Finally Scott asked her what she wanted Scottie (whom Zelda still referred to as Patricia Scott Fitzgerald) to be when she grew up. 'Not great and serious and melancholy and inhospitable, but rich and happy and artistic. I don't mean that money means happiness, necessarily. But having things, just things, objects makes a woman happy. The right kind of perfume, the smart pair of shoes. They are great comforts to the feminine soul. ... I'd rather have her be a Marilyn Miller than a Pavlowa. And I do want her to be rich.'

Zelda had said very little about their domestic life, other than 'Home is the place to do the things you want to do. Here we eat just when we want to. Breakfast and luncheon are extremely moveable feasts. It's terrible to allow conventional habits to gain a hold on a whole household; to eat, sleep and live by clock ticks.'

Scott's last question was to ask Zelda what she would do if she had to earn her own living. Her answer was prophetic: 'I've studied ballet. I'd try to get a place in the Follies. Or the movies. If I wasn't successful, I'd try to write.'

Zelda worked harder at her writing than she admitted. During 1922–23 she sold two short stories, a review, and at least two articles, earning $1,300 for her efforts. Scott helped her with one of her short stories, called 'Our Own Movie Queen', which she completed in the month after the preceding interview was published. When Scott listed the story in his Ledger he noted that 'two thirds [were] written by Zelda. Only my climax and revision.' The story was not published until 1925, when it won two stars in O'Brien's short-story collection for that year. Zelda was not, however, given credit for having written it, and the story was published under Scott's name alone. He was paid $1,000 for it, which they split.

It has been assumed that Scott gave Zelda help with her writing, and various notations in the record-keeping section of his Ledger point to the times when he did. There was never, however, a similar record kept of Zelda's assistance to him, and it is only from friends' remarks and a close reading of Scott's letters to his editor that a hint comes through of what it was. He once commented that he had to stop 'Referring everything to Zelda – a terrible habit; nothing ought to be referred to any-body until it's finished'. It was Zelda who insisted that the 'happy ending' of the serialized version of *The Beautiful and Damned* be cut, and who told Scott to stick to his guns about the title of his last collection of short stories, *Tales of the Jazz Age*. And it was Zelda who would convince him of the aptness of the title for his next novel, *The Great Gatsby*, and while he was working on *The Vegetable* he wrote Edmund Wilson, who liked it very much, 'Zelda and I have concocted a wonderful idea for Act II of the play'. Certainly, as we have seen, Fitz-gerald drew almost ruthlessly upon her letters and diaries, al-though Zelda gave no sign that she disapproved; for Fitzgerald was the professional and not Zelda.

In June 1923 Fitzgerald had begun his third novel, but in the press of summer guests and parties he could not seem to get on with it. By the fall all his effort went into his play, which, after having been turned down three times, was accepted for produc-tion. In October *The Vegetable* went into rehearsal in New York and Fitzgerald was completely involved in those rehear-sals; for, besides being vastly intrigued with the theatre, Scott staked everything on his having a Broadway hit. He counted on making $100,000 from it, and he considered that a conservative estimate. In November the play opened in Atlantic City, and he and Zelda went down and promenaded on the broadwalk with the Lardners for the photographers. 'It was', he wrote later, 'a colossal frost. People left their seats and walked out. ... After the second act I wanted to stop the show and say it was all a mistake but the actors struggled heroically on.' He spent a week trying to revise it and then gave up and returned to Great Neck in gloom. They had made $36,000 that year, had spent all of it and were $5,000 in debt. It took Scott the entire spring, writing in a large bare room over his garage, to work himself into a secure enough financial position to get back to his novel. When he summarized the year in his Ledger he labelled it 'The most miserable year since I was nineteen, full of terrible failures and acute miseries.'

Zelda wrote in her unpublished novel, *Caesar's Things*, that life during the one and a half years on Long Island was 'a matter of rendez-vous and reward'. 'There were many changing friends and the same old drinks and glamour and story swept their lives up into the dim vaults of lobbies and stations until, as one said, evenements accumulated. It might have been Nemesis incubating.'

They were tired of their friends, of the destructive pace of their lives, and of the unending struggle to get their finances in shape. They accepted Ring Lardner's offer to help them rent their house, and by mid-April, with a capital of $7,000, deciding that they could live more cheaply in Europe, they sailed for France. Lardner said goodbye in a poem 'To Z.S.F.'.

> Zelda, fair queen of Alabam',
> Across the waves I kiss you!
> You think I am a stone, a clam;
> You think that I don't care a damn,
> But God! how I will miss you!
>
> *
>
> So, dearie, when your tender heart
> Of all his coarseness tires,
> Just cable me and I will start
> Immediately for Hyeres.
>
> To hell with Scott Fitzgerald then!
> To hell with Scott, his daughter!
> It's you and I back home again,
> To Great Neck, where men are men
> And booze is ¾ water.

8

New York lay behind them. The forces that produced them lay
behind them. That Alabama and David would never sense the
beat of any other pulse half so exactly, since we can only
recognize in other environments what we have grown familiar
with in our own, played no part in their expectations.

ZELDA FITZGERALD, *Save Me the Waltz*

The Fitzgeralds were fleeing Long Island and New York as
they had previously fled Westport, Montgomery, and St Paul,
but this time it was in a conscious attempt to end the disarray
of their lives. In May of 1924 Scott badly wanted to get back
to work on his novel. It was with this in mind that they arrived
in Paris, their expectations high. Paris that spring was, to use a
favourite word of the twenties and of Scott's, gorgeous. Lawton
Campbell spotted them strolling on the Champs Elysées: 'They
were so smartly dressed and striking. . . . They were beautiful –
the loveliness . . .' Wearing an immaculately tailored suit, Scott
stood beside Zelda, tapping a silver-headed cane on the sidewalk. And Zelda, catching sight of Campbell, stretched out her
arms toward him, crying, 'Lawton!'

'She was dressed in a lovely frock which she said she had
designed; it was military blue and she told me at once it was
brand new. "This, Lawton, is my Jeanne d'Arc dress", she
quipped. Zelda as St Joan gave one a turn, but the dress did
look innocent and sweet.'

During the several days they spent in Paris they acquired a
nanny for Scottie (whom they had mistakenly 'bathed . . . in the
bidet . . . and she [Scottie] drank a gin fizz thinking it was lemonade and ruined the luncheon table next day'). They also met
Gerald and Sara Murphy, who told them of a paradise in the
South of France – the Riviera, off season.

The Murphys lived in Paris on private incomes from their
families. Sara was a beautiful heiress from Ohio, and Gerald,
who had been Skull and Bones at Yale, had been unable to
decide upon a career for himself. He loathed the idea of enter-

ing his father's prosperous New York leather-goods store, Mark Cross. They came to Paris in 1921 to escape formidable family pressures at home and because the rate of exchange in France was favourable to the dollar. Neither of the Murphys was as conventional as their backgrounds and wealth might have suggested. Gerald Murphy was a fair, slender, and precisely elegant man who sported a pair of flourishing sideburns. He had recently decided that he wanted to paint. He said they had left America because 'there was something depressing to young married people about a country that could pass the Eighteenth Amendment. The country was tightening up and it was so unbecoming. You really resented being herded into the basements of old sandstone houses. It was, I suppose, the tone of life in America that we all found uncongenial.' The nuances implicit in his phrase 'the tone of life' distinguished the Murphys, for their own mastery of it was not essentially artistic, but social. They took the old Spanish adage 'Living well is the best revenge' as their motto. They did not join the expatriates in the established American colony about the Étoile, because it had a decidedly Jamesian air about it, which they found stuffy. Instead the Murphys sought, cultivated, and entertained artists living in Paris whose paintings were utterly different from anything they had seen before. Soon they came to know Picasso, Miró and Juan Gris. Both of the Murphys studied scene design with Natalie Goncharova of the Ballet Russe of Diaghilev and through that contact came to know Stravinsky, Léon Bakst, and Braque. They met their friends at the new exhibitions, at recitals and at art galleries. Paris was, as Sara said, 'like a great fair, and everybody was so young'.

By the time the Fitzgeralds first met the Murphys, Gerald and Sara were already close friends of Archibald MacLeish, John Dos Passos and an unknown young writer, Ernest Hemingway. Sara Murphy said, 'You see, most of us had given up something to come to France. Archie, for instance, a law career; it took courage to simply chuck it and come to France to write. Now, Hemingway was without a penny.'

The Murphys discovered the Riviera off season through Cole Porter, who had been a friend of Gerald's at Yale. They were so taken by the lushness of its gardens and the closeness of the sea that they were building their own villa at Antibes. They told the Fitzgeralds about it and the tiny beach – the Garoupe – which Gerald had begun to clear, and they made plans to meet there that summer.

Scott and Zelda left for the South of France at the end of May. Zelda's description of their trip from Paris down to the Riviera in *Save Me the Waltz* evokes the spell Provence held for her: 'The train bore them down through the pink carnival of Normandy, past the delicate tracery of Paris and the high terraces of Lyon, the belfries of Dijon and the white romance of Avignon into the scent of lemon, the rustle of black foliage, clouds of moths whipping the heliotrope dusk – into Provence, where people do not need to see unless they are looking for the nightingale.'

They stopped at Grimm's Park Hotel in Hyères, but the small city was primarily a resort for invalids taking the cure and it was mercilessly hot. In June they came to St Raphaël and Scott wrote, 'It was a red little town built close to the sea, with gay red-roofed houses and an air of repressed carnival about it. . . .' Although the Fitzgeralds had come to France to economize they forgot their resolutions once they found the Villa Marie. Situated high above the sea, surrounded by terraced gardens of lemon, palm, pine, and silver olive trees, with a winding gravel drive leading to its entrance and with Moorish balconies of brilliant white-and-blue tiles, it faced the Mediterranean like an exotic fortress.

The Murphys remembered the beautiful terraced rock garden at the Fitzgeralds' villa, where one afternoon Zelda and Scott staged a mock crusaders' battle. 'Zelda must have spent days making the intricate cardboard battlements and castle. There were lead soldiers [from Scott's collection] and Scott had fashioned a series of interconnecting moats that flooded at the proper time in the siege. The children loved it.' The summer seemed a perfect one, and the Murphys took an especial liking to Zelda. 'I don't think we could have taken Scott alone', Gerald said. 'Zelda had her own personal style; it was her individuality, her flair. She might dress like a flapper when it was appropriate to do so, but always with a difference. Actually, her taste was never what one would speak of as à la mode – it was better, it was her own.'

In many ways the climate of Provence was like that of Alabama. There were delirious heat and acid sunlight, a similar extravagance of greenery. But it was a far more dramatic setting than the American South, with the immediacy of the sea, the exotic food, and the foreignness of the French themselves. That summer the air of the Riviera was perfumed by the aroma of burning eucalyptus from a series of fires behind the beaches. Zelda loved the Riviera from the first. She wrote, '(Oh, we are going to be so happy away from all the things that almost got us but couldn't quite because we were too smart for them!)' They bought beach umbrellas and bright-coloured cotton bathing suits and espadrilles from the sailors' quarter in Cannes and settled in for the summer.

It began well, with Scott writing every day. There was a nanny to look after Scottie and there was plenty of household help to run the spacious Villa Marie. They met a group of French aviators stationed nearby at Fréjus, with whom they drank and danced at night in the casino behind the *plage*. Zelda swam and baked in the sun; she tried very hard to keep out of Scott's hair during the day while he wrote; she read a little, but her eyes bothered her and she preferred being active to the immobility of reading. She was left alone with little to do. 'After all, Scott had his writing. Zelda had Scott – and she didn't have very much of him while he was working', Gerald Murphy remarked. So she swam strenuously, as though it were necessary for her to have some form of physical release, and soon she was as deeply tanned as she had been in her girlhood. Yet the days were monotonous for her and when she recalled them in *Save Me the Waltz* Zelda had the heroine ask her husband, ' "What'll we *do* . . . with ourselves?" ' He replies that ' "she couldn't always be a child and have things provided for her to do" '.

Zelda wrote Edmund Wilson: '. . . everything would be perfect if there was somebody here who would be sure to spread the tale of our idyllic existence around New York. . . .' She felt, she said, 'picturesque', adding, 'It's fine to be away from the continual necessity of revolt of New York.' She had, however, begun a private revolt of her own.

Casually at first, Zelda and one of the young aviators, Édouard Jozan, began to meet in the afternoons to swim together. They were seen lying on the wide canvas beach mats in the sun, sunburned and laughing together while they 'invented new cocktails'. No one paid much attention to them and they seemed content to be in each other's company without joining the other bathers. Scott was pleased that Zelda had at last found someone to help her pass the time. Jozan was handsome, his hair dark and curling, his body even more deeply tanned than Zelda's. He was, in contrast to Scott, tall and slender and athletic. It was astonishing how closely he resembled the dashing young officers from Montgomery who had adored Zelda and to whom she had been attracted before her marriage to Scott. Obviously infatuated with her, he stunted his airplane above their villa, dipping dangerously close to its red-tiled roof, as if emulating those Montgomery flyers who had paid her similar homage. His black hair gleamed from beneath its net in the bright sunlight.

It was June 1924, Zelda was not quite twenty-four, and Jozan was a year and two days older than she. Édouard Jozan cannot remember any longer how he first met the Fitzgeralds, but a small group of young officers and friends – himself, Bellando, René Silvy (who was a civilian, the son of an attorney in Cannes) – all bachelors, would come down to the beach whenever they could to swim and have picnics. And because of their youth, he says, it was not necessary to have formal introductions. They just met. All the young men fell a little in love with Zelda, who was, Jozan remembers, 'a shining beauty'; and they all admired Scott's intelligence and quick conversation. Soon there were excursions taken together, dancing in the cabarets along the coast, and endless conversations about art and literature. Jozan recalls: 'Zelda and Scott were brimming over with life. Rich and free, they brought into our little provincial circle brilliance, imagination and familiarity with a Parisian and international world to which we had no access.'

Scott seemed to Jozan very intellectual – 'I would even say "intellectualist" ' – and from a far more sophisticated world than any Jozan had known. Fitzgerald was looking for an explanation of a world which had not yet stabilized itself after the upheaval of World War I. 'But in his search for new trends Scott paid great attention to the resources of society: social position, the effectiveness and the force of money, of which, being a good American, he knew both the power and the burden. "Ford", he said, "runs modern society and not the politicians who are only screens or hostages." ' And their discussions together were often heated and passionate, for they did not share the same point of view. It was human bravery, the sort of courage he had seen displayed in the war, that turned Jozan toward an entirely different life. He wanted to earn honour and glory; he had a taste for risk, for knowledge without commercial profit. 'In short, we were young romantics arguing with a man better versed in the practicalities of life.

'Zelda was a creature who overflowed with activity, radiant with desire to take from life every chance her charm, youth, and intelligence provided so abundantly.' And she did not seem like a complicated woman to him; her pleasures were simple ones: 'the relaxed life on beaches gilded by the sun, trips by car, informal dinners'. The little group took her as their centre and would come and go according to the demands of their missions. Then, suddenly, 'One day the Fitzgeralds left and their friends scattered, each to his own destiny.'

Jozan went on to a distinguished military career, holding one of the highest ranks of the French navy. In 1940 he commanded a naval flotilla at Dunkirk; in 1952 he became Vice-Admiral of the French navy; and two years later he commanded the French maritime forces in the Far East. Among his numerous decorations were the Grand-Croix de la Légion d'honneur, the Croix de guerre 1939–45, and the Grand-Croix au Mérite de l'Ordre de Malte.

Even in the summer of 1924, as a young officer, he showed that quality of leadership that was to distinguish him during his long military career. There was an air of assurance about him, a quality of natural leadership that Zelda respected and responded to. Leadership, athletic prowess, a smart military air were precisely those qualities Scott Fitzgerald lacked. It was as if Jozan and Fitzgerald were opposite sides of a coin, each admiring the other's abilities, gifts, and talents, but the difference in the equipment they brought to bear on life was clear. When Zelda described him in *Save Me the Waltz*, she caught it: 'Jacques moved his sparse body with the tempestuous spontaneity of a leader.'

Zelda called her young officer Jacques Chevre-Feuille in *Save Me the Waltz*: 'The head of the gold of a Christmas coin ... broad bronze hands. ... The convex shoulders were slim and strong. ...' And when she described the progress of their romance that summer it was in explicitly sensual terms. 'He drew her body against him till she felt the blades of his bones carving her own. He was bronze and smelled of the sand and sun; she felt him naked underneath the starched linen. She didn't think of David. She hoped he hadn't seen; she didn't care. She felt as if she would like to be kissing Jacques Chevre-Feuille on the top of the Arc de Triomphe.'

Scott was used to young men falling in love with his wife, and it amused, perhaps even flattered, rather than irritated him. He was not, however, prepared to find Zelda seriously reciprocating the attention. Sara Murphy thought that Zelda 'always had to chase around after Scott, follow up after him', and that she hadn't liked to. Sara wondered whether 'Jozan wasn't someone for her to talk to; I must say everyone knew about it but Scott'. The Murphys had seen Zelda and the young officer on the beach together and dancing at the casino; they said it was impossible not to notice what was happening. Gerald Murphy said: 'I don't know how far it really went, I suspect it wasn't much, but it did upset Scott a good deal. I wonder whether it wasn't partly his own fault?'

Then, abruptly, Zelda and Jozan were no longer seen on the beach together. When Zelda reappeared she swam alone. No one knew exactly what had happened. Scott wrote in his Ledger: 'The Big Crisis – 13th of July. ... Zelda swimming everyday.'

At that point not more than six weeks had passed since Zelda first met Jozan. At the beginning of August Gilbert Seldes and his bride arrived at St Raphaël to spend a few days of their honeymoon with the Fitzgeralds at the Villa Marie. There was not a hint of discord between Scott and Zelda apparent to either Seldes or his wife during their entire visit. They talked a good deal about the novel that Scott was working on; Seldes could recall only a few incidents from their time together.

One occurred the morning after their arrival. Seldes, upon opening the shutters of the window to his room, looked up and saw Scott standing on the balcony of his bedroom, which faced the sea. He was motionless as he gazed out, and then, sensing Seldes's presence, he quietly said, 'Conrad is dead'. Joseph Conrad had died in England on 3 August and Scott, who was a great admirer of his writing, would one day write in his introduction to *The Great Gatsby* (the novel he was working on that summer) that 'never before did one try to keep his artistic conscience as pure as during the ten months put into doing it. ... I had just reread Conrad's preface to *The Nigger*, and I had recently been kidded half haywire by critics who felt that my material was such as to preclude all dealing with mature persons in a mature world. But, my God! it was my material, and it was all I had to deal with.'

Seldes also remembers the trips he and his new wife made with the Fitzgeralds down to the beach together. 'The road from their villa had been built for carriage traffic and there was one point at which it dangerously narrowed and curved. Every time, just at this point, Zelda would turn to Scott, who was driving, and say, "Give me a cigarette, Goofo." ' In the moments of terrified silence that followed, Scott always managed both to give Zelda her cigarette and to straighten out the Renault along the narrow turn, but it was harrowing and the Seldeses both thought it peculiar of Zelda to make her request repeatedly at just that hazardous point in the road.

It would appear that the 'Big Crisis' Fitzgerald referred to in mid-July had not particularly disrupted their lives. Certainly they presented a united front to the Seldeses. In August Scott wrote in his Ledger, 'Zelda and I close together'. But between the time the Seldeses left the Fitzgeralds' villa and the beginning of September there was another crisis which went unrecorded in Scott's Ledger.

The Murphys were still living in their temporary quarters at the Hôtel du Cap, awaiting the completion of the Villa America. At about three or four one morning Scott knocked at the Murphys' door. 'He was green faced, holding a candle, trembling – Zelda had taken an overdose of sleeping pills. We went with him, and Sara walked her up and down, up and down, to keep her from going to sleep. We tried to make her drink olive oil, but Zelda said, "Sara, . . . don't make me take that, please. If you drink too much oil you turn into a Jew."' This attempted suicide occurred at approximately that period when Scott had written, 'Zelda and I close together'. It throws into question not only their reconciliation but Scott's understanding of how deeply Zelda had been affected by her romance with Jozan.

There were no explanations offered to the Murphys as to why Zelda had taken the pills, and the incident was never referred to again between the couples. From the Murphys' point of view Zelda's suicide attempt was inexplicable, but in retrospect they were certain it had some connection with Jozan. In Fitzgerald's eyes she had broken the trust between them in their marriage, as indeed she had, but why she had, what had compelled her toward Jozan, he neither understood nor sought to understand. It was not until much later in his life that he would write, 'That September 1924 I knew something had happened that could never be repaired.' But at the time even that 'something' went unnamed and unadmitted. Refusing to acknowledge Zelda's desperate unhappiness, her uneasiness at being locked out of his world as he wrote, her dependence upon him, his entries in his Ledger continued optimistically. In September he wrote, 'Trouble clearing away', and in October, 'Last sight of Josanne'.

Years later Scott told a relative that Zelda had come to him that July, telling him that she loved Jozan and asking for a divorce. Furious, Scott insisted upon a showdown among the three of them. He told Zelda that Jozan had to face him in Zelda's presence and ask for her himself. Then, in a burst of anger, he locked her in her rooms at the villa. The confronta-

tion did not take place; Zelda apparently accepted Scott's ultimatum passively and the subject of divorce was dropped. Jozan
says that he was not involved in the scenes which took place
between the Fitzgeralds, and it is altogether possible that he
was unaware of Zelda's predicament. He insists that Zelda's
infidelity was imaginary. 'But they both had a need of drama,
they made it up and perhaps they were the victims of their own
unsettled and a little unhealthy imagination.' He left the Riviera
without knowledge of what had passed between Scott and
Zelda, and he never saw either of the Fitzgeralds again. In *Save
Me the Waltz*, Alabama says: 'Whatever it was that she wanted
from Jacques, Jacques took it with him. . . . You took what you
wanted from life, if you could get it, and you did without the
rest.'

The sea turned the colour of gun-metal and the cold winds of
the mistral blew down from the Alps Estérel. The Fitzgeralds
remained on the Riviera while Scott tried to clear everything
from his mind but the manuscript of *The Great Gatsby*, which
he had nearly completed. He told Maxwell Perkins that it would
not reach him before 1 October 'as Zelda and I are contempla-
ting a careful revision after a week's complete rest'. He said the
summer had been a fair one. 'I've been unhappy but my work
hasn't suffered from it. I am grown at last.' That was the only
clue he gave to any of his friends at that time of the blow that
had been struck at their marriage. At the end of October
Gatsby was sent to Scribner's and the Fitzgeralds decided to
follow what little sun there was to Italy. Zelda was reading
Roderick Hudson and suggested to Scott that they winter in
Rome. In November Scott entered in his Ledger: '. . . ill feeling
with Zelda', but there were no explanatory notes to accompany
his comment.

Rome was an unfortunate choice for both of them. It was
damp and cold and they were ill intermittently throughout the
dreary winter months. Scott disliked the Italians, got in scrapes
with the police, and began to drink heavily. Yet, when the
proofs of *Gatsby* began to arrive from New York, he worked
soberly and in full control as he revised them. He worried about

the title of the novel. Should it have been *Trimalchio in West Egg*, the title he'd put on the book; simply *Trimalchio*, or *Gatsby*? He had two alternative titles which he rejected for their lightness: *Gold-hatted Gatsby* and *The High-bouncing Lover*. But Zelda preferred *The Great Gatsby* and he trusted her instinct.

She read aloud to him from a novel by Will James about cowboys, in order, he said, to spare his mind, and when he had difficulty visualizing Gatsby, she drew pictures until her fingers ached, attempting to capture his image for Scott. The result was, he wrote Perkins, 'I know Gatsby better than I know my own child.'

By the first of the new year they set off for Capri to recuperate. Zelda became ill with colitis and her attacks were painful. They were to come and go fitfully during the entire year and made them both anxious over her health. The ailment came on the heels of her failed love affair and there was probably a connection between the two. It was in Capri that Zelda first began to paint; it was to become a lifelong pursuit. Scott wrote, '. . . me drinking', while he assured John Peale Bishop: 'Zelda and I sometimes indulge in terrible four-day rows that always start with a drinking party but we're still enormously in love and about the only truly happily married people I know.'

In April they travelled back to southern France in their Renault; its top had been damaged and was removed at Zelda's insistence, for she preferred open cars. When the car broke down in Lyon they abandoned it and continued on to Paris by train. That spring in Paris was composed for them of '1000 parties and no work', but they did meet Ernest Hemingway.

The previous fall, Fitzgerald, upon reading something of Hemingway's in the *transatlantic review*, predicted to Perkins that he had 'a brilliant future. . . . He's the real thing.' Meeting him in Paris, Scott took to Hemingway immediately; he liked his tough-guy charm, his engaging lopsided grin. Ernest Hemingway was three years younger than Scott and a half foot taller. There was an athletic swagger to his walk; he wore a moustache and swore in cliché French. 'Parbleu!' and 'Yes, we have no bananas!' were his favourite expressions. Soon Hemingway was calling Scott his best friend and a guy he liked to talk to most of the time. '

Shortly after they met, Scott invited Hemingway to join him in a trip to Lyon to pick up the Fitzgeralds' abandoned Renault. It was on the two-day trip that Scott first told Hemingway about Zelda's romance with Jozan. Less than ten months had passed since the crisis in the Fitzgeralds' marriage According to Hemingway's posthumously published memoir, *A Moveable Feast*, on their return from Lyon Scott tried to put a call through to Zelda in Paris. While waiting for the call he and Hemingway had several drinks and Scott began to talk about his life with Zelda. It was then that he revealed what Hemingway said 'was truly a sad story and I believe it was a true story'. He was later in the same book to remark that during the course of his friendship with Scott the story of Zelda's romance was told several times, and altered with each retelling. Hemingway said he heard about it so often that he could picture the tragic romance (it became increasingly tragic as Scott repeated it) in his mind's eye. But this first time Scott was at pains to tell Hemingway everything about it – how it had disturbed him, and exactly what had happened.

Hemingway's first wife, Hadley, to whom he was married when he met the Fitzgeralds in 1925, remembers the Fitzgeralds' joint recital of Zelda's romance. She says: 'It was one of their acts together. I remember Zelda's beautiful face becoming very, very solemn, and she would say how he had loved her and how hopeless it had been and then how he had committed suicide.' That last detail was only one of the dramatic embellishments added to give the affair tragic significance. Hadley continued: 'Scott would stand next to her looking very pale and distressed and sharing every minute of it. Somehow it struck me as something that gave her status. I can still see both of them standing together telling me about the suicide of Zelda's lover. It created a peculiar effect.'

Scott had helped to fictionalize the affair, thereby giving it a heightened meaning and value, which he, having created, could come to share. It was all of a piece with his having married the heroine of his stories and novels; of his feeling, which by this time, dangerously, had become *their* feeling, that he somehow possessed a right to Zelda's life as his raw material.

Hemingway perceptively noticed two kinds of jealousy in the Fitzgeralds' marriage. Zelda was jealous, he said, of Scott's work while Scott was jealous of Zelda. Zelda tried to keep Scott from writing, and Scott tried to keep Zelda from other people. Instinctively Zelda realized that a part of her attractiveness for Scott lay in her ability to provoke his jealousy, but that in no way mitigated her own. It might, in fact, have created a tension within her to maintain that ability, especially since it was something she could not wholly understand or control.

Hadley feels that Zelda 'was a charming, lovely creature. She lived on what Ernest called the "festival conception of life".' She believes that Zelda was essentially 'a frivolous kind of woman'. There were from the start problems between the two couples. Hadley says: 'They were inconvenient friends. They would call on the Hemingways at four o'clock in the morning and we had a baby and didn't appreciate it very much. When Scott wrote I don't know.'

Their writing was what drew the two men into friendship, and Scott eventually succeeded in having Scribner's take on the as yet largely unknown Hemingway. But it was never Hemingway's considerable talent alone that attracted Scott to him. There was a purity about Hemingway then, a dedication to his art, a seemingly total lack of affectation that impressed Scott as it had others. And Hemingway, by his own admittance, was curious about Fitzgerald, the best-selling author, the writer of *The Great Gatsby*.

Gatsby, which was published in April 1925, was a critical rather than a financial success. In the first week of its publication Perkins cabled Scott in Marseille that the reviews were superb, but the sales uncertain. When Scott had finished it he had written John Peale Bishop that 'my book has something extraordinary about it. I want to be extravagantly admired again.' Fitzgerald had decided that *Gatsby* must sell seventy-five thousand copies, and he was depressed by Perkins's wire. He told Perkins: 'In all events I have a book of good stories for the fall. Now I shall write some cheap ones until I've accumulated enough for my next novel.' If that collection did not succeed, 'I'm going to quit, come home, go to Hollywood and learn the movie business. I can't reduce our scale of living and I can't stand this financial insecurity. Anyhow there's no point in trying to be an artist if you can't do your best. I had my chance back in 1920 to start my life on a sensible scale and I lost it. . . .' The reviews which he saw irritated him.

Then Gilbert Seldes reviewed it intelligently and sensitively in *The Dial*: 'Fitzgerald has more than matured, he has mastered his talents and gone soaring in a beautiful flight, leaving behind him everything dubious and tricky in his earlier work, and leaving even farther behind all the men of his own generation and most of his elders.' In May Gertrude Stein wrote Scott: 'You are creating the contemporary world much as Thackeray did in his *Pendennis* and *Vanity Fair* and this isn't a bad compliment.' In June Fitzgerald learned that the dramatic rights to *Gatsby* were being sold and his financial worries were for the moment in abeyance. Although *Gatsby* sold less than twenty-five thousand copies, the personal letters Scott received about it from people like Wilson and Stein and especially T. S. Eliot made him rightly proud of his achievement. Eliot wrote him, '. . . it seems to me to be the first step that American fiction has taken since Henry James. . . .'

Hemingway and Fitzgerald were then 'very thick' and they saw a lot of each other. Neither Zelda nor Hadley was included in their literary discussions, but met on a more purely social level, as the wives of writers. Zelda seemed to Hadley a canny woman, and she recalls Zelda saying with a smile, ' "I notice that in the Hemingway family you do what Ernest wants." ' Ernest didn't like that much, but it was a perceptive remark. He had a passionate, overwhelming desire to do some of the things that have since been written about, and so I went along with him – with the trips, the adventures. He had such a powerful personality; he could be so enthusiastic that I became caught up in the notions too. It could work in reverse, that persistence. Once he took a dislike to someone you could absolutely never get him back [to them]. If he took exception to anyone, that was it; there was no reasoning with him about it. He eventually turned on almost everyone we knew, all his old friends.

In an anecdote which has become a part of the Fitzgerald-Hemingway canon, Ernest upon meeting Zelda for the first time is supposed to have drawn Scott aside and told him that Zelda was crazy. Zelda's reaction to Hemingway on the other hand was no more complimentary, for she considered him 'bogus'. Scott had hoped that Zelda would be as taken with Ernest as he himself was, and he was both puzzled and disappointed in their mutual distrust.

'At that time', Gerald Murphy said, 'the word [bogus] just didn't seem to fit; there wasn't anyone more real and more himself than Ernest. Bogus, Ernest? Of course, who knows how right she may prove to be?'

Hadley did not remember Ernest saying that Zelda impressed him as crazy, but he may, of course, have told only Scott. She said: 'The portrait of Zelda – of both of them – in *A Moveable Feast* seemed quite brutal. But Ernest could be brutal. Zelda and he didn't take to each other. He was too assured a male for her. Maybe she caught this and resented it. . . . He was then the kind of man to whom men, women, children, and dogs were attracted. It was something.'

In August the Fitzgeralds left Paris for Antibes. They returned to the South of France because, as Scott wrote, 'One could get away with more on the summer Riviera, and whatever happened seemed to have something to do with art.' They were to spend only a month there, but it was a month marred by a chilling episode.

The Fitzgeralds joined the Murphys one evening for dinner at an inn located at St-Paul-de-Vence in the mountains above Nice. Its dining terrace was built about two hundred feet above the valley and there was a sheer drop from the outer walls of the terrace. Gerald Murphy took a seat with his back to the parapet and a series of ten stone steps. It was perhaps ten o'clock and they had just finished their meal. The only lights other than those that ringed the harbour like a necklace across the Bay of Angels were two candles on their table. At a nearby table sat Isadora Duncan surrounded by three admirers. Gerald Murphy said: 'Scott didn't know who she was, so I told him.

He immediately went to her table and sat at her feet. She ran her fingers through his hair and she called him her centurion. But she was, you see, an old lady [she was 46] by this time. Her hair was red, no, purple really – the colour of her dress – and she was quite heavy.'

Zelda was quietly watching Scott and Duncan together and then suddenly, with no word of warning or explanation, she stood up on her chair and leaped across both Gerald and the table into the darkness of the stairwell behind him. 'I was sure she was dead. We were all stunned and motionless.' Zelda re-appeared within moments, standing perfectly still at the top of the stone stairs. Sara ran to her and wiped the blood from her knees and dress. Gerald said, 'I don't remember what Scott did. The first thing I remember thinking was that it had not been ugly. I said that to myself over and over again. I've never been able to forget it.' *

An incident such as this, so obviously self-destructive and shot through with gratuitous violence, was to blight subsequent meetings between the Murphys and Fitzgeralds. 'You see,' Gerald Murphy commented, 'they didn't want ordinary pleasures, they hardly noticed good food or wines, but they did want something to happen.' It was as though the Fitzgeralds were straining for some definite mode of action that they barely understood, or, not needing to understand, acted out. Their code, which was never simply the hedonistic one of the twenties, had begun to make demands upon them.

In September Scott summarized the year: 'Futile, shameful useless but [for] the $30,000 rewards of 1924 work. Self disgust. Health gone.' It got no better in Paris that winter. Their apartment, which was near the Étoile, had little charm and Zelda took no interest in decorating it or in preparing meals. It was a damp and cheerless place on the rue de Tilsit, a five-flight walk-

---

*Several years later, writing about the scene, Zelda severely altered her own role. She said that she was able to steal 'Two glass automobiles for salt and pepper ... from the café in Saint-Paul (Alpes-Maritimes). Nobody was looking because Isadora Duncan was giving one of her last parties at the next table. She had got too old and fat to care whether people accepted her theories of life and art, and she gallantly toasted the world's obliviousness in lukewarm champagne.'

up with faded gold-and-purple wallpaper. Its air of former elegance accented its current dilapidation and neglect. In January Zelda's colitis again flared up and they decided to rest at Salies-de-Béarn, a small town in the Pyrénées, where Zelda took the cure. She wrote: 'We had a play on Broadway and the movies offered $60,000, but we were china people by then and it didn't seem to matter particularly.'

In early March 1926, they returned to the Riviera, taking less elaborate living quarters in Juan-les-Pins at the Villa Paquita. A reporter for *The New Yorker* magazine captured something of the aura about Scott and Zelda that spring on the Riviera. He said that the Riviera was quiet until the Fitzgeralds arrived, sunburned from tennis the day before, with everyone waiting for them, talking about them. There were remedies for their burns, as if they were wayward children in need of benevolent advice. 'That the Fitzgeralds are the best looking couple in modern literary society doesn't do them justice. . . . Scott really looks more as the undergraduate would like to look, than the way he generally does.'

Then Scott asked if the reporter knew that he was 'one of the most notorious drinkers of the younger generation' as though it were an established fact, a feat in which one took pride. The money was pouring in too, Scott admitted, but he complained that they had nothing to show for it – Zelda hadn't even a pearl necklace.

In May the Hemingways joined the Fitzgeralds, the Murphys and the MacLeishes on the Riviera. Each family was convinced that it was a perfect place to work and play. The Hemingways were to stay with the Murphys at their Villa America. Gerald and Sara had a small guesthouse, a *bastide,* at the foot of their property, which would suit them nicely. 'Any place that Sara touched became exquisite', Hadley recalls, and the *bastide* was hardly primitive. 'Ernest, Bumby [their son], and I went to Antibes. Sara and Gerald were impressive friends, you know; they were both very good looking, fine featured and blond. Somehow they matched each other. We grownups would sit on mats in the sand in the sun and Sara and Gerald added their own particular charm to the Mediterranean's.' There were games which Gerald, the perfect host, carefully organized, festive lunches on the beach brought down by Sara. However, as luck would have it, the Hemingways' son came down with whooping cough after they had been in Antibes only about a week. Sara, according to Hadley, 'was terrified; I really think their children had never had any of the ordinary childhood illnesses like measles and chicken pox. When Bumby became ill she told us that we'd have to go and I understood how difficult a position she was in. Then Scott and Zelda came in from their place, which was further away in Juan-les-Pins. Scott told us they had six weeks or so to go on their villa and offered it to us. It was terribly kind of them and we took the offer. Then we'd sit by ourselves on the beach; we were in quarantine and couldn't go calling. I'll never forget yardarm time with the MacLeishes, the Murphys, and the Fitzgeralds. Three cars would pull up outside our place just beyond the iron fence and by the time we left at the end of the summer that fence was covered with glass bottles artfully arranged. It was great fun.'

Having offered the Hemingways their villa, the Fitzgeralds took another larger place also in Juan-les-Pins called the Villa St Louis, where they remained until the end of 1926. Scott wrote: 'The mistral is raging outside like the end of the world and the idea of writing is anathema to me. We are wonderfully situated in a big house on the shore with a beach and the Casino not 100 yards away and every prospect of a marvelous summer.'

Zelda was not seen during the day and Mrs MacLeish says: 'I don't know what she did or where she was. Sometimes we swam together, but I rarely saw her with Scottie at the *plage*. You'd see Scottie alone with her nanny.' In a film taken during the summer there is a glimpse of Zelda sitting with Scott and several friends around a large circular table with a beach parasol over them. She is wearing a brightly striped French sailor's jersey, and her short hair is blowing back from her face and looks springy and dark. Nervously she plays with her hands on the table top, and looking up once into the camera, clearly embarrassed, she waves and laughs.

When Zelda indulged in high jinks that summer there was a quality about the performance that was striking; she seemed unconcerned about the presence of others and that gave her actions an unforgettable touch. One evening the Murphys and the Fitzgeralds were sitting at a table in the Casino at Juan-les-Pins. It was very late and nearly everyone had gone home. Zelda rose from the table and raising her skirts above her waist began to dance. Motionless, Scott sat watching her. When the orchestra caught on it played to her. A first the Murphys were startled, and then, Gerald said, 'I remember it was perfect music for her to dance to and soon the Frenchmen who were left gathered about the archways leading to the small dance area near our table gaped at her – they expected to see a show, something spectacular. Well, it was spectacular, but not at all in the way they had expected it to be. She was dancing for herself; she didn't look left or right, or catch anyone's eyes. She looked at no one, not once, not even at Scott. I saw a mass of lace ruffles as she whirled – I'll never forget it. We were frozen. She had this tremendous natural dignity. She was so self-possessed, so absorbed in her dance. Somehow she was incapable of doing anything unladylike.'

Scott's impact on people was entirely different from Zelda's. Mrs MacLeish remembers: 'Oh, you could talk to him. He was such a sunny man. But he'd ask the most personal questions. I remember one night out dancing when he followed two young French boys around the dance floor asking them if they were fairies. I think I was dancing with one of them. He could be terrible. Zelda was nothing like that.' Zelda was aloof and remote; it was not that she did not pay attention to what one was saying, but a strange little smile would suddenly, inexplicably cross her face. She answered questions if they were put to her, but otherwise she remained distant. Mrs MacLeish remembers Zelda as a night person. 'I remember how she'd do these things – dancing on tables and so forth. But there was no mirth. No fun. "This is what we do and now I'll proceed to do it." Those were the Fitzgerald Evenings which we learned to avoid like the plague. They seemed intent upon living this lurid life; the ordinary evening wasn't enough.'

Gerald Murphy described the way Scott and Zelda seemed to work together that summer – like 'a pair of conspirators'. 'They would begin together in the evening; you would see some look come over them as though they had been drawn together – and then they were companions. Then they were inseparable. They would stay out all night. It was as though they were waiting for something to happen; they didn't want entertainment, or exotic food; they seemed to be looking forward to something fantastic. That's the only way I can put it; something had to happen, something extravagant. It was that they were in search of, and they went for it alone.'

That June Zelda had her appendix removed at the American hospital in Neuilly outside of Paris. It was not a serious operation and she recovered quickly; they were able to return to the Riviera by the beginning of July. Prior to the operation, however, Zelda had suffered not only from colitis but also from 'ovarian troubles'. She and Scott had apparently been trying to have another child with no success. It was after the appendectomy that those ovarian troubles lessened, but she still did not become pregnant.

Sara Mayfield, who had known Zelda as a girl in Montgomery, was visiting in Paris while Zelda was in the hospital. She was having drinks one afternoon with the son of the Spanish ambassador to the United States and Michael Arlen, whose novel *The Green Hat* was creating a sensation abroad, when Scott saw her and joined them at their table. He complimented Arlen on his success, and told him that he would probably be his successor as the most popular fiction writer of the day. The compliment was a little backhanded, but Arlen took it debonairly. Politely he in turn praised *The Great Gatsby*. After an amiable half-hour or so the two men crossed over their estimation of Ernest Hemingway's writing. Scott angrily accused Arlen of being 'a finished second-rater that's jealous of a coming first-rater'. It was with difficulty that someone managed to interrupt the train of the conversation and steer Scott off the subject. At last Scott invited Miss Mayfield to join him for a visit to Zelda at the hospital. First, however, they would all have dinner together. They would stop at Harry's New York Bar and see if Hemingway had returned from Pamplona. At the bar a newspaperman suggested that Scott was promoting Hemingway and a fight was narrowly avoided. They never did get around to visiting Zelda, for Scott passed out in Les Halles and Sara took a taxi back to her hotel without him. More and more Scott's nights and days were passed in this way; no work done, drinking and talking with friends, passing out and being put into a taxi and sent home alone.

Miss Mayfield remembers a specific conversation involving the Fitzgeralds' opposing attitudes toward Hemingway. Zelda had told her that the Hemingways had left the Riviera earlier in the summer because of domestic difficulties but that before they left Hemingway had brought over his novel *The Sun Also Rises*.

When I asked what his novel was about, Zelda said, 'Bullfighting, bullslinging, and bullsh –'

'Zelda!' Scott cut her description short. 'Don't say things like that.'

'Why shouldn't I? . . .'

'Say anything you please,' Scott growled, 'but lay off Ernest.'

'Try and make me!' she retorted. 'He's a pain in the neck – talking about me and borrowing money from you while he does it. He's phony as a rubber check and you know it.'

Zelda had become jealous of Hemingway, or more specifically, of his relationship with Scott. But it was not a one-way vendetta. Years later Hemingway wrote about her effect upon Scott, 'If he could write a book as fine as *The Great Gatsby* I was sure that he could write an even better one. I did not know Zelda yet, and so I did not know the terrible odds that were against him.'

There was a strong element of hero worship in Scott's attitude toward Hemingway, and he deeply admired Hemingway's physical prowess: his boxing, his hunting, his being wounded in Italy during the war. Scott had always had some friend whom he considered his mentor, but Hemingway was the first whom Zelda regarded as a threat to her relationship with Scott. She was unrelenting in her opinion that Hemingway was a poseur. But her jealousy also grew out of her own weakening tie to Scott. Perhaps it also had something to do with her lessening self-regard. She had accomplished very little during those two years abroad. She had written nothing, she had become entangled with Jozan, and as fond as she was of Scottie her relationship to her was remote.

They returned to the Riviera, to the parties, and to the Murphys, who now saw them every day. But Scott's behaviour sometimes irritated even their good friends. Sara Murphy remembered a time Fitzgerald casually began to cast their delicately blown Venetian glasses over the edge of their garden. When he had thrown two Gerald stopped him: 'I think that was the time I told him he couldn't come back for a while.'

And Murphy said: 'You know, Scott liked people to be accessible and easy. He could be, for instance, very simple-minded about Zelda. I mean, even when he seems to use her as a fictional model she is so one-sided. But she was far more complex; he never really caught that. Somehow we always felt that her mind made different connections than most people's – and it was this extraordinary, intuitive lucidity of hers which distinguished her. She very rarely said things lightly or for effect. She would say whatever occurred to her.' She once asked Gerald, out of the blue, 'Gerald, don't you think that Al Jolson is just like Christ?' Murphy was stunned. 'There was someone else there with us at the time who did not know her and I didn't want to embarrass her by pushing the topic further. She had a ruminative mind. She didn't small-talk at all, and really no intellectual talk either. She spoke only of things that came into her mind at the time. It gave her conversation a freshness and a certain edge that was part of her charm.'

Sara added: 'She never, never spoke personally – I mean about herself – and she never spoke a word about Scott. We knew they rowed, all married people row, don't they? Oh, they did have terrific rows, but never in public and never in front of their friends. One heard of it the next day; or one saw Zelda's trunk out on the street where she had left it the night before.' Whenever they fought, Zelda threatened to pack up and leave.

She threw everything she owned into her trunk and dragged it out to the street. 'There she would wait – one never knew what for. When she got sleepy she'd go back to bed, but the trunk was left behind. One always knew when the Fitzgeralds had rowed; the trunk marked the night.'

Still, she was absolutely loyal to Scott. Sara tells of a time in a taxi when Scott was sitting next to her: 'He had been drinking and we were all crammed into the tiny back seat; Scott began to act silly, outrageous, grabbing at me and making terrible noises, so I said, "Scott, stop that, you smell awful!" Zelda immediately said, "I think he smells wonderful." We all roared. What, after all, can one say back to that?'

The Murphys knew the Fitzgeralds at their peak; Scott had finished *Gatsby* and Zelda was still lovely. 'She was not a legitimate beauty – thank God!' said Gerald Murphy. 'Her beauty was not legitimate at all. It was all in her eyes. They were strange eyes, brooding but not sad, severe, almost masculine in their directness. She possessed an outstanding gaze, one doesn't find it often in women, perfectly level and head-on. If she looked like anything it was an American Indian. She couldn't have been anything but American really. You know in their early days they were two beauties – I mean that – Scott's head was so fine, really unbelievably handsome. They were the flawless people.'

Sara interrupted: 'But Zelda could be spooky. She seemed sometimes to be lying in ambush waiting for you with those Indian eyes of hers.'

Gerald said, 'She was the only woman I've ever known who could wear a peony in her hair or on her shoulder and not look silly. She would pluck a brilliant peony and put it square on the top of her head. To see her with that tousled dark blonde hair, quite short in back but always a few pieces of it falling across her forehead, those piercing eyes peering from beneath the bangs – topped by a fuchsia peony, well, it was something!

'She could get away with it too,' Gerald added.

'She wasn't trying to get away with anything', Sara quickly put in.

'No, I guess not, and that's exactly why she did.'

But there were times that summer when Zelda's behaviour was more cryptic and destructive. It was useless to play the cross aunt and uncle to the Fitzgeralds, but the Murphys did feel called upon once in a while as friends to caution them. One never got far with Zelda, for she simply did not let anyone close enough to criticize her. She did not allow a disagreement to surface – at least not to the point where it could be discussed. Sara once warned them about their diving from the rocks high above the sea. 'One had to be a superb diver in order to make it during the day. There were notches cut in the rock at five feet, ten, up to thirty. Now, that's a high dive, a dangerous dive any time, but especially at night, one had to have a perfect sense of timing or one would have been smashed on the rocks below. Zelda would strip to her slip and very quietly ask Scott if he cared for a swim. I remember one evening when I was with them that he was absolutely trembling when she challenged him, but he followed her. It was breathtaking. They took each dive, returning from the sea all shivering and white, until the last, the one at thirty feet. Scott hesitated and watched Zelda until she surfaced; I didn't think he could go through with it, but he did.' When Sara remonstrated with them, Zelda said very sweetly in her low, husky voice, ' "But Sayra – didn't you know, we don't believe in conservation." And that was that!'

At the end of the year they left Europe for the United States. Zelda had been ill throughout the year and Scott's Ledger bears witness to it: 'Zelda sick', 'Zelda drugged', 'Zelda better', 'Zelda sick in Genoa'. (On one occasion at the Villa St Louis, apparently after a considerable amount of drinking, Zelda went so completely out of emotional control that a doctor was sent for and she was given a shot of morphine to calm her. The episode terrified both of them.) Their money had nearly run out and Scott was returning home without the manuscript of the new novel. He stubbornly insisted, however, that the years abroad had not been wasted. 'God', he wrote Perkins, 'how much I've learned in these two and a half years in Europe. It seems like a decade and I feel pretty old but I wouldn't have missed it, even its most unpleasant and painful aspects.' Although they had indulged themselves, Scott had written *Gatsby,* and even if he had not completed his new novel, he was deeply absorbed by it.

It was Zelda who had little to show for those years in Europe. She was still insisting as she had in 1924 upon the benefits of being a flapper; they had not, however, accrued in value. Zelda was quoted in a newspaper article just before they left Europe as saying: ' "I'm raising my girl to be a flapper", says Zelda Sayre Fitzgerald, [wife of] popular novelist of flaming youth fiction. "I like the jazz generation, and I hope my daughter's generation will be jazzier. I want my girl to do as she pleases, be what she pleases, regardless of Mrs Grundy." ' But there was something a little desperate in these plans for the child who was just five, and much as she loved Scottie and very much wanted and needed to draw closer to her, Zelda quite clearly saw in Scottie's future only the mirroring of her own best dreams: ' "I think a woman gets more happiness out of being gay, light-hearted, unconventional, mistress of her own fate, than out of a career that calls for hard work, intellectual pessimism and loneliness. I don't want Pat to be a genius. I want her to be a flapper, because flappers are brave and gay and beautiful." '

Years later Zelda realized that for herself and Scott 'there aren't any roots. They asked a lot of life and gave freely of what they had. . . . So they lived cutting off the complicated and replacing it with the simple till there was little left. . . .' In December 1926, there was still a lot left: they would return to America; they would not allow life to become a losing game; they would try to move through life more securely.

Upon their return to America Scott was offered a job in Hollywood with United Artists to write a screenplay for Constance Talmadge. He had never written for the movies, but there was a fortune to be made writing film scripts and Scott was sure he could make it easily. He would be paid $12,000 if United Artists took his script, $3,500 if they didn't use it. It was a tempting offer and, short of capital, Scott took the gamble and travelled West. As soon as they arrived, Zelda wrote to Scottie, who had stayed with her nanny in Washington, where Scott's parents were living:

It is so hot here we can't wear coats and even Daddy sleeps under one blanket. It is the most beautiful country imaginable – just long avenues of palm trees and Eucalyptus and Poinsettas grow as tall as trees. It is really the tropics ... Daddy got so nervous [on the train trip West] he thought he had an appendicitis so we had to get out and spend the night at a place called El Paso on the Mexican border – but he was all well by the time we got to the hotel.

The Ambassador Hotel in Los Angeles had a large central garden with bungalows grouped about it, one of which was the Fitzgeralds'. The setting was luxurious and Zelda liked it, but even with Pola Negri and John Barrymore as their neighbours, Zelda remarked to Scottie that Hollywood was not what the magazines said it was, for the stars were rarely seen in public. She tried to recreate something of the atmosphere of the city in her letters to her daughter:

Last night we went with some old friends to dance. It was all decorated with palm trees and had a real water-fall at the end of the room. On the ceiling of the place, clouds moved and there were stars that twinkled just as if they were real. And in every tree there was a huge stuffed monkey that had big lights for eyes.

Hollywood, however, palled rather quickly on Zelda and more than once she thought nostalgically of France:

This weather here makes me think of Paris in the spring and I am *very* homesick for the pink lights and the trees and the gay streets. So is Daddy, also for the wine and the little cafés on the sidewalk. I'd like more than anything to be touring from Paris to the Riviera along the white roads. I think we ought to buy us a gipsy caravan and start out. But most of all we are very lonesome for you. There are not many pie-faces in California and when you get used to having one around – Well! you know how it is! ... I wish I were there to nibble a little teeny hole just in one side of your cheek. Maybe I'd find a diamond. That's the way they found the Chantilly diamond: somebody bit on it while they were eating an apple.

Her letters to Scottie were adorned with charming sketches of round-faced smiling little creatures, snowmen, boys and girls playing, illustrating the points in her letters. After hearing that Scottie had visited the White House, Zelda admitted:

Personally, I think this country is awful and there's *nothing* to do and I am trying to make 'ole Massa' let me come east alone *now* – this very minute – but NO is all I get in answer. If we ever get out of here I will *never* go near another moving picture theatre or actor again. I want to be in New York where there's enough mischief for everybody – that is, if I can't be in Paris ... There's nothing on earth to do here but look at the view and eat. You can imagine the result since I do not like to look at views.

Although Zelda's dislike of Hollywood seemed to stem from boredom and restlessness, there were other more serious causes which she could not express to the child. Scott had met a young actress, Lois Moran, with whom he was instantly charmed. The seventeen-year-old screen star was, as George Jean Nathan recalled, 'a lovely kid of such tender years that it was rumoured she still wore the kind of flannel nightie that was bound around her ankles with ribbons, and Scott never visited her save when her mother was present'. Whether they were chaperoned or not,

Zelda did not take the infatuation lightly. Outwardly, she was polite and even friendly to the girl, but her irritation showed itself to Scott. At first he insisted that he simply admired Lois Moran, but as they quarrelled about her, he told Zelda that at least the girl did something with herself, something that required not only talent but effort. Zelda was stung by his remark and in a moment of injured pride, while he was at dinner with the young star, she burned in the bathtub of their bungalow all of the clothes which she had designed for herself. It was an odd gesture of fury and Fitzgerald, ignoring the peculiarity, told her she was behaving childishly.

In Zelda's letters to Scottie, there is only one mention of Lois Moran and that is in an offhand remark, apparently added as an afterthought: 'Daddy was offerred a job to be leading man in a picture with Lois Moran!! But he wouldn't do it. I wanted him to, because he would have made so much money and we could all have spent it, but he said I was silly.' Scott was actually rather eager and curious to see himself as an actor and did take a screen test, but he did not go through with the motion of making a film.

Fitzgerald's attitude toward Lois Moran took material form in a story written that spring called 'Jacob's Ladder'. In the story the girl's youth is seen as a shield against the passion of an older man who loves her: 'She did not know yet that splendor was something in the heart; at the moment when she should realize that and melt into passion of the universe he could take her without question or regret.' Her lack of awareness eventually leads the man to indulge in a reverie of possession in which his passion is transformed: 'Silently, as the night hours went by, he molded her over into an image of love – an image that would endure as long as love itself, or even longer – not to perish till he could say, "I never really loved her." Slowly he created it with this and that illusion from his youth, this and that sad old yearning, until she stood before him identical with her old self only by name.

'Later when he drifted off into a few hours' sleep, the image he had made stood near him, lingering in the room, joined in mystic marriage to his heart.'

Zelda told Scottie that the weather had turned rainy and they no longer went swimming; they went to parties instead. 'And we have seen so many pretty girls that I did not think there were so many in the world. How would you like to be a moving picture actress when you are a lady? They have pretty houses and lots of money. Last night we went to a house way up in the hills and down below all the lights of Los Angeles were spread out like a beautiful field of daffodils.' She added that she wanted to learn to do the Black Bottom, 'but it is very hard and I am sure I will fall right on my nose when I try. Everybody here is very clever and can nearly all dance and sing and play and I feel very stupid.'

Samuel Goldwyn gave a costume party for the Talmadge sisters at which Scott and Zelda appeared uninvited. They were found at the street door on all fours, barking, and said they were strangers to Hollywood and couldn't they please come to the party? Colleen Moore remembers that as she was about to get her coat to leave Zelda came in, and they went upstairs together. To her surprise Zelda went into the bathroom and turned on the bath faucets. The young star waited to see what would happen next; Zelda slipped out of her clothes and took a bath. When she emerged, she patted her hair dry, put her clothes back on, and went downstairs to the party.

After nearly eight weeks of gruelling work Scott's script was finished. Zelda wrote Scottie: 'He says he will never write another picture because it is too hard, but I do not think writers mean what they say about their work.' United Artists decided against using Scott's story and the Fitzgeralds left California for the East. Zelda had come to that point in her life where she wanted a home of her own, and she told Scottie to make a drawing of the sort of house she would like to live in when they were settled. Zelda herself had been making a scrapbook with pictures of houses. 'I am *crazy* to own a house. I want you to have a lovely little Japanese room with pink cherry-blossoms and a ducky little tea-table and a screen – Would you like it? And perhaps you could make a little garden – I want a garden full of lilac trees, like people have in France – Daddy says we must rent a house first, tho, to see if we are going to like America.'

On the train trip East, Zelda and Scott again quarrelled about Lois Moran (he had invited her to visit them once they were settled) and Zelda threw her diamond and platinum wristwatch from the window of the train. The watch was the one he had given her during their courtship in Alabama and it was the first object of value, both sentimental and actual, that she received from him.

At the beginning of March the Fitzgeralds leased a house called Ellerslie near Wilmington, Delaware. It was through the assistance of Scott's old friend and room-mate from Princeton, John Biggs, that they discovered it. Biggs and Perkins thought that the atmosphere in Wilmington, which was not at all literary, might prove less distracting to Scott's work on his novel than another move to the environs of New York. Scott and Zelda agreed, and were charmed by the huge old mansion with its pillared portico and great lawns stretching down to the Delaware River. The rent was reasonable and it was quiet. Before Scott left Europe he had predicted to Perkins, 'I'll be home with the finished manuscript of my book about mid-December.' He was now far behind schedule, and Ellerslie's calm was just what he needed.

Zelda later evoked the archaic charm of the area: 'A friend took us to tea in the mahogany recesses of an almost feudal estate, where the sun gleamed apologetically in the silver tea-service and there were four kinds of buns and four indistinguishable daughters in riding clothes and a mistress of the house too busily preserving the charm of another era to separate out the children. We leased a very big old mansion on the Delaware River. The squareness of the rooms and the sweep of the columns were to bring us a judicious tranquility.'

The tall and elegant rooms of Ellerslie proved difficult to decorate, for their size diminished the few pieces of furniture Scott and Zelda possessed after years of living in furnished houses and apartments. Zelda cleverly had outsized furniture made in Philadelphia. The giant couches and huge overstuffed chairs made the people sitting in them seem dwarfed and child-like, but it was a striking solution to the problem.

They had no sooner settled in Wilmington than Lois Moran visited them. She was staying in New York and managed a weekend at their home. Zelda must have concealed her resentment well, for Miss Moran sensed no conflict with her and recalls only 'the very intent, piercing look in those marvelous eyes'. During the weekend, which included 21 May, the day Lindberg landed at Le Bourget, she remembers picnicking on the breakwater by the Delaware River and one glorious moment afterward when they all stood quietly out on the lawn gazing toward the sky as if they might at any moment miraculously see Lindbergland.

It was shortly after their move to Wilmington that Zelda began to write again. She had done nothing since the pieces for *McCall's* in 1924, but during the remainder of 1927 she worked energetically on four articles, three of which were published the following year. The first, 'The Changing Beauty of Park Avenue', was signed by both Fitzgeralds, but in his Ledger Scott gave Zelda credit for the article. The style was obviously hers and relied heavily on physical description. She captured the strutting elegance of the avenue when she described the morning promenade of nannies with their fashionable young charges: 'They clutch in gloved hands the things that children carry only in illustrations and in the Bois de Boulogne and in Park Avenue: hoops and Russian dolls and tiny Pomeranians.' And she told of the small glass-fronted shops which looked like dolls' houses from a dream, 'where one may buy an apple with as much ritual as if it were the Ottoman Empire, or a limousine as carelessly as if it were a postage stamp'. There were minor corrections on the manuscript which are in Scott's hand (he wrote in both the title and authors' names, putting his own name first); one can see by comparing his revisions to the published version that the manuscript was, however, revised once more before publication, either by Zelda or by the editors and some of Scott's revisions were eliminated.

Zelda's second article was called 'Looking Back Eight Years', and was also attributed to both Fitzgeralds. Two sketches of the Fitzgeralds done by James Montgomery Flagg framed the article. It was, as the title suggests, a reminiscence, but of the entire postwar period, not simply of their own lives. 'Success', Zelda wrote, 'was the goal for this generation and to a startling extent they have attained it, and now we venture to say that, if intimately approached, nine in ten would confess that success is only a decoration they wished to wear; what they really wanted is something deeper and richer than that'. The sentiment of that sequence reminds one of the epigraph to *Gatsby*.

> Then wear the gold hat, if that will move her;
>   If you can bounce high, bounce for her too,
> Till she cry 'Lover, gold-hatted, high-bouncing lover,
>   I must have you!'

For all visible purposes the Fitzgeralds had for some time worn the gold hat, yet as the piece continued their private bogies crept into it. It was not, Zelda wrote, prosperity or the softness of life, or any instability that marred the war generation; it was a great emotional disappointment resulting from the fact that life moved in poetic gestures when they were younger and had since settled back into buffoonery. '. . . surely some of this irony and dissatisfaction with things supposedly solid and secure proceeds from the fact that more young people in this era were intense enough or clever enough or sensitive or shrewd enough to get what they wanted before they were mature enough to want the things they acquired as an end and not merely as a proof of themselves'.

Their retreat to Wilmington did not bring the hoped-for tranquillity. Soon Scott and Zelda were throwing what Dos Passos calls 'Those delirious parties of theirs; one dreaded going. At Wilmington, for instance, dinner was never served. Oh, a complete mess. I remember going into Wilmington – they lived some miles out, trying to find a sandwich, something to eat. A wild time.' And that was not an exceptional party; it could have occurred on any given weekend when the Fitzgeralds were celebrating. They would assemble a collection of their literary and theatre friends in Wilmington on Friday and have them stay over until Monday. Edmund Wilson once remarked, 'The aftermath of a Fitzgerald evening was notoriously a painful experience.' Still, their parties always began in a spirit of revelry and their invitations were sought after. Scott was splendidly at his ease with the women, charming them with his graciousness and his interest in them. If that charm soured, it was always because of his having drunk too much. Then it became apparent that what he wanted from the woman he was talking to was her story, and one sensed a certain coolness, a detachment in him, which could be chilling. Zelda, their friends noticed, might disappear at some point in the evening, and reappear refreshed by a nap.

During those first several months at Ellerslie she wrote Carl Van Vechten frequently, and some of her letters contain an undercurrent of unhappiness and remorse.

May 27, 1927: From the depths of my polluted soul, I am sorry that the week-end was such a mess. Do forgive my iniquities and my putrid drunkenness. This *was* such a nice place, and it should have been a good party if I had not explored my abyses in public. Anyhow, please realize that I am sorry and contrite and thoroughly miserable with the knowledge that it would be just the same again if I got so drunk.

Two days later she sent him an amusing thank-you note for a cocktail shaker he had given them; she signed it, 'Marie, Queen of Romania' (who had been visiting in America).

June 9, 1927: I love 'Squeeze Me' so much that it has distracted me from being taken up by Philadelphia society a little ... These high-church agnostics remind me of something in the puzzle sections of the Sunday World ... I shall see that you are rewarded with a moon-skin full of wine and a shining sword which collapses like a rubber dagger – That your eyes are bathed with blackberry juice, which you know will make it so you never never want to sleep, and that all your shaving suds turn into whipped cream –

June 14, 1927: Cheer up – Nobody is ever going to be like we think they are – The only consolation I know is that my intuitions are always wrong. I cling to it desperately –

With great devotion and disloyalty,
Zelda

I forgot something that will change the course of history: we got two dogs out of the pound. One of them is splotchy but mostly white with whiskers although he is sick now, so his name is Ezra Pound. The other is named Bouillabaisse, or Muddy Water or Jerry. He doesn't answer to any of them so it doesn't matter.

June 24, 1927: 'Crescent Ltd.' *En Route.* Dear Carl – We are getting away from it all.

Urgently,
Scott and Zelda

September 6, 1927: [Zelda is trying to persuade Van Vechten to come to a party.] Anyway I will have the Coolidges and the Indian guide from the Stillman case and the bath-tub girl from Earl Carroll's chorus and the Sistine Madonna and John Charles Thomas – Good Simple People and all intimate friends –

October 14, 1927: Please forgive my not writing sooner – It seems that life went to pieces. I joined the Philadelphia Opera Ballet and guests came and everybody has been so drunk in this country lately that I am just finding enough chaos to pursue my own ends in, undisturbed, again . . . You were very kind and thoughtful and unlike yourself to send it [*Peter Whiffle*, a novel of Van Vechten's] and I couldn't like it better – unless of course I'd written it myself.

– And now that we've got delirium tremens we are going to sit here and brood until Christmas. Our house is full of every ghost that Fanny Ward and Conan Doyle imagined and I hope that I will never again feel attractive –

Little Bright Eyes

At the beginning of summer Sara Murphy wrote Zelda:

But why Wilmington? . . . and your house – (according to Esther) [Mrs Murphy's sister-in-law] – is palatial and then some – You keep, it appears only 14 of the 27 bedrooms open and only 3 drawing rooms – and you and Scott have a system of calls and echoes to locate each other readily. Do you ever have a hankering for Villa St Louis?

People have now started to crowd onto our beach, – discouragingly undeterred by our natural wish to have it alone. However, by means of teaching the children to throw wet sand a good deal, and by bringing several disagreeable barking dogs and staking them around – we manage to keep space open for sunbathers.

The old guard of last year has changed, giving place to a new lot of American Writers and Mothers ... Every now and again I think I see your old rat Renault whipping around a corner. Is Scott working? And how's the book coming on?

Scott did very little writing that summer and he and Zelda began to quarrel with increasing frequency. He was drinking heavily and Zelda, too, drank and smoked too much. One evening a doctor had to be called from Wilmington to give Zelda a morphine injection; it was the second time this had happened (the first was at the Villa St Louis), and on both occasions the Fitzgeralds had been drinking heavily and quarrelling. Zelda became hysterical. These bitter rows continued to centre around the dispute that had begun with Lois Moran; Zelda felt Scott was reproaching her for not working at something professionally.

By the middle of the summer Zelda had decided to take dancing lessons again. She considered painting as a career, but her eyes bothered her and she refused to wear glasses. She determined on dancing, 'to be', in her own words, 'a Pavlova, nothing less'. She was twenty-seven years old when she began her lessons as a student of Catherine Littlefield in Philadelphia. Miss Littlefield, who directed the Philadelphia Opera Ballet Corps, had studied in Paris with Madame Lubov Egorova (the Princess Troubetskoy) of the Diaghilev ballet. Zelda's decision to become a dancer did not at first trouble Scott. He knew that she had taken dancing lessons as a child, and had been highly praised in Montgomery. Obviously, that was a far cry from becoming a first-rate ballerina, but Zelda had dabbled in writing and painting in the past and Scott no doubt decided to go along with her dancing lessons as another whim. He once told John Biggs that a woman ought to have something to do in case she had to earn her keep, and he was trying to decide whether Scottie ought to learn to type or take dancing lessons. In the end she was sent to Philadelphia with Zelda to dance.

Anna Biggs accompanied Zelda during one of her frequent trips into Philadelphia. They shopped for furniture. 'One of the objects that caught her fancy was a gigantic gilt mirror, nineteenth century, I think. It was surrounded by scrollwork and cherubs and wreaths in the best heavily decorated style. She loved it. At Ellerslie when I next saw it, it was hung in the front room beside her Victrola. She had run a ballet bar in front of it and practised there all day. She would sometimes dance the entire time that we were there – whether it was for dinner, for a long afternoon's talk, whatever. She'd perhaps stop for a few minutes for a drink or something, but then continue. It was madness.' Her husband added that he had heard 'The March of the Wooden Soldiers', which Zelda practised to, so repeatedly that he suspected the melody was engraved on every organ he possessed.

Scott's favourite cousin, Mrs Richard Taylor, a pretty woman who was slightly older than he and with whom he had always been a little in love, had a daughter, Cecilia, who was her namesake. Scott was partial to her and invited the young girl up from Norfolk for a gala weekend at Ellerslie that autumn. Cecilia was just twenty-two and eager for adventure. Scott met her train, explaining that Zelda had a skin irritation (which may have been her first attack of eczema) and wouldn't go to dinner with them that night because of it. He had decided to give a dinner dance for Cecilia and went to New York alone to pick up a suitcase of wine and gin for the festivities. Cecilia remembers that Zelda was not especially warm to her, but did not in any way make her feel unwelcome. 'Scott seemed to be the moving spirit in almost everything. . . . He hired an orchestra for the dinner dance. He seemed to tell the several coloured servants what to do. I think Zelda was perfectly capable of handling things, but she seemed perfectly willing to let Scott do it. She was painting then. She had done a screen, which I vaguely remember had seashore scenes on it, and a lampshade of Alice-in-Wonderland characters for Scottie.'

One of Zelda's first projects at Ellerslie had been to design a doll's house for Scottie, which she had built herself, papering and painting it until it looked like a palace with elegant pieces of furniture and mirrors and glass windows. She was also busily painting a group of lampshades decorated with scenes from the various places they had lived in Europe and America. Some were fanciful, with animals and illustrations of fairy tales; others were humorous sketches of members of their family. Cecilia recalled that it was Scott who paid attention to Scottie's studies and who seemed in charge of correcting her when it was necessary.

Zelda's taste in clothes had definitely improved from her earlier days in New York. She now dressed expensively and with chic, choosing simple lines in brilliant colours (reds and pinks were her favourites) and plain fabrics. Her Southern accent was very much in control. She seemed to enunciate carefully, with a special timing to her phrases. She spoke very slowly, huskily, drawling her words slightly. It seemed to Scott's cousin that she affected her accent, for she sounded like no other Alabaman this Virginian had heard. 'She talked intensely when she was interested, but she was not terribly vivacious. ... Her features were rather large and to some extent she had the look of a grown-up child. ... I cannot say why she was so distinctive. Partly her sort of tawny coloring. Blond but nothing washed out about it.'

The weekend of the party was chaotic from beginning to end. A game of 'croquet-polo on plow horses' was improvised on their lawn and an inscribed silver trophy was awarded to the winner, who was, of course, Cecilia. It read, 'The Fitzgerald all Silver Beaker for fast and clean croquet, won by ——. God sees everything.'

Among the many people at the party were Dick Knight and John Dos Passos. Dick Knight, who was a lawyer from New York, was a strange fellow, with a peculiarly misshapen large head. He told the Fitzgeralds and Cecilia that he had had to identify his brother at the morgue before he came, but he said it merrily without a trace of sadness or seriousness. Zelda and he seemed quite fond of each other.

After the party Scott and Zelda and Cecilia went to New York and visited several speakeasies. There was also a theatre party and after that Zelda suggested a trip to Harlem. Young Cecilia was dropped off at their hotel, but to her surprise Scott and Zelda returned almost immediately. On their trip back to Wilmington the following day they stopped in Philadelphia for Zelda's ballet lesson. To Scott's young cousin (who had taken ballet lessons herself) she appeared to be a dreadful dancer. Scott made it obvious that he did not feel that Zelda was any good and motioned to Cecilia that he wanted to leave the studio and go have a drink. By the time they caught the train for Wilmington later that afternoon Scott was on the verge of passing out. Zelda, who was entirely sober, seemed oblivious of the situation and completely ignored Scott. Cecilia was left to manage him, his wallet, and their baggage by herself. At last the conductor, who was rewarded with their last bottle of gin, got them off and into a taxi. And for Cecilia, who had expected gaiety, the weekend turned flat and even a little frightening.

During one of Scott's trips to New York that fall H. L. Mencken and his young assistant on *The American Mercury*, Charles Angoff, visited him at his hotel. Angoff remembers that Scott had been drinking and was rather remote toward Mencken, which displeased the critic. After a little conversation about George Jean Nathan, Scott got up and paced the room. He said

'Henry, I got another idea for a novel going through my head. Have a lot of it written up. It's about a woman who wants to destroy a man, because she loves him too much and is afraid she'll lose him, but not to another woman – but because she'll stop loving him so much. Well, she decides to destroy him by marrying him. She marries him, and gets to love him even more than she did before. Then she gets jealous of him, because of his achievements in some line that she thinks she's also good in. Then, I guess, she commits suicide – first she does it step by step, the way all people, all women, commit suicide, by drinking, by sleeping around, by being impolite to friends, and that way. I haven't got the rest of it clear in my head, but that's the heart of it. What do you think, Henry?'

'Well, it's your wife, Zelda, all over again,' Mencken said.

Scott sat down for a moment, sipped his drink, then stood back up and without looking at Mencken told him it was not only the 'dumbest piece of literary criticism' he'd ever heard, but 'I spill out my insides to you, and you answer with . . . Zelda.' He said Mencken had no compassion. '"Of all the times to mention Zelda to me! Or all the goddamn times to mention her!"' Then he burst into tears. Mencken's reaction after they left Fitzgerald was to tell Angoff that Scott would never amount to anything until he got rid of his wife.

In November 1927 Scott wrote Ernest Hemingway that although he had wasted the summer insofar as his writing was concerned, he had accomplished a lot during the fall. He hoped, he said, to complete his novel by the first of December. Zelda was dancing three times a week in Philadelphia, as well as painting. 'Have got nervous as hell lately – purely physical but scared me somewhat – to the point of putting me on the wagon and smoking denicotinized cigarettes.' The purpose of the letter was to congratulate Hemingway on the recent publication of his collection of stories *Men Without Women*. Scott wrote: 'The book is fine. I like it quite as well as *The Sun*, which doesn't begin to express my enthusiasm. In spite of all its geographical and emotional rambling, it's a unit, as much as Conrad's books of Contes were.' Zelda liked it a lot, he said, and thought his best story was 'Hills Like White Elephants'. But, for all Scott's genuine admiration, there was a defensiveness about his letter, the first sign of the professional competitiveness that was to mar his friendship with Hemingway. He let Hemingway know, for instance, that '*The Post* pays me $3500 – this detail so you'll be sure who's writing this letter.'

In fact, Fitzgerald had done little writing of any sort in 1927. He had been working since the summer of 1925 on his novel and he now very much exaggerated his progress to Hemingway, for he was making almost none. The book had gone through various drafts and would go through more before its publication as *Tender Is the Night* in 1934. It was going to be a sensational novel about American expatriate life on the Riviera, and its hero, Francis Melarky, a film technician, would be driven to murder his mother. Fitzgerald had been stimulated by both the Ellingson and Leopold-Loeb* cases as sources for his novel.

*Dorothy Ellingson, who was a sixteen-year-old girl, murdered her mother in January of 1925 during a quarrel about the girl's wild living. Both this case and the Leopold-Loeb sensational murder in 1924 fascinated Fitzgerald and he followed the newspapers' reporting with great interest. Later, according to Matthew Bruccoli, in his study *The Composition of Tender Is the Night*, he mentioned them as sources for the novel to both Harold Ober and Hemingway.

The novel went through a number of titles, *Our Type, The World's Fair*, and somewhat later *The Melarky Case* and *The Boy Who Killed His Mother*, which was apparently Zelda's suggested title.

Zelda's sister and brother-in-law Rosalind and Newman Smith spent a weekend with the Fitzgeralds in February 1928. The visit was, Scott noted in his Ledger, a catastrophe. He had been invited to Princeton to speak at Cottage Club. There was an enormous amount of drinking and when he returned home late that night he was on a weeping jag. During the course of an argument Scott threw a favourite blue vase of Zelda's into the fireplace. When Zelda cuttingly referred to his father as an Irish policeman, Fitzgerald retaliated by slapping Zelda hard across the face. As a result her nose bled and her sister, outraged by what she had seen, left the house the following morning. She was convinced that Scott was behaving basely toward her sister and felt that Zelda should leave him. Zelda, however, ignored her sister's pleas and told her that she and Scott chose to live the way they did and she would tolerate no interference from her family.

Fed up with Wilmington and with themselves they decided upon another trip to Europe that spring. 'They were on their way to Paris', Zelda wrote. 'They hadn't much faith in travel nor a great belief in a change of scene as a panacea for spiritual ills; they were simply glad to be going.'

They took an apartment in the rue Vaugirard opposite the Luxembourg Gardens, so that Scottie could have a place to play. Zelda wrote Eleanor Browder, who had recently married, that they had left New York in too much of a mess to send her a present for her wedding; 'we are vaguely floating about on the surface of a fancy French apartment. It looks like a setting for one of Mme Tausand's gloomier figures but we have got moved in. . . . It looks as if we'll never stay anywhere long enough to see how we like it . . .'

Gerald Murphy introduced Zelda to Madame Lubov Egorova, who was the head of the ballet school for the Diaghilev troupe, the same woman who had been Catherine Littlefield's teacher. Madame Engorova had a great gift for instruction, according to Murphy, and although she had once been a leading ballerina with the Ballet Russe, the most exciting group performing in the world at that time, it was as a coach that she excelled, for she was a superb technician. Murphy said, 'I had the feeling that unless one went through with it [arranging Zelda's introduction] something awful would happen. I suppose that was why I helped her to begin with. There are limits to what a woman of Zelda's age can do and it was obvious that she had taken up the dance too late.' Nevertheless, Zelda worked feverishly under Egorova's demanding supervision, practising eight or more hours a day. What had begun as a defiant response to Scott's praise of Lois Moran's ambition and energy had become Zelda's sole preoccupation. She was determined to become a superb ballerina.

Scott later said that it was at Ellerslie in 1928 that he first began to use liquor as a stimulant for his work. Until then he had drunk only when he was not working; now he drank in order to be able to work. In 1927 and again in 1928 he was making more money from his writing, nearly $30,000, than he ever had before. But his drinking was a serious problem for both Fitzgeralds; Zelda was unable to stop him and felt that he was growing indifferent to her because he preferred the company of his drinking companions. Scott felt that Zelda's dancing was executed in a spirit of vengeance against him and needled her about her commitment to it. But it was not simply vengeance that motivated Zelda; it was a desire to find something of her own that might give her release from her life with Scott.

Zelda described in *Save Me the Waltz* what she sought from her dancing:

It seemed to Alabama that, reaching her goal, she would drive the devils that had driven her – that, in proving herself, she would achieve that peace which she imagined went only in surety of one's self – that she would be able, through the medium of the dance, to command her emotions, to summon love or pity or happiness at will, having provided a channel through which they might flow. She drove herself mercilessly . . .

'Zelda wanted immediate success. She wanted to dance for

the world', Gerald Murphy said. One day she invited the Murphys to the studio to watch her dance. They went with trepidation. 'The stage of the training room was built on an incline, it was perhaps two feet higher at one end than at the opposite. The effect was that one looked up at her the entire time she danced. The view was not a flattering one, for it made her seem taller, more awkward than she was. There was something dreadfully grotesque in her intensity – one could see the muscles individually stretch and pull; her legs looked muscular and ugly. It was really terrible. One held one's breath until it was over. Thank God, she couldn't see what she looked like. When I watched Zelda that afternoon in Paris, I thought to myself, she's going to try to hold on to her youth. You know, there's nothing worse; it ruins a woman.'

The Murphys felt close to Zelda, which sometimes upset Scott; he would ask them if they liked Zelda better than they liked him. Or, if he felt they were giving her too much attention, he would say, 'Sara, look at me!' Zelda didn't like everybody, as Sara was well aware; 'she was choosy, she didn't take to many people'. Sara remembered being with Zelda once while they were introduced to several people at a luncheon. 'Each time someone was brought to be introduced, she would smile at them sweetly and as she took their hands say under her breath, "I hope you die in the marble ring". Of course no one suspected that she was saying anything but the usual pleasantries; I heard her because I was standing right next to her. She was so charming and polite as she said it – must have been one of her childhood taunts.' But it was not; it was an utterance from the interior.

None of them realized that Zelda was poised on the edge of a vast and troubling doubt about herself, and if she and Scott quarrelled less, it was only because they had become silent and watchful toward each other. Zelda later recalled 'long conversations about the ballet over sauerkraut in Lipp's, and blank recuperative hours over books and prints in the dank Allée-Bonaparte. Now the trips away had begun to be less fun.'

Scott's description of the summer was no less sombre. His entry for July in the Ledger read: 'Drinking and general unpleasantness.' In August the situation had not improved, 'General aimlessness and boredom.'

When they returned to America in September of 1928 he wrote that they were 'back again in [a] blaze of work and liquor'. And on the occasion of his thirty-second birthday he summarized the year as 'Ominous [underlining it three times]. No Real Progress in any way and wrecked myself with dozens of people.' It was unfortunately not an exaggeration.

Back at Ellerslie, where they had a few more months to go on their two-year lease, Zelda began her dancing lessons in Philadelphia with renewed vigour. But at home she kept entirely to herself, brooding and silent. She practised in front of the great ornate mirror, sweating profusely, stopping only for water, which she kept beside the Victrola, and ignoring Scott's remarks as he watched her leap and bend. He hated the glass, which he called their 'Whorehouse Mirror'.

Scott had brought back to the United States with them a Paris taxi driver and ex-boxer, Philippe, to be their chauffeur and his drinking companion. Zelda thoroughly disliked him; she said he was insubordinate to her and stupid. She hated it when he and Scott boxed together. Even John Biggs got a little tired of calls at three or four in the morning to pull Scott and Philippe out of the scrapes they always managed to get into. The household situation was further complicated by the presence of Mademoiselle, Scottie's French governess, whom Zelda also disliked. Zelda's relationship with Scottie had deteriorated to the point where they seemed to friends to be two children playing together. Zelda was obliquely describing how she felt about Scottie when she wrote:

And there was the lone and lovely child knocking a croquet ball through the arches of summer under the horse-chestnut trees and singing alone in her bed at night. She was a beautiful child who loved her mother. At first there had been Nanny but Nanny and I quarrelled and we sent her back to France and the baby had only its mother after that, and a series of people who straightened its shoes. I worried. The child was unhappy and thought of little besides how rich people were and little touching, childish things. The money obsession was because of the big house and going to play with the

Wanamakers and the DuPont children. The house was too immense for a child and too dignified.

Their return to Wilmington brought them no more satisfaction than their period of departure had and the endless litany of their discontent continued. When the lease on Ellerslie ran out, with Scott's novel still uncompleted, they again left America. In the brittle spring chill of 1929, nearly a decade since the beginning of the Jazz Age, the Fitzgeralds, with their blue-bound leather copies of Scott's books and their scrapbooks, Scottie and her dolls, and Zelda in her old fur coat, boarded the ship for Genoa. Scott wrote Maxwell Perkins: 'I am sneaking away like a thief without leaving the chapters . . . I haven't been able to do it. I'll do it on the boat and send it from Genoa. A thousand thanks for your patience – just trust me a few months longer, Max – it's been a discouraging time for me too but I will never forget your kindness and the fact that you've never reproached me.'

3. Breaking Down

10

A rout of dancers then came in: Dancers who were young in
dances that were dead.

JOHN PEALE BISHOP

From the Port of Genoa, where their boat docked, the Fitzgeralds travelled along the Mediterranean coast toward Nice.
They stopped there briefly as if to gather strength and refresh-
ment from the Riviera and then continued up to Paris. Zelda
immediately arranged with Egorova for her dancing lessons to
begin: class lessons in the morning with a private afternoon
lesson. Painful as it was for Scott, he impotently stood by while
Zelda's entire world was once again consumed by those exhaust-
ing lessons. Zelda said: 'I worked constantly and was terribly
superstitious and moody about my work; full of presentiments.
... I lived in a quiet, ghostly, hypersensitized world of my own.
Scott drank.' When she returned home from the ballet Scott
was rarely there, and if he was, a barrier of indifference held
them apart. It was impossible for him to share her conviction
that she would one day become a dancer of the first rank. He
did not object to the lessons, but they were an irritant between
them. Daily Zelda sent her teacher armfuls of fresh flowers. She
saw Egorova in her poverty and dedication as an ideal figure
whom she wished to emulate. One evening Scott and Zelda
took Egorova to dinner at a splendid restaurant, George V;
during the dinner Scott flirted mildly with the older woman
and to Zelda's surprise Egorova was pleased and rather
charmed. Scott enjoyed the situation, and chided Zelda about
her reaction, which was first one of shock and then of annoy-
ance. He thought it was ridiculous of her to insist on regarding
Egorova as an exemplar of dedication to the dance and impatiently he told her so.

Although Ernest Hemingway was living in Paris that spring the Fitzgeralds saw very little of him. A certain coolness had developed in their friendship, which Scott could not at first fathom. Hemingway seemed more irritable and avoided many of those drinking companions and cronies he had chummed around with the year before at the Closerie des Lilas and Lipp's. He had recently remarried and Scott knew he was working to complete his new novel, *A Farewell to Arms*, for Hemingway had allowed him to read it in manuscript. Scott had not done the amount of work on his own novel that he had hoped to do and felt guilty before Hemingway's progress. There was also an increasing tension between Zelda and Hemingway. They were polite to each other, but Scott was well aware of their mutual dislike. Therefore, when the men saw each other they were usually alone together. Morley Callaghan, a young Canadian writer who had known Hemingway in Toronto, was visiting Paris for the first time that spring; he was surprised to find that Fitzgerald and Hemingway were not on closer terms. Perkins, who was his editor as well as theirs, had told him that they were good friends. Callaghan, too, noticed the change in Hemingway. He suspected Hemingway of testing him, of wanting to engage in bouts where he would come off the victor, whether it was boxing or drinking. When the Callaghans met the Fitzgeralds they were impressed by their handsomeness, their air of superb confidence. But they were surprised when Zelda, whom they had expected to be gay and madcap, sat silent, studying them.

At their first meeting, Callaghan reports, Scott read him portions of *A Farewell to Arms* from the manuscript copy he had. When he had finished he asked if it wasn't beautiful. Callaghan wasn't sure, maybe it was, but as his reluctance became clear, Scott seemed a little injured. Zelda, however, was pleased by Callaghan's reaction and said Hemingway's prose sounded 'pretty damned Biblical' to her. With that Scott put the manuscript away. Then, after some talk on Zelda's part about writing in general, Scott, who seemed to them to be watching her closely, letting her talk while saying little himself, abruptly told her she was tired and should go to bed. He explained to the Callaghans about her ballet lessons, said that she had to be up early, and hoped they would understand. They didn't quite, but all the same Zelda left them.

The next time they met, Callaghan remembers, Zelda suddenly began to talk about her own writing; she was at pains to insist that she too wrote, and wrote well. He was taken aback by her assertion, not so much because he thought she did not write well, but because of her intense insistence. The two couples had been having dinner together, and when they were finished, 'Zelda laughed out loud, looking around. She had the restless air, the little sway of a woman seeking some new exhilaration, a woman in Paris who knew the night should be just beginning. She kept saying, "What'll we do? Let's do something" ', and then she suggested that they go roller-skating together. The Callaghans had agreed, when to their surprise Scott, who had been politely demurring, grabbed Zelda by the wrist and told her it was time for her to go home to bed. He put her into a taxi, and as he did so they noticed that Zelda's entire manner changed; Callaghan wrote: '... it was as if she knew he had command over her; she agreed meekly. ... And suddenly she had said good night like a small girl and was whisked away from us – and Scott dismissed the little scene almost brusquely.' Again he explained about the strain of her ballet lessons, and when Callaghan asked him why Zelda wanted to dance, he told him it was quite simple, she 'wanted to have something for herself, be something herself'.

In the winter of 1928–9 Zelda began writing the first in a series of short stories that dealt with the lives of six young women. Harold Ober made a note to himself in February about the Fitzgeralds' arrangement with *College Humor*. 'SF said that Z would do six articles for College Humor, that he would go over them and fix them up and that the articles would be signed with both their names. He said that as he remembered, they paid $200 for one article that Zelda did, and $250 for another. He said we had better leave the price until they did the first article. They are to be articles about different types of girls. I should think they ought to pay $500 for them, if they are 4 or 5 thousand words in length.'

Each story was written in an astonishing but hazardous burst of energy, for Zelda was at the same time continuing her ballet lessons and her strength, although seemingly boundless, was taxed to the breaking point. By June 1929, Zelda's fourth sketch had been sent to Ober. Five of these stories were to be published in *College Humor*, which had taken two of her articles in 1928 and considered her talented in her own right. Nevertheless, without exception the stories were published under both Fitzgeralds' names. Later Scott wrote Ober asking for $1,000 for the best of the stories. He said that if *College Humor* could only pay $500, Zelda's name should stand alone. Most of the stories, he told Ober, 'have been pretty strong draughts on Zelda's and my common store of material. This is M— for instance [probably in reference to the last story in the series, published by *College Humor*, 'The Girl with Talent', for which they received $800] and the 'Girl the Prince Liked' was J— both of whom I had in my notebook to use.'

The sixth story, 'A Millionaire's Girl', was published by the *Saturday Evening Post*, and although it was Zelda's story, Scott's name alone was signed to it. (A wire from New York assured him that the *Post* would pay $4,000 if Zelda's name was omitted, and it was.) Scott later wrote that the story 'appeared under my name but actually I had nothing to do with it except for suggesting a theme and working on the proof of the completed manuscript. This same cooperation extends to other material gathered ... under our joint names, though often when published in that fashion I had nothing to do with the thing from the start to finish except supplying my name.'

The stories attracted considerable notice at the time. Sometime about July 1930, Scott in a letter to Perkins told of three more stories that he was sending on to Harold Ober to place. Those stories were not published and were eventually lost. Zelda had written them, Scott said, 'in the dark middle of her nervous breakdown. I think you'll see that apart from the beauty and richness of the writing they have a strange haunting and evocative quality that is absolutely new. I think too that there is a certain unity apparent in them – their actual unity is a fact because each of them is the story of her life when things for a while seemed to have brought her to the edge of madness and despair.' The same might have been said of the stories which were published during 1929, for the breakneck speed at which they were written did not impair their effectiveness, and they remain a remarkable expression of Zelda's considerable talent as an essentially descriptive writer.

From the titles of the stories one notices that each is the portrait of a girl rather than a woman, although their ages range from sixteen well into the thirties, and although all but one have married (four have children as well). The husbands and children are, however, vague presences, placed in the stories, one suspects, as proof of a certain adequacy – that the girls have passed through a phase of life successfully – rather than as significant figures in themselves. The girls are adventuresses: sleek but restless and lonely women who are always exceptionally pretty. They are ambitious; they wish to distinguish themselves without fully knowing how to do so. And they share an immunity toward the everyday aspects of life by being in the main heiresses or actresses or dancers. There is something disquieting about these figures of allure, for they are imbued with a selfishness that is nearly as total as their attractiveness. What they suffer from is boredom of spirit. As she says of one of them, 'She wanted to get her hands on something tangible, to be able to say, "That is real, that is part of my experience, that goes into this or that category, this that happened to me is part of my memories."'

But they do not quite succeed in coming to life. Seen always from a distance by a detached and omniscient narrator about whom we know nothing (we are not even sure whether that observer is male or female), the girls do not interact with life. Rather, they are moved through it. Dialogue is almost non-existent. Zelda states again and again that they are courageous girls, but we do not see that courage tested or at work. What she does is to describe the characters, not develop them.

If they are not entirely satisfactory as characters, the skill Zelda exercises in describing their situations and their backgrounds is nevertheless impressive. These are the fashionable, 'rose-gold', and formidable girls that the nineteen-twenties cherished and whom Zelda took as her material. They are *le beau monde*. They live in silver apartments 'with mulberry carpets', surrounded by 'pastel restraint'. Their boyishness, their air of being children of the world, their carelessness, we are told, is only a decoy for their total control of social situations. Yet they seem to have no control whatsoever over their lives, through which they float without urgency, and ultimately, for all the author's insistence to the contrary, they are passive and elusive women.

In July the editor of *College Humor* sent Zelda some copy written to accompany one of her stories, 'Southern Girl'.

You know how sweethearts have a song between them, one they have grown to like very much. When they are separated and this song is played, *their song*, for them it immediately recalls the happiness they shared, and those dusty words, 'I love you.'

Examine very carefully *Southern Girl*, which the Fitzgeralds have done for this issue. There is not a line of conversation in it, but with very few words they have struck out a soft pattern of beauty and characters which were so real in their own lives that they come alive in your own ... I am so happy to have it because it marks an important milestone in the literary career of Zelda Fitzgerald. I cannot imagine any girl having a richer background than Zelda's, a life more crowded with interesting people and events. She is a star in her own right.

This, then, was the public image of the Fitzgeralds, cultivated by the slick magazines and the tabloids. Its variance from their private lives in the summer of 1929 was staggering.

Later in her life Zelda said she wrote to pay for her dancing lessons; she hated to take Scott's money for them, because she wanted her dancing to be her exclusive possession. At the time, however, the vehemence of her thoughts on this score were concealed from Scott. He was astonished by her productivity and even resented it in comparison to his own vexing inability to move forward on his novel. The strain of her pace began to show in fatigue, and she began to give way in her outward behaviour. She was easily distracted and even the simplest conversations were difficult for her to maintain. She took refuge in an impenetrable and unnerving silence. She and Scott attended few parties together, and when they did Scott was watchful for those first signals of tension that spelled ruinous quarrels if Zelda was not sent home immediately to rest. Zelda for her part had her hands full when Scott drank excessively, and she was frequently humiliated by his conduct. They avoided being alone together in their drab apartment. The tacit motivation for their behaviour was more similar than they were able to admit, and as desperately as they needed each other, they blindly strove to disentangle themselves from each other. They became engaged in a contest for personal survival very much like the one between Nicole and Dick Diver, which Scott would write about in *Tender Is the Night*. He has Dick say, ' "I can't do anything for you any more. I'm trying to save myself." '

The contest between the Fitzgeralds was no more pretty than that between the Divers; all rules of conduct were void. There were delirious parties that ended at Maxim's or the Coupole. Zelda wrote, 'Nobody knew whose party it was. It had been going on for weeks. When you felt you couldn't survive another night, you went home and slept and when you got back, a new set of people had consecrated themselves to keeping it alive.' And the Fitzgeralds were seen stepping from taxis, their handsome faces half hidden in the shadows of the night. Those were the evenings, indistinguishable from each other, spent in the company of the lively and exotic Kiki, or with Dolly Wilde, Oscar's niece, who had kohl-rimmed eyes and a total lack of discretion. Scott would make her an American girl in a cancelled episode in *Tender Is the Night* and name her Vivian Taube: 'To be a tall rich American girl is a form of hereditary achievement. ... Nevertheless it was increasingly clear to him that Miss Taube had more immediate concerns – there was a flick of the lip somewhere, a bending of the smile toward some indirection, a momentary lifting and dropping of the curtain over a hidden passage. An hour later he came out of somewhere to a taxi whither they had preceded him and found Wanda limp and drunk in Miss Taube's arms.' This was later cut from the manuscript, as were most of the other descriptions of homosexuals.

On the boat to Europe Zelda had mentioned to Scott that she thought a friend from the ballet was a homosexual. Now, desperately uncertain of herself, she accused Scott of a homosexual liaison with Ernest Hemingway. Scott, who had gone without Zelda to have a drink one evening with Hemingway and his wife, had returned home intoxicated and had fallen into a deep sleep. In his sleep he had murmured, 'no more baby', which was taken by Zelda as absolute proof of her suspicions. Fitzgerald was dumbfounded. They quarrelled violently, each making increasingly wild accusations against the other. Scott did not once question Zelda's sanity.

If the origin of such an unhappy rupture in the Fitzgeralds' marriage can be dated, it would be early in 1926. For it was then that Scott worriedly told the wife of a friend of theirs that Zelda complained of his inability to satisfy her. It was also in the winter of 1926–7 that they had begun trying to have another child, for they very much wanted a son. Several months later Robert McAlmon told Hemingway that Scott was a homosexual. Hemingway must have relayed the accusation to Fitzgerald, for Scott mentioned it in a letter to Maxwell Perkins: 'Part of his [McAlmon's] quarrel with Ernest some years ago was because he assured Ernest that I was a fairy – God knows he shows more creative imagination in his malice than in his work. Next he told Callaghan that Ernest was a fairy. He's a pretty good person to avoid.' Zelda knew of McAlmon's canard. By the spring of 1929, the Fitzgeralds' own physical estrangement all but complete, Zelda turned that charge against Scott. It took surprising effect. For a while at least Scott had begun to believe her.

Morley Callaghan, in his memoir of this spring in Paris, reports an incident that struck him as peculiar at the time. He and his wife had gone into the St Sulpice Church, which was near the Fitzgeralds' apartment. Scott was with them but he refused to enter the church and waited outside. Then they came back out and began to cross the square together. Scott said quietly, ' "I was going to take your arm, Morley . . ." '

' "Well, so . . ." '

' "Remember the night I was in bad shape? I took your arm.

Well, I dropped it. It was like holding on to a cold fish. You thought I was a fairy, didn't you?"

' "You're crazy, Scott," I said. But I wished I had been more consoling, more demonstrative with him that night.'

By the time the Fitzgeralds left Paris for the Riviera in July not only their marriage, but their very identities were in peril.

They stayed at the Villa Fleur des Bois in Cannes that summer. Zelda looked weary and haggard; her complexion, which had always been fresh, was ashen and colourless. Even her speech seemed to have changed. Gerald Murphy remembered her sudden bursts of laughter for no discernible reason, which came more as spasms of reaction than from enjoyment. He said: 'The laughter was her own, not like a human voice. Something strange in it, like unhinged delight. It was ecstatic, but there was a suppressed quality about it, a low, intimate sound that took one completely off guard.' And he remembered going to a movie at the local cinema near Antibes that summer with the Fitzgeralds and Sara. It was a documentary about underwater life and had been filmed in an aquarium. 'There were all sorts and varieties of strange fish swimming by the camera; there were myriad reeds and seaplants swaying in the water, and then the movie began to show photos of the predatory fish in their natural habitat. Quite nonchalantly an octopus, using his tentacles to propel himself, moved diagonally across the screen. Zelda, who had been sitting on my right, shrieked and threw herself all the way across my lap onto my left shoulder and, burying her head against my neck and chest, screamed, "What is it? What is it!" Now, we had all seen it and it moved very slowly – it was perfectly obvious that it was an octopus – but it had nevertheless frightened her to death. She was hardly a timid woman; I mean, she was really absolutely fearless and she was an expert swimmer. One simply didn't think she would have been so frightened by what she had seen, unless, of course, she had seen it as a distortion of something horrible.'

All through that summer Zelda sank more deeply into her private world, becoming increasingly remote from Scott and

Scottie. She continued her ballet lessons and danced professionally for the first time at brief engagements in Nice and Cannes. She was encouraged by her success, minor as she knew it was, and hoped that upon her return to Paris she could begin dancing with a major ballet company like Diaghilev's.

Scott quarrelled with the Murphys that summer too, and the escapades of the Fitzgeralds that had once had such élan now took on a sinister cast of self-destructiveness that was unavoidably clear to their friends. Sara Murphy said, 'I don't think he knew much about women and children.' She once wrote Scott: 'You don't even know what Zelda or Scottie are like – in spite of your love for them. It seemed to us the other night (Gerald too) that all you thought and felt about them was in terms of *yourself.* . . . I feel obliged in honesty of a friend to write you that the ability to know what another person feels in a given situation will make – or ruin lives.'

At the end of the summer, with the accumulation of grievances bearing down hard upon him, Scott wrote Hemingway:

My latest tendency is to collapse about 11:00 and, with tears flowing from my eyes or the gin rising to their level and leaking over, tell interested friends or acquaintances that I haven't a friend in the world and likewise care for nobody, generally including Zelda, and often implying current company – after which the current company tend to become less current and I wake up in strange rooms in strange palaces. The rest of the time I stay alone working or trying to work or brooding or reading detective stories – and realizing that anyone in my state of mind, who has in addition never been able to hold his tongue, is pretty poor company. But when drunk I make them all pay and pay and pay.

Scott's pallor had become such that when he slept beneath the striped umbrellas on the *plage* he looked unearthly. What hopes the Fitzgeralds had invested in the Riviera as a place which would revive their troubled spirits vanished, and they returned to Paris in October. It was on the automobile trip back to Paris along the Grande Corniche through the mountainous and steep roads of the south of France that Zelda grabbed the steering wheel of their car and tried to put them off the cliff. To her it seemed that the car had a will of its own, that it swerved as though by its own volition: '... it seemed to me it was going into oblivion beyond and I had to hold the sides of the car'.

Hemingway answered Scott's letter by reassuring him that the summer was a disheartening time of year to work. Death, he said, was not in the air as it was in autumn. In the fall of 1929 Paris filled with Americans. Zelda wrote, 'There were Americans at night, and day Americans, and we all had Americans in the bank to buy things with.' But the dollar was about to collapse, and the gala spree, the ceaseless and unrelenting party, was nearly over for all of them. Zelda said, 'We went [to] sophisticated places with charming people but I was grubby and didn't care.' Her nervousness made Scott edgy, and there were dinners taken together when Zelda held the sides of the table in order to endure sitting through the entire meal. She was nearly fifteen pounds under her normal weight. She continued her dancing lessons as if driven, and indeed she was.

On 23 September 1929, Zelda was invited to join the ballet school of the San Carlo Opera Ballet Company in Naples. She was offered a solo role in *Aïda* as her début, with the promise of other solos in other operas during the season. Madame Julia Sedova, who ran the school as well as the ballet company, added in her letter of invitation that living in Naples was inexpensive; one would be able to have a complete pension for thirty-five lire a day. It was Zelda's chance and it was not such a bad one, but inexplicably she did not take it. Scott never acknowledged that Zelda had come this close to a serious career as a ballerina. As late as 1936 he was writing that Zelda had been hoping to get 'bits' in the Diaghilev Ballet and that the only people who came to the studio to watch her 'who she thought were emissaries of his and who turned out to be from the Folies Bergères ... thought they might make her into an American shimmy dancer'.

In what had by now become a pattern with them, they travelled to North Africa in February 1930, as much to escape as to vacation. 'It was a trying winter', Zelda wrote, 'and to forget bad times we went to Algiers'. Since they were fleeing from themselves, they did not find respite. They took a series of snapshots which they carefully saved in one of their scrapbooks, dated 1929–31. Scott was tanned and his hair was thinner, but Zelda looked ravaged in the harsh and telling light. It was characteristic of her to appear entirely different in each of her pictures, but in these the effect was eerie; she is wraithlike, as if haunted. Her shoulders are hunched, deep lines surround her eyes, her mouth is unsmiling always. She looks furtive and distracted.

One afternoon after the Fitzgeralds' return from North Africa, the Murphys, who were living in Paris for the spring, went to the Fitzgeralds' apartment on the rue Pergolése to pick up Zelda, whom they were taking to an art exhibition. As they approached the apartment they saw both Fitzgeralds and John Bishop leaving the building. 'We immediately sensed something wrong between them. You know the way one can tell if there has been something embarrassing or upsetting that has happened. Zelda was surprisingly quiet and didn't say anything to us, which was not her usual form; in fact, she hardly spoke to us. Suddenly she turned to both of them and said, "Were you talking about me?" She was watching them very closely and they were embarrassed. Scott turned away toward me as though to say, "You have no idea of what we have been through this afternoon." They had all been having luncheon together at the Fitzgeralds'. Can you imagine her suspecting that they were talking about her? I mean, she was sitting right there with them!'

But such incidents were no longer rare. Undoubtedly as Zelda's own behaviour became more clearly peculiar her friends did reflect something of their discomfort in her company. Zelda's reaction was to become suspicious of all those people who had formerly been considered their friends – now she thought of them as Scott's friends.

Inevitably the break came. During a luncheon party in April which the Kalmans, old friends of theirs visiting from St Paul, attended, Zelda became afraid of missing her ballet lesson and abruptly left the table to catch a taxi. Kalman, noticing how nervous she seemed, went with her. In the taxi, while Zelda changed into her practice clothes, he tried to persuade her to take a rest from the ballet. But she did not appear to hear him and mumbled something unintelligible. As the taxi paused at a crossing, Zelda ran from the car toward her studio. Kalman returned to Scott, told him what had happened, and suggested that there was something seriously wrong with Zelda.

Madame Egorova, too, had begun to notice a change in Zelda. One afternoon Zelda invited her to tea. They were alone in the apartment and it became clear to the older woman that there was something strange happening to Zelda – her gestures, her face, and even her voice seemed increasingly peculiar. When they had finished their tea, Madame Egorova sat down on the couch facing Zelda. Suddenly Zelda threw herself down on her knees at Egorova's feet. Trying to prevent the situation from going any further, Egorova rose calmly and told Zelda that it was late and that she had to go home, and quietly left the apartment.

On 23 April 1930, slightly more than a decade after their marriage, Zelda entered a hospital called Malmaison on the outskirts of Paris. She was in a state of extreme anxiety, and restlessly paced the room, saying: 'It's dreadful, it's horrible, what's to become of me, I must work and I won't be able to, I should die, but I must work. I'll never be cured. Let me leave, I must go to see "Madame" [Egorova], she has given me the greatest possible joy; it's like the rays of the sun shining on a piece of crystal, to a symphony of perfumes, the most perfect harmonies of the greatest musicians.' She was slightly intoxicated on her arrival and said that she found alcohol a necessary stimulant for her work. On 2 May Zelda abruptly left the hospital against her physician's advice.

Unfortunately, when she returned to their apartment, Scott was involved in a series of wedding parties and bachelor dinners for Powell Fowler (the brother of Ludlow Fowler). There was a lot of drinking and no time for convalescence. Scott wrote Perkins at the time that 'Zelda got a sort of nervous breakdown from overwork and consequently I haven't done a line of work or written a letter for twenty-one days.' But Zelda's collapse was far more serious than Scott implied. She returned to her ballet lessons with a frenetic exuberance. Less than two weeks later she was dazed and incoherent. She heard voices that terrified her, and her dreams, both waking and sleeping, were peopled with phantoms of indescribable horror. She had fainting fits and the menacing nature of her hallucinations drove her into an attempted suicide. Only an injection of morphine could comfort her. The demonic dreams which she experienced became more real for her than reality and Scott could not let her out of his sight. She entered Valmont, a clinic in Switzerland, on 22 May. But Valmont handled gastrointestinal ailments primarily and the physicians there recognized that Zelda's illness was of a deeply psychological nature. At the request of her physician, Dr Oscar Forel was called in to examine her. The report from Valmont was ominous.

At the beginning of her stay Mrs Fitzgerald declared that she had not been sick and that she had been taken by force to a sanitarium. She repeated daily that she wanted to return to Paris in order to resume her work in ballet, in which she believed she could find her only satisfaction in life ... The husband's visits often were the occasion of violent arguments, provoked especially by the husband's attempts to reason with the patient and to refute the patient's insinuations suspecting the husband of homosexuality. Mrs Fitzgerald became highly excited at the thought that ... she was losing precious time....

At calm moments the patient understood quite well that she was at the end from a physical and nervous [psychological] standpoint and that she badly needed to take care of herself, but then an hour later she again wanted to know nothing about that and insisted on her return to Paris. Numerous discussions with her were fruitless because of all her real thoughts she expressed only a few incoherent ones.

From an organic standpoint there is nothing to report, no signs of mental illness.* It became more and more clear that a simple rest cure was absolutely insufficient and that psychological treatment by a specialist in a sanitarium was indicated. It was evident that the relationship between the patient and her husband had been weakened for a long time and that for that reason the patient had

* In the sense of an ailment such as a tumour or injury to the brain.

not only attempted to establish her own life by the ballet (since the family life and her duties as a mother were not sufficient to satisfy her ambition and her artistic interests) but that she also [had withdrawn] from her husband. As far as her 8 year old daughter is concerned she expressed herself as follows to the question: 'What role did her child play in her life?': [in English] 'That is done now, I want to do something else.'

In view of the necessity of psychological treatment for this complicated case, a consultation with Dr Forel of the Clinic of Prangins near Nyon was requested, with the request that he advise from a therapeutic standpoint. After he studied the case, Dr Forel declared his willingness to receive the patient in his clinic if she wanted to go there of her own will. He insisted that treatment could only be psychotherapy, based on an analysis of all the factors which were able to lead the patient into such a complicated situation. Admission to Prangins would be possible only on the condition of a temporary separation from her husband.

On the evening of the consultation (3 June) the patient said herself that she felt very tired and sick and that she very much needed treatment. One had the impression that she agreed to go to Prangins. The next morning she was again in a bad mood and unreasonable. She is leaving the clinic with her husband.

On 4 June Zelda left Valmont. Rosalind's husband, Newman Smith, who had been living in Brussels, arrived to try to help Scott cope with the situation. He not only lent his moral support but he tacitly represented Zelda's side of the family. Somehow they persuaded Zelda to enter Les Rives de Prangins for extensive psychiatric treatment. Later she was to write of that journey to the asylum:

Our ride to Switzerland was very sad. It seemed to me that we did not have each other or anything else and it half killed me to give up all the work I had done. I was completely insane and had made a decision: to abandon the ballet and live quietly with my husband. I had wanted to destroy the picture of Egorova that I had lived with for four years and give away my tou-tous and the suitcase full of shoes and free my mind from the thing. The light in which the thing presented itself to me was: I had got to the end of my physical resources. ... If I couldn't be great, it wasn't worth going on with though I loved my work to the point of obsession. It was all I had in the world at the time.

Ahead of them would be the slow agony of putting the pieces of their lives together again. They did not yet realize the extent of Zelda's breakdown, nor the amount of time that it would take to 'cure' her, nor even if she could be cured. She was diagnosed by Dr Forel as a schizophrenic, and not simply a neurotic or hysterical woman. It was as if once Zelda had collapsed there was no escape other than her spiralling descent into madness. Except, of course, it was not a simple descent; it was upheaval, spin and skid into a treacherous insanity where nothing was what it seemed. To record her breakdown is to give witness to her helplessness and terror, as well as to explore again the bonds that inextricably linked the Fitzgeralds.

Les Rives de Prangins was located on the shoreline of Lake Geneva near Nyon, twenty-two kilometres from Geneva. It had opened that year under the direction of Dr Oscar Forel and was quickly becoming established as the foremost sanitarium for the treatment of mental illness in Europe. (James Joyce's daughter, Lucia, was diagnosed as a schizophrenic by Dr Forel and was placed under his care at Prangins briefly in the summer of 1933 and again in 1934.) Prangins looked like a splendid resort hotel for the wealthy; most of its hundred acres of grounds was immaculately groomed, with trees trimmed into cones and pyramids, and exact rows of sculptured hedges. There were winter gardens, tennis courts, farms, and seven villas (four of which were reserved for patients, who were called guests). The atmosphere was intended to be homelike rather than institutional and the number of patients admitted was limited to ensure close psychiatric care. The physicians and their families lived on the grounds and participated in the life of the institution.

Zelda arrived at Prangins late in the afternoon of 5 June with Scott and Newman Smith. She showed no signs of resistance to being there, but the first night was difficult, for she was naturally anxious and ill at ease. The following day she said that she wished to be cured and that she would cooperate with the doctors; she also said she wanted to paint indoors. Dr Forel noted that Zelda was afraid of contact with other patients and shied away from direct conversation about herself.

On 8 June the first in a series of ruminative letters from a member of Zelda's family arrived for Dr Forel, written in an effort to provide him with a picture of Zelda's background and heritage. The Sayres were described as intellectuals of simple and temperate habits, and, the writer added, there was no history of insanity in their family. Zelda's childhood had been entirely normal. The only person she had ever been attached to was her mother, toward whom she was extraordinarily loving. Although thoroughly spoiled by Mrs Sayre, Zelda had been the most vigorous and healthy of the Sayres' children, with the others inclining toward nervousness and depression. Perhaps those traits had developed because of the character of Judge Sayre and the tenseness that resulted from it in the family. The Judge was described as a solitary man in the most thoroughgoing sense; he was silent, not at all sociable, and possessed no sympathy toward youth. Their home life was consequently not happy. He was devoted to their mother, who was a gay and warm woman, but on his own terms; he did not show affection and his restraint eventually cast an oppressive aura over the entire family.

Scott wrote to Dr Forel on the same day. He tried to give the background of Zelda's life, but solely within the context of their marriage. The letter revealed more about his own attitude toward Zelda and their life together than it did about Zelda herself. Scott selected five elements that seemed crucial to him for an understanding of Zelda's current condition, but he began by assuring Forel that he was in absolute agreement with him about her and that, as slow as her recovery might be, he would abstain from seeing her until 'the moment when her attitude toward me will change'.

Zelda, he wrote, was the child of parents who were over forty years old when she was born. She had always been something of a defeatist, 'or at least a fatalist, opposed to my ability of finding ways to fight against difficulties or obstacles'. He mentioned that they had tried several times to have more children, but always without success, and that the failure had deeply distressed him. The 'lessening of our sexual relationship' was not due to 'coldness' on his part, he wrote,

as she would have it understood ... but rather to the facts of her growing absorption in the ballet, and that I have been drinking too much during the last 18 months, as well as to the animosities and hostilities caused by all of this. After having worked all day at home, I would want to go out at night – my wife, on the contrary, having been gone all day, wanted only to stay home and go to bed. ... The last six months she did not even take any interest in our child. ... Before she devoted herself to the ballet she took care of all her duties and more.

In closing he mentioned that he had a story with him that Zelda had written while at Valmont and he wondered if she was well enough to revise and correct it before he sent it off to America. If he could not see her, could he have flowers sent to her every other day? And lastly he asked, 'When could I without danger start sending her short notes, mentioning neither the misunderstandings of these last days nor her sickness?'

In an undated, pencilled letter (which may have been a draft of a letter never sent) he wrote to Zelda about how he felt while looking at a snapshot of her. The letter speaks for itself of how deeply wounded Scott was, and of how deeply he loved Zelda.

When I saw the sadness of your face in that passport picture I felt as you can imagine. But after going through what you can imagine I did then and looking at it, I saw that it was the face I knew and loved and not the metalic superimposition of our last two years in France. ... The photograph is all I have; it is with me from the morning when I wake up with a frantic half dream about you to the last moment when I think of you and of death at night. The rotten letters you write me I simply put away under

L in my file.... If you choose to keep up your wrestling match with a pillar of air I would prefer to be not even in the audience.

I am hardened to write you so brutally by thinking of the ceaseless wave of love that surrounds you and envelopes you always, that you have the power to evoke at a whim – when I know that for the mere counterfiet of it I would perjure the best of my heart and mind. Do you think the solitude in which I live has a more amusing decor than any other solitude? Do you think it is any nicer for remembering that there were times very late at night when you and I shared our aloneness? I will take my full share of responsibility for all this tragedy but I cannot spread beyond the limits of my reach and grasp, I can only bring you the little bit of hope I have and I don't know any other hope except my own. I have the terrible misfortune to be a gentleman in the sort of struggle with incalculable elements to which people should bring centuries of inexperience; if I have failed you is it just barely possible that you have failed me ... I love you with all my heart because you are my own girl and that is all I know.

Scott had written to the Sayres about Zelda's breakdown as soon as it occurred, but he did not stress the seriousness of her collapse. He told them it was a case of nervous exhaustion as a result of overwork, and that she was taking a cure in Switzerland. Mrs Sayre was not taken in by the evasion. Zelda had written to her mother regularly once a week and those letters had now stopped. She wrote Scott, 'I get frantic for news from my little baby.' Although she was upset by her daughter's breakdown, her reaction was one of resignation. She had gone through similar periods with her oldest daughter, Marjorie, and with the Judge. Zelda, she realized, would have to remain in Europe and rest; they would all have to guard against relapses; and, she wrote Scott, 'we might just as well face facts for there is no dodging them'.

At the end of June Zelda was no better and she wrote Scott:

Just at the point in my life when there is no time left me for losing, I am here to incapacitate myself for using what I have learned in such a desperate school – through my own fault and from a complete lack of medical knowledge on a rather esoteric subject. If you could write to Egorowa a friendly impersonal note to find out exactly where I stand as a dancer it would be of the greatest help to me – Remember, this is in no way at all her fault. I would have liked to dance in New York this fall, but where am I going to find again these months that dribble into the beets of the clinic garden? Is it worth it? And once a proper horror for the accidents of life has been instilled into me, I have no intention of joi[n]ing the group about a corpse. My legs are already flabby and I will soon be like A.———, huntress of corralled game, I suppose, instead of a human being recompensed for everything by the surety of a comprehension of one manifestation of beauty – Why can't you write me what you think and want instead of vague attempts at reassurance? If I had work or something it would be so much decenter to try to help each other and make at least a stirrup cup out of this bloody mess.

You have always had so much sympathy for people forced to start over late in life that I should think you could find the generosity to help me amongst your many others – not as you would a child but as an equal.

I want you to let me leave here – You're wasting time and effort and money to take away the little we both have left. If you think you are preparing me for a return to Alabama you are mistaken, and also if you think that I am going to spend the rest of my life roaming about without happiness or rest or work from one sanatorium to another like K.——— you are wrong. Two sick horses might conceivably pull a heavier load than a well one alone. Of cource, if you prefer that I should spend six months of my life under prevailing conditions – my eyes are open and I will get something from that, too, I suppose, but they are tired and unhappy, and my head aches always. Won't you write me a comprehensible letter such as you might write to one of your friends? Every day it gets harder to think or live and I do not understand the object of wasting the dregs of me here, alone in a devasting bitterness.

Zelda

In a postscript she added:

Please write immediately to Paris about the dancing. I would do it but I think the report will be more accurate if it goes to you – just an opinion as to what value my work is and to what point I could develop it before it is too late. Of cource, I would go to another school as I know Egorowa would not want to be bothered with me – Thanks.

Dr Forel was absolutely certain that the way to Zelda's recovery did not lie in further dancing, and he too thought that Scott should write to Egorova. But he suggested that Fitzgerald make clear to her their preference that in her answer she discourage Zelda, even if it was a gross deception. Zelda, Forel decided, had to be made to realize that dancing was not her vocation. She wanted to begin working again, but in Forel's opinion it was medical treatment that she urgently needed rather than more dancing. The weekend before, Zelda had gone out with her nurse and tried to run away. It was only with the assistance of several nurses that she was brought back to Prangins and he found it necessary to transfer her to the Villa Eglantine, where patients were placed under restriction. It was a severe blow to both Zelda's and Scott's hopes for her rapid recovery.

Scott did write to Egorova, but he could not bring himself to suggest to her that they deceive Zelda about her potential as a ballerina. He asked very specifically, however, just what her abilities were in comparison with the professionals in Mme Egorova's studio. Egorova did not equivocate. She wrote that Zelda had started dancing too late to become a dancer of the first rank; she could, however, become a good dancer; she could dance with success important roles in the Ballet Massine in New York. But among Madame's pupils there were many who were superior to her and who would always be. She would never equal stars such as Nemtchinova. For Zelda, Egorova's judgement (when and if she learned of it) would be a crushing blow, but to Scott and Dr Forel it was far more positive than they had anticipated.

Zelda, meanwhile, in an effort to understand her own condition, began writing letters to Scott that were a recapitulation of their life together. She had no idea that she would remain at Prangins under treatment for the next fifteen months. And these letters to Scott, whom she was allowed to see only once every few weeks, had a voice and tone of their own. They were unlike anything she had written during the course of their marriage; strangely enough, they were perhaps most like the candid letters she had written to him during the period of separation in their courtship during the spring of 1919 – but without the girlishness, without the absolute self-confidence. They permit access to the terrain of her anguish.

Every day it seems to me that things are more barren and sterile and hopeless – In Paris, before I realized that I was sick, there was a new significance to everything: stations and streets and façades of buildings – colors were infinite, part of the air, and not restricted by the lines that encompassed them and lines were free of the masses they held. There was music that beat behind my forehead and other music that fell into my stomach from a high parabola and there was some of Schumann that was still and tender and the sadness of Chopin Mazurkas – Some of them sound as if he thought that he couldn't compose them – and there was the madness of turning, turning, turning through the deciciveness of Litz. Then the world became embryonic in Africa – and there was no need for communication. The Arabs fermenting in the vastness; the curious quality of their eyes and the smell of ants; a detachment as if I was on the other side of a black gauze – a fearless small feeling, and then the end at Easter – But even that was better than the childish, vacillating shell that I am now. I am so afraid that when you come and find there is nothing left but disorder and vacuum that you will be horror-struck. I don't seem to know anything appropriate for a person of thirty: I suppose it's because of draining myself so thoroughly, straining so completely every fibre in that futile attempt to achieve with every factor against me – Do you mind my writing this way? Don't be afraid that I am a meglomaniac again – I'm just searching and it's easier with you –

You'll have to re-educate me – But you used to like giving me books and telling me things. I never realized before how hideously dependent on you I was – Dr Forel says I won't be after. If I can have a clear intelligence I'm sure we can use it – I hope I will be different [. I?] must have been an awful bore for you.

Why do you never write me what you are doing and what you think and how it feels to be alone –

There were also letters that were accusing, sometimes incoherent, plaintive, questioning, violent, and loving. It was at great cost and pain that Zelda admitted her illness, admitted her own need for psychiatric help. And her recapitulation, although often a line of defence, was never that alone. She faced her madness and by way of explaining it to herself tried to express it to Scott. What she could not fully grasp was the extent of her damage or her own part in it.

Dear Scott:

There is no use my trying to write to you because if I write one thing one day I think another immediately afterwards. I would like to see you. I don't know why I have constantly a presetiment of disaster. It seems to me cruel that you cannot explain to me what is the matter since you will not accept my explanation. As you know, I am a person, or was, of some capabality even if on a small scale and if I could once grasp the situation I would be much better able to handle it. Under existing conditions, I simply grovel about in the dark and since I can not concentrate either to read or write there does not seem to be any way to escape. I do not want to lose my mind. Twice horrible things have happened to me through my inability to express myself: once peritonitis* that left me an invalid for two years and now this thing. Won't you please come to see me, since at least you know me and you could see, maybe, some assurance to give me that would counteract the abuse you piled on me at Lausanne when I was so sick. At any rate one thing has been achieved: I am thoroughly and completely humiliated and broken if that was what you wanted. There are some things I want to tell you.

Zelda

Dear Scott:

To recapitulate: as you know, I went of my own will to the clinic in Paris to cure myself. You also know that I left (with the consent of Proffessor Claude) knowing that I was not entirely well because I could see no use in jumping out of the frying-pan into the fire, which is what was about to happen, or so I thought. I also went, practically voluntarily but under enormous pressure to Valmont with the sole idea of getting back enough strenghth and health to continue my work in America as you had promised me. There, my head began to go wrong ... During all this time you, knowing everything about me, since in all this dreary story I have never tried to conceal the slightest detail from you, but have on the contrary urged you to manifest some interest in what I was doing, never saw fit to either guide or enlighten me. To me, it is not astonishing that I should look on you with unfriendly eyes. ... if you had

*See Notes for Chapter 8.

explained to me what was happening the night we had dinner with John Bishop and went to the fair afterwards which left me in hysterics. The obligation is, after all, with the people who understand, and the blind, of necessity, must be led. I offer you this explanation because I know I owe you one and because it is like this that I began this abominable affair.

My attitude towards Egorowa has always been one of an intense love: I wanted to help her some way because she is a good woman who has worked hard and has nothing, or lost everything. I wanted to dance well so that she would be proud of me and have another instrument for the symbols of beauty that passed in her head that I understood, though apparently could not execute. I wanted to be the first in the studio so that it would be me that she could count on to understand what she gave out in words and of cource I wanted to be near her because she was cool and white and beautiful.... at home there was an incessant babbling it seemed to me and you either drinking or complaining because you had been. You blamed me when the servants were bad, and expected me to instill into them a proper respect for a man that they saw morning after morning asleep in his clothes, who very often came home in the early morning, who could not sit, even, at the table. Anyhow, none of those things matter. I quite realize that you have done the best you can and I would like you to try to realize that so have I, in all the disorder. I do not know what is going to happen, but since I am in the hands of Doctor Forel and they are a great deal more powerful than yours or mine, it will probably be for the best. I want to work at something, but I can't seem to get well enough to be of any use in the world. That's not all, but the rest is too complicated for me now. Please send me Egorowa's letter –

Zelda

Knowing how defeated she would feel by Egorova's letter, Scott suggested that Dr Forel use caution in showing her the reply: 'Poor girl, I am afraid it will be taking away from her what appears to her as her last *refuge*.'

By mid-June Zelda had developed a severe eczema that covered her face, neck, and shoulders. It came on the heels of a visit from her daughter, when Zelda had made a valiant effort to appear normal so that Scottie would see none of the traces of her illness. The strain was too great. Zelda had suffered from eczema before, but always for brief periods of time, and at those times it had been thought that the skin irritation was due to drugs she had been taking. This time there was an obvious psychological link, and the eczema was virulent and painful. None of the medicines tried at Prangins were effective against it. For the rest of July, all of August, and early September Zelda suffered its debilitating pain, which Scott was later to make use of in *Tender Is the Night*, where he wrote:

On her admittance she had been exceptionally pretty – now she was a living agonizing sore. All blood tests had failed to give a positive reaction and the trouble was unsatisfactorily catalogued as nervous eczema. For two months she had lain under it, as imprisoned as in the Iron Maiden. She was coherent, even brilliant, within the limits of her special hallucinations.

Zelda wrote to Scott, at the onset of the affliction:

Please, out of charity write to Dr Forel to let me off this cure.... For a month and a week I've lived in my room under bandages, my head and neck on fire. I haven't slept in weeks. The last two days I've had bromides and morphine but it doesn't do any good. – All because nobody ever taught me to play tennis. When I'm most miserable there's your game to think of. If you could see how awful this is you would write lots more stories, light ones to laugh about. I want to get well but I can't it seems to me, and if I should whats going to take away the thing in my head that sees so clearly into the past and into dozens of things that I can never forget. Dancing has gone and I'm weak and feeble and I can't understand why I should be the one, amongst all the others, to have to bear all this – for what? ...

I can't read or sleep. Without hope or youth or money I sit constantly wishing I were dead.

Mamma does know whats the matter with me. She wrote me she did. You can put that in your story to lend it pathos. Bitched once more.

Dear Scott:

The panic seems to have settled into a persistent gloom punctuated by moments of bombastic hysteria, which is, I suppose a relatively wholesome state. Though I would have chosen some other accompaniment for my desequilibrium than this foul eczema, still ... I am waiting impatiently for when you can come to see me if you will – Do you still smell of pencils and sometimes of tweed?

Yesterday I had some gramophone discs that reminded me of Ellerslie. I wonder why we have never been very happy and why all this has happenned – It was much nicer a long time ago when we had each other and the space about the world was warm – Can't we get it back someway – even by imagining?

The book came – thanks awfully –

Dear, I will be so glad to see you –

Sometimes, it's desperate to be so alone – and you can't be very happy in a hotel room – we were awfully used to having each other about –

Zelda

Dr Forel told me to ask you if you had stopped drinking – so I ask –

In early fall Scott wrote Maxwell Perkins from Geneva, where he was living: 'Zelda is almost well. The doctor says she can never drink again (not that drink in any way contributed to her collapse), and that I must not drink anything, not even wine, for a year, because drinking in the past was one of the things that haunted her in her delirium.' Scott not only exaggerated the rate of Zelda's improvement, but he was unable to admit the hold that alcohol had over him. However, in a letter to Dr Forel that summer, he stated that he could not give up all drinking permanently. Although he was as trapped in alcoholism as Zelda was in her madness and eczema, he avoided coming to terms with it by placing the blame on Zelda.

Dr Forel ...
When I last saw you I was almost as broken as my wife by months of horror. The only important thing in my life was that she should be saved from madness or death. Now that, due to your tireless intelligence and interest, there is a time in sight where Zelda and I may renew our life together on a decent basis, a thing which I desire with all my heart, there [are] other considerations due to my nessessities as a worker and to my very existence that I must put before you.

During my young manhood for seven years I worked extremely hard, in six years bringing myself by tireless literary self discipline to a position of unquestioned preeminence among younger American writers; also by additional 'hack-work' for the cinema ect. I gave my wife a comfortable and luxurious life such as few European writers ever achieve. My work is done on coffee, coffee and more coffee, never on alcohol. At the end of five or six hours I get up from my desk white and trembling and with a steady burn in my stomach, to go to dinner. Doubtless a certain irritability developed in those years, an inability to be gay, which my wife – who had never tried to use her talents and intelligence – was not inclined to condone. It was on our coming to Europe in 1924 and upon her urging that I began to look forward to wine at dinner – she took it at lunch, I did not. We went on hard drinking parties together sometimes but the regular use of wine and apperatives was something that I dreaded but she encouraged because she found I was more cheerful then and allowed her to drink more. The ballet idea was something I inaugurated in 1927 to stop her idle drinking after she had already so lost herself in it as to make suicidal attempts. Since then I have drunk more, from unhappiness, and she less, because of her physical work – that is another story.

Two years ago in America I noticed that when we stopped all drinking for three weeks or so, which happened many times, I immediately had dark circles under my eyes, was listless and disinclined to work. I gave up strong cigarettes and, in a panic that perhaps I was just giving out, I applied for a large insurance policy. The one trouble was low blood-pressure, a matter which they finally condoned, and they issued me the policy. I found that a moderate amount of wine, a pint at each meal made all the difference in how I felt. When that was available the dark circles disappeared, the coffee didn't give me excema or beat in my head all night, I looked forward to my dinner instead of staring at it, and life didn't seem a hopeless grind to support a woman whose tastes were daily diverging from mine. She no longer read or thought, or knew anything or liked anyone except dancers and their cheap satellites. People respected her because I concealed her weaknesses, and because of a certain complete fearlessness and honesty that she has never lost, but she was becoming more and more an egotist and a bore. Wine was almost a nessessity for me to be able to stand her long monologues about ballet steps, alternating with a glazed eye toward any civilized conversation whatsoever.

Now when that old question comes up again as to which of two people is worth preserving, I, thinking of my ambitions once so nearly achieved of being part of English literature, of my child, even of Zelda in the matter of providing for her – must perforce consider myself first. I say that without defiance but simply knowing the limits of what I can do. To stop drinking entirely for six months and see what happens, even to continue the experiment thereafter if successful – only a pig would refuse to do that. Give up strong drink permanently I will. Bind myself to forswear wine forever I cannot. My vision of the world at its brightest is such that life without the use of its amentities is impossible. I have lived hard and ruined the essential innocense in myself that could make it possible, and the fact that I have abused liquor is something to be paid for with suffering and death perhaps but not with renunciation. For me it would be as illogical as permanently giving up sex because I caught a disease (which I hasten to assure you I never have.) I cannot consider one pint of wine at the days end as anything but one of the rights of man.

Does this sound like a long polemic composed of childish stubborness and ingratitude? If it were that it would be so much easier to make promises. What I gave up for Zelda was women and it wasn't easy in the position my success gave me – what pleasure I got from comradeship she has pretty well ruined ... Is there not a certain disingenuousness in her wanting me to give up all alcohol? Would not that justify her conduct completely to herself and prove to her relatives and our friends that it was my drinking that had caused this calamity, and that I thereby admitted it? Wouldn't she finally get to believe herself that she had consented to 'take me back' only if I stopped drinking? I could only be silent. And any human value I might have would disappear if I condemned myself to a life long ascetism to which I am not adapted either by habit, temperament or the circumstances of my metier.

For portions of August and mid-September Scott vacationed in Caux. He finished 'One Trip Abroad' and 'A Snobbish Story' during those periods of relative peace. But he did nothing with his novel. He had begun to work on a sixth draft in the spring of 1930, but with Zelda's illness he apparently put it aside and turned to writing short stories for quick cash. At the beginning of 'One Trip Abroad' (which Matthew Bruccoli rightly calls 'a miniature of *Tender Is the Night*') Fitzgerald wrote about 'the young American couple' Nicole and Nelson Kelly: 'Life is progressive, no matter what our intentions, but something was harmed, some precedent of possible non-agreement was set. It was a love match, though, and it could stand a great deal.' The Kellys, who showed signs of being modelled after both the Fitzgeralds and the Murphys, did stand a great deal, until restlessness and their own inner resources began to give way. At the end of the story Nicole says, ' "It's just that we don't understand what's the matter. . . . Why did we lose peace and love and health, one after the other? If we knew, if there was anybody to tell us, I believe we could try. I'd try so hard." '

During that time Zelda wrote to Scott:

I hope it will be nice at Caux. It sounds as if part of its name had rolled down the mountain-side. Perhaps when I'm well I won't be so afraid of floating off from high places and we can go to-gether.

Except for momentary retrogressions into a crazy defiance and complete lack of proportion I am better. It's ghastly losing your mind and not being able to see clearly, literally or figuratively – and knowing that you can't think and that nothing is right, not even your comprehension of concrete things like how old you are or what you look like –

Where are all my things? I used to always have dozens of things and now there doesn't seem to be any clothes or anything personal in my trunk – I'd *love* the gramophone –

What a disgraceful mess – but if it stops our drinking it is worth it – because then you can finish your novel and write a play and we can live somewhere and have can have a house with a room to paint and write maybe like we had with friends for Scottie and there will be Sundays and Mondays again which are different from each other and there will be Christmas and winter fires and pleasant things to think of when you're going to sleep – and my life won't lie up the back-stairs of music-halls and yours won't keep trailing down the gutters of Paris – if it will only work, and I can keep sane and not a bitter maniac –

Dear Scott:

I wish I could see you: I have forgotten what it's like to be alive with a functioning intelligence. It was fine to have your post-card with your special reaction to Caux on it. Your letters are just noncommital phrases that you might write to Scottie and they do not help to unravel this infinite psychological mess that I'm floundering about in. I watch what attitude the nurse takes each day and then look up what symptom I have in Doctor Forel's book. Dear, why has my ignorance on a medical subject which has never appeared to me particularly interesting reduced me to the mental status of a child? I know that my mind is vague and undisciplined and that I know only small smatterings of things, but that has nothing to do with cerebral processes. . . .

I don't know how we're going to reverse time, you and me; erase and begin again – but I imagine it will be automatic. I can't project myself into the past no matter how hard I try. There are lots of days when I think it would have been better to give me a concise explanation and let it go – because I know so much already. One illusion is as good as another.

Write me how you are and what you do and what the world is like at Caux – and Love Zelda

As the summer passed Zelda wavered between a seeming re-cuperation and yet deeper illness. Once when things seemed very black indeed for her recovery Dr Forel asked her as part of his therapy to write out a summary of the way she felt about her family and herself. In this document she was able to reveal something of herself to Forel for the first time, with fewer of the restraints and disguises she usually employed. She wrote quickly and in a highly idiosyncratic French. (The following are excerpts from a translation of that record, which in the original runs to about seven pages.) Dr Forel asked Zelda to describe her parents. She remembered her mother as being ex-tremely indulgent of others' faults, an artistic woman who wrote, played the piano and sang. Zelda said Mrs Sayre had a passion for flowers and birds. She saw her mother in terms of a mood photograph: 'I can always see her sitting down in the opalescent sunlight of a warm morning, a black servant combing her long grey hair.' But no such images of her father came to mind. She described him exclusively in terms of what he was and did. He was a man of 'great integrity'. 'I had an enormous respect for my father and some mistrust.' Then he asked her about their marriage.

When I was a child their relationship was not apparent to me. Now I see them as two unhappy people: my mother dominated and oppressed by my father, and often hurt by him, he forced to work for a large family in which he found neither satisfaction nor a spiritual link. Neither of them complained.

When asked about her parents' influence on her, Zelda insisted that they had had absolutely none.

Her relationship toward her brother and sisters she simply described as 'vague'. She was a great many years younger than they and did not have memories of a youth passed together. Her sisters were pretty; she quarrelled with them constantly. Her favourite was Rosalind, who 'appeared elegant, perfumed, sophisticated'.

The great emotional events of her life were:

My marriage, after which I was in another world, one for which I was not qualified or prepared, because of my inadequate education.

And:

A love affair with a french aviator in St Raphael. I was locked in my villa for one month to prevent me from seeing him. This lasted for five years. When I knew my husband had another woman in California I was upset because the life over there appeared to me so superficial, but finally I was not hurt because I knew I had done the same thing when I was younger.

I determined to find an impersonal escape, a world in which I could express myself and walk without the help of somebody who was always far from me. I had begun dancing in Paris, with a great ballet dancer, but I was obliged to leave her because of my illness. ... When I returned to Paris I went again into the same school. I have worked four hours a day and in the evening, and Sundays, during the holidays, on the boat when I was travelling. I began to understand it.

Suddenly last spring I began to see all red while I worked or I saw no colors – I could not bear to look out of windows, for sometimes I saw humanity as a bottle of ants. Then we left for Cannes where I worked on technique and where after the lessons I had the impression that I was an old person living very quietly in winter. I loved my ballet teacher in Paris more than anything else in the world. But I did not know how. She had everything of beauty in her head, the brightness of a greek temple, the frustration of a mind searching for a place, the glory of cannon bullets; all that I saw in her steps. From Christmas on I was not able to work correctly anymore, but she helped me to learn more, to go further. She always told me to look after myself. I tried to, but it was worse. I was in a real 'mess'. ... One day the world between me and the others stopped – I was dragged like by a magnet – I had headaches and I could jump higher than ever, but the day after I was sick. I left my lessons, but without them I could not do anything. It was Easter, I wanted to do something for my little girl, but I could not stop in a shop and Madame came to encourage me. Enough to give me the strength to go to Malmaison. There the doctors told me that I was well and I came back to the studio, unable to walk in the streets, full of medicine, trying to work in an atmosphere which was becoming more and more strange.... My husband forced me to go to Valmont – and now I am here, with you, in a situation where I cannot be anybody, full of vertigo, with an increasing noise in my ears, feeling the vibrations of everyone I meet. Broken down.

Then, perhaps in a moment of recognition, she added:

I am dependent on my husband, and he told me that I must get cured. I accept, but as I am lost about anything with him, with his life in which there is nothing for me except the physical comfort, when I get out of your clinic it will be with an idea: to arrange myself in any condition to be able to breathe freely. Life, beauty or death, all that is equal for me.

I must add another thing: this story is the fault of nobody but me. I believed I was a Salamander* and it seems that I am nothing but an impediment.

That summer Scott sent Harold Ober three of Zelda's stories, asking him to show them to Maxwell Perkins for possible publication in *Scribner's Magazine*. After Perkins had seen them he wrote Scott,

I have read Zelda's manuscripts over several times – they came to me while I was away – and I do think they show an astonishing power of expression, and have and convey a curiously effective and strange quality. But they are for a selected audience, and not a large one, and the magazine thinks that on that account, they cannot use them. One would think that if she did enough more they might make a book. Descriptively they are very rare, and the description is not just description. It has a curious emotional content in itself. But for the present I shall have to send them back to Ober. I think one of the little magazines might use them. I wish we could.

*Zelda may have been referring to the mythical salamander, which was able to live in fire and endure it without harm.

I am terribly sorry about Zelda herself. But if she has made progress maybe it should become more rapid, and everything will come out right.

Scott replied that he

was sorry of course about Zelda's stories – possibly they mean more to me than is implicit to the reader who doesn't know from what depths of misery and effort they sprang. One of them, I think now, would be incomprehensible without a waste-land footnote. She has those series of eight portraits that attracted so much attention in *College Humor* and ... I think a book might be got together for next spring if Zelda can add a few more during winter.

But that was wishful thinking, for Zelda was not able to concentrate on anything consistently throughout the rest of the summer and fall of 1930, so completely was she in the relentless grip of the eczema. She wrote to Scott:

... *Please* help me. Every day more of me dies with this bitter and incessant beating I'm taking. You can choose the conditions of our life and anything you want if I don't have to stay here miserable and sick at the mercy of people who have never even tried what its like. Neither would I have if I had understood I *can't* live any more under these conditions, and anyway I'll always know that the 'door is tacticly locked' – if it ever is.

There's no justice – no quiet place of rest left in the world, and the longer I have to bear this the meaner and harder and sicker I get....

Please Please let me out now – Dear, you used to love me and I swear to you that this is no use. You must have seen. You said it was too good to spoil. What's spoiling is me, along with it and I don't see how any-body in the world has a right to do such a thing –

Zelda needed Scott's reassurance and, even more than that, she expected that he alone could explain to her the causes of her malady, and rescue her from them. She wrote desperately to him:

I seem awfully queer to myself, but I know I used to have integrity even if it's gone now – You've *got* to come to me and tell me how I was. Now I see odd things: people's arms too long or their faces as if they were stuffed and they look tiny and far away, or suddenly out of proportion.

... *Please explain* – I want to be well and not bothered with poissons big or little and free to sit in the sun and choose the things I like about people and not have to take the whole person – because it seems to me that you can't see the parts so you can never write about them or even remember them very well –

In September the eczema had grown worse and Dr Forel tried a completely different and experimental approach. He hypnotized Zelda and the results were dramatic. Zelda fell into a deep hypnotic sleep that lasted for thirteen hours and when she awoke the eczema was almost completely gone. It was to reappear again, but in a milder form. Immediately after the treatment Zelda told him that she had felt the eczema oozing in her trance, and she added that she thought there was a link between the eczema and her psychological condition. When she felt normal and realized the danger in her conjugal conflicts the eczema appeared. It came, she thought, as a sort of warning device. Her behaviour toward Scott vacillated between being loving and being nasty. She was impulsively affectionate at moments when Scott least expected it, yet she might turn on him as he responded to her affection.

Looking at the letters which she wrote to Scott during the autumn, one catches the wild fluctuations of her moods. Scott was to incorporate portions of these letters into *Tender Is the Night* to indicate the progress of the relationship between Nicole and Doctor Dick Diver. He moved freely among those letters of Zelda's which were the most peculiarly disordered to those which were intensely loving. However, one notices that even among the latter letters there were often currents of strangeness. She seemed now to need to express her dependence upon Scott, as though it was proof of her sanity.

Goofy, my darling, hasn't it been a lovely day? I woke up this morning and the sun was lying like a birth-day parcel on my table so I opened it up and so many happy things went fluttering into the air: love to Doo-do and the remembered feel of our skins cool against each other in other mornings like a school-mistress. And you 'phoned and said I had written something that pleased you and so

I don't believe I've ever been so heavy with happiness.... Darling
– I love these velvet nights. I've never been able to decide whether
the night was a bitter enemie or a 'grand patron' – or whether I
love you most in the eternal classic half-lights where it blends with
day or in the full religious fan-fare of midnight or perhaps in the
lux of noon – Anyway, I love you most and you 'phoned me just
because you 'phoned me to-night – I walked on those telephone
wires for two hours after holding your love like a parasol to
balance me. My dear –

I'm so glad you finished your story – Please let me read it Friday. And I will be very sad if we have to have two rooms. Please.

Dear. Are you sort of feeling aimless, surprised, and looking
rather reproachful that no melo-drama comes to pass when your
work is over – as if you [had] ridden very hard with a message to
save your army and found the enemy had decided not to attack –
the way you sometimes feel – or are you just a darling little boy
with a holiday on his hands in the middle of the week – the way
you sometimes are – or are you organizing and dynamic and mend-
ing things – the way you sometimes are –

I love you – the way you always are.

Dear –

Good-night –

Dear – dear dear dear dear dear dear

Dear dear dear dear dear dear

Dear dear dear dear dear dear

Dear dear dear dear dear dear

Dear dear dear dear dear dear dear ... [etc.]

Although by the end of October the eczema was nearly cured
there was no essential change in Zelda's mental attitude. She
continued to complain about 'something' in her head which
was not normal. When she was left alone during the day she
daydreamed, and she was unresponsive to questions put directly
to her. She appeared dull and expressionless. Dr Forel began to
fear organic brain damage. By 10 November 1930 the eczema
had reappeared and Zelda grew worse. Dr Forel transferred
Zelda once again to the Eglantine. Scott considered this to be
a major setback and he was dissatisfied with the progress of her
treatment. He played what he called 'a sort of American hunch'

and asked Forel if something else couldn't be tried to expedite her cure. On the 22nd Dr Forel called in Dr Paul Eugen Bleuler for consultation. Bleuler was a distinguished authority on psychosis (specifically schizophrenia, which he had named) in Europe at that time.

Dr Forel says he called in Bleuler to clear his own diagnosis. It was extremely important that he arrive at a correct diagnosis, for the treatment depended upon it. 'The more I saw Zelda, the more I thought at the time: she is neither a pure neurosis (meaning psychogenic) nor a real psychosis – I considered her a constitutional emotionally unbalanced psychopath – she may improve, never completely recover. It was a great help to discuss this difficult patient with Bleuler.' He also mentioned that he had not been able to psychoanalyse Zelda for fear of disturbing and perhaps sacrificing what precious little equilibrium she possessed. Dr Forel wrote, 'Mrs Fitzgerald is more intuitive than intelligent, more brilliant than cultivated.' He noticed that she liked to pretend she was more childish than she actually was; she was also sneaky and, he said, always found ways of avoiding the discipline of the hospital.

Scott wrote Judge and Mrs Sayre telling them of the consultation with Bleuler. He was careful to give all the details of both Forel's and Bleuler's professional standing. '. . . Forel's clinique is as I thought *the best* in Europe, his father having had an extraordinary reputation as a pioneer in the field of psychiatry, and the son being universally regarded as a man of intelligence and character.' Bleuler had been chosen after careful consideration. Dr Jung was Scott's alternative choice, but Jung handled cases of neurosis primarily. The consultations were expensive ($500) and Scott did not want questions of medical etiquette to complicate an already thorny case.

Bleuler spent an afternoon with Zelda and the evening with Forel and Scott. Zelda's personal reaction to Bleuler was succinct; she thought him 'a great imbecile'. Bleuler told Scott that three out of four cases such as Zelda's were discharged as cured, 'perhaps one of those three to resume perfect functioning in the world, and the other two to be delicate and slightly eccentric through life – and the fourth case to go right down hill into total insanity'. Zelda must absolutely not be moved from the clinic to America at the risk of her sanity. Bleuler additionally felt that Zelda's re-entry into the world was going perhaps a little more quickly than it should and that she must be brought along slowly. He reassured Scott (and Scott reassured the Sayres, as well as himself): 'This is something that began about five years ago. Let us hope it is only a process of re-adjustment. Stop blaming yourself. You might have retarded it but you couldn't have prevented it.' Scott asked both doctors if a change in his attitude toward Zelda would help her since, as he explained, Zelda had always shown a preference 'for men of a stable and strong character'. They told him that it was 'possible that a character of tempered steel would help, but Mrs Fitzgerald loved and married the artist in Mr Fitzgerald'.

Once Scott took up residence in Lausanne he began to see Zelda for brief visits once every two or three weeks as Dr Bleuler had recommended. He planned to visit Scottie in Paris once a month for four or five days. It was unsatisfactory, but her life had to continue with as little interruption as was possible under the circumstances of her mother's illness. It was best for her to remain in Paris and continue her schooling there among her friends.

Zelda was not able to write often and her letters to her daughter were therefore few. Her world was not comprehensible to a child and Zelda must have realized how distant she had become from Scottie. She wrote that she wanted Scottie to continue her dancing lessons:

It is excellent to create grace and interest in the arts and I was not pleased that you had to stop, and I hope in the spring you will be capable of going on again as you did before – The saddest thing in my life is that I was no good at it having begun so late – but thats only an excuse on my part, as you have easily guessed I suppose.

She said she missed her 'darling baby' and she was tired of the Swiss landscape, the endless winter, and her own sickness.

If Scott did not actually blame himself for Zelda's collapse he was nevertheless aware of having contributed to it. The very style of their life together was conducive to instability; they had lived hard amidst increasing disorder. It was necessary for Scott to try to comprehend in the most personal terms the calamity that had befallen them. In order to do that he had to write about it. In a manuscript or a letter which was intended for Zelda, or at any rate addressed to her ('Written with Zelda gone to the Clinique'), he attempted to recover those days from their past when things had first begun to go wrong. It is not simply a recapitulation, but the *cri de coeur* of a man who while wounding had been himself deeply wounded.

I know this then – that those days when we came up from the south, from Capri [February–March 1925; Scott had completed *Gatsby* in November 1924], were among my happiest – but you were sick and the happiness was not in the home.

I had been unhappy for a long time then – when my play failed a year and a half before, when I worked so hard for a year twelve stories and novel and four articles in that time with no one believing in me and no one to see except you and before the end your heart betraying me and then I was really alone with no one I liked. In Rome we were dismal and [I] was still working proof and three more stories and in Capri you were sick and there seemed to be nothing left of happiness in the world anywhere I looked.

Then we came to Paris and suddenly I reallized that it hadn't all been in vain. I was a success – the biggest one for the moment in my profession everybody admired me and I was proud I'd done such a good thing. I met Gerald and Sara who took us for friends now and Ernest who was an equal and my kind of an idealist. I got drunk with him on the Left Bank in careless cafés and drank with Sara and Gerald in their garden in St Cloud but you were endlessly sick and at home everything was unhappy. We went to Antibes and I was happy but you were sick still and all that fall and that winter and spring at the cure and I was alone all the time and I had to get drunk before I could leave you so sick and not care and I was only happy a little while before I got too drunk. Afterwards there were all the usual penalties for being drunk.

Finally you got well in Juan-les-Pins and a lot of money came in and I made [one] of those mistakes literary men make – I thought I was a man of the world – that everybody liked me and admired me for myself but I only liked a few people like Ernest and Gerald and Charlie McArthur and Sara who were my peers. Time goes bye fast in those moods and nothing is ever done. I thought then that things came easily – I forgot how I'd dragged the great Gatsby out of the pit of my stomach in a time of misery. I woke up in Hollywood no longer my egotistic, certain self but a mixture of Ernest in fine clothes and Gerald with a career – and Charlie Mc-Arthur with a past. Anybody that could make me believe that, like Lois Moran did, was precious to me.

Ellerslie, the polo people and Mrs Chanler, the party for Cecilia were all attempts to make up from without for being undernourished now from within. Anything to be liked, to be reassured not that I was a man of little genius but that I was a great man of the world. At the same time I knew it was nonsense – the part of me that knew it was nonsense brought us to the Rue Vaugirard.

But now you had gone into yourself just as I had four years before in St Raphael – and there were all the consequences of bad appartments through your lack of patience ('Well, if you want a better appartment why don't you make some money') bad servants through your indifference ('Well, if you don't like her why don't you send Scotty away to school') Your dislike for Vidor, your indifference to Joyce I understood – share your incessant enthusiasm and absorption in the ballet I could not. Somewhere in there I had a sense of being exploited, not by you but by something a resented terribly no happiness. Certainly less than these had ever been at home – you were a phantom washing clothes. . . . I remember desolate trips to Versaille to Phienis, to LaBaule undertaken in sheer weariness of home. I remember wondering why I kept working to pay the bills of this desolate menage I had evolved. In despair I went from the extreme of isolation, which is to say isolation with D———, or the Ritz Bar where I got back my self esteem for half an hour, often with someone I had hardly ever seen before. On the evenings sometimes you and I rode to the Bois in a cab – after awhile I preferred to go to Cafe de Lilas and sit there alone remembering what a happy time I had had there with Ernest, Hadley, Dorothy Parker and Benchley two years before. During all this time, remember I didn't blame anyone but myself. I complained when the house got unbearable but after all I was not John Peale Bishop – I was paying for it with work, that I passionately hated and found more and more difficult to do. The novel was like a dream, daily farther and farther away.

Ellerslie was better and worse. Unhappiness is less acute when one lives with a certain sober dignity but the financial strain was too much. Between Sept when we left Paris and March when we reached Nice we were living at the rate of forty thousand a year.

But somehow I felt happier. Another Spring – I would see Ernest whom I had launched, Gerald and Sarah who through my agency had been able to try the movies. At least life would [seem] less drab; there would be parties with people who offered something, conversations with people with something to say. Later swimming and getting tanned and young and being near the sea.

It worked out beautifully didn't it. Gerald and Sara didn't see us. Ernest and I met but it was a more irritable Ernest, apprehensively telling me his whereabouts lest I come in on them tight and endanger his precarious lease. The discovery that half a dozen people were familiars there didn't help my self-esteem. By the time we reached the beautiful Rivierra I had developed such an inferiority complex that I couldn't face anyone unless I was tight. I worked there too, though, and the unusual combination exploded my lungs.*

You were gone now – I scarcely remember you that summer. You were simply one of all the people who disliked me or were indifferent to me. I didn't like to think of you. – You didn't need me and it was easier to talk to or rather at Madame Bellois and keep full of wine. I was grateful when you came with me to the Doctors one afternoon but after we'd been a week in Paris and I didn't try any more about living or dieing. Things were always the same. The appartments that were rotten, the maids that stank – the ballet before my eyes, spoiling a story to take the Troubetskoys to dinner, poisoning a trip to Africa. You were going crazy and calling it genius – I was going to ruin and calling it anything that came to hand. And I think everyone far enough away to see us outside of our glib presentations of ourselves guessed at your almost meglomaniacal selfishness and my insane indulgence in drink. Toward the end nothing much mattered. The nearest I ever came to leaving you was when you told me you [thought] that I was a fairy in the Rue Palatine but now whatever you said aroused

---

*At various periods in Fitzgerald's life he referred to having had tuberculosis. Usually it was a pretext to cover his drinking. And because he was something of a hypochondriac it is difficult to decide if he suffered from tuberculosis to the degree that he thought he did. According to his biographer Arthur Mizener, Scott did suffer a mild attack in 1919, and in 1929 'he had what subsequently proved to have been a tubercular hemorrhage . . .'

a sort of detached pity for you. For all your superior observation and your harder intelligence I have a faculty of guessing right, without evidence even with a certain wonder as to why and whence that mental short cut came. I wish the Beautiful and Damned had been a maturely written book because it was all true. We ruined ourselves – I have never honestly thought that we ruined each other.

The letter breaks off here, incomplete. Zelda was in even less of a position to cope with the fissures within their marriage than Scott. In a letter that may have been a reaction to this one of Scott's, she struck back.

Your letter is not difficult to answer with promptitude since I have done nothing but turn over cause and effect in my mind for some time. Also your presentation of the situation is poetic, even if it has no bearing on the truth: your working to preserve the family and my working to get away from it. If you so refer to giving your absolute minimum of effort both to your work and to our mutual welfare with no hope or plans for the future save the vague capricices which drive you from one place to another, I envy you the mental processes which can so distort conditions into a rectitude of attitude for you. You have always told me that I had no right to complain as long as I was materially cared for, so take whatever comfort you may find in whatever self-justification you can construct. Also, I quite understand the restless dissatisfaction which drives you from existing conditions since I have been through it myself, even to the point of being completely dependent on a mentality which had neither the desire nor the necessity of touching mine for the small crumbs of beauty that I found I must have to continue. This is not a treatise of recriminations, but I would like you to understand clearly why there are certain scenes not only toward the end which could never be effaced from my mind. I am here, and since I have no choice, I will try to mister the grace to rest peacefully as I should, but our divergence is too great as you must realize for us to ever be anything except a hash to-gether and since we have never found either help or satisfaction in each other the best thing is to seek it separately. You might as well start whatever you start for a divorce immediately.

When you saw in Paris that I was sick, sinking – when you knew that I went for days without eating, incapable of supporting contact with even the servants – You sat in the bathroom and sang 'Play in your own Backyard'. Unfortunately, there wasn't any yard: it was a public playground apparently. You introduced me to ———— and sat me beside ———— one moment and the next disparaged and belittled the few friends I knew whose eyes had gathered their softness at least from things that I understood. Some justification has always been imperative to me, and I could never function simply from the necessity for functioning not even to save myself as the King of Greece once told Ernest Hemmingway was the most important thing of all as you so illuminatingly told me.

You will have all the things you want without me, and I will find something. You will have some nice girl who will not care about the things that I cared about and you will be happier. For us, there is not the slightest use, even if we wanted to try which I assure you I do not – not even faintly. In listing your qualities I can not find even one on which to base any possible relationship, except your good looks, and there are *dozens* of people with that: the head-waiters at the Plaza and ———— and my coiffeur in Paris – as you know, my memories are mostly lost in sound and smell, so there isn't even that, I'm sorry. In Paris, I hope you will get Scottie out of the city heat now that she has finished school.

Later, in a calmer mood, she wrote again:

I am tired of rummaging my head to understand a situation that would be difficult enough if I were completely lucid. I cannot arbitrarily accept blame now when I know that in the past I felt none. Anyway, blame doesn't matter.... Try to understand that people are not always reasonable when the world is as unstable and vacillating as a sick head can render it – that for months I have been living in vaporous places peopled with one-dimensional figures and tremulous buildings until I can no longer tell an optical illusion from a reality – that head and ears incessantly throb and roads disappear, until finally I lost all control and powers of judgement and was semi-imbecilic when I arrived here.

At the end of November Zelda wrote Dr Forel:

Can't you please explain to me why I should spend five months of my life in sickness and suffering seeing nothing but optical illusions to devitalize something in me that you yourself have found indespensible and that my husband has found so agreeable as to neglect shamefully his wife during the last four years.... I am forced to bear the hopeless months of the past and God knows what in the future. Exalted sophistries are not much of a prop. *Why do I have to go backwards when everybody else who can goes on? ... and if you do cure me whats going to happen to all the bitterness and unhappiness in my heart –* It seems to me a sort of castration, but since I am powerless I suppose I will have to submit, though I am neither young enough nor credulous enough to think that you can manufacture out of nothing something to replace the song I had.

Christmas 1930: the nightmare darkened. Although Zelda had asked to see Scottie, she behaved badly when confronted by her, breaking the ornaments on their tree and talking incoherently. Scott took Scottie skiing at Gstaad to try to mitigate what must have been a painful and upsetting scene for the child.

Suddenly, at the end of January, Scott's father died in Washington. Deeply sorrowful at the loss, he planned to return to America immediately for the funeral. Before he left there was a final meeting with Zelda. In his detailed report to Dr Forel, he said that, although a first-year medical student could phrase it better than he could, he had a theory about Zelda which he wished to put forth. He then plotted the course of her illness in outline form from age fifteen to the present. His notion was that some 'uneliminated poison attacks the nerves'.

In brief my idea is this. *That the eczema is not relative but is the clue to the whole business. I believe that the eczema is a definite concurrent product of every struggle back toward the normal, just as an alcoholic has to struggle back through a period of depression.* ... I can't help clinging to the idea that some essential physical things like salt or iron or semen or some unguessed at holy water is either missing or is present in too great quantity.

Scott felt that Zelda needed some intense form of physical activity to aid her in the cure. Her poor eyesight and her highly developed artistic sense made embroidery, carpentry, and bookbinding insufficiently involving; nor were these activities, he felt certain, any real substitute for sweating.

Zelda, too, was moved by his father's death, as well as by Scott's grief. He said she literally clung to him for an hour.

Then she went into the other personality and was awful to me at lunch. After lunch she returned to the affectionate tender mood, utterly normal, so that with pressure I could have manoeuvred her into intercourse but the eczema was almost visibly increasing so I left early. Toward the very end she was back in the schizophrania.

Zelda realized that their meeting had not been satisfactory and wrote him a note in an effort to reach him before he was at sea. 'I would have been so happy to help you. A neurose is not much good in times of distress to others. . . .'

With Scott in America Zelda suddenly began to improve. No one on the staff linked her beginning recovery to Scott's absence, but it must have been related for it was astonishing how rapidly she now began to take hold. She ate her meals at the table regularly with the other patients, and the odd little smile which had uncontrollably marked her expression from the beginning of her illness disappeared. She also began to ski every day at nearby St Cergues when the snow was good. There were photographs taken of her smiling happily in her chamois jacket, her hair flying. It was as if the skiing itself were an indication that the tide of her illness had turned in her favour. Scott had guessed right when he said that she needed physical exercise. She apparently needed distance from him.

During Scott's stay in America he managed a brief trip to Montgomery to see the Sayres about Zelda. The Judge was ill with the flu, and the visit was only a partial success. It did, however, serve to reassure Mrs Sayre about Zelda's recovery, and she was grateful to Scott for having come.

As the spring passed it became clear that Zelda had definitely improved. The tone of her letters changed and her relationship to Scott was slowly evolving into one more loving and less charged with bitterness and recrimination. She thought back on good times they had shared together.

I keep thinking of Provence and thin brown people slowly absorbing the deep shade of Aix – the white glare on the baking dust of a country pounded into colorless oblivion by an incessantly rotating summer – I'd like awfully to be there – Avignon must be

perfect now, to feel the wide quiet of the Rhone, and Arles obliter-
ating its traces with the hum of cafés under the great trees – I'd
like to be eating the lunch we had at Chateau Neuf du Pap, where
the air was not vibrant and full of the whole spectrum – looking
over a deep valley full of grape-vines and heat and far away the
palace of the Popes like a mirage –

I would like to be walking alone in a Sirocco at Cannes at night
passing under the dim lamps and imagining myself mysterious and
unafraid like last summer –

At the end of the letter her tone changed into something other
than poetic reminiscence, as if she were trying to ascertain
what degree of change comparable to her own might have taken
place in Scott.

I would like to be working – what would you like? Not work, I
know, and not lone places. Would you like to be in New York
with a play in rehearsal like you always said? and to have decorative
people about you – to be reading Spengler, or what? It is not possible that you should really want to be in the hurry and disorder
of the Ritz Bar and Mont Matre and the high excitability of scenes
like the party we went to with McGowan where you passed so
much of your time recently –

She asked that Scott send her books to read; she wanted Spengler's *The Decline of the West* and a book on playwriting that
he had once promised her. 'I have been reading Joyce and find
it a nightmare in my present condition. . . .' She did not want
anything in French, 'since I have enough difficulty with English
for the moment and *not* Lawrence and *not* Virginia Wolf or
anybody who writes by dipping the broken threads of their
heads into the ink of literary history, please –'

Throughout the spring and into June she and Scott were able
to see more of one another without the side effects of eczema
or irritation that their earlier meetings had provoked in Zelda.
It rained steadily on the lake now, and the dreariness of the
days made her a little sad.

I can't write. I tried all afternoon – and I just twisted the pencil
round and round. . . . When you can't write you sit on the bed and

look so woe-begone like a person who's got to a store and can't remember what they wanted to buy –

Good-night, dear. If you were in my bed it might be the back of your head I was touching where the hair is short and mossy or it might be up in the front where it make[s] little caves about your forehead, but wherever it was it would be the sweetest place, the sweetest place.

When they met now, there were day trips taken together at Lausanne and Geneva for shopping, or luncheons of hot chocolate and apricot tarts and whipped cream at the cafés. When they could not meet, Zelda wrote to him telling him how she felt and what she was doing, and how much she missed him.

And theres always my infinite love – You are a sweet person – the sweetest and dearest of all and I love you as I love my vanished youth – which is as much as a human heart can hold –

It continued to rain and the sky, Zelda wrote, was

filled with copper clouds like the after-math of cannon-fire, pre-war, civil-war clouds and I feel all empty and bored and very much in love with you, my dear one, my own. I wish you were here so we could stretch our legs down beside one another and feel all warm and hidden in the bed, like seeds beaten into the earth. Why is there happiness and comfort and excitement where you are and no where else in the world, and why is there a sleepy tremulo in the air when you are near that's promising and living like a vibrating fecundity?

And then her last line, to tease and please him : 'excuse me for being so intellectual. I know you would prefer something nice and feminine and affectionate.'

Gerald Murphy, who was living with his family in Switzerland, recalled Fitzgerald's coming to see him that spring : 'Scott called me and said, "At last she is asking to see someone. She wants to see you, Gerald." We knew how important that was. It was a breakthrough. But he warned me that it might be a terrible experience and he didn't want to press me into going if I felt I couldn't. I remember telling him that of course I would go – and feeling absolutely terrified at the same time.'

Dr Forel screened him carefully before letting him see Zelda. He explained what she had been through and cautioned Gerald against mentioning certain things that were known to upset her.

'She had chosen basket therapy when she was well enough and she was outside in a courtyard working on one when I went to visit her. I remember spotting her near a lovely old house – there was a fig tree near her and I noticed that she was watching me without seeming to do so. I had to cross the entire courtyard and that was the most God awful long walk that I have ever made. She looked altered, *distrait*. I moved as calmly as I could and when I reached her I smiled and said that all my life I had wanted to make baskets like hers – great, heavy, stout baskets. She accepted that, smiled back at me and asked, 'Where did you come from?' I told her where we were living and that I was on my way to Geneva, I had just stopped to say hello. Actually, I stayed less than five minutes with her, but it was a harrowing experience.'

Zelda began to take trips with other patients (rather than in the company of nurses) into Berne and Geneva, and she asked Scott how he could love 'a silly girl who buys cheese and plaited bread from enchanted princes in the public market and eats them on the streets. . . .' As her world expanded she tried to let Scott know how delicious her freedom was, as well as how much she missed his presence.

Darling –

I went to Geneva all by myself with a fellow maniac and the city was thick and heavy before the rain. . . . and I wanted to be in Lausanne with you – . . . Have you ever been so lonely that you felt eternally guilty – as if you'd left off part of your clothes –

. . . .

I hope you know they are kisses splattering you[r] balcony to-night from a lady who was once, in three separate letters, a princess in a high white tower and who has never forgotten her elevated station in life and who is waiting once more for her royal darling

Good-night, honey –

In July there were two idyllic weeks that Zelda spent with
Scott and Scottie at Annecy. They said they would 'never go
there again because those weeks had been perfect and no other
time could match them'. They played tennis and fished and
danced in the warm nights by the lake, 'white shoes gleaming
like radium in the damp darkness. It was like the good times
when we still believed in summer hotels and the philosophies
of popular songs.'

When she was back she teased him playfully, lovingly:

My dearest and most precious Monsieur,
   We have here a kind of maniac who seems to have been inspired
with erotic aberrations on your behalf. Apart from that she is a
person of excellent character, willing to work, would accept a nomi-
nal salary while learning, fair complexion, green eyes would like
correspondance with refined young man of your description with
intent to marry. Previous experience unnecessary. Very fond of
family life and a wonderful pet to have in the home. Marked behind
the left ear with a slight tendency to schitzoprenie.

Toward the end of the summer Dr Forel suggested that the
Fitzgeralds take another trip together – a trial run so that Zelda
might work her way back into society. The Murphys had taken
up residence at an old manor house in the Austrian Tyrol; they
likened it to a hunting lodge, with its sanded floors and white
walls. It was simple and solid and it stood amid beautiful fields
of grain. As it was not far from Switzerland, the Fitzgeralds
decided to visit them there. Zelda would be with people she
liked, she could relax, and the atmosphere was both refreshing
and calming. 'At first we were petrified at the idea of their
coming', Gerald Murphy said. 'But once she was there she
enjoyed it so, relished it, really. Scott was delighted with the
place and enormously reassured by Zelda's behaviour.' One
incident marred the long weekend that the Fitzgeralds spent
with them, but it had nothing to do with Zelda. The Murphys
had brought with them their nursemaid for their own three
children. In the evening when it was time for their baths the
nurse asked Scottie (who was nearly ten) if she wanted her
bath as well. Scottie rebelled. 'She was sure the bathwater was

dirty; she thought Mademoiselle had used the same water to bathe each of the three Murphy children. It was cloudy and she ran and told her mother and father. Zelda took it beautifully, but Scott – well, Scott behaved like a child, he made a great deal of fuss over the whole thing.' Bath salts, which clouded the water, had been used to soften it, and Scottie thought it was dirty. Scott may also have been more worried than he let on about the tuberculosis of one of the Murphy sons. He had always thought of himself as tubercular and he must have been anxious about Scottie's coming in contact with it. Gerald Murphy said: 'Well, it's all written into *Tender Is the Night* – changed a little of course. But we were stunned, we would never have dreamed of washing them all in the same water!'

Zelda had passed those various tests of her ability to cope with her life with Scott and her child. She was now able to reassure Scott when he felt blue about their future together.

Please don't be depressed: nothing is sad about you except your sadness and the frayed places on your pink kimona and that you care so much about everything – You are the only person who's ever done all they had to do, damn well, and had enough left over to be dissatisfied ... Can't you possibly be just a little bit glad that we are alive and that all the year that's coming we can be to-gether and work and love and get some peace for all the things we've paid so much for learning? Stop looking for solace: there isn't any, and if there were life would be a baby affair ...

Stop thinking about our marriage and your work and human relations – you are not a showman arranging an exhibit – You are a Sun-god with a wife who loves him and an artist – to take in, assimilate and all alterations to be strictly on paper –

On 15 September 1931, after a year and three months of treatment, Zelda was released from Prangins. Her case was summarized as a 'reaction to her feelings of inferiority (primarily toward her husband). . . .' She was stated to have had ambitions which were 'self-deceptions' and which 'caused difficulties between the couple'. Her prognosis was favourable – as long as conflicts could be avoided.

The Fitzgeralds motored to Paris and from there went on to board the *Aquitania* for the United States. On a sunny day during the crossing, with Scottie playing shuffleboard next to them, Scott took a snapshot of Zelda sitting on a canvas deck chair. She is wearing sturdy low-heeled shoes and her hair is pushed back clumsily beneath a pale beret. She is smoking a cigarette and on her lap balances a large sketching pad. She is not smiling, but scowls against the sun. If it were not that the photograph is included in the Fitzgeralds' scrapbook and labelled 'Homeward bound on the Aquitania' one could not identify Zelda, for she is altered and aged beyond recognition. She has lost her good looks and what remained was a face hardened by suffering and despair.

Earlier that year when it had seemed to her that she might recover she had written Scott: 'I can't make head or tails out of all this dreary experience since I do not know how much was accidental and how much deliberate – how big a role circumstance played and what proportion was voluntary – but if such a thing as expiation exists it is taking place and I hope you will forgive me the rest of my part –'

They stayed in New York only a few days before travelling to Alabama to see Zelda's anxious family. They were considering settling in Montgomery, perhaps even buying a house. At last Scott would be able to return to his novel, which he had not touched thus far in 1931, while Zelda set up housekeeping.

Montgomery was a haven from the Depression, which seemed to have had no effect upon life there, and even the passage of time left the city unaltered. Zelda wrote, 'In Alabama, the streets were sleepy and remote and a calliope on parade gasped out the tunes of our youth.' 'Nothing', she added, 'had happened there since the Civil War.'

The Fitzgeralds searched for a house and found one at 819 Felder Avenue, which was on the edge of Montgomery's first suburb, Cloverdale. It was, as usual, an improbable place, far too large for them. They hired a Negro couple to take care of housekeeping and cooking as well as the secondhand Stutz they had just bought. They acquired a white Persian cat, which they called Chopin, and a bloodhound, named Trouble. Life settled down to a quiet routine of football games, tennis, and golf, and visiting old friends. By October Scott was bored and wrote in his Ledger, 'life dull'.

Zelda seemed peculiar to her friends, few of whom knew about her recent breakdown, and her appearance startled them. She was haggard and her mouth fell into a slight smile, as if she were permanently amused. The Fitzgeralds had always provided Montgomerians with a topic of conversation and gossip, but now it was no longer entirely out of envy that their names came up. Someone overheard them quarrelling about a suicide pact made in the early days of their marriage when they had promised that at thirty-five they'd call it quits. The notion had definitely lost its appeal for Scott, who turned thirty-five that September. He wrote at the top of his Ledger, 'Recession and Procession', adding, 'Zelda well, worse, better. Novel intensive begins.'

Zelda began to feel increasingly uncomfortable in Montgomery. She felt surrounded by women of limited horizons. 'You know the kind: women of fifty still known as "Baby".' She gave a friend a copy of Faulkner's new novel, *Sanctuary*, and was delighted when she learned that the woman was sleepless after reading it. She wondered if it mightn't do many of the women in Montgomery good to be shocked out of their complacency.

Judge Sayre was gravely ill. He had not recovered from the influenza of the previous spring and the strain of his long sickness exhausted Mrs Sayre. Outwardly she was composed, even calm, but she tended to reminisce more than she had before, as if her memories gave her comfort. It was in the midst of this atmosphere of illness and impending death that Scott announced his plans to go to Hollywood. An offer came via Harold Ober to work on a film script under the direction of Irving Thalberg, and Scott felt he could not turn it down. The money was good and he was eager to try his hand at films again after his rankling failure in 1927. He would be gone no more than eight weeks and be home by Christmas.

Even before Scott left, Zelda had begun to work on her writing. It was the only field she felt remained open to her in which she might be able to accomplish something professionally. Dancing was now permanently out of the question, for she was no longer in top physical condition and she realized the limitations of both her age and her ability. She felt her talents as a painter were second-rate and, besides, her poor eyesight made painting difficult and tiring. She had attracted a modest amount of attention as a short-story writer in the *College Humor* pieces and she hoped there would be a market for the kind of stories she wanted to write. Writing regularly, with an astonishing degree of self-discipline and speed, she finished at least seven stories and began planning a novel during the period Scott was in Hollywood. Only one of the stories was a revision from the previous summer, and they were usually mailed to Harold Ober just as soon as they were typed. Unfortunately, only one of the stories was published and none survive in manuscript. The synopses kept by Ober give us our only clue to their general content.

Two stories were Southern in their locale and in both there was a clutter of sensational events: miscegenation, attempted incest, a shooting, and automobile accidents were elements about which the stories turned. The others centred on the chic worlds of Long Island and Europe. But no matter what their themes were, Ober could not sell them.

In notes accompanying the stories, Zelda asked Ober what he thought about them and suggested where they might be published. '*Please* tell me your *frank* opinion. . . . I wish we could sell something. Can't we *give* them away? I feel sure 'Nuts' is a good story, why won't Scribner's take it? It's so satisfactory to be in print.' Scribner's did eventually take it (if 'Nuts' refers, as it seems to, to 'A Couple of Nuts') and it was published the following summer. It was a good story, possibly the best of Zelda's short fiction. It possesses a Fitzgeraldian aura of romance falling apart but it is unmistakably Zelda's. All too frequently her stories had failed because they became homilies on conduct overly laden with description of setting. Her characters froze into prototypes rather than growing as memorable and separate people. But in 'A Couple of Nuts' Zelda was in control of her talent.

The story is about a young American couple, Larry and Lola, who play the banjo and sing in a club in Paris. They are 'young and decorative' and 'In those days of going to pieces and general disintegration it was charming to see them together'. Their innocent youthfulness and good looks soon made them a fashionable pair among the rich. They attract a patron who introduces them on the Riviera, where they become a success. 'Their stuff was spectacularly American and they made a killing at it, being simple kids.' Within a year they are a vogue, but they've also become calculating. Lola is romantically involved with their patron and careless; Larry's role is to ignore the situation, which he does. There is a casual reference to an abortion, which they have to borrow money to cover. Eventually Larry persuades Lola to leave with him for America, where, he believes, they can make a name for themselves. We learn of their flop in the States through the patron, who had been instrumental in providing them with an introduction to the smart club in America where they failed. The plot becomes complicated at this point as Mabel, the patron's ex-wife, falls for Larry. Lola retaliates by bringing a lawsuit for a hundred thousand dollars against them. It saddens the narrator to think back on the couple, for 'They had possessed something precious that most of us never have: a jaunty confidence in life and in each other. . . .' At the end of the story Larry and Mabel are drowned on Mabel's yacht. Lola survives with a lonely existence before her. The narrator remembers the times they had shared together and the night he was given their Paris address: 'I had promised to send them some songs from home – songs about love and success and beauty.'

Those three words were the themes of Zelda's fiction, and of her life before her breakdown. The missing word was *ruin*. She understood that a failure of love made meaningless the otherwise potent nouns *success* and *beauty* – each of which was liable to impermanence. There is in the story an indictment of the rich as seducers nearly as strong as Hemingway's was to be in *A Moveable Feast*. Except that Zelda points out both the responsibility and the foolishness of those who take their attention as anything more than part of an intricate game, in which the rich play as masters with little at stake.

The story was reviewed in St Paul by James Gray, who knew the Fitzgeralds. He called it a companion piece to *Gatsby*, and added that a dual egotism had sustained the main characters – an absorption in each other was the first thing that distinguished them – as it had Scott and Zelda, he might have added.

That absorption in each other had already left its mark on both their lives, and now that Scott was in Hollywood Zelda felt intensely her need for him, his company, and his reassurance. During the eight weeks that Scott was gone Zelda wrote him thirty-odd letters. In these letters she again and again told him of her dependence upon him. She had sensed Scott's boredom in Montgomery, feeling bored to some extent herself, but she was more than a little uneasy about his abrupt trip to Hollywood without her.

Roaming Montgomery during her morning walks, she found the old blind bugler from the Civil War who had sold candy to her and Scott when they were courting, and bought a cream bar from him for remembrance's sake. She continued working on her short stories and she began to read one of Scott's stories every night before falling asleep. Once while reading 'The Offshore Pirate' she wrote him, 'You were younger than anybody in the world once – what fun you must have had in that curious place that's younger than life.' In full admiration of the excellence of 'Absolution' she told him, 'I will never be able to write like that.'

Rereading his stories was in part a gesture of love made in his absence, but Zelda was also reading them in order to learn how to construct fiction. It was inevitable that she would model her work on his. The social and emotional territory of their work had always been strikingly similar. She now became deeply aware of Scott's skill as a writer, and her opinion of her own work suffered by comparison. Unfortunately this stimulated one of the symptoms of her illness, competitiveness toward Fitzgerald. For what she was doing now was measuring her abilities as a writer against his – and finding her own lacking.

In her letters to him she constantly belittled her own attempts and insisted that her writing was not going well: '. . . my stuff (the last two since you left) has got too thin and spiritless to be worth the effort. With some ruinous facility junk flows and is utterly worthless.' Still, she finished her stories and continued with others, all the while writing him, 'I do not believe I can write.' When she did not hear immediately from Ober she began to think she was writing for herself. No one, or at least neither Scott nor Zelda nor the Sayres, questioned the intense speed at which she was working. The isolation she must have required in order to write did not then strike Fitzgerald as being at all out of hand, nor did it remind him of that period just prior to her breakdown in Paris when she was extremely productive, writing at a tremendous clip, while continuing her ballet.

Suddenly in early November the Judge grew worse. 'Daddy is sinking rapidly the Doctors say. I only go once a day and take Mamma for a long drive, since he is completely unconscious and does not know us or seem to want anybody about.' On the night of 17 November he died. Zelda was notified the following morning. She wired Scott of the Judge's death and when she had a moment to herself she wrote to him in those abstract terms with which she had learned to describe her father, calling his death 'the end of another brave, uncompromising effort to preserve conceptions –'. She added as an afterthought, 'I wonder what ironic sequence, what stamina of spirit Daddy has carried over that made him think so little of the world and so much of justice and integrity?'

At his death the State of Alabama paid him its highest honours. At the capitol the main entrance to the supreme court chamber was draped with black crepe and the flag flew at half staff. Roses were cut from the grounds of the capitol and placed around his casket. A simple burial sermon was read and there were no hymns, for the Judge had requested that manifestations of sentiment be avoided. Zelda bought a blanket of flowers for the Judge's coffin because, she wrote Scott, no one else in the family had the money to do it and 'I knew how you felt towards Daddy and that you would have wanted us to.' She told him the Judge looked 'very little in his clothes', and she said simply, 'It's just the little personal things we care about in people. . . . Who cares what good or evil dies? And all of us care that we will never hear a certain chuckle again or see the fingers meet a certain way.'

In an obituary in the Montgomery newspaper, after the Judge had been praised for his excellence and fairness it was noted: 'The remarkable thing about his success before the people is that he was in no sense a politician. We doubt if any holder of a State office in the last 20 years has known so few Alabamians personally as Judge Sayre. He did not make speeches, he did not go about over the State much, he was not a joiner.'

A few days after the funeral, Zelda and her mother went to the capitol and closed the Judge's office. Zelda told Scott how it had looked, 'musty and masculine and cerebral', with a gorgeous butterfly pinned over a map of the L & N railroad lines, some dusty cotton shirt samples and a copy of Josephus.

Zelda managed to keep her equilibrium throughout the difficult ordeal of her father's illness and death, but she began to suffer signs of distress that were all too familiar to her. She wrote to Scott that her eyes were bothering her, that she had been sleepless with asthma* and had recently noticed touches of eczema 'which I could not trace since I have done my best to lead as healthy a life as possible so you would find me fresh and cheerful when you got back'. Her father's death had filled the house with relatives and that climate of bereavement was a great strain on her. It was doubly difficult without Scott. She wrote him, 'Life is horrible without you because there's not another living soul with whom I have the slightest communion.'

On her mother's birthday, which was only a few days after the Judge's death, Zelda invited her family to lunch.

Anthony's wife is awfully nice and Tilde is pretty and Marjorie is good and kind and there we were: All Daddy had to leave behind. Mamma sat in that more aristocratic world where she and Daddy have always lived. She is so sweet and foolish and infinitely courageous.

But even with her family around her she felt isolated and out of place.

I feel like a person lost in some Gregorian but feminine service here – I have come in on the middle and did not get the beginning and cannot stay for the end but must somehow seize the meaning – It's awful to think that Daddy isn't here any more – I would like to pick up Mamma and go –

Her family fatigued her and she felt remote from them, yet

* Zelda first developed asthma when she was twenty-three. Fitzgerald later told Dr Forel she was allergic to moose hair.

obliged to make an attempt to understand them and keep in their company. When Scott wrote back to her about Hollywood Zelda replied that if he again mentioned 'Lily Dalmita or Constance I will go off to Florida for a week and spend our money and make you jealous of my legs à la Creole when you get home'.

Then, as her asthma grew more harassing she did decide to spend a long weekend on the coast of Florida to recuperate. She told Scott that although she had everything in the world in Montgomery, except him, she needed to get away.

I know I am nervous and too introspective and stale – . . . just long riding rolling along will give me back the calm and contentment that has temporarily disappeared with my physical well-being. Please understand and do not think that I leave in search of any fictitious pleasure. After the utter solitude of Prangin there have been many people lately and people that I love with whom my relations are more than superficial and I really think I need a day or two by myself.

But Scott did not understand and had misgivings about her travelling alone. Zelda in turn was hurt by his lack of confidence in her. 'If you feel that I am such an irresponsible person you should have left me in the clinic.' She added that she did not intend to do anything to injure him or herself.

I wish you could believe that though I may have transitory and uncorrelated ideas and impulses which make it difficult to appear as a solid individual, still they are more fleeting always and my actions accord with what I would like to be – as well as I am able.

Scott did not want to rob her of her self-confidence just when she was doing so well and he relented. Before she left she wrote him:

Scottie and I have had a long bed-time talk about the Soviets and the Russian idea. . . . You will be absolutely ravished by her riding trousers and yellow shirt and Scottie rearing back in her saddle like a messenger of victory. Each time she goes she conquers herself and the pony, the sky, the fields and the little black boy who follows on a fast shaven mule. I wish I were a fine sweet person like you two and not somebody who has to go 200 miles because they have a touch of asthma.... I hope you haven't worked yourself to death. We *must* reduce our scale of living since we will always be equally extravagant as now. It would be easier to start from a lower base. This is sound economics and what Ernest and most of our friends do.

She travelled to Florida, and as a compromise took along a trained nurse.

The day before Thanksgiving Zelda received a recording of Scott's voice which delighted both her and Scottie. 'It made me feel all safe in the centre of things again and important.' She played it over and over. She told him she was busy writing, but 'Fantastic exhuberance has deserted me and everything presents itself in psychological terms for novels.' Certainly she had been working very hard on her stories, but as yet none of them had been sold and perhaps a novel would do better. She said she wanted to send her stories to Scott, 'but I know you are absorbed in your own so I'll do the best I can and send it on to Ober. Darling I miss you so not having anyone to trust and talk to intellectually. There's no use asking anybody else's opinion because I don't care what it is.'

The fact that Zelda did not show Scott her stories for his opinion or approval, while reiterating her deep need for him, is worth notice. The ambivalence that lay behind it would reappear when she completed the manuscript of her novel, with disastrous consequences.

On Thanksgiving Day after the turkey dinner at her mother's she wrote Scott again:

It makes me remember all the times we've been to-gether absolutely alone in some suspended hour, a holiday from Time prowling about in those quiet place alienated from past and future where there is no sound save listening and vision is an anesthetic.... My story limps homeward, 1,000 words to a gallon of coffee.... I have a *wonderful* plot for a short thing that I will get at as soon as I can. It's for your Christmas.... It's fun thinking of Christmas and the night you will get home and how you'll look as you come out the gate. I will be surprised at your mondanity [?] and very amazed that you are concise and powerful and I will be very happy that you are so handsome and when I see how handsome you are my stomach will fall with many un-pleasant emotions like a cake with too many raisins and I will want to shut you up in a closet like a dress too beautiful to wear.

It was only with Scott gone that she realized how dependent upon him she had become; it was as if he were a source of energy for her to draw upon. It was not that she hadn't ideas of her own; it was that she needed him to confirm them and herself. She asked him repeatedly, 'Do you love me so *very* much like I do you?' 'Is it possible for a person to be as absolutely perfect as I think you are.' The tone grew to be obsessional.

Deo, my love, my one, my person, I miss you so terribly. It seems a year since you went and it's very pale and pathetic just trailing about in the wake of your thoughts. When you are not there everything presents itself only in terms of your impressions and I have no independent self save the one that lives in you – so I'm never thoroughly conscious except when you're near.

She left Scott's hat in the hallway and his cane on their bed, '... and you could not tell that it's all just a bluff and a make-shift without you'. She kept the light on in his study at night so that she would think he was there when she woke up. And she said her disposition suffered in his absence; maybe it was the result of her asthma attacks. 'I am going to dig myself a bear-pit and sit inside thumbing my nose at the people who bring me carrots and then I will be perfectly happy.' Caught up among her own imaginings she told Scott some bears were lovely and pleasant and lived on honey and wildflowers. 'But I will be a very dirty bear with burrs in my coat and my nice silky hair all matted with mud and I will growl and move my head about disconsolately.' She said he must never go off without her again.

These letters suggest that without Scott Zelda's own existence and estimation of herself were impaired. She may have exaggerated her sense of dependence on him in order to demonstrate to him and to herself how perfectly normal she had become, for part of Forel's cure had been a somewhat mysterious 're-education' of Zelda in terms of her role as wife to Scott. That may have instilled in Zelda a standard of normality against which she tried to measure herself. That it seems to have been foreign to her individual temperament and personality was not taken into consideration. Certainly it seems strained for Zelda to write, 'We are like a lot of minor characters at table waiting for the entrance of the star.' But in 1931 that was her tone.

In late November Scott wrote Dr Forel from Hollywood about Zelda. He said that she was well, living cautiously, and drinking no alcohol whatsoever. He said that their relationship had never been better. He also mentioned that Zelda had begun writing. The death of the Judge, which he said they had expected, Zelda had taken in her stride. He had felt no hesitation about leaving her to go to Hollywood.

Scott mocked Hollywood and he never entirely got over the feeling that there was something demeaning about going there to write. But it intrigued him as a place of false glamour against which a part of him competed for attention. He went to the parties and allowed his real charm to dissolve in alcohol. In early December he must have written Zelda about his dissatisfaction at the studios; for she replied:

I'm sorry your work isn't interesting. I had hoped it might present new dramatic facets that would make up for the tediousness of it. If it seems too much drudgery and you are faced with 'get to-gether and talk-it-over' technique – come home, Sweet. You will at least have eliminated Hollywood forever. I wouldn't stay and waste time on what seems an inevitable mediocrity and too hard going.

Although Zelda never directly told Scott of her anxieties about Hollywood, they once took shape in a nightmare, which clearly revealed her sense of impending panic about Scott and herself.

Dearest, My Love:
I had the most horrible dream about you last night. You came home with a great shock of white hair and you said it had turned suddenly from worrying about being unfaithful. You had the big leather carry-all trunk you have always talked about buying and in it were two huge canvasses, landscapes, with the trees stuffed and made of cloth and hanging off like doll's arms. O Goofo! I love you so and I've been mad all day because of that dream.

She added that she missed him and wanted him near; then, astonishingly, she wrote: 'It's wonderful that we have never had a cross word or done bad things to each other. Wouldn't it be awful if we had?' She said that Scott was all she cared about on earth, 'the past discredited and disowned, the future has doubled up on the present; give me the peace of my one certitude – that I love you. It's the only instance in my life of my intelligence backing up my emotions – That was an awful dream – awful dear. I didn't want to live and you were only formally sorry.' In the last sentence she said she didn't mean anything she had written: 'I want you to have a good time and take what you can from everywhere and love me if you want to and be kind –' She did not, of course, mean that at all. She wanted him home with her where she could be sure of him – and of herself.

Continuing to read his short stories, she wanted to cry over 'The Sensible Thing', a story Scott had written about their abortive courtship and his losing her:

Reading your stories makes me curious more than ever about you. I don't suppose I really know you very well – but I know you smell like the delicious damp grass that grows near old walls and that your hands are beautiful opening out of your sleeves and that the back of your head is a mossy sheltered cave when there is trouble in the wind and that my cheek just fits the depression in your shoulder.

In the December issue of *Scribner's Magazine* a story of Zelda's appeared, 'Miss Ella' (sometimes referred to as 'Miss Bessie', possibly its title in manuscript), which had been written in Switzerland. It was an ambitious story and as closely constructed as Zelda could make it at that time.

'Miss Ella' was one of Zelda's Southern stories, and it is hard to imagine either the situation of the story or its central character as existing in any other area of the world than the American South. Ella is a Victorian spinster who lives a highly ordered life in which everything has its proper place. She keeps fit by standing up twenty minutes after each meal; she naps until the hot midday sun has cooled, and at five she goes for a drive in a carriage with her ancient aunt. The grounds of her home are hidden behind a high wall, which the children of the neighbourhood climb only after the departure of Miss Ella. On the other side of the wall is a wooden playhouse which charms them. The playhouse is half hidden in a thicket by masses of overgrown flowers and it conceals inside a rusting shotgun and some dried apple blossoms pasted to the walls. A proprietary Negro tends the gardens and scolds the children severely when he catches them invading the grounds around the playhouse.

Miss Ella's life seems as orderly as her garden; she has, however, a story, 'which like all women's stories was a love story and like most love stories took place in the past'. In her youth she had been engaged to a Mr Hendrix, who courted her formally and conventionally. After a proper length of time he asked her to marry him and she agreed. At Christmastime during a Sunday school party to which they had all gone, Andy Bronson lighted a firecracker and from its explosion a spark caught fire to Ella's dress. Instantly her skirts flamed up and Andy dashed to her side, the first to reach her, smothering the flames with his hands. In the weeks that followed the accident he began to send Miss Ella gifts of flowers, and silks and beads, a fan, and 'an exquisite miniature of himself when his face was smaller than his great soft eyes – treasures'. Ella discovered that 'she loved him with desperate suppression. One night he kissed her far into the pink behind her ears and she folded herself in his arms, a flag without a breeze about its staff.' They planned to marry, but Ella had of course to break her engagement to Mr Hendrix, 'saving and perfecting dramatically the scene she hopefully dreaded'. He took it wordlessly and stiffly and she was relieved when he left.

The following spring on the afternoon of her marriage to Bronson, while she was upstairs dressing, Mr Hendrix quietly entered her garden and shot his head off on the steps of the playhouse. 'Years passed but Miss Ella had no more hope for love. She fixed her hair more lightly about her head and every year her white skirts and peek-a-boo waists were more stiffly starched.' The story ends by repeating an image from the opening paragraph: the rims about Miss Ella's eyes 'grew redder and redder, like those of a person leaning over a hot fire, but she was not a kitchen sort of person, withal'. She avoids all contact with heat, that of the day as well as that of love. In fact, carefully placed images of heat and fire establish and underline the motion of the story, which is a glimpse of a frustrated woman. 'Bitter things dried behind the eyes of Miss Ella like garlic on a string before an open fire' is the first sentence of the story. Her memories has 'acrid fumes'; her hair is red. When Miss Ella is first introduced by the narrator of the story she is 'dodging the popping bits of blue flame' from the coal fire before the hearth. It is a flame which ignites Ella's skirts and draws her into contact with Andy Bronson. Even he is first seen by the reader in 'The church [which] was hot. . . . There in the smoky feminine confusion stood Andy Bronson.'

Zelda had read Faulkner before she wrote this story (we know she was reading him in Switzerland before her return to America in the fall of 1931); she was nurtured by a kindred South. She had also been reading psychological studies while at Prangins and what she had learned about repression informed her description of this Victorian spinster. 'Even her moments of relaxation were arduous, so much so as to provoke her few outbursts of very feminine temper and considerable nervous agitation.' Zelda was also sharply aware of those disguises of self that mask the neurotic feminine personality. The apparent orderliness of Miss Ella's person matches the orderliness of the grounds of her home, yet both are façades: the one for the erotic attraction she has felt toward the flamboyant Bronson, the other as a mask before the playhouse, the scene of violent and self-inflicted death.

Stories of suicide were a part of Zelda's youth and natural material for her to draw on. Although Ella does nothing violent herself, she provokes violence. Just why she no longer believes in love after the suicide of Hendrix is never made clear. What is clear is the extent to which she lives within herself after the shock of that suicide. She retires from anything that smacks of life. She swings herself in a hammock, dressed entirely in white, rocking herself as no lover would be permitted, yet 'you would never have guessed how uncomfortable she was or how in-

Top left: Minnie Machen,
'The Wild Lily of the Cumberland'

Top right: Anthony Dickinson
Sayre, aged nineteen

Right: Zelda Sayre

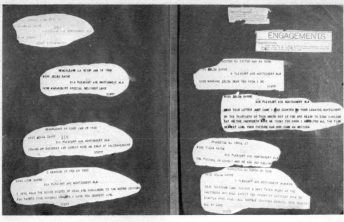

Above: A page of telegrams from Scott in Zelda's scrapbook

Left: Zelda's scrapbook, 1918

Below: Scott Fitzgerald in front of 6 Pleasant Avenue, May 1919

Right: Mr and Mrs F. Scott Fitzgerald, February 1921, New York

Above: Westport, Compo Beach, 1920. From left: Tanaka, John D. Williams, Zelda, George Jean Nathan, Scott, and Alexander McKaig

Left: Scott and Zelda, Dellwood, September 1921, the month before Scottie's birth

OPPOSITE PAGE

Above: First trip abroad, 1921

Right: Zelda and Scottie, summer of 1922, White Bear Lake, Minnesota

SCOTT AND ZELDA FITZGERALD

Left: A baby party in St Paul, from Zelda's scrapbook, 1922

Bottom left: The F. Scott Fitzgeralds, 1923. Zelda always called this portrait her 'Elizabeth Arden Face'

Right: Zelda, Scott and Scottie on the Riviera, 1924

Below: The Fitzgeralds in Paris, 1925

Left: Scottie and Scott on the plage, about 1925

Right: Scott at Arles, 1929

BELOW

Left: Zelda at the gorge at Constantine, February 1930

Right: Scott and Zelda in North Africa, February 1930

Left: Christmas at Gstaad, 1930

Bottom left: 'Recovered', 1931

Below: 'A Real Reunion', taken shortly after Fitzgerald's father's death, January 1931

Right: Zelda at Prangins

Fitzgerald's chart for *Tender is the Night* paralleling Zelda's case and Nicole Diver's

Self-portrait, probably done in the early forties

Above: Mrs Sayre, Scott and Zelda in North Carolina, about 1938

Left: A late snapshot of Zelda, taken near Ashville

tensely she disliked hammocks'. Within this woman there is sexual energy in restraint that Zelda tries to depict, and to do so she reaches back in time, describing a woman familiar in the South but hardly one of the romantic figures of her own youth. Ella is not a belle; she is an ordinary, if neurotic, spinster who no longer likes or tolerates disorder within her person. Trying to seat herself comfortably in her hammock she 'invariably loosened the big silver buckle that held her white-duck skirt in place'; she worries about an immodest showing of her legs and once in the hammock she tries to maintain 'a more or less static position'.

Zelda was no longer content to write the slight ironic and fashionable sketches she had written earlier. She was consciously trying to extend herself in her fiction. This story did not entirely flounder in an abundance of poetical description, and what descriptive materials were included had a cutting edge of meaning to them. The flaw was still a lack of sufficient development of the characters in terms of their relationships to each other. It was not enough to plant images; those images needed to accumulate into a fuller portrait of Miss Ella and her suitors.

One of the things Zelda was trying to get at was the attempt at revolt of a conventional young woman. Ella's alliance with Hendrix promised to be stifling from the beginning. Their plans for a life together were 'modest stable plans. ... He told her how things were to be, and she acquiesced.' She hears his quiet voice filling the air 'like smoke in an airless room'. Her one chance to avoid suffocation is to love Bronson. He gives her exotic gifts: deep red roses whose petals 'shone like the purple wings of an insect', lavish silks from Persia, which underline the sexual and feminine aspects of Ella. Only an act of violence stops her from marrying him, but once stopped she never risks herself again. This aspect of the story never clearly emerges. We are told too many things at a remove, the characters are not allowed to speak for themselves, and finally the torpor that envelops Miss Ella envelops the reader.

The publication of Zelda's story caused a stir in Montgomery that delighted her. She wrote Scott that she had sent Dr Forel a copy of *Scribner's Magazine* 'from sheer vanity'. Intoxicated with the pleasure of being published, she nevertheless fell back into her role of pupil-wife. 'I do not dare read the story. Knowing it is not first rate, I don't want to be discouraged – I *wish* you could teach me to write.'

From Hollywood Scott wrote Zelda that if his film was really successful he might make $75,000. Zelda was ecstatic and immediately made plans about how to spend it. 'We could build us a house. . . . A great denuded square I want with frank windows that frame the world in cold impersonal rigidity. And it is to be all over yellow. We will have all the children we can, and call them Dementia Praecox Fitzgerald – Dear, how gruesome!'

Zelda wrote about how she sat with her mother in the parlour of her house during the long rainy afternoons, talking about the Civil War and Zelda's grandfather, but she connected it all to something else. 'It's so nice to have important men and I'm so glad that you are one. I want you to come home and for us to have a son and lots of vital things we own.'

It rained nearly every day from the end of November to mid-December and Zelda wrote that she not only missed Scott and was lonely, but had a 'sore throat, asthma, grippe and indigestion'. On the good days, she said, a joyous release of pent-up excitement was likely to overcome her. She had a pistol without any bullets that she kept in a bureau drawer for protection.

I love climbing out on the tin roof and brandishing my empty pistol and yelling 'Who's there?' as if I had a mob at bay. But I am, secretly, always the escaping criminal. My bravado instincts do not function on the side of law and order, as do not also a great many other interesting facets of myself: i.e., to me, interesting, of cource.

. . . .

I miss my Daddy horribly. I am losing my identity here without men. I would not live two weeks again where there are none, since the first thing that goes is concision, and they give you something to butt your vitality against so it isn't littered over the air like spray[s] of dynamite.

In the wake of the Judge's death she could bear reminiscences of her mother's, for she knew they gave her relief from her grief, but she was bored and impatient with the conversation of friends from her girlhood.

This place is like one of those cracked phonograph records that plays always in the same place where you have to push the needle over but each revolution it sticks till you push it again and you never can come to the tune. Save me, Deo, from the darkness and the blight.... I am drugged with atmosphere. It's a shock moving about as we do – or is it growing old – suddenly finding yourself on unremembered corners surrounded by a flood of forgotten association.

It was nearly Christmas, and the household was in a flurry of preparations for the holidays and Scott's return on the 20th. The ornaments for their Christmas tree had been stored for so long that Zelda said they had lost their 'sex appeal', but they were unbroken and she decided not to buy any more, 'though there's nothing so beautiful as shining red balls dangling like the evolution of a jewel before your eyes. I s'pose thats why savages like things like that: they are both at the same level.'

Scottie hung a sign on her door, 'Voici la chambre mystérieuse', and four red wreaths at her windows. Her closet was filled with gifts wrapped in silver paper. She was a little glum about her discovery that there was no Santa Claus and decided that she wanted an electric train to help soothe her disillusionment. With Scott away Zelda had drawn closer to Scottie. But closer in the rather special sense of observing her, rather than doing things with her. Scottie came sometimes to dress herself in front of the fire in Zelda's room and Zelda wrote Scott, '... it's a joy to watch her long sweet delicate body and the cool of her pale hair quenching the light from the flames'. Scottie was, Zelda decided, like her father, a moon person. Zelda never said what kind of a person she thought she was, but it is unlikely that she thought of herself in terms of the moon. Scottie, who was now ten, was already being consciously nurtured by her father in a manner that he hoped would help her to avoid the pitfalls of her mother's character, as well as his own. He did not, for example, want her educated in the South. He was suspicious of the languidness he thought the climate encouraged. And he insisted upon a far more rigorous education than Zelda could possibly oversee. In the main Zelda agreed with him, but she left to Scott, as she always had, those important choices of education and direction.

Scott was back. Christmas was more strenuous than they had planned, with many relatives in the house, and Zelda's asthma grew ominously worse. Finally she and Scott decided to escape to Florida, where the clear, hot air might relieve her. They would both work on their novels. Their Negro chauffeur, Freeman, drove them to the Don Ce-Sar Hotel in Saint Petersburg.

It was splendid in the sun. Zelda was gentle and loving toward Scott, they swam together, and Zelda tanned herself copper. She got the rest she needed and the asthma disappeared. Buoyed by their holiday, Scott wrote Maxwell Perkins: 'At last for the first time in two years and a half I am going to spend five consecutive months on my novel. I am actually six thousand dollars ahead. Am replanning it to include what's good in what I have, adding 41,000 new words and publishing. Don't tell Ernest or anyone – let them think what they want – ...'

Without warning a spot of eczema appeared on Zelda's neck. It left two hours later only to reappear in two days for another tense two hours. Scott thought it might have been due to a deep-sea fishing trip, which had made her seasick, 'or worry about her novel which she thought was not going so well. ...' The eczema scotched all plans for remaining in Florida, and they prepared to leave for Montgomery at once. The first night spent on the road Zelda was sleepless. Moving restlessly about their room while Scott slept, she found a flask in his suitcase and drank everything in it. She woke Scott at 5 A.M. and told him that dark things were being done to her secretly. Finally, after hours of talking together, with Scott trying to calm her, Zelda said that she wanted to go to a clinic.

They were desperately unhappy; it was a crushing blow to their hopes for a normal life together. They returned to Montgomery, with Scott hoping it had been just a passing attack brought on by the liquor. On 1 February 1932 Scott wrote Dr

Forel for advice about Zelda. Until the night before there had been no further trouble.

She had been working all day hard and complained of her eyes which are terribly strained. At dinner she was merry and a little excited. After dinner in the middle of a chess-game (which I was winning) she complained of her eyes, quit, began an arguement and for an hour behaved distinctly irrationally – I do not mean she behaved like last winter in Prangins. More as she did in Paris before she broke down two years ago. Each time the dominant idea is that someone is causing the eczema and the eye hurting, with my connivance. This has disappeared utterly in the morning (she wanted to work some more last night but I made her go to bed) but the asthma is bad and I dread the day and the evening. She is affectionate but this time is not sorry for last night or won't admit it; I wanted her to walk rather than work or smoke but, she answers 'Dr Forel told me when I did not feel stable I ought to work.'

Scott was worried and told Forel: 'For the first time in three years I have money enough to work on my novel on which my whole fortune depends.' Scott was willing to move in the spring, but he desperately wanted to stay put for the time being and not have to break up housekeeping or put Zelda in a clinic, which would use all his reserves. 'It seems terrible because we have both been so utterly happy, happier almost than we have ever been. What the moral effect on me would be, I do not know and I hardly dare to think what it would be on her.'

A week later, after spending some hours working on her novel, Zelda had another period of hysteria. It lasted no more than two hours, but it terrified both of them.

On 10 February, Scott wired Dr Adolf Meyer, the director of the Henry Phipps Psychiatric Clinic of the Johns Hopkins University Hospital, that he was bringing his wife to Baltimore for treatment. At Zelda's suggestion they left Montgomery immediately by train. 'My haste', Scott later wrote Forel forlornly, 'was that she begin to turn against me again ...'

13

No one has schizophrenia, like having a cold. The patient has not
'got' schizophrenia. He is schizophrenic.

R. D. LAING, *The Divided Self*

On 12 February 1932, Zelda entered the Phipps Clinic. She
spoke very little that first day, but what she did say supported
Scott's fears of her growing irrationality. Quietly, as if to herself,
she asked: 'Isn't it terrible when you have one little corner of
your brain that needs fixing – Dr Meyer can do it, can't he? It's
this asthma and eczema that has just disrupted our home when
it was running so well.' She complained of not being able to
sleep and of being under a terrific strain due to the death of her
father during her husband's absence. 'I was left alone with my
daughter and it was just too much.'

Scott gave the young resident physician who would be in
charge of Zelda a detailed case history. He described Zelda's
youth as wild – she was 'the town scandal' – and said that she
had been his mistress for a year before their marriage. He
stressed her relationship to her mother, saying that it was 'unusual – she was spoiled and never thwarted in any way'. When
asked about her family, Scott said that Judge Sayre was a brilliant idealist and the only man he had ever admired without
qualification, but he thought that Mrs Sayre tried to have Zelda
succeed where she had failed. Mrs Sayre was the saint of the
family, and its centre.

He also tried to describe Zelda's personality; he explained
that Zelda, although outgoing and on the surface friendly, had
never been able to establish any close friendships. Her friends
were followers and as such her position in relation to them was
a superior one. He said she was proud and vain and always
jealous of him. He stressed his opinion that she could not take
criticism of any sort and became obstinate in the face of it, then

he contradicted himself and said that ultimately she could be reasoned with because of her logical mind.

He said almost nothing about himself in relation to Zelda, and he did not once mention his drinking. He told fairly sketchily about his romance in 1927 with Lois Moran in order to explain Zelda's reaction to it. But he now considered the extremity of her reaction a forewarning of her first breakdown. His only other reference to himself was to state that he had been unjustly accused by Zelda of a homosexual attachment to Ernest Hemingway.

The following day Scott returned to Alabama. Zelda appeared to be cheerful and optimistic in his absence, but when she replied to questions put to her by the doctors her sentences were long and peculiarly involved. Upon occasion she would break off abruptly for no apparent reason and make plays on words which had no meaning the doctors could fathom. Her replies were nonetheless revealing. Routinely she had been asked how old she was when she began school. 'Six, and then I left and then I – I know what keeps me from getting well is shyness, and then a terrible inferiority complex that drives one to attempt anything. . . . A feeling of being thrown into complete pandemonium when you see someone who can do more. I am not easy with people. I have never had any intimate friends. My husband and I have been very complete with each other. Everything is impersonal.'

Those sudden switches in midstream of her thoughts had always been characteristic of her, and when they were noted as examples of formal thought disorder, for the purposes of classifying her psychosis, the judgement was perhaps only partially right. Not knowing Zelda well, the doctors could not yet perceive the kinds of connections she was able to make from within her apparent disorder. Scott, for example, who knew Zelda better than anyone else, very rarely had trouble following her. Her earliest letters to him, written when she was eighteen and nineteen, were marked by a similar lack of conventional continuity and were full of sudden turns. But they were also marked to an extraordinary degree by special insights into herself and Scott. Even then she did not rely entirely upon the logical linking construction of language. Her thoughts moved rapidly by description and an appeal to the senses. She felt the death of a Confederate soldier; she could smell the aroma of loss that pervaded the South. If her thoughts were unruly, they nevertheless carried enormous meaning to Scott and it was from an emotional rather than a rational language of meaning that she wrote. Its limits, and they were severe, were that she depended on too private a mode of communication. In the end it severed her from ordinary communication with other people. It could be argued that this is precisely the limitation of the insane: they have withdrawn into a mode, habit, or even style of thought so exclusive that it seals them within their own interior, out of which they are no longer able to escape.

Now Fitzgerald kept in constant touch with the clinic, serving as a commentator on Zelda's illness. Later in the same week, although she remained largely uncommunicative about her illness, she admitted to having had hallucinations in the form of optical illusions at Prangins; 'you know just schizophrenia', she remarked nervously. When pressed to describe her relationship to Scott, she said: 'We are both monogamists so far as I know. We have both been absorbed in our love for each other and our hatred for each other. I am not a monogamist in theory.'

Soon Zelda had settled into the routine deemed necessary for her recovery. She pointedly refused to discuss her problems, but she was sleeping well, painting and writing two hours of each day. There was, however, a marked difference between the self she presented to the doctors and the self she revealed to the nurses who observed and assisted her daily. She was apt to be coy with the young resident, Dr Mildred Squires, and epigrammatic with Dr Meyer. And she was not beyond putting him on. For instance, Meyer would ask her about her friends. Had she made many? 'Good Lord, no. There is no one I distrust like my friends – Oh, no! [a long pause] I have cat thoughts that chase the mouse thoughts and sometimes they will get all the mouse thoughts caught and I read Aeschylus to put myself to sleep.'

She remarked later to a friend that Dr Meyer wouldn't be able to do anything for her and she thought she'd spend the rest of her life in sanitariums. She smiled at inappropriate times and tried to cover it by pretending she had thought of something funny, but in reality that smile was uncontrollable and it terrified her. She insisted that the nurses walk on her left side, for she said she couldn't see them if they were on her right.* She continued sketching and writing, spending more and more of her free time working on her novel.

It is a classic symptom among schizophrenics that they are rarely able to form intimate relations with people and are generally quite isolated from ordinary human contact. Dr Meyer repeatedly asked about her friends; one suspects that he was trying to bring Zelda into some sort of admission of her isolation to herself. Exasperated by his insistence upon this theme she said: 'I can't tolerate my friends. I hate them – the ones I used to love. I can only tolerate my acquaintances and enemies. So you see where that puts me. It makes me unfit to live in the world, but I'm not unhappy.'

She asked Dr Squires to read her novel, a section of which she had just had typed. The doctor wrote Scott saying she found the style very similar to that of 'Miss Ella'; it was vivid and it had charm, but it noticeably tended to break off and leave the reader stranded. However, she expected that Zelda would revise this first draft. So far, on the surface, things were going smoothly.

At the end of February Zelda wrote Scottie:

I am very glad that you and Daddy have found something to do in the evenings. Chess is such a good game – do learn to play it well. I have never been able to endow it with much of an existance apart from Alice-in-Wonderland and my pieces usually spend most of the game galloping in wild pandemonium before the onslaughts of Daddy. But we must play when I get home. You will soon be an

* Upon her entry to the clinic Scott told the doctors that she was practically blind in one eye. Years after her death, a member of her family mentioned that Zelda's doctor in Montgomery, who had treated her from childhood, thought the retina of her right eye was 'missing'. Zelda had a lorgnette, which she never wore, saying that it did no good. Scott assumed it was out of vanity that she refused to wear it. She did suffer from headaches caused by eyestrain, but there is no other evidence of a defective or detached retina.

accomplished dame-de-compagnie for him and I shall have to sit cutting paper-dolls and doing my chemical experiments while you two amuse yourselves. . . . I expect you to keep the house supplied with soap, flowers and tapdancers during my absence. . . . Take care of Daddy. See that there's plenty of spinach and Dinasaurus meat for Sunday. And profit by my absence to be as bad as you can get away with.

You are a darling and it is very, very, very lonely not to be able to work myself into a grouch by coming into cover you up when I think you're cold.

Are you practicing standing up straight in your long hours of doing nothing – straight on your hands, I mean. You will be an unsuccessful debutante if it isn't perfected by the time you're twenty –

Send me a blossom from your garden –

> With all my love –
> Mummy

Scott returned to Montgomery feeling depressed about Zelda's relapse and its meaning in terms of his novel. Certainly he found it difficult to write now, and he was simply waiting until the lease ran out on their house before he left for Baltimore to try to find them another there. He also wanted Scottie to finish the school year without further interruptions. In his Ledger he wrote, 'Scotty sick, me sick, Mrs Sayre playing the fool . . . everything worser and worser.' Worrying that Zelda's illness might exhaust them financially, Scott again set about writing stories for the *Post*. Zelda seemed to understand how deeply disappointed he was: 'It seems so awful that you should have to leave your novel. I've cut my cigarettes way down and am getting enough exercise to give me a muscular hemmorage and I can't write very well, so I ought to be better soon. Darling, what an awful struggle you have.'

As unhappy as he was, early one evening he took Scottie to dinner at the country club, perhaps for company, perhaps for a treat. A friend of theirs remembers Fitzgerald gently leading Scottie out to the edge of the dance floor, talking to her quietly, and then very slowly swinging the little girl out in graceful arcs to a slow fox trot. They were not recognized in the dim light until someone pointed them out and said, 'That's Scott Fitzgerald and his little girl.' They stopped as quietly as they had begun and left the club arm in arm.

Zelda missed Scott and wrote to him:

We always have such fun pricking each others aesthetic pompousities, which we pretend to take very seriously. Sometimes I almost believe that our fundamental attraction is an intellectual suspicion.... Anyway, I am *very* lonely for you.

She mentioned her own writing and the two-hour limit she had to work within according to her doctors' schedule for her.

I am reading Ian Gordon's Modern French Painters. He speaks of the sense of growing things in Van Gogh's work. Those crawling flowers and venomous vindictive blossoms are the hallucinations of a mad-man – without organization or rhythm but with the power to sting and strangle.... I loved them at Prangins. They reassured me.... Dearest – I suppose I will spend the rest of my life torn between the desire to master life and a feeling that it is, au fond, a contemptuous enemy. If there weren't you + Scottie, melancholia is about as happy a state as any other I suppose. There's a woman here who wanders tentatively about the halls like the ghost in a poor detective story. It is impossible to feel sorry for crazy people since their realities do not coincide with our normal conceptions of tragedy etc. And yet, a woman's brother came to pay a visit. I thought how awful and poignant – that boney casket full of nothing that the man had ever loved and he was saying that he wanted her to come home again. It made me feel very sorry. I presume he was addressing his past – ... Anyway, there's nothing so sordid as being shut up – When a man is no longer his own master, custodian of his own silly vanities and childish contentments he's nothing at all – being in the first place only an agent of a very experimental stage of organic free will –

I love you –

Dear, My Own – My love

March began with Dr Squires feeling certain that Zelda was making definite progress. He wrote Scott saying that Zelda's tenseness had decreased, and that she had completed the second chapter of her novel by 2 March. Dr Squires told Scott that this chapter was superior to the first and that if Zelda could keep it up the book would be a success. Working consistently, Zelda had made great strides toward its completion and wrote Scott:

> I am proud of my novel, but I can hardly restrain myself enough to get it written. You will like it – It is distinctly École Fitzgerald, though more ecstatic than yours – Perhaps too much so. Being unable to invent a device to avoid the reiterant 'said' I have emphasized it a la Ernest much to my sorrow. He is a very determined writer, but I shall also die with my boots on.

Scott was naturally curious about the novel and Dr Squires's letter to him about it prompted him to write her back: 'The lack of continuity in her novel doesn't worry me. She isn't a "natural storyteller" in the sense that I am, and unless a story comes to her fully developed and crying to be told she's liable to flounder around rather unsuccessfully among problems of construction. Anyhow the form of so many modern novels is less a progression than a series of impressions, as you know – rather like the slowly-turned pages of an album.' He added: 'Like all Americans she is in some ways and to some extent a puritan and literally can't survive without some code, and she has too much tendency to submerge herself in my turbulent Irish anarchism.'

Dr Squires answered his letter the following day with the astonishing news that Zelda had, that morning, 9 March, completed her novel. Zelda sent it immediately to Maxwell Perkins at Scribner's with the following note: 'Scott, being absorbed in his own [novel], has not seen it, so I am completely in the dark as to its possible merits, but naturally, terribly anxious that you should like it. ... As soon as I hear that you have safely received the copy, I want to mail the ms. to Scott, so could you wire?' Then Zelda wrote Scott. She told him she was sure Scribner's would refuse it; she did not send the manuscript with her letter, but promised to mail it to him the following Monday.

On 14 March Scott wrote Dr Squires in a fury. He had just received Zelda's manuscript. For four years, he wrote, he had been forced to work intermittently on his novel, 'unable to proceed *because* of the necessity of keeping Zelda in sanitariums', Zelda had heard fifty thousand words of his novel and 'literally one whole section of her novel is an imitation of it, of its rhythm, materials . . . there are only two episodes, both of which she has reduced to anecdotes *but upon which whole sections of my book turn*, that I have asked her to cut. Her own material – her youth, her love for Josanne, her dancing, her observation of Americans in Paris, the fine passages about the death of her father – my criticisms of that will be simply impersonal and professional.' She had even named one of the main characters Amory Blaine (the name of Scott's hero in *This Side of Paradise*).

Fitzgerald was angry and things had to calm down, he wrote, if he was to continue turning out his stories for the *Post*. 'It is getting more and more difficult in this atmosphere of suspicion to turn out the convinced and well-decorated sophisms for which Lorimer pays me my bribe.' He was living in a state of 'mild masturbation and a couple of whiskeys to go on' until his lease ran out in mid-April. His anger did not subside and two days later he wired Scribner's that Zelda's novel would 'seriously compromise what literary future she may have and cause inconceivable harm in its present form . . .'

Zelda had for the first time directly invaded what Scott considered his own domain, and the violence of his reaction was telling. Her novel was intensely, even naïvely autobiographical, and as she drew on her own life, so she drew on her life with Scott, for it was her material as well as his. Scott strenuously disagreed. The psychiatrists at Phipps were surprised by the vehemence of his reaction and could only apologize for having allowed Zelda to mail the novel to Scribner's without first gaining Fitzgerald's release. They wired him to say that she had switched addresses at the last moment without their knowledge. They promised it would not happen again, but clearly no one had anticipated his fury.

It is probable that when in 1930 Scott abandoned his idea for a novel which would turn upon matricide, he was very much under the influence of Zelda's first illness. In January 1932 he proceeded to sketch out a longer novel than he had originally

intended to write, salvaging what he could use from his earlier
drafts, while immersing his fresh version in Zelda's insanity
and his own complex reactions to it. He called his seventh draft
The Drunkard's Holiday and it was about Nicole and Doctor
Dick Diver. Zelda had undoubtedly heard or read portions of
his revised plot in Florida and Montgomery as she worked on
her own novel.

In early spring Scott drew up his 'General Plan' (but it is un-
clear whether in Montgomery or in Baltimore, where he was to
move in April, because none of the manuscript is dated); he
wrote:

> The novel should do this. Show a man who is a natural idealist,
> a spoiled priest, giving in for various causes to the ideas of the
> haute Burgeoise, and in his rise to the top of the social world
> losing his idealism, his talent and turning to drink and dissipation.
> Background one in which the liesure class is at their truly most
> brilliant & glamorous such as Murphys.

*

> The hero born in 1891 is a man like myself brought up in a
> family sunk from the haute burgeoisie to petit burgeoisie, yet ex-
> pensively educated. He has all the gifts and goes through Yale
> almost succeeding but not quite getting a Rhodes scholarship which
> he caps with a degree from Hopkins, & with a legacy goes abroad
> to study psychology in Zurich. At the age of 26 all seems bright.
> Then he falls in love with one of his patients who has a curious
> homicidal mania toward men caused by an event in her youth.
> Aside from this she is the legendary *promiscuous* woman. He
> 'transfers' to himself & she falls in love with him, a love he
> returns.

In a 'Further Sketch' he added, '*The Drunkard's Holiday* will
be a novel of our time showing the break up of a fine personality. Unlike *The Beautiful and Damned* the break-up will be
caused not by flabbiness but really tragic forces such as the
inner conflicts of the idealist and the compromises forced upon
him by circumstances.' Later, he very carefully drew up outlines of Dick's and Nicole's lives. It is Nicole's life that is of
especial interest in relation to Zelda.

Nicole's Age
Always one year younger than century.
Born July 1901
  courtship for two and one half years before
  that, since she was 13.
Catastrophe June 1917 Age almost 16
Clinic   Feb. 1918 Age 17
             To middle October bad period
             After Armistice good period
             He returns in April or May 1919
             She discharged June 1, 1919. Almost 18
             Married September 1919. Aged 18
Child born August 1920
Child born June 1922
  2nd Pousse almost immediately to October
    1922 and therafter
  Frenchman (or what have you in summer of
    1923 after almost 4 years of marriage.
In July 1925 when the story opens she is just 24
  (One child almost 5 (Scotty in Juan les Pins)
  One child 3 (Scotty in Pincio)
In July 1929 when the story ends she is just 28

The heroine was born in 1901. She is beautiful on the order of Marlene Dietrich or better still the Norah Gregor-Kiki Allen girl with those peculiar eyes. She is American with a streak of some foreign blood. At fifteen she was raped by her own father under peculiar circumstances – work out. She collapses, goes to the clinic and there at sixteen meets the young doctor hero who is ten years older. Only her transference to him saves her – when it is not working she reverts to homicidal mania and tries to kill men. She is an innocent, widely read but with no experience and no orientation except what he supplies her. Portrait of Zelda – that is, a part of Zelda.

We follow her from age 24 to age 29.

Then, after a brief description of 'Method of Dealing with Sickness Material' and a 'Classification of the Material on Sickness', he charts in detail Nicole's case history against Zelda's.

Various elements of Nicole's background are pure invention.

For instance, Zelda was not raped by her father, and she showed no homicidal tendencies toward men, but the degree to which Scott used Zelda in a fictional counterpart is otherwise explicit enough. How much of this was clearly worked out in 1932 we do not know, but the basic elements of Dick's and Nicole's characters probably were. At last Fitzgerald had found his theme. That it involved a use of Zelda, that she might object to it, be wounded by it, did not seem to have disturbed him. He saw it only from a writer's point of view.

He had spent years in a quandary about this novel; he had not published a novel since *Gatsby* in 1925, seven years before. He clearly resented the time he put into short-story writing, although that resentment now seems completely out of proportion. His income in 1931 was at its apex: he had earned $37,599 in the middle of the Depression. But writing short stories was more than just economically profitable for Fitzgerald. His stories were usually not the hack work he seemed to feel compelled to call them. The best of them, written for the top magazines in the country, have withstood whatever scrutiny was directed toward them, and many of the others were exploratory exercises in his craft. He stripped and mined the latter mercilessly for scenes and characters and moods to be incorporated into his novels. As such, these stories, about 160 in his relatively brief career, were not a compromising of his talent, as he liked to think, but a disciplining of it. They made him money and they kept him writing while he floundered with his fourth novel.

Although furious with Zelda, Scott had not written directly to her about her novel. Learning of his reaction through her doctor, she tried to soothe his irritation with a letter of careful explanation.

Dr Squires tells me you are hurt that I did not send [my] book to you before I mailed it to Max. Purposely I didn't – knowing that you were working on your own and honestly feeling that I had no right to interrupt you to ask for a serious opinion. Also, I know Max will not want it and I prefer to do the corrections after having his opinion. Naturally, I was in my usual rush to get it off my hands — You know how I hate brooding over things once they are finished: so I mailed it poste haste, hoping to have yours and Scribner's criticisms to use for revising.

Scott, I love you more than anything on earth and if you were offended I am miserable. We have always shared everything but it seems to me I no longer have the right to inflict every desire and necessity of mine on you. I was also afraid we might have touched the same material. Also, feeling it to be a dubious production due to my own instability I did not want a scathing criticism such as you have mercilessly — if for my own good given my last stories, poor things. I have had enough discouragement, generally, and could scream with that sense of inertia that hovers over my life and everything I do. So, Dear, My Own, please realize that it was not from any sense of not turning first to you — but just time and other ill-regulated elements that made me so bombastic about Max.... Goofo, please love me — life is very confusing — but I love you. Try, dear — and then I'll remember when you need me too sometime, and help.

Scott was having none of it. He scored sections of the first paragraph in red pencil and made a note to himself in the margin: 'This is an evasion. All this reasoning is specious or else there is no evidence of a tornado in the sta ...' and the rest was made illegible by a smudge of ink. His resentment, however, was clearly enough expressed; he was not just suspicious, he was sure she was purposely trying to harm him. In the latter part of her letter when she wrote, 'I was also afraid we might have touched the same material', she had, in Scott's opinion, given herself away.

Zelda knew perfectly well that if any portion of her book imitated or even echoed Scott's novel he would insist that she change it. If she had sent it first to Perkins as a ploy to avoid Scott's criticism or his demand that certain changes be made before he would allow its publication, she failed utterly. Certainly she must have known that sending it to Scott's editor was hardly a way of keeping it from Scott. Her action could not have been as underhanded as Scott felt it was, but neither was it as innocent as Zelda maintained: she *had* heard portions of his novel and throughout the past four months she had consciously tried to learn from his style. Her motives were mixed.

But Scott's reaction, especially since he was the more balanced of the two, was completely out of proportion.

Scott must have written Zelda in the same accusing and defensive vein as he had Dr Squires – she had been able to complete a novel in, at the most, three months, while he had been forced to discontinue his. At this point he was totally insensitive to Zelda's precarious state. She answered:

Dear – You know that if I could sell any of my stories I would not have written this book. Ober is swamped with my things, and it seems worthless to plague him with more. The fact that I have had time to write it while you have had to put aside your own is due to circumstances over which I had no control and cannot bring myself to feel a sense of guilt. You, of all people, certainly would not have preferred my folding of hands during my long unoccupied hours.... Believe me, dear, I quite appreciate the strain and depression under which you are existing.... I realize that there is little that your life has to offer as a substitute, but I wish you could drink less – do not fly into a rage, I know you stay *sober* – but you need some rest and I can't think how you can get it except by using those miserable moments that gin helps to dispel and turn into activity by resting.

I love you D.O. – I would have collapsed years ago if I'd had me on my hands ...

Evidently he again wrote to her, this time insisting on specific changes in the novel. We have only Zelda's reply.

Of cource, I glad[ly] submit to anything you want about the book or anything else. I felt myself the thing was too crammed with material upon which I had not the time to dwell and consequently lost any story continuity. Shall I wire Max to send it back? The real story was the old prodigal son, of cource. I regret that it offended you. The Pershing incident which you accuse me of stealing occupies just one line and will not be missed. I willingly relinquish it. However, I would like you to thoroughly understand that my revision will be made on an aesthetic basis: that the other material which I will elect is nevertheless legitimate stuff which has cost me a pretty emotional penny to amass and which I intend to use when I can get the tranquility of spirit necessary to write the story of myself versus myself. That is the book I really want to write. As you know my contacts with my family have always been in the nature of the raids of a friendly brigand. I quite realize that the quality of this book does not warrant so many excursions into the bizarre – As for my friends: first, I have none; by that I mean that all our associates have always taken me for granted, sought your stimulus and fame, eaten my dinners and invited 'The Fitzgeralds' place[s]. You have always been and always will be the only person with whom I have felt the necessity to communicate and our intimacies have, to me, been so satisfactory mentally that no other companion has ever seemed necessary. Despised by my supiors, which are few, held in suspicion by my equals, even fewer, I have got all external feeding for my insignifigant flames from people either so vastly different from myself that our relations were like living a play or I have cherished my inferiors with color ... and the friends of my youth. However, I did not intend to write you a treatise on friendship in which I do not believe.

She signed herself, 'With dearest love, I am your irritated Zelda.'

The novel reopened the rift between them and it was Scott who, on the surface, was the more deeply wounded. Zelda had used him, he insisted – his writing, his life, his material – to her own advantage. Yet at the end of March just before he left Alabama for Baltimore he wrote to Dr Squires (who, astonished by the vehemence of his reactions, had apparently suggested to him that if he and Zelda could not survive together a separation might be in order):

My whole stomach hurts when I contemplate such an eventuality – it would be throwing her [Zelda] broken upon a world which she despises; I would be a ruined man for years –

On the other hand, he could not

stand always between Zelda and the world and see her build this dubitable career of hers with morsels of living matter chipped out of my mind, my belly, my nervous system and my loins. Perhaps 50% of our friends and relatives would tell you in all honest conviction that my drinking drove Zelda insane – the other half would assure you that her insanity drove me to drink. Neither judgment would mean anything: ... these two classes [of friends and relatives] would be equally unanimous in saying that each of us would be well rid of the other – in full face of the irony that we have never been so desperately in love with each other in our lives. Liquor on my mouth is sweet to her; I cherish her most extravagant hallucinations.

Her affair with Eduard Josanne in 1925 and mine with Lois Moran in 1927, which was a sort of revenge shook something out of us, but we can't both go on paying and paying forever. And yet I feel that that's the whole trouble back of all this.

14

'But I warn you,' she said, 'I am only really myself when I'm somebody else whom I have endowed with these wonderful qualities from my imagination.'

ZELDA FITZGERALD, *Save Me the Waltz*

Zelda told Scott she found the title for her novel, *Save Me the Waltz*, in a Victor record catalogue. It is an evocative request, with a bitter edge, and like an old song it stirs memories. In the novel Zelda probes her childhood in Montgomery as well as her life with Scott Fitzgerald. Inevitably her awareness of Scott's process of creating fiction had deeply influenced her. And she too stripped portions from various of her short stories, like 'A Couple of Nuts' and 'A Millionaire's Girl', and added them to her novel. The surface structure of the novel is quite simple; there are four chapters, which are each divided into three sections. But she has trouble sustaining a longer narrative and *Save Me the Waltz* is not an easy book to read. Its force depends on the cumulative effect of its vignettes rather than on an orderly flow of events. Her style is turgid, and extended chunks of poetical description, an oddity of language, as well as incorrect grammar and mis-spellings seriously mar the novel. (It did not appear to have been copy-edited by Scribner's at all, as several of the reviewers pointed out.) Yet, as eccentric a novel as it is, as uneven and flawed, it is nonetheless charged with her own fictional energy and voice. It becomes a good deal more than the curio of a deranged sensibility working over the grievances of a life with Scott Fitzgerald, or of a life shattered by mental illness.

Zelda recreates the life of an American girl in the Deep South before World War I, who later, in the twenties, is exposed, through the extraordinary success of her artistic husband, to a gaudy and unstable life in New York, Paris, and the Riviera. Few women could have written about it with greater authenticity or poignancy. Again and again the autobiographical impulse seeks release in the novel, ensnaring the reader who has a prior knowledge of Zelda's life. Perhaps that is the larger problem presented by this novel – that because it is so deeply autobiographical, the transmutation of reality into art is incomplete. We read it against the life, or as a gesture of release from the life. If Zelda is telling her side of the story, Scott's turn will come within two years with the publication of *Tender Is the Night*. Both of the Fitzgeralds would corrupt and alter the story by seeing it through their private angles of vision. *Save Me the Waltz* is not a defence; it is Zelda's view of that complex tangle of selves within wedlock in those postwar years when, as she wrote, 'People were banking in gods . . .'

The original manuscript, as well as Zelda's revisions of that first draft, have been lost. What exists are a typed manuscript used probably as printer's copy, two consecutive sets of heavily revised galley proofs (each with a duplicate also reworked in Zelda's handwriting) and one set of clean page proofs. There must also have been a duplicate set of pages which were reworked, for there are changes in the published version of the novel that were not made on any of the existing galleys or pages.

From evidence in Zelda's letters to Scott, and in Scott's correspondence with Maxwell Perkins prior to even the signing of the contract, we know that there were earlier, extensive revisions, but we do not know specifically what they were. An indication of Zelda's rewriting is given in a letter Scott wrote to Perkins at the end of April or the beginning of May: 'Zelda's novel is now good, improved in every way. It is new. She has largely eliminated the speakeasy-nights-and-our-trip-to-Paris atmosphere. You'll like it. It should reach you in ten days. I am too close to it to judge it but it may be even better than I think.' Then he asked Perkins to keep whatever praise he wished to give Zelda *'on the staid side'*, for Scott said it was important to the doctors at Phipps that Zelda not be made to feel too jubilant about the fame and money that might come to her through publication. '. . . I'm not certain enough of Zelda s present stability of character to expose her to any superlatives. If she has a success coming she must associate it with work done in a workmanlike manner for its own sake, and part of it done fatigued and uninspired, and part of it done when even to remember the original inspiration and impetus is a psychological trick. She is not twenty-one and she is not strong, and she must not try to follow the pattern of my trail which is of course blazed distinctly on her mind.' This was all as much an indication of Scott's feelings about his own work on his novel as it was about Zelda's possible reactions toward hers.

In a second letter to Perkins, written about two weeks later, Scott sent him *Save Me the Waltz*. He wrote: 'Here is Zelda's novel. It is a good novel now, perhaps a very good novel – I am too close to tell. It has the faults and virtues of a first novel. It is more the expression of a powerful personality, like *Look Homeward, Angel,* than the work of a finished artist like Ernest Hemingway. It should interest the many thousands interested in dancing. It is *about something* and absolutely new, and should sell.'

Somewhat cavalierly Fitzgerald added that he would withdraw his restraint on praise if Scribner's decided to take the book; Perkins might even write to Zelda directly about it. His advice was given, he said, in order to protect Zelda's mental stability for fear of her 'incipient egomania . . . but she has taken such a sane common-sense view lately – (At first she refused to revise – then she revised completely, added on her own suggestion and has changed what was a rather flashy and self-justifying "true confessions" that wasn't worthy of her into an honest piece of work. She can do more with the galleys but I can't ask her to do more now).' Finally, he suggested that Perkins not mention Zelda's novel to Hemingway, who would also have a book published that season by Scribner's. It was not that there was a 'conflict between the books'; it was rather because of the conflict between Zelda and Hemingway – which was in part a struggle for prominence. Fitzgerald hinted that if Perkins praised or even mentioned the book to Hemingway there might be 'curiously grave consequences – curious, that is, to un-jealous men like you and me'. He also asked Perkins not to discuss the terms of her contract with Zelda should Scribner's take the novel; he would handle that himself.

Scribner's did decide to publish the book and the contract for *Save Me the Waltz* was signed on 14 June 1932. A clause added to the agreement stipulated that one-half the royalties earned would be retained by Scribner's to be credited against 'the indebtedness of F. Scott Fitzgerald', until a total of $5,000 had been repaid. Publication was planned for the following October.

In the first chapter of *Save Me the Waltz* we are introduced to the heroine, Alabama Beggs; her parents, Millie and Judge Beggs; as well as her two older sisters, Dixie and Joan. By the close of the chapter Alabama has gone to New York and married a twenty-two-year-old artist, David Knight, whom she met when he was a lieutenant stationed in the South during World War I.

Chapter 2, which is the longest in the novel (and the only one for which an earlier version exists; Zelda completely rewrote the opening thirty-three pages in galleys, reducing them to twenty-five pages, and revised ten pages of Section III), takes us from David's extraordinary success as a painter in New York and the birth of their daughter, Bonnie, through the Knights' journey to the Riviera, where Alabama falls in love with a French aviator, to a series of ludicrous parties in Paris, where David is lionized and Alabama is completely unhappy. By the end of this chapter a distraught Alabama has decided to become a ballet dancer, although she is aware that she is too old to be beginning. Her decision is made in retaliation against David's attraction to a lovely movie actress, Gabrielle Gibbs. Alabama has overheard David telling Miss Gibbs that her breasts are like 'a sort of blancmange', and that he has heard she has 'the most beautiful blue veins all over [her] body'. Alabama, who is at the dinner table with them, observes, 'David opened and closed his personality over Miss Gibbs like the tentacles of a carnivorous maritime plant.' The following morning, when David comes home after having spent the night out,

Alabama wonders why 'Men . . . never seem to become the things they do, like women. . . .' She tries to tell herself that she doesn't care, but she does.

' "I can't stand this any longer", she screamed at the dozing David. "I don't want to sleep with the men or imitate the women, and I can't stand it!" '

When David tells her that he understands, ' "It must be awful just waiting around eternally," ' Alabama tells him to ' "shut up!" ' and promises him, ' "I am going to be as famous a dancer as there are blue veins over the white marble of Miss Gibbs." ' But she has also turned to the dance in an effort to bring order and meaning into a life 'so uselessly extravagant'. This duality of motivation is important, for as Alabama becomes immersed in dancing it is far more because of her feelings of having wasted her life than out of jealousy. It is, however, the intermeshing of both strains that tightens the texture of the book.

The third chapter describes Alabama's increasing dedication to the ballet; she becomes possesed by it. Her dancing is also seen as a defence against the collapse of her marriage, and she spends less and less time with her husband and child. She exhausts herself practising, and she is infuriated when a member of the ballet studio asks her why she tries so hard when she already has a husband who will take care of her. Alabama says, ' "Can't you understand that I am not trying to get anything – at least, I don't think I am – but to get rid of some of myself?" ' At the end of the chapter, as the Knights plan to return to America, Alabama, in a sudden reversal of plans, accepts an invitation to dance her solo début in the opera *Faust* with the San Carlos Opera in Naples.

The first and second sections of Chapter 4 deal with her success in Naples, where she is living without David and Bonnie, who are in Switzerland. These sections are perhaps the only departures from Zelda's own life, in the sense that Zelda did not go to Naples to dance and has probably transmuted her memories from Switzerland into the Italian setting. Bonnie visits her mother in Naples, and it goes badly; the child eagerly returns to her father in Switzerland. David gets a telegram from

America notifying them that Alabama's father is dying. At the same time Alabama has suddenly fallen seriously ill in Naples with blood poisoning caused by an infection in her foot. Her foot is operated on and the tendons are severed; she will be able to walk, but never to dance again. David comes to her side during her illness, and his devotion brings them together again. As soon as Alabama is well enough to travel they return to America and the Judge's bedside. He dies in November 1931.

At the end of the novel the Knights have decided to leave the South and they realize that they will return only to visit Alabama's family.

Clearly Zelda patterned her novel closely upon her own life. Judge Beggs is much like her own father, Judge Sayre, and Millie, Alabama's mother (whose name in an interesting combination of Scott's mother's first name, Mollie, and Minnie Sayre's), shares many of Mrs Sayre's traits, as well as her place within the marriage and family. She is their harmonizer. There are also certain resemblances between Dixie, Alabama's oldest sister, and Rosalind. The job as society editor she holds in the novel was one Rosalind held in Montgomery, and there is the same age difference between the two sisters as there was between Rosalind and Zelda. David is twenty-two when Alabama meets him, as was Scott; Alabama and David honeymoon at Room 2109 in the Biltmore, as did Zelda and Scott; and they take a house in the Connecticut countryside shortly after their marriage, with the same intentions the Fitzgeralds had when they moved to Westport. Their Japanese houseboy is Tanka; the Fitzgeralds' was Tanaka. But a listing of these relatively minor details is not the main concern; rather, it is with how *Save Me the Waltz* works as a novel, as well as with what it tells us about Zelda, for it provides a key to those images of self that Zelda projected into her fiction.

At the heart of the novel is the characterization of Judge Beggs. It is with him that the novel opens and closes. His standards of judgement serve Alabama as a model against which she measures her life, and his austere infallibility is the pivot about which the entire motion of the novel turns. It was not until the death of Judge Sayre that Zelda began to form her book and it would seem that his death provided a kind of psychological freeing for her that stimulated her into reviewing her life up to his death. She establishes the Judge's importance at the beginning of the book: ' "Those girls", people said, "think they can do anything and get away with it." That was because of the sense of security they felt in their father. He was a living fortress.'

The Judge has only one flaw: he is completely inaccessible. In a fortress that is an ideal quality, but in a father it is nearly disastrous. Images of defence and imprisonment from a feudal society – castles, impregnable keeps, drawbridges, strongholds, and ramparts – are carefully used by Zelda to describe the Judge's character. He is 'entrenched . . . in his integrity', the 'lord of the living cycle', and his strength of character is formidable and unchallengeable, for he is always on the side of right and justice. But he stands for an ideal of conduct Alabama cannot hope to find in either herself or her own generation. When beaux come to pick her up for dates and whistle from their cars for her, she is ashamed of them. But more importantly she is ashamed also of herself for wanting to go out with them. Good manners, however, are the lightest of the burdens the Judge places on his children; they are permitted no deviation from his code of integrity, no vacillations of purpose or errors of judgement. As a result his children never learn to deal with the world on their own terms, but try to emulate his. By comparison their own efforts are inadequate. Zelda understood that failure clearly. 'By the time the Beggs children had learned to meet the changing exigencies of their times, the devil was already upon their necks. Crippled, they clung long to the feudal donjons of their fathers. . . .' Zelda also implies that as long as the Beggs children remain within the household they are safe; it is only when they move out into larger worlds where choices are less clear that they are uncertain. Their final crippling is due to their inability to exercise their own faculties of reason and judgement.

Pitted against the Judge is his wife. She is as vague and soft as the Judge is harsh and unremittingly correct. It is to her that the girls turn for relief from their father, for 'the Judge became, with their matured perceptions, a retributory organ, an inexorable fate, the force of law, order, and established discipline'. This relationship between the Judge and his wife instills in their youngest daughter, Alabama, a mode of masculine feminine role-playing that, much as she tries to rebel against it, has formed her. The male partner may be the stronger, may possess the keener intelligence, but his authority is undercut by the rather passive deviousness of the female, who by fooling him gets her own, or in Millie's case, her children's way.

Millie, who had never had a very strong sense of reality, was unable to reconcile that cruelty of the man with what she knew was a just and noble character. [The Judge and Millie have just lost their only son; the Judge's reaction to his son's death is to turn 'savagely to worry fleeing from his disappointment' and to fling the bill for the boy's funeral at Millie, asking how she expects him to pay for it.] She was never again able to form a judgment of people, shifting her actualities to conform to their inconsistencies till by a fixation of loyalty she achieved in her life a saintlike harmony. . . . The sum of her excursions into the irreconcilabilities of the human temperament taught her also a trick of transference that tided her over the birth of the last child. . . . Confronted with the realism of poverty, she steeped her personality in a stoic and unalterable optimism and made herself impervious to the special sorrows pursuing her to the end.

When Dixie dates someone whom the Judge deeply disapproves of, Millie suggests that rather than 'bother' her father she 'could make [her] arrangements outside'; in other words she tries not only to be the peacemaker in the family, but attemps to have Dixie avoid confrontation with the Judge by subterfuge.

The wide and lawless generosity of their mother was nourished from many years of living faced with the irrefutable logic of the Judge's fine mind. . . . Millie Beggs, by the time she was forty-five, had become an emotional anarchist. It was her way of proving to herself her individual necessity of survival. Her inconsistencies seemed *to assert her dominance* [my italics] over the scene. . . .

In her introduction of Alabama, Zelda takes special care to stress her heroine's primary concern: Alabama's quest for her own identity. And, although the novel begins with a description of the Judge in relation to his family, Alabama's sense of herself is first described within her mother's orbit. Alabama's quest for her own identity will grow throughout the novel, but it is here marked by a peculiar distinction.

'Tell me about myself when I was little,' the youngest girl insists. She presses against her mother in an effort to realize some proper relationship.

'You were a good baby.'

The girl had been filled with no interpretation of herself, having been born so late in the life of her parents that ... childhood [had] become more of a concept than the child. She wants to be told what she is like, being too young to know that she is like nothing at all. ... She does not know that what effort she makes will become herself. It was much later that the child, Alabama, came to realize that the bones of her father could indicate only her limitations.

Uncertain about who she is, the author steps in and states that Alabama 'is like nothing at all. ...' Zelda describes 'The girl' in terms of a vessel, an object which has not been 'filled', but it is a strangely impersonal figure of speech: Alabama as container.

In an interchange with her mother which immediately follows the preceding one, Alabama tries another tactic to rouse a more meaningful response from Millie. But her mother characteristically veers from a pertinent answer. Alabama asks,

'And did I cry at night and raise Hell so you and Daddy wished I was dead?'

'What an idea! All my children were sweet children.'

But Alabama does not want to know about 'all' of her mother's children, she wants something specific about herself; the very intensity of the language of her question is a push for a genuine emotional response from her mother.

Just before Alabama's bedtime that evening she overhears the Judge asking Millie the whereabouts of Dixie (who is out with Randolph McIntosh, whom the Judge considers a wastrel). Millie tells him, ' "She's out with some friends." Sensing the mother's evasiveness, the little girl draws watchfully close, with an important sense of participation in family affairs.' (We would expect Alabama to say 'her mother', but instead Zelda uses 'the', an impersonal article, which reinforces Alabama's sense of estrangement from her mother.) The Judge suspects that Dixie is out with Randolph and tells Millie that if she is, ' "she can leave my house for good" '. Millie takes Alabama to bed 'and the little girl lies in the dark, swelling virtuously submissive to the way of the clan'. As she falls asleep the aroma of pears from an orchard fills her room; she hears a band practising 'waltzes in the distance'.

White things gleam in the dark – white flowers and paving-stones. The moon on the window panes careens to the garden. . . . The world is younger than it is, and she to herself appears so old and wise, grasping her problems and wrestling with them as affairs peculiar to herself and not as racial heritages. There is a brightness and bloom over things; she inspects life proudly, as if she walked in a garden forced by herself to grow in the least hospitable of soils. She is already contemptuous of ordered planting, believing in the possibility of a wizard cultivator to bring forth sweet-smelling blossoms from the hardest of rocks, and night-blooming vines from barren wastes, to plant the breath of twilight and to shop with marigolds. She wants life to be easy and full of pleasant reminiscences.

In this passage Zelda weaves back and forth between two strains that she will use consistently throughout the novel. Images of flowers and gardens reinforce the development of her central characters and establish not only mood but the interior direction of these characters' lives. Sometimes, however, that imagery extends beyond what the reader could be prepared to accept about a character within the time sequence of the novel. For example the following passage is infused with images drawn from Zelda's memories and hallucinations at Prangins – within the context of the novel at this point the passage does not make much sense. But within the context of Zelda's life it is explosive with autobiographical meaning.

She grows older sleeping. Some day she will awake to observe the plants of Alpine gardens to be largely fungus things, needing little sustenance, and the white discs that perfume midnight hardly flowers at all but embryonic growths; and, older, walk in bitterness the geometrical paths of philosophical Le Nôtres rather than those nebulous byways of the pears and marigolds of her childhood.

(Much later in the novel when Alabama is ill in Naples, she too will have fantasies, but not of 'Alpine gardens' in southern Italy.)

When the war comes Alabama plans 'to escape on the world's reversals from the sense of suffocation that seemed to her to be eclipsing her family. ... Relentlessly she convinced herself that the only thing of any significance was to take what she wanted when she could. She did her best.' She falls in love with the romantic figure of Lieutenant David Knight, who carves a 'legend' in the doorpost of the country club, 'David ... David, David, Knight, Knight, Knight, and Miss Alabama Nobody.' Insistently he tells her how famous he will become. He asks her to tell him she loves him.

> 'Say, "dear," ' he said.
> 'No.'
> 'You love me. Why won't you?'
> 'I never say anything to anybody. Don't talk.'
> 'Why won't you talk to me?'
> 'It spoils things. Tell me you love me.'

He does. But Alabama withholds from him her own pledge of love. When Zelda describes Alabama's love for David she says it is like pressing her nose against a mirror and looking into herself: 'So much she loved the man, so close and closer she felt herself that he became distorted in her vision. ...' She feels 'the essence of herself pulled finer and smaller like those streams of spun glass that pull and stretch till there remains but a glimmering illusion'.* She does not break, but remains in a sort of

* R. D. Laing in his book *The Divided Self* uses an astonishingly similar description of schizophrenics: 'His whole life has been torn between his desire to reveal himself and his desire to conceal himself. ... the person whom we call "schizoid" feels both more exposed, more vulnerable to others than we do, and more isolated. Thus a schizophrenic may say that he is made of glass, of such transparency and fragility that a look directed at him splinters him to bits and penetrates straight through him. We may suppose that precisely as such he experiences himself.

'We shall suggest that it was on the basis of this exquisite vulnerability that the unreal man became so adept at self-concealment.'

suspension of self within David; she feels 'very small and ecstatic. Alabama was in love'.

Alabama, then, in a fantasy, enters David's head, which is 'gray and ghostly'; she looks into 'the deep trenches of the cerebellum'. She runs to 'the front lines' and becomes lost in 'a mystic maze [of] folds and ridges [rising] in desolation; there was nothing to indicate one way from another'. She falls and reaches the 'medulla oblongata'. 'Vast tortuous indentations led her round and round. Hysterically, she began to run.' This entire scene takes place during a kiss. The mirror image at the opening is crucial, for what Alabama loves is something of herself in David. It is when she enters his head that she is terrified, and images of a bleak terrain of the mind, a deserted battlefield, are used to reinforce her terror. What she seems to be afraid of is not simply being there, but the emptiness, the oddly directionless mindscape she is within. It is immediately after this scene that David tells her he is going to see her father about marrying her.

David Knight is Alabama's rescuer from her father's world. A knight is a young man whose job it is to rescue princesses from their imprisonments. David Knight promises to take Alabama away with him into a world without restraint, without fortresses; a world in which law plays little part. It is the artistic world of New York.

When Knight is in New York for embarkation he describes it to Alabama in terms of a fairy tale, and his letters probably echo Scott Fitzgerald's: ' "The tops of the buildings shine like crowns of gold-leaf kings in conference – and oh, my dear, you are my princess and I'd like to keep you shut forever in an ivory tower for my private delectation." ' The third time David writes about his locked-in princess Alabama asks him (as Zelda had asked Scott) 'not to mention the tower again'. In a sense she seems to believe she is a princess in a tower, but a tower like the one described in the opening of the book, which has been built by her father. She is eager to escape from it through Knight, but certainly she will not accept a change of domains on similar terms of imprisonment. However, David differs decidedly from the Judge and Alabama is attracted to him because he does. He is open-handed, an artist, a man who is comfortable with people and playful; he is also as restless and filled with dreams as Alabama is. What he lacks is the Judge's inexorable strength and single-mindedness. One day, long after David's splendid first successes, Alabama will find herself repelled by him, and it will be largely because she misses that quality of authority she had resented in her father. A fortress, Zelda seems to be saying, had protected as well as imprisoned. Alabama turns to memories of her father for sustenance: 'She thought of the time when she was little and had been near her father – by his aloof distance he had presented himself as an infallible source of wisdom, a bed of sureness. She could trust her father. She half hated the unrest of David, hating that of herself that she found in him.' Frightened then by the disintegration of her marriage, she tries to make 'a magic cloak' out of the 'strength of her father and the young beauty of her first love with David. . . .'

With Chapter 2 begins the story of the Knights' marriage. In time, six novels written by the Fitzgeralds would grow out of their love affair and marriage: *This Side of Paradise*, *The Beautiful and Damned*, *The Great Gatsby*, *Save Me the Waltz*, *Tender Is the Night* and Zelda's unfinished manuscript *Caesar's Things*. What Zelda cut out of the chapter probably tells us something about the kind of material to which Scott objected. Still some of it was not cut entire, but recast and in the recasting Zelda kept what she wanted.

Alabama's peculiar genius lay in possessing a rapacious engulfing ego that swallowed her world in the swift undertow of its ebb and flow. . . . Alabama was proud of David. Used to the plugging, slow, and costly successes of the life about her in the South, David's triumphs filled her with an anticipatory sense of uneasiness, as if she had ordered some elaborate appurtenance and, penniless, awaited the bill.

The first sentence was altered to read 'Possessing a rapacious, engulfing ego *their* particular genius swallowed *their* world in its swift undertow and washed its cadavers out to sea' (my italics). The change was clearly intended to include David as well as Alabama.

Mention of money, debt, and drinking were pared down; and the single reference to Alabama's jealousy in the galley proof was drastically altered by the time it was published. But the primary difference between what was published and what appeared in the galleys before revision is in Alabama's attitude toward her family. In both versions Alabama's parents come to visit the Knights while they are living in Connecticut. Their visit is a disaster. In a comic scene, while the Knights are trying to present themselves as models of conventional young marrieds to the Beggses, two of David's friends appear drunk on a hammock in the Knights' back yard. Unable to think of a way to get rid of them, Alabama manages to manoeuvre her mother upstairs for a rest. 'From the sense that she had nothing whatever to do with herself which radiated from the girl as she descended from her parents' room David knew that something was wrong.' This reads pretty much the same in the galleys except that there are additional sentences which explain why she is the way she is: 'Alabama had a way of abnegating under difficulties. It wasn't that she shirked, but her mother had led her to believe that she could have no connection whatever with anything but perfection from babyhood.' These sentences did not appear in the published version.

The two friends eventually wander off, but they return in the early hours of the morning. David goes downstairs to quiet them and winds up drinking gin and tomato juice with them. Alabama is furious with David, tries to grab the bottle from him, and as he pushes her away she falls against the door. It smacks her in the face, giving her not only a bloody nose, but two black eyes. She tries to hide her face under layers of powder, but it is useless. As soon as the Judge sees her he decides to leave immediately for Alabama's sister's apartment in the city. 'Alabama had known this would be their attitude but she couldn't prevent a cataclysmic chute of her insides.' As the Judge disapproves, Alabama reacts against him, but she does not express herself directly; she 'sat silently', she 'said defiantly to herself', or 'to herself bitterly', but not once, until the very end of the scene, does she speak out.

'Understand,' the Judge was saying, 'that I am not passing a moral judgment on your personal conduct. You are a grown woman and that is your own affair.'

'I understand,' she said. 'You just disapprove, so you're not going to stand it. If I don't accept your way of thinking, you'll leave me to myself. Well, I suppose I have no right to ask you to stay.'

'People who do not subscribe,' answered the Judge, 'have no rights.'

In the galley version Alabama, at David's suggestion, follows her parents into the city and plans to spend the night with them and her sister. David, who has just made an important sale of some frescoes, is going up to New Haven.

'Wouldn't you mind?' she said.
'Why should I?'
Her spirits sank in disappointment.
'I don't know,' she said. It gave her a desperate feeling to think that nothing held her – also an experimental excitement. Though she knew in her heart that she'd never have half as much fun without David as she did with him, still there was a pleasurable leap of her insides at the thought of being without him.

As she enters the elevator of Dixie's apartment she realizes her jealousy of David's increasing fame. Alabama's evening with her parents and Dixie is a débâcle from beginning to end. They lecture her about her and David's extravagance; they do not listen as she tries to tell them about David's sale of his frescoes, and when she suggests dinner out at the Ritz, they tell her it costs too much. At her insistence they go anyway. No one but Alabama has dressed for dinner; it is too early to dine properly, the Judge wants 'something plain ... some spinach' and everyone else orders club sandwiches. 'The club sandwiches were awful. The Ritz wasn't accustomed to serving club sandwiches at the dinner hour.' Alabama then suggests going to a show. This time the entire family balks. 'Alabama took a deep breath of the warm air. The streets of New York smelled acrid and sweet to her like imagined drippings from the mechanics of a night-blooming garden.'

Alabama decides to go out with one of David's bachelor friends and leaves her family back at Dixie's apartment. Alabama thinks, 'If they hadn't been so completely impervious to her she would have tried to explain.' When she does not return by 3 a.m. her family calls David, who races back to New York and is furious with Alabama. The scene ends with the Judge's and Millie's goodbyes. Alabama reflects, ' "Another tie broken. . . . The tie will be there but it will be different – I'm no longer part of them which they criticize but have to accept, but something foreign which they reject at will." ' David tells her that she must ' "understand that you can't run roughshod over the world as you evidently think you can, doing everything you like and leaving others to check up after you" '. He suggests that she compromise. From then on her mother's letters to her ask her to behave. At the close of the cut galleys, 'Wedged in between glowing accounts of their activities, she wrote that she was going to have a baby.'

In the published version there is a little more attention given to the birth of Bonnie, but not much. It is handled piecemeal and skittishly. Interrupting the story of whether Alabama is or is not pregnant are fine passages of description of New York City. This nervous, jagged interrupting of the narrative line works effectively to quicken the tempo of these pages and to propel us into the mood of the Knights' early married life.

The top of New York twinkled like a golden canopy behind a throne. David and Alabama faced each other incompetently – you couldn't argue about having a baby.

'So what did the doctor say?' he insisted.

'I told you – he said "Hello!" ' '

'Don't be an ass – what else did he say? – We've got to know what he said.'

'So then we'll have the baby,' announced Alabama, proprietarily.

David fumbled about his pockets. 'I'm sorry – I must have left them at home.' He was thinking that then they'd be three.

'What?'

'The bromides.'

'I said "Baby."'
'Oh.'
'We should ask somebody.'
'Who'll we ask?'
Almost everybody had theories: ... but nobody knew how to have a baby.
'I think you'd better ask your mother,' said David.
'Oh, David – don't! She'd think I wouldn't know how.'
'Well,' he said tentatively, 'I could ask my dealer – he knows where the subways go.'

Breaking into their disjointed conversation about having a baby is another descriptive passage about New York and the popularity of the Knights. Then David says:

'I'll have to do lots of work.... Won't it seem queer to be the centre of the world for somebody else?'
'Very. I'm glad my parents are coming before I begin to get sick.'
'How do you know you'll get sick?'
'I should.'
'That's no reason.'
'No.'
'Let's go some place else.'

It is after this, in the published version, that Alabama's parents come for their visit and Alabama remarks that 'she hadn't been absolutely sure of how to go about anything since her marriage had precluded the Judge's resented direction'. Six pages later, almost as an aside, Zelda wrote:

Vincent Youmans wrote a new tune. The old tunes floated through the hospital windows from the hurdy-gurdies while the baby was being born and the new tunes went the luxurious rounds of lobbies and grills, palm-gardens and roofs.

(Zelda's treatment of the birth of Bonnie is reminiscent of Fitzgerald's attempt in *The Beautiful and Damned* to handle Gloria's supposed pregnancy. In both novels the reader is left uncertain about the basic facts. In Scott's the fact that Gloria is not with child is written about as an aside. Bonnie's birth is, after the build-up, similarly oblique.) After this passage Zelda slips in another about New York, but this one is marked with ominous descriptive material.

> The New York rivers dangled lights along the banks like lanterns on a wire; the Long Island marshes stretched the twilight to a blue Campagna. Glimmering buildings hazed the sky in a luminous patchwork quilt. Bits of philosophy, odds and ends of acumen, the ragged ends of vision suicided in the sentimental dusk. The marshes lay black and flat and red and full of crime about their borders. Yes, Vincent Youmans wrote the music.

The final sentence would seem to tie this material to that about the birth of Bonnie, but there is no direct commentary about the baby at all. She is born, that's it. We don't know what she looks like or, more importantly, how her parents feel about her. Suddenly the novel switches direction and the Knight *ménage* is off for Europe.

> It costs more to ride on the tops of taxis than on the inside; Joseph Urban skies are expensive when they're real ... a thread of glamor, a Rolls-Royce thread, a thread of O. Henry ... their fifty thousand dollars bought a cardboard baby-nurse for Bonnie, a second-hand Marmon, a Picasso etching ... two white knickerbocker suits exactly alike ... and two first class tickets for Europe.
>
> In the packing case a collection of plush teddy bears, David's army overcoat, their wedding silver and four bulging scrapbooks full of all the things people envied them for were ready to be left behind.
>
> ....
> Alabama said to herself they were happy – she had inherited that from her mother. 'We are very happy,' she said to herself, as her mother would have said, 'but we don't seem to care very much whether we are or not. I suppose we expected something more dramatic.'

When the Knights at last escape New York for the Riviera there is a return to the images of physical description that Zelda had used at the beginning of the novel in connection with Judge Beggs and the South. There is the scent of fruit trees, but this time there is the hint of something threatening within the setting. The foliage is 'black', there are 'keeps' and 'battlements' and 'ancient moats', and the scene is '*bound* in tangled honey-

suckle; fragile poppies *bled* the causeways; vineyards *caught* on
the jagged rocks' (my italics).

The name of the villa they take is 'Les Rossignols', the Night-
ingales, and when Alabama describes it she says, 'Pastel cupids
frolicked amidst the morning-glories and roses in garlands
swelled like goitres or some malignant disease.' Alabama wonders whether it is going to be as 'nice as it seems'. David tells her
they are now in Paradise '– as nearly as we'll ever get'. Alabama
asks him if he's going to work all the time and David replies
that he hopes to. ' "It's a man's world", Alabama sighed. ...
' "This air has the most lascivious feel –" ' David's reply, ' "Well,
I can't paint at night, you know. We shall have plenty of private
life" ', was cut from the published version. But somehow they
do not have much private life; David works and Alabama is
left very much to herself. She tries to occupy herself reading,
but she resents being left alone while David works. 'When she
was a child and the days slipped lazily past in the same indolent
fashion, she had not thought of life as furnishing up the slow
uneventful sequence, but of the Judge as meting it out that way,
curtailing the excitement she considered was her due. She began
to blame David for the monotony.'

Alabama has met Jacques, a French aviator, whose surname
Chevre-Feuille (honeysuckle) is a conscious attempt to link him
to the setting. Chevre-Feuille is, as David was when Alabama
fell in love with him, in military uniform and a lieutenant.

Eventually Jacques asks her to come to his apartment. She
says, ' "Yes – I don't know. Yes." ' And David, although he
does not know exactly what has passed between the two, tells
Alabama she is 'sick ... insane' and threatens that if she sees
Jacques any more he will go back to America without her. She
tells Jacques that if she does not come to him he must not visit
her any more. He asks what she will say to David.

'I'll have to tell him.'
'It would be unwise,' said Jacques in alarm. 'We must hang on to
our benefits –'

Although it is never made explicit, what Jacques has seemed to
say is that he wants Alabama, but not on a permanent basis. In

other words, she is not to tell David and thereby threaten her marriage, or Jacques is clearly not prepared to offer Alabama anything more than an invitation to an affair. Up to this point they have done nothing more than kiss, and as it turns out (although they do meet once again in David's company) Alabama does not go to his apartment. Jacques Chevre-Feuille gets himself transferred to 'Indo-Chine' and leaves Alabama with a photograph of himself and a letter in French which she cannot read. She rips up the letter, and 'Though it broke her heart, she tore the picture too. ... What was the use of keeping it? ... There wasn't a way to hold on to the summer. ... Whatever it was that she wanted from Jacques, Jacques took it with him to squander on the Chinese. You took what you wanted from life, if you could get it, and you did without the rest.' This is an almost exact repetition of Alabama's earlier resolve, when the war began, 'to take what she wanted when she could'. Except, of course, Alabama had not done so in this case. She had not taken Jacques Chevre-Feuille, whom she had apparently wanted; she had let him go, with regret perhaps, but she had not ventured very far.*

Which brings us to the centre of both the novel and the characterization of Alabama Beggs. Alabama has not fulfilled her promise to herself and she begins to see her life with David in terms of the sense of suffocation and eclipse she once felt with her family in the South. Once she had sought a definition of herself, but her marriage has brought her no answers to her quest. It is only when the Knights leave the Riviera for Paris ('a perfect breeding place for the germs of bitterness they brought with them') that, caught up in the endless wave of parties, amid the debris of her marriage, she finds her answer. And in the manner Zelda has established earlier in the novel, her flower imagery gives the clue to her fiction. In Paris the flowers are artificial: 'They made nasturtiums of leather and rubber and

---

* Scott, however, took *Save Me the Waltz* as proof of Zelda's love affair with Jozan. He wrote one of Zelda's doctors: 'As soon as she could feel I was safe at home she immediately betrayed me. She did it by her own confession. You only have to read her book. And I was doing the best work in my life.' (He was writing *The Great Gatsby*.)

wax gardenias and ragged robins out of threads and wires. They manufactured hardy perennials to grow on the meagre soil of shoulder straps and bouquets with long stems for piercing the loamy shadows under the belt.'

In that Parisian world of parties, at which no one is French, but English and American – with a peppering of Russians from the ballet – Alabama feels 'excluded by her lack of accomplishment'. She is not as elegant as the other women and feels 'clumsy' when she compares herself to Gabrielle Gibbs, with whom David is obviously charmed. (The ten-page revision of Section III of this chapter cuts out some of the small talk of the parties and gives a sharper sense of Alabama's growing removal and isolation and insecurity.)

After a dinner party at which David and Miss Gibbs flirt they all go to the theatre to see a Stravinsky ballet. The ballet seems to Alabama to offer her a chance for distinction. Her friends completely misunderstand her reasons for wanting to dance, but provide an interesting glimpse into what Zelda knew they thought of Alabama/Zelda: ' "I think ... that it would be the very thing for Alabama. I've always heard she was a little peculiar – I don't mean actually batty – but a little difficult. An art would explain." '

When Zelda was first at Phipps she had written Scott:

Life has become practicly intolerable. Everyday I develop a new neurosis until I can think of nothing to do but place myself in the Confederate Museum at Richmond. Now it's money: we must have more money. To-morrow it will [be] something else again: that I ran when Mamma needed me to help her move, that my hips are fat and shaking with the vulgarities of middle-age, that you had to leave your novel ... a horrible sickening fear that I shall never be able to free myself from the mediocrity of my conceptions. For many years I have lived under the disastrous pressure of a conviction of power and necessity to accomplish without the slightest ray of illumination. The only message I ever thought I had was four pirouettes and a feueté. It turned out to be about as cryptic a one as [a] Chinese laundry ticket, but the will to speak remains.

In Chapter 3 she wrote as fully as she was able of her consuming involvement with the ballet. This chapter moves at a higher pitch than the first two and the world of the young girls who dance at Madame's studio behind the stage of the Olympia Music Hall comes vibrantly to life. The curiously female and narcissistic atmosphere of the dance is emphasized by the incessant quarrelling of the girls as they manoeuvre for positions of excellence before their teacher's eyes. Alabama pushes her body beyond the pain of the stretches, the 'Miles and miles of *pas de bourré*', toward excellence, but it is a punishing effort. In one of the sentences from the first galleys that were eliminated in the published version we are given a clue to Alabama's development: 'Of all things on earth she had never wanted anything quite so much as to possess herself, as it seemed to her, that she would if she could attain a perfected control.' Her consuming interest is in the perfection of her body. But, as she drives herself, David is left spending his time drinking with friends at the Ritz bar.

'Why will you never come out with me?' he said.

'Because I can't work next day if I do.'

'Are you under the illusion that you'll ever be any good at that stuff?'

'I suppose not; but there's only one way to try.'

'We have no life at home any more.'

'You're never there anyway – I've got to have something to do with myself.'

'Another female whine – I have to do my work.'

And this time when Zelda writes of flowers, they are a heady, lush, exotic contribution to the prose. They are flowers for the dance; flowers for Madame.

Yellow roses she bought with her money like Empire satin brocade, and white lilacs and pink tulips like moulded confectioner's frosting, and deep-red roses like a Villon poem, black and velvety as an insect wing, cold blue hydrangeas clean as a newly calcimined wall, the crystalline drops of lily of the valley . . . She bought lemon-yellow carnations perfumed with the taste of hard candy, and garden roses purple as raspberry puddings, and every kind of white flower the florist knew how to grow. She gave Madame gardenias like white kid gloves and forget-me-nots from the Madeleine stalls, threatening sprays of gladioli, and the soft, even purr of black tulips. She bought flowers like salads and flowers like fruits, jonquils and narcissus, poppies and ragged robins, and flowers with the brilliant carnivorous qualities of Van Gogh.

Alabama does have her work to do, but David makes a distinction between what she can hope to accomplish in hers and what he has done in his. ' "You're so thin" ', said David patronizingly. "There's no use killing yourself. I hope that you realize that the biggest difference in the world is between the amateur and the professional in the arts."

' "You might mean yourself and me –" she said thoughtfully.' Moments later Alabama reflects that 'David's success was his own – he had earned his right to be critical – Alabama felt she had nothing to give to the world and no way to dispose of what she took away.' David's success had deeply impressed her and she badly wants her own. Zelda reveals in her fiction the story of her own frustrated desire for accomplishments that would match Scott's. But the collapse of Alabama's dreams is as total as Zelda's had been. In Alabama's case a physical accident, the infection of her foot, destroys any chance she has to become a ballerina, as in Zelda's life her mental breakdown destroyed hers.

One of the levels on which *Save Me the Waltz* moved at its opening was that of the fairy tale – Alabama as princess to her Knight. Zelda seems to have dropped the implications of her fairy tale only to pick up the threads again in Chapter 4 when Alabama is in Italy without David and Bonnie. Bonnie, at David's suggestion, comes to visit her, but the timing of her visit is unfortunate. Alabama is preparing to dance in *Le Lac des Cygnes*; she gets permission to miss a rehearsal and meets Bonnie and Mademoiselle at the train. When Alabama sees her daughter she notices: 'The bones had begun to come up in her nose; her hands were forming. She was going to have those wide-ended fingers of a Spanish primitive like David. She was very like her father.' But Bonnie is disappointed to find out that her mother has none of the conveniences she is used to in her father's company. There is no car, but 'a flea-bitten horse-cab'; the boarding house in which Alabama has been living in Naples smells of 'damp and urine'. Both Mademoiselle and Bonnie are clearly disappointed, and it seems to Alabama that her child has become a snob. Bonnie gets a rash from the food; Alabama plans a party for Bonnie at which the child is bitten by a monkey. To make her feel better Alabama takes her on her lap before the other children and begins to tell her a story; it is about Greek temples, but when Alabama finally gets everyone's attention, she cannot think of a story to tell. Bonnie gets sick from the monkey bite, or maybe the climate, and Alabama goes back to her rehearsals. Bonnie and Mademoiselle leave Italy to return to David.

'We should have taken the train-de-luxe,' said Bonnie. 'I am in rather a hurry to get to Paris.'

'This is the train-de-luxe, snob!'

Bonnie gazed at her mother in impassive skepticism.

'There are many things in the world you don't know, Mummy.'

'It's just barely possible.'

When Bonnie arrives in Switzerland (the reference to Paris above must be an error), David wants to know if she had a good time. As Bonnie looks about her she notices 'Ladies in lace with parasols, ladies in linen with white shoes. ...' And as she turns to look at her father she sees that he is 'Dressed in a catalogue of summer ... his clothes were a little amazing, suggesting a studied sartorial selection. He was dressed in pearly grey and he looked as if he had stepped down inside his angora sweater and flannel pants with such precision that he hardly deranged their independent decorative purpose.' He is handsome and Bonnie is proud of him. She tells him that Alabama 'was dancing'. Then as they enter the hotel, Zelda makes her point: ' "The rooms, Prince", said the sad, suave hotel man. . . . The valet carried their luggage to a white-and-gold encrusted suite. . . . "How would the royal visitor like her bath?" said David.'

The separate worlds of David and Alabama Knight have changed. David has become, in his success and fame and handsomeness, a prince, and Bonnie a princess. Together, daughter and father move into the world of fairy tale without

Alabama. And it seems to be a brighter, richer world than Alabama's had ever been.

Riding home through the flickering night, the country passed in visions of twinkling villages and cottage gardens obstructing their passage with high sunflower stalks. The children, wrapped in the bright armor of Bonnie's father's car, dozed against the felt cushions. Safe in the glittering car they rode: the car-at-your-disposal, the mystery-car, the Rajah's-car, the death-car, the first-prize, puffing the power of money out on the summer air like a seigneur distributing largesse. Where the night sky reflected the lake they rode like a rising bubble through the bowl of the mercurial, welded globe. They drove through the black impenetrable shadows clouding the road like fumes from an alchemist's laboratory and sped across the gleam of the open mountain top.

At the end of the novel Alabama returns with David and Bonnie to the small Southern town of her girlhood for her father's final illness and death. Alabama confronts her past in the person of her dying father. At each step of the way from the railway station to her father's bedside she is overcome by remembering things that had formed her. She recalls the infallibility of her father and her own delight when something went wrong for him; it was a small reminder of his humanity, and thereby brought him closer to her. When at last she is alone with him her tenderness toward him overwhelms her. When she speaks to him it is again for guidance, for some measure of direction from him for her own life, and she disguises her feeling in abstract questions.

'Oh, my father, there are so many things I want to ask you.'
'Baby,' the old man patted her hand. His wrists were no bigger than a bird's. How had he fed them all?
'I never thought you'd known till now.'
She smoothed the gray hair, even Confederate gray.
'I've got to go to sleep, baby.'
'Sleep,' she said, 'sleep.'
She sat there a long time. She hated the way the nurse moved about the room as if her father were a child. Her father knew everything. Her heart was sobbing, and sobbing.
The old man opened his eyes proudly, as was his wont.

'Did you say you wanted to ask me something?'

'I thought you could tell me if our bodies are given to us as counter-irritants to the soul. I thought you'd know why when our bodies ought to bring surcease from our tortured minds, they fail and collapse; and why, when we are tormented in our bodies, does our soul desert us as a refuge?'

The old man lay silent.

'Why do we spend years using up our bodies to nurture our minds with experience and find our minds turning then to our exhausted bodies for solace? Why, Daddy?'

'Ask me something easy,' the old man answered very weak and far away.

In what is the first admission of the deep love she feels for her father, Alabama is nevertheless unable to the end to reach him, unable to elicit from him any answers to her questions about life itself. Zelda tries to parallel Alabama's feelings toward the Judge with those of Alabama's mother to her father, and of Bonnie toward David. It is as if generations of fathers passing before her imagination give some mute testament of life to their daughters, some comfort. 'Her father!' she had written before Alabama left Europe for home. 'Without her father the world would be without its last resource.

' "But" ', she remembered with a sudden sobering shock, "it will be me who is the last resource when my father is dead." '

After her father's death Alabama searches for some token of direction left behind by him, but she finds nothing. ' "He must have forgot," Alabama said, "to leave the message." ' She tries to remember things he has said, but can bring little to mind other than his last words that his illness was expensive. 'Once he had said, "If you want to choose, you must be a goddess." That was when she had wanted her own way about things.' She says that she is heir to ' "many doubts" '.

As the Knights make ready to leave the South they give a farewell party, and the people attending the party compliment them and tell them they are lucky, that they ' "have an easy time" '. Alabama says: ' "We grew up founding our dreams on the infinite promise of American advertising. I *still* believe that one can learn to play the piano by mail and that mud will give you a perfect complexion." ' But no matter what her protests people insist that the Knights are 'happy'. As the party guests leave 'the pleasant place' Zelda undercuts the well wishing of their departures by repeated use of the words 'death' and 'dead' until it becomes death in the first person:

'We've talked you to death.'
'You must be dead with packing.'
'It's death to a party to stay till digestion sets in.'
'I'm dead, my dear. It's been wonderful.'

Alabama says they will come back to visit her family, and then, to herself, thinks, 'Always ... we will have to seek some perspective on ourselves, some link between ourselves and all the values more permanent than us of which we have felt the existence by placing ourselves in our father's setting.' The party over, Alabama begins to empty ashtrays. She tells David it is ' "very expressive of myself. I just lump everything in a great heap which I have labelled "the past", and, having thus emptied this deep reservoir that was once myself, I am ready to continue." '

The Knights will continue as they have been, the novel points to no fresh departures for they believe in none, and it gives little hope of a brighter future for them. They sit together, staring at each other among the silver debris of glasses and trays of their last party and watch the twilight come in upon the living room and themselves.

15

O Darling! My poor dear – watching everything in your life
destroyed one by one except your name. Your entire life will
soon be accounted for by the toils we have so assiduously
woven – your leisure is eaten up by habits of leisure,
your money by habitual extravagance, your hope by
cynicism and mine by frustration, your ambition
by too much compromise.

ZELDA, in an undated letter to Scott.

During Zelda's first month (February 1932) at Phipps her conversations with the psychiatrists had been evasive and unpro-
ductive. They were no closer to understanding her than when
she arrived, for she treated their calls on her as social visits. But
after *Save Me the Waltz* was written the doctors changed their
tactics; instead of only talking with her, they asked her to write
out what she thought had happened to her. The result was a
strangely distorted autobiographical sketch, studded with expressions of distrust and recrimination – a semi-fantasy of her
life with Scott. It confirmed some of the things Scott had mentioned, and it gave her doctors Zelda's perspective toward those
things. Portions of this document are puzzling, for some of the
biographical references are inaccessible, lost in the tangle of
Zelda's mind. But once again she demonstrated her uncanny
ability to express the undercurrent drifts of her feelings. She
began writing at the remove of the third-person narrator, as if
this were a story, but as the intensity of her revelations gained
momentum, the game of story writing fell away and she wrote
as *I*.

The eyes of the psychiatrist moved back and forth under the
heavy lashes, like the shuttle of a loom weaving a story from the
dark heavy thread.

'So write the story with no embellishments,' said the voice. There
was that excitement about the voice of waiting un-committed; the
excitement of the inveterate gambler with many systems, who yet
takes his money haphazard; the excitement of inveterate super-
stition.

'Very well,' began the sick one patiently, 'but it is the story of a fathomless solitude, of a black detachment of nothing. A vacuum can only exist, I imagine, by the things which enclose it.'

A pretense that the invalid made sense fluttered over the fine face. The face had nothing to do with the psychiatry. She inspected it like an interloper she might have found in her room, returned to the patient and said, 'Go on.'

'We lived in a big house by the river [Ellerslie in Wilmington]. The rooms were high and full of the immensity of beautiful proportions. The house was so perfect that the doors grew smaller at the top like the columns of a Greek temple. A circular stair-well plumbed its depth. There were trees outside the windows that rose like rockets and spread in sprays at their ultimate point across the wide panes. A gaunt barn with a burnt sienna roof and walls that had faded to a gangrenous sheet of bilious green, rested on thin posts like the niches of a cathedral. Violets grew in the abandoned traces of an ante-bellum garden and yellow roses like crumpled bits of tissue paper climbed the fence. Outside the stark luxuriance of the yard, cinders stretched for miles and miles, to a government buoy station whose red roofs lay like a canopy over the sandbars and to a boiler factory bound by a white rose hedge.

....

'There were many things to brood about. There was Marie, a wonderful negro maid, high and gawky, who laughed and danced bare-foot about the Christmas tree on the broken balls, and there was Phillipe, a Paris taxi-driver who wanted to run the house like a cab at night, who was stupid and insubordinate, and boxed with his master and worked too hard in his official capacity as butler. He had an air of being always startled, perhaps in his uncertainty of his present role. We called him from the kitchen with a French auto-horn attached to the dining room chair. There was Ella who sang spirituals in the kitchen and sat like a dark ejection of the storm in the candle-light of the dining room when thunder blew up the Maryland lightning belt at night and whipped and cracked over the river. And there was Mademoiselle, nervous and reeking of sachet, whose great brown eyes followed a person about like a mop and who cried and wept and grew hysterical about Phillipe....

'The first company came: a young actress like a breakfast food that many men identified with whatever they missed from life since she had no definite characteristics of her own save a slight ebullient hysteria about romance. She walked in the moon by the river. Her hair was tight about her head and she was lush and like a milkmaid.

Carl [Van Vechten] came. Carl is divine; he spent six months in prison rather than pay his wife alimony. He is an experimentalist and a connoisseur. He brought suppressed nigger records and a cock-tail shaker and saved my letters and collects first editions in friends whom he vivisects with rapt interest. He's a dramatist at heart. Our relations were very impersonal but Carl was a fine friend.

'Teddy [Theodore Chanler] came. Teddy is an instrument of our lost republic. He could understand why an amusement park is the best place to be amorous – it's something about the whitewashed trees and the smell of peanuts and the jogging of the infernal machines for riding. . . .

. . . .

'Dick [Richard Knight] came. I do not know why he is attractive. He flung a pot of mustard at the dining room door, his head is too big for his body, he is a lawyer. One lost afternoon in a black lace dress we drank cocktails in a New York apartment and sat afterwards a long time on the stairway, oblivious with a kind of happy desperation. . . . We would have made scenes but there was trouble. . . . I forgot him during rehersals for the Opera Ballet. I was too tired to care and too full of brooding except when something external drove me to him: the night Scott came home drunk from Princeton and smashed my nose about some conflict of his own and my sister left the house and never forgave him, poor man. I telephoned Dick. He has the most magnetic voice I've ever known. Dick had to go; . . . I don't think though Scott had a world of his own which made no provision for our lives together except to kick about rehersals because once I got drunk in an Italian restaurant with some girls from the ballet after I'd finished a story in the Phila. library during the afternoon, and he was angry. He left me so much alone that I was very ashamed of wanting him once. . . . He was thinking of the actress: he said so. I said I wanted to leave him but he wouldn't let me go. We fought.

'My dancing teacher was a protege of Nijinsky. I ate lunch with him at Rubens and went with him to his apartment. There was nothing in the commercial flat except the white spitz of his mistress and a beautiful collection of Leon Bakst. It was a cold afternoon. He asked me if I wanted him to kill me and I said I would cry and [he?] left me there. I ran to my lesson through the cold streets. I always wore white. . . .

'I do not know what Scott was doing during that year. He went to New York: I didn't want to go. He worked a little, we lived in the cinders and the wind from the river and sometimes, rarely, we did things together.

'On the boat he had friends and I was very unimaginative about a dark man who thought it was nice that he had a brown jacket and I had a blue one.... They all came down and we drank champagne. I think I wanted him to see a new nightgown I had.

'In Genoa, Scott and I slept together.

'In Nice, I worked at a studio which I did not like, with Nevalskaya. Scott and I were happy in the bright, incisive sun, watching the frog swallower on the promenade and the awful comedies at the Casino. He was mad because I wouldn't go to a French version of Broadway and liked me when I told him why the Place Gallieni was charming: about the faded Baroque painted houses and the one-dimensional quality of that sun-sterile stone. He hated the child's nurse. We drank aperitifs at a blue cafe in front of the Jetée and I loved walking to the hotel from my dancing. The sapphire twilight was deep and mysterious and I hummed the songs that the old man played; mostly Strauss waltzes.... The studio piano was out of tune. The hotel bedroom was red plush and the bed was brass and the rooms were on the sea and I loved him very much.

'We went to Paris. You have the history of the studio there in my book. It was like living in a dream. Scott drank almost always. ... I thought always of my dancing and of Egorova. I wanted to do something for her terribly. I was very tired and cried once for 2 hours when she asked me to work with a girl who did not dance as well as I. The girl came dressed in a new cerise ballet-dress which faded afterwards on the chair of the dressing room. I could not get it off, the stain, with eau-do-cologne.

'Scott went out with King Vidor and Andre Champson and hated the apartment and our dreary lunches. I was working and unattractive. We bought a black cat that had diarrhea and had to give him back.... I didn't think much about him [Scott] because I felt like a priest about my work. We went once to church. I hated taking his money for my lessons: I wanted my dancing to belong to me, so I wrote to pay for them.

'He came out with me to Egorova's to dinner. He passed out. It was an awful meal. I adored her. She lived in poverty and seemed very poignant. Once we took her to a Russian cabaret and I filled her champagne glass with daisies. She was a great artist. I used to carry lemonade to the hot studio.... She seemed to me like a gardenia, so I gave her gardenias and found some Oriental gardenia perfume for her. She was reticent and I don't know what she thought. She was very good and kind and always gave me lessons, the famous dancers clamored for her hours.

'Scott and I went to Cannes. We quarrelled there that year: everybody did. It was a nightmare. I worked everyday in Nice, largely to escape....

'Scott had half a novel done. It was fine. He brought some friends home with him drunk, and I found it all over the floor the next morning. He was sick with tb and drank. I drank sherry and ginger-snaps – not much after swimming. I wrote a ballet called "Evolution" and made the scenery and costumes on the beach. I hardly saw my child because I hated the nurse she had, who snored and was mean to Scottie. Scott did not want to fire her. I was half-crazy and thought the people looked like embryos, and wanted to get back to Paris. Scott and I were completely alienated. He went some with his friends, exotic, interesting people who sat up all night. I couldn't: I was working on grand pirouettes.... He talked and talked and talked at table with the governess about French politics. I couldn't stand much talking.

'We came back to Paris through the Cévennes. The trip was fun and we would have been closer but when the car swerved to the crest of a hill, it seemed to me it was going into oblivion beyond and I had to hold the sides of the car. I wrote a story about those mountains. I felt like Cardinal Ballou in the car and wanted to leave him at Tours, but I felt too sorry to think of his driving alone thru the rain – or maybe I did come home on the train: I can't remember. Anyway, I was very sorry for Scott.

'In Paris I worked and wrote and went to Algiers. In Algiers I thought of my teacher always and wrote many letters from Biskra and Bou Saad and was miserable in the gorge of Constantine and unhappy at Tungaad and nervous in the big, tearing bus. There were apple trees in bloom on the bleak hills and velvet nights and wonderful smells and goat cheese and lamp-light along the way at dusk.

'On the boat coming home, I was sick. An English lady called out "Cheerio" with every rock of the boat, and I was utterly alone and thought the boat was sinking. Scott had found companions. He is a popular man. The stewards were sick; everybody was sick. We ate Brioche and marmalade on the pier, when we landed. I brought

Egorova a bandana handkerchief filled with perfume and silk for a green dress and amber chips from Africa. The moon in Bou Saada had been white and hot and the Ouled-Naïls had brown bodies to churn when they danced. Soft cries muffled the night; the Arabs ate nougat under the gas flares and the streets were baked and caked with dust. . . . It was an awful trip, though there was a pleasant half-hour with Scott in Biskra. Somehow those dreadful passages have a way of assuming qualities that they did not possess at the time, in retrospect. It is one of the places I should like to go again. Algiers will always remain colored for me by my impatience and drive to get back, my jealousy of Scott's ability to amuse himself, and an implacable sense of desperation that haunted me constantly like a person crossing a dangerous stream, not daring to look further ahead than the next stone . . .

'In Paris again, I saw a great deal of Nemtchinova after classes and my friend of the Opera. I worked constantly and was terribly superstitious and moody about my work, full of presentiments about the sun and the rain and the wind. I lived in a quiet ghostly, hyper-sensitized world of my own. Scott drank. One night he told me that he had spit up a cup of blood. I cried all night and next day he said it wasn't true. He said he was sick and that he couldn't work and we lived like strangers. He had other friends and so did I. I had grown to resent the people we knew who did not work, no matter how attractive they were and to feel contemptuous of them.

'We went to a party somewhere that ended at Maximes. . . . All this time passed in A DAZE.

'. . . I was sick. . . . All I cared about was my lessons. Every day I took flowers to the studio. . . . Then at four o'clock one after-noon, after my lesson, Michael Arlen was at home drinking with Scott. He was very pleasant and told me to go to a clinic. I quar-relled with Scott violently because I felt that I needed him and he so obviously preferred being with Michael.

'I went to MalMaison and flirted outrageously with the Doctor.

'I came back and went to work. Egorova came to see me and gave me a present. I knew I could not dance again and I was utterly heartbroken when I told her goodby. . . .'

She said that from the dance she had learned exaltation 'and a feeling for the flights of the human soul divorced from the person'. When she found that she could not understand some-thing she had only to transpose it into choreographic terms and it became clear. At the end of what she called 'this … fairy tale' she left five blank lines for the psychiatrist to fill in with her opinions. Zelda had again disdainfully eluded those she called The Authorities. But had she? What was clear to them now was her refusal to confront her illness directly; she would neither admit nor accept their assistance.

At about the same time this document was written, Zelda wrote Scott in an entirely different mode:

Darling, Sweet D.O. –

… I have often told you that I am that little fish who swims about under a shark and, I believe, lives indelicately on its offal. Anyway, that is the way I am. Life moves over me in a vast black shadow and I swallow whatever it drops with relish, having learned in a very hard school that one cannot be both a parasite and enjoy self-nourishment without moving in worlds too fantastic for even my disordered imagination to people with meaning. Goofo – I adore you and worship you and I am very miserable that you be made even temporarily unhappy by those divergencies of direction in myself which I cannot satisfactorily explain and which leave me eternally alone except for you and baffled. You are absolutely all in the world that I have ever been able to think of as having any vital bearing on my relations with the evolution of the species. … I love you and I would like us to be covered with the flake of dried sea water and sleeping to-gether on a hot afternoon. That would be very free and fine. Dear Heart!

I have got so fetid and constantly smell of the rubbery things about here – It's ghastly, really. I do not know to what depths the human soul can sink in bondage, but after a certain point everything luckily dissolves in humor. I want to fly a kite and eat green apples and have a stomach-ache that I know the cause of and feel the mud between my toes in a reedy creek and tickle the lobe of your ear with the tip of my tongue.

If Trouble still bites give him a good kick in the ass for me.

Darling, I love you so.
Zelda

Zelda was far more upset by her second collapse than she revealed to the doctors or to Scott, and she tried to hide from all of them her fury toward Scott for holding up her novel. She was overheard saying to herself, 'I have always done whatever I wanted to do, whenever I could possibly manage it. My book is none of my husband's Goddamned business.'

Scott arrived in Baltimore to hunt for a house, and until he found one he stayed at the Rennert Hotel in the centre of town, a few minutes from Phipps. He spent a great deal of time trying to provide the psychiatrists with his own point of view on Zelda's breakdown. In this effort, he had written a sketch about Mrs Sayre pinpointing the significance of her relationship to Zelda, which he sent to Dr Squires on 4 April 1932. He felt that their early attachment gave a clue to Zelda's troubles.

'It all went back to Zelda whom she [Mrs Sayre] suckled until, as Zelda afterwards remarked she could probably have chewed sticks. Zelda was a beauty – a wild, gallant child, precociously passionate because of the early cultivation that her mother had made of her nervous system, lazy and half contemptuous of her own talents and selfish up to a point where the other members of the family, Judge Sayre and Zelda's sisters, refrained from a constant protest that would have amounted to echolalia, only because of the strange mystic power of her mother's fixation upon her.' He insisted that Zelda had learned very early to assert herself even when that assertiveness was inappropriate and without motivation. As an adolescent she had naturally begun to pull away from her mother, but rather than accept this, Mrs Sayre had cultivated her position as confidante; she waited on Zelda, and tried to act as her conscience. '. . . it destroyed Zelda's personal integrity (in later years she was never able quite to comprehend the meaning of the phrase) and it attached her by the silver cord forever'. Zelda had learned to 'beguile', Scott said, rather than stand on her own.

By mid-April Scott was able to visit Zelda daily at the clinic, but their meetings were spoiled by constant quarrelling. The visits began to have a pattern. Scott behaved badly and grew insulting and angry when Zelda would refuse, for example, to show him a story she was writing. They would quarrel and Zelda would put up a good front at the time, then weep during the night. She was sleeping only four to six hours out of twenty-four.

Zelda gave no details of their quarrels to her doctors, whereas Scott was quite willing to discuss them. He struck the doctors as acting martyred, lacking in understanding, and uncertain of himself. After their quarrels they would write remorseful letters to each other.

Scott would try patiently to explain to Zelda what was the matter with her:

Honey, when you come out into the world again I wish you would try to realize what I can only describe as the:

Nub (N U B) of Experience

The fact that in your efforts you have come up *twice* against insuperable facts 1st against L.——— 2nd against me – both times against long desperate heart-destroying professional training beginning when we . . . were seven, probably.

There has never been any question as to your 'value' as a personality – there is however a question as to your ability to use your values to any practical purpose. To repeat the phrase that became an athema in my ears during the last months of our trying to make a go of it *'expressing oneself'* I can only say there isn't any such thing. It simply doesn't exist. What one expresses in a work of art is the dark tragic destiny of being an instrument of something uncomprehended, incomprehensible, unknown – you came to the threshold of that discovery and then decided that in the face of all logic you would crash the gate. You succeeded merely in crashing yourself, almost me, and Scotty, if I hadn't interposed.

Zelda would, equally patiently, try to tell Scott that she was not reacting against him, but an uncontrollable part of her illness objected to his advice and struck out against Dr Fitzgerald. Writing to Scott to say that she would rather stay at Phipps for a while until she was better, she added: 'We have been so close this last year and have so many pleasant memories of things we've done that I'd hate to spoil it in any way. I think we're all agreed that your role is *not to be that of a doctor* and in my present condition you have to mother me and bear with a lot of unpleasantness which is not part of how I feel towards you at all but the result of my health, simply –'

As their correspondence continued Scott kept returning to the issue of her writing, and in an unpublished sketch, which he probably wrote at this time, he made the basis for his objections quite clear.

ANALOGY

Supposing Nikitma was going to create La Chatte in London. Supposing she had for many years supported a younger sister, a neophyte of the ballet but much less experienced and probably less talented. The performance has been delayed and will indeed be still longer delayed from Nikitma's necessity of taking care of her sister.

Suddenly she finds that the sister has been secretly rehearsing La Chatte with the idea of giving it in London.

'That's out,' says Nikitma. 'Rehearse anything else and I'll back you but not that. If your London performance comes before mine, with the name I've made I'm done for. Nobody could beat that handicap.'

SISTER: 'But I want to express myself.'

NIKITMA: 'Nevertheless that's out.'

SISTER: 'But I saw the script the same day you did.'

NIKITMA: 'But I chose it and bought it and paid for it.'

SISTER: 'But I would if I could.'

NIKITMA: 'But I did.'

SISTER: 'You're horrid. You have bad habits.'

NIKITMA: 'So would you if I didn't watch you.'

SISTER: [']Besides I've seen you rehearse so many times I think I could do it nearly as well as you.'

NIKITMA: 'When I've tried it you can try it. Not till then.'

SISTER: 'But I'm going on rehearsing.'

NIKITMA: 'Not on this stage. Not with these lights and this music.'

SISTER: 'I promise I won't do it until you do.'

NIKITMA: 'Then why are you so eager to rehearse at once. No, no, little girl, I've been in this game too long.'

SISTER: 'But I want to express myself.'

NIKITMA: 'All right. Whatever that means. But you can't exploit your relation to me to do me harm.'

Scott gave an interview to the Baltimore *Sun* in which he mentioned Zelda's forthcoming novel. The headline for the article ran, 'He Tells of Her Novel', with subtitle, 'Work Sent to Publisher Is Autobiographical at Suggestion of Her Husband'. That must have been hard for Zelda to swallow. Actually, he said next to nothing about *Save Me the Waltz* and talked about the economic health of the nation. But he had covered himself.

Dr Meyer continued to try to tell Zelda some of the things he felt she had to learn in order to exist successfully again in the outside world. And Zelda at Scott's urging tried to be more open with Meyer. But communication between them always fell short of the trust that had to exist if she was to make significant progress under his care. Dr Meyer wanted Zelda to face her sickness squarely, not passively in the fixed terms of dementia praecox and schizophrenia that she would prattle about as an evasive tactic. He wanted her to avoid the terrific strain she had felt when she was involved in the ballet and seek a middle course. That was not a line of argument congenial to Zelda's temperament and she once told him flatly to stop insisting upon it. 'I went into dancing because I was miserable in my personal life and I thought I could dance – that was a delusion.' That was as far as they got. A colleague of Dr Meyer's who would one day work closely with Zelda at Phipps says: 'It is easy to understand why Dr Meyer never got close to her; he was too heavy and ponderous and germanic ... none of the quick comeback and wit that appealed to Zelda. I don't think Zelda's responses to Dr Meyer or me were of a psychotic nature. I think she would have turned away from both of us before she was ever ill.'

Dr Forel had suggested that if Zelda did not seem to be improving at Phipps Scott should transfer her to a private and elegant nursing home in New York State, Craig House, under the direction of a friend of his, Dr Slocum. Forel knew that there was a certain bias against such places by psychiatrists like Meyer (who had received his training at a state institution), but he felt certain that Zelda would profit by the environment that Craig House could offer. Phipps, in the centre of Baltimore, could not provide the same air of gracious country living. But for the time being, although Scott investigated other clinics, Zelda remained at Phipps.

On 20 May 1932 Scott found a house on the outskirts of Baltimore, in Towson. It was called La Paix, and Zelda described it as 'a very feminine [house] – dowager grandmother', adding that she had always chosen 'masculine houses with staring windows'. Scott wrote Dr Squires that he wanted Zelda to take the move very slowly. For the first week she should spend only the mornings at the house and return to Phipps at 1.30 to resume her routine, and 'when she comes to the house for good, on, let us say, the 8th of June it will be with an absolutely air-tight schedule agreed upon for the summer'. One reason Fitzgerald wanted these precautions was to avoid fatiguing Zelda; another was 'the fact that since the whole burden of a mistake falls on me *I should be able to dictate the conditions. . . .*'

By the beginning of June Zelda was able to spend half of her time at La Paix and the remainder at Phipps. Aside from a few outbursts of temper she was doing quite well. There was of course a certain strain in resuming her normal life with Scott.

Scott felt he had to have some authority over Zelda to use as leverage if she fell off stride; Zelda resented his exercising any authority over her whatsoever. Dr Meyer urged Zelda to resist an all-or-nothing attitude toward her work, which created yet another strain between her and Scott. But she said she had to contribute something to life; if one didn't one was 'as useful as an appendix. My work is unproven. My work is not a strain. All I ask to do is to work.' On 26 June Zelda was discharged from Phipps. Her condition was unimproved.

La Paix was what was once called a Victorian cottage. It had gables and porches, fifteen or sixteen rooms, and it was full of night sounds, dark, and rather down at the heels. But it was set on the estate of Mr and Mrs Bayard Turnbull, and the grounds surrounding it were handsome. Zelda described it in a letter to John Peale Bishop.

We live in a nice Mozartian hollow disciplined to elegance by imported shrubbery of the kind which looks very out of place any-where. In this very polite Maryland atmosphere we write things. We have black-gums over the tennis court and pink dog-wood trees over the pond and the place looks as if it were constructed to hide bits of Italian marble from the public. Scott likes it better than

France and I like it fine.... We are more alone than ever before while the psychiatres patch up my nervous system.

This 'they say' is the way you really are – or no, was it the other way round?

Then they present you with a piece of bric-a-brac of their own forging which falls to the pavement on your way out of the clinic and luckily smashes to bits, and the patient is glad to be rid of their award.

Don't *ever* fall into the hands of brain and nerve specialists unless you are feeling very Faustian.

Scott reads Marx – I read the Cosmological philosophers. The brightest moments of our day are when we get them mixed up.

The Turnbulls' son Andrew, who was eleven then, remembered when Zelda first came to La Paix; he watched a taxi coming out from Phipps with a form in the back seat and someone said, 'That's Mrs Fitzgerald; she's sick.' His impression was of someone for whom everything was organized. He remembered her sitting under the oak trees in high laced white shoes, biting her lips, picking at her face. 'There was something not wholesome about her', he said. When she went swimming at the quarry she wore a two-piece maroon suit, but her figure seemed peculiar to him. 'She was odd; she had to be explained.' Zelda would dance around the living-room table to the tune of her gramophone and her face twisted quirkily. She was a frail and somehow pathetic figure to the little boy. 'When things were going well for them [the Fitzgeralds] you sensed it immediately; they possessed a sort of very clean fragrance, as though they were fresh from the bath, and then theirs was a bandbox freshness, a daintiness. She played a better game of tennis than Scott, but as might be expected, hers was an uneven game.'

She talked very little to anyone, and nothing stuck in the memory of Andrew or his mother. It was Scott who made the more vivid impression on the Turnbulls. Mrs Turnbull found him a charming man: 'He was the only man I've ever known who would ask a woman a direct question about herself. ... He did seem to care and he always told you plain truths about yourself.' She remembers him playing with their children and

Scottie, the 'marvellous quality of his voice when he recited poetry to the children. How magical that voice was, how it held one – he could have been an excellent actor.' His drinking had bothered her, for the Turnbulls were teetotallers, but a respect for his literary genius eclipsed her memory of that. Mrs Turnbull remembers, 'He was terribly sensitive to criticism – perhaps he was a little guilty about Zelda ... he talked a lot about Zelda; she was his invalid. But he only spoke of her charm, her appeal for men, and her brilliance.' She said that he often spoke of Zelda's great fascination and magnetism – 'a true admiration of her judgment'. He seemed sometimes to depend upon her approval. But Mrs Turnbull could remember no evidence of Zelda's revealing herself to her. 'Oh, she spoke a great deal about trees and used the same words to describe them – repeated herself a good deal. But then we never really spoke to each other. She stayed very much to herself. I used to see her walking like a small shadow along the path by the flower garden. She often walked there, quietly and alone. I thought of her as an invalid. She struck one like a broken clock.'

A woman who worked as Fitzgerald's secretary from the time they moved into La Paix until 1938, when she recalls herself 'still trying to untangle their bills', saw Scott and Zelda from a far less romantic point of view than the Turnbulls. When Scott hired her one of his requirements was that the person not be the sort of woman with whom he could possibly fall in love. And vice versa. Scott offered twelve dollars a week for the job and there were lines of women applying for it. This was in the middle of the Depression, and if twelve dollars wasn't good, if it was steady it wasn't bad. 'It sounded really simple – I didn't know there would be calls at midnight or four o'clock in the morning! I was a companion, I drove their car, bought canvases and paints for Zelda, played tennis, rode and swam with her.'

In July Zelda was kept busy correcting proofs of *Save Me the Waltz*. She was living at home all the time and seeing a psychiatrist at Phipps once a week. By the end of August she had trouble keeping to the schedule set up for her before she left Phipps. Her relationship with both Scott and Scottie grew ominously tense. Frequently she would flare at one of them and then run to her room, locking herself in; on such occasions Scott would try to talk her back downstairs, and if that failed he might slip a note such as this one beneath her door.

Dearest: I'm writing because I don't want to start the day with an arguement – though I had thought that what has become controversial was settled before you left the clinic.

Darling when you shut yourself away for twenty four hours it is not only very bad for you but it casts a pall of gloom and disquiet over the people who love you. To spend any reasonable time in your room has been agreed apon as all right, but this shouldn't be so exaggerated that you can't manage the social side any further than sitting at table. It would help everything if you could enter a little into Scotty's life here on the place, and your reluctance to play tennis and swim is a rather reckless withdrawal; for whatever of the normal you subtract from your life will be filled up with brooding and fantasy. If I know that there is exercise scheduled for morning and afternoon and a medical bath in the afternoon & that you have half an hour for us after supper and you stop work at ten, my not very exigent list, *insisted upon by Dr. Myers*, is complete. When you throw it out of joint I can only sit and wait for the explosion that will follow – a situation not conducive to work or happiness. If this week has been too much it is easy to return to the clinic for three days and it needn't be done in a spirit of dispair any more than your many returns to Prangins.

I believe however you are not giving it, giving us, a fair trial here. If I didn't love you so much your moods wouldn't affect me so deeply and excitedly. We can't afford scenes – the best protection is the schedule and then the schedule and again the schedule, and you'll get strong without knowing it.

Scott was hospitalized for two weeks that summer. The doctors thought he was ill with typhoid fever; he was not, but he was run down and needed a rest. Maxwell Perkins visited him and described his impressions of their visit in a letter to Hemingway: 'Scott and Zelda are living about forty minutes out from Baltimore in a house on a big place that is filled with wonderful old trees. I wanted to walk around and look at the trees, but

Scott thought we ought to settle down to gin-rickeys. .... It was really a fine sort of melancholy place. .... Scott did not look so well, but he was in fine spirits, and talked a lot.' Scott was drinking hard and at the same time working on *Tender Is the Night*. He entered in the Ledger, 'The novel now plotted and planned, never more to be permanently interrupted.'

Dr Thomas Rennie had taken over Zelda's case at Phipps and Zelda began to feel a far greater rapport with the handsome bachelor than she had with Meyer. The young doctor, who was intensely interested in literature and who had once wanted to become a playwright, was fascinated by both of the Fitzgeralds. He could not, however, help noticing that Zelda's relations with Scott were growing increasingly difficult, and he tried to check the downward trend. Scott's drinking and daily quarrels with Zelda had reduced their relationship to a constant wrangle. When Zelda was on schedule she wrote in the morning, played tennis before lunch, and painted in the afternoon. In the evening she tried not to have an outburst of temper, but if she did she retired to her own room. She began to plan a new novel, which would deal with madness. The main characters, a man and his wife, were being driven to an asylum by their heartless and selfish daughter. Zelda told Dr Rennie she wanted to draw a picture of insanity that would be so near the normal that the reader would not discover until the novel's end that the two characters were already in an asylum. It was a dangerous course she had set out on, because the central theme of Scott's much revised novel dealt with psychiatry too, and the madness of Nicole Diver, the psychiatrist's wife. Zelda knew this perfectly well and certainly she realized how distressed Scott had been about *Save Me the Waltz*, but she again ignored the similarity of their territory.

On 29 August the Fitzgeralds had a fierce row and Zelda called Rennie, demanding that she be sent to Sheppard-Pratt, a nearby clinic for the treatment of nervous diseases. Rennie explained to her that the goal of therapy was to keep her out of the hospital and help her to function on her own. Both of the Fitzgeralds came to the Phipps clinic late in the afternoon. Scott looked unkempt and clearly had been drinking.

Apparently they had argued about Scottie. Rennie set up a rigid schedule for Zelda to follow; she was to try it for a week as a test and see what effects it had on their marriage. She seemed relieved that something definite was expected of her and followed the schedule to the letter – for a while.

Dr Rennie saw the Fitzgeralds' problem in three parts. The first was the struggle between them as creative artists, each jealous of the other. The second was the conflict caused within Zelda by trying to have a career as a writer while at the same time fulfilling the obligations of her home and marriage. The third was their sexual relation to each other. What Rennie had noticed was the growing discrepancy between the Fitzgeralds' ideas of the roles of husband and wife and the part they were individually prepared (or able) to play. Neither of them was at this point fulfilling his role to the satisfaction of his partner. Scott told Rennie: 'In the last analysis, she is a stronger person than I am. I have creative fire, but I am a weak individual. She knows this and really looks upon me as a woman. All our lives, since the days of our engagement, we have spent hunting for some man Zelda considers strong enough to lean upon. I am not. However, I am now so near the breaking point myself that she realizes she has me against the wall and that she can drive me no further. She is a little afraid of me at the present time.' Rennie hoped that the publication of *Save Me the Waltz* would settle the question of whether or not Zelda was a literary artist of major calibre, and that once that was resolved some of their other problems would fall into place. Events were to prove it a naïve expectation.

Save Me the Waltz was published in October 1932. Zelda had designed a jacket for the book, but Scribner's received her work too late to use it. Nevertheless, she wrote Perkins:

We are delighted with the book. The two figures on the cover are rather reminiscent of some of my own drawings – It's fine. I only hope it will be as satisfactory to you as it is to me. It certainly is tremendously thick if bulk bulges sales any.

Scott's novel is nearing completion. He's been working like a streak and people who have read it say its wonderful. We wait now till each other's stuff is copy-righted since I try to more or less absorb his technique and the range of our experience might coincide.

The novel did not sell well. It is difficult to determine how many copies were printed, but for a first novel in the middle of the Depression the run was probably less than three thousand copies. Zelda wrote Perkins unhappily after publication: 'Do you suppose a small add on the "dance" page of the Times or Tribune would help any? Naturally, I am distressed for your sake and mine that the response has been so slight. I had the idea that those special enthusiasts might be interested.'

Critical reaction to *Save Me the Waltz* was mixed. Zelda wrote to Perkins, asking him to send for her scrapbook any additional reviews that she might not have seen, and when she received them she thanked him, but said she was sorry she had asked.

Zelda liked a review written by William McFee for the New York *Sun* the best; she told Perkins it was 'the only intelligible (to me) criticism of the book that I've seen so far'. McFee wrote that the novel was obviously autobiographical; he hoped that it would not be denied an audience because the public no longer wanted to be reminded of that era – the period of postwar hoopla among American expatriates on the Riviera and in Paris. He continued:

... here is a peculiar talent, and connoisseurs of style will have a wonderful time with 'Save Me the Waltz'. In this book, with all its crudity of conception, its ruthless purloinings of technical tricks and its pathetic striving after philosophical profundity, there is the promise of a new and vigorous personality in fiction.

McFee felt that the best scenes were those that dealt with the world of ballet, but that 'Alabama's personality is not sufficiently distinct to sustain interest'.

In the desperate attempt to be contrary and enigmatic she resembles an insane child. But one has to go on and on to discover what happens to this essentially American marriage. The author occasionally has only the vaguest notion of the meanings of many words she uses, but the effect of the accumulated fantastic metaphors is fascination for all that. Veteran word-mongers will read

[it], with envy and a kind of dizzy delight. . . . Passages [like one he had just quoted] give the book an almost alcoholic vitality. Mrs. Fitzgerald's next novel will be an interesting event.

Not surprisingly many reviewers noticed that although Zelda covered much of the same ground as Scott she wrote in an entirely different tone. Her work was highly stylized, and the main negative criticism of the novel was its overwriting and lack of careful editing and proof-reading. In the book section of the *New York Times* the reviewer wrote:

It is not only that her publishers have not seen fit to curb an almost ludicrous lushness of writing but they have not given the book the elementary services of a literate proofreader.

Another reviewer wrote:

There is a warm, intelligent, undisciplined mind behind *Save Me the Waltz*. Mrs. Fitzgerald should have had the help she needed to save her book from becoming a laughingstock.

This was the most strongly expressed criticism of that aspect of the novel, but it came to grips with one of its essential defects. Critics complained of Zelda's 'miasma of a glittering surface smartness' and her reduction of various scenes potentially tragic to a 'harlequinade'.

At about the same time her book was published she was interviewed in Baltimore by a reporter. Zelda told the woman, ' "Lives aren't as hard as professionals" ' (which was a line from *Save Me the Waltz*). Of the peace-denoting name of La Paix she quipped that she had not named it: ' "I'd have called it Calvin Coolidge, Jr. . . . because it's so pleasantly mute." ' She said that a woman must be a goddess to direct her own life (a sentiment she had put in Judge Beggs' mouth in her novel) and a goddess is one who manages to keep her purposes aloof from a woman's ordinary lot: ' "In working hard for a goal . . . a woman pushes out her own horizons." ' The article continued, quoting Zelda:

Security, Mrs. Fitzgerald defines as something rather like money in the bank.

'And whether you make it or some one else does, represents the two kinds of peace in this world – to me, of course. But I don't mean that happiness or the glorious sense of using what abilities we have has any financial side to it.... When I was nineteen ... I thought Botticelli was unbeautiful because the women in the Primavera did not look like the girls in the Follies.

'But now I don't expect Ann Pennington to hold the same charm for me as a Matisse odalisque.

'And for me, it's easier to take than give, since the sense of my own needs has become stronger for me than my sense of other people.'

Save Me the Waltz sold 1,392 copies. Its poor sales plus the high cost of Zelda's revisions in both galley and page proofs made the clause about $5,000 from her royalties being used to pay off Scott's indebtedness to Scribner's meaningless. Zelda earned $120.73 from her novel and Max Perkins sent her a cheque for the full amount on 2 August 1933. Perkins told her:

Maybe I ought to have warned you about corrections for they came to a great deal. I knew they would, when the proofs began coming back, but I knew you wanted to get the book the way you thought it ought to be. The result won't be encouraging to you, and I have not liked to ask you whether you were writing any more because of that fact, but I do think the last part of that book in particular, was very fine; and that if we had not been in the depths of a depression, the result would have been quite different. But as it was, nothing got any show unless it were by some writer already noted for earlier successes, or had some very special salience.

Malcolm Cowley, too, had read *Save Me the Waltz,* and thought well enough of it to write Fitzgerald:

It moves me a lot: she has something there that nobody got into words before. The women who write novels are usually the sort who live spiritually in Beloit, Wisconsin, even when they are getting drunk at the Select. Zelda has a different story to tell.

Throughout the fall Zelda worked on her new novel, the one that dealt with psychiatric material and her own hospitalization. Scott was beside himself with anger and in a long forceful letter to Dr Rennie said he thought they had all agreed that he was to finish his novel before Zelda took up any extended piece of fiction, and she was violating that promise. 'But in her subconscious there is a deathly terror that I may make something very fine in the use of this material of "ours", that I may preclude her making something very fine.'

Her hopes collapsed with the failure of *Save Me the Waltz,* and her small reserve of balance imperilled by her arguments with Scott, Zelda began to storm at Scottie. On the surface her complaint was that she thought Scottie was thoroughly spoiled, but shot through it all was Zelda's fear that Scottie was growing away from her before she had ever known her, that she no longer had any voice in her daughter's life. 'I can't help her at all', she told Rennie. 'I'm like a stranger in the house.' But recognizing her unfairness to Scottie didn't seem to help her control herself. She told Rennie: 'Instantly I lose my temper when I get up. It's awfully unfair to my husband and child. It's destructive to her. . . . Our relationship has been very bad. In order not to think of her, I say I don't care about her. That's silly. Of course I care about her. But I give her nothing – have not for three years. It's torture to her. My child is gone from the present – out of my life. It isn't fair and I make terrible kicks against it.' Zelda's position was made even more unbearable by her own knowledge of what she was doing. 'If I approach her and her hair smells bad and I get nauseated – I just have to go away from her. I know her hair doesn't smell bad, but it makes me sick anyway.'

What she concealed from Dr Rennie was the difficulty she was having keeping herself in hand at all times, and not only in connection with Scottie. When she sat down to dinner in the presence of guests, she found herself thinking about their feet or wondering if the women were pregnant. On the tennis courts she could no longer control her game, and would move drowsily, doing each of the actions as if something were curiously wrong, walking to the wrong court, thinking it was her own serve instead of Scott's. Scott was impressed enough by the regularity of her wrongness to make a note of it to himself.

16

When I like men I want to be like them – I want to lose the
outer qualities that give me my individuality and be like them.
I don't want the man; I want to absorb into myself all the
qualities that make him attractive and leave him out. I cling
to my own innards. When I like women I want to own them,
to dominate them, to have them admire me.

F. SCOTT FITZGERALD, Notebooks, K

Throughout the summer and fall of 1932 Zelda had worked
on a farce that she called *Scandalabra*. When she could not
proceed on her new novel, either because of Scott's objections
or her own instability, she turned to her play for relief. In a
rush of energy she completed it late in October and sent it off
to Harold Ober, with a note suggesting who might produce it.
She also wrote to Perkins, saying that she'd 'read every play
ever written with the hope that some dramatic sense would
seep into my nonsense'. The play made the rounds of pro-
ducers for a few months, but no one in New York was interested in putting it on.

Scott, harassed by his troubles with Zelda, drinking more
than was good for him, also began to suffer from the tension
of trying to pull his novel into shape. He fretted over every
phrase of his manuscript-in-progress, for he staked his entire
future on its success. Sitting at his table in an old bathrobe,
toying with a pencil, the smells of gin and cigarette smoke
filling the study, he worked. His secretary remembered those
days of anxious writing. 'He just wasn't a stationary man –
even when he wrote he kept moving around, walking back and
forth. . . . Zelda kept out of the way while he wrote. I'll never
forget him wandering around that spooky house, talking all
the time to himself.

'I think I typed *Tender Is the Night* completely three times
– and sections of it many more times than that. I can quote
whole passages. . . . Zelda's memory was good and he would
go up to her room and ask advice about things they had done
together, conversations they had. . . . He couldn't write about

anything he didn't know. Some of those stories were terrible that he turned out during that time – we all knew it. He was convinced he was dead and buried.'

In an article written during this period and published in the *Saturday Evening Post,* called 'One Hundred False Starts', he tried to pinpoint his problems as a writer; he said that he was thirty-six now and 'For eighteen years, save for a short space during the war, writing has been my chief interest in life, and I am in every sense a professional.

'Yet even now when . . . I sit down facing my sharpened pencils and block of legal-sized paper, I have a feeling of utter helplessness.' He said that writers repeat themselves, and that much as he tried to grapple with fresh plots, new material, or old notes jotted down to be resuscitated in bright settings, it was no good.

We have two or three great moving experiences in our lives – experiences so great and moving that it doesn't seem at the time that anyone else has been caught up and pounded and dazzled and astonished and beaten and broken and rescued and illuminated and rewarded and humbled in just that way ever before.

Then we learn our trade, well or less well, and we tell our two or three stories – each time in a new disguise – maybe ten times, maybe a hundred, as long as people will listen. . . . Whether it's something that happened twenty years ago or only yesterday, I must start out with an emotion – one that's close to me and that I can understand. . . . What you aim at is to get in a good race or two when the crowd is in the stand.

But the crowd no longer seemed to him to be in the stands; his income had dropped in 1932 to $15,823, less than half of what it had been in 1931.

His mother would sometimes visit from Washington, where she lived after the death of her husband. She brought Scott little bags of candy that she thought he'd like, in the hope that sweets would make him drink less. But it never worked and he was infuriated by her simple ploy. Zelda was kind to her and took her side in disputes, but that only irritated Scott more. First he blamed his mother, then Zelda; he would draw his secretary aside, telling her, 'I am as I am because of my wife.'

But there were still good times together. His secretary remembered them talking to each other – 'that seemed at the heart of the matter; they talked and talked and talked. One of them would remember something that had happened and off they'd go laughing and chatting.' It was just that the good times seemed brief in comparison to their states of siege. Their help learned to gauge what was going to happen by listening to their sounds as they retired for the night. They slept in the same room and Scott, who frequently had trouble falling asleep, would begin to pace the floor, talking. Their help could tell as soon as they entered the door in the morning if things had gone sour the night before. 'It depended upon what kind of discussion they had had. You just sensed that they upset each other. She [Zelda] took a lot from him, it seemed to me, and I never remember her criticizing him. Of course, she had no say.' Scott felt that Zelda had to be protected from everything; she could not drink, for if she did she lost control completely, and she saw guests only on those occasions when it seemed unlikely that their presence would set her off.

In December 1932 Dr Meyer wrote Dr Forel in Switzerland, telling him of the progress of Zelda's case. He felt that she was beginning to improve, but that Scott was headed downhill. His situation was, in the doctor's opinion, worse than Zelda's; he was drinking a lot and had begun treatment at Phipps with one of Meyer's colleagues. The strain of trying to be a nurse to Zelda and a shield to Scottie, of maintaining a semblance of balance in the household as well as working to complete his final draft of *Tender Is the Night,* had taken its toll. He was also, as he told Dr Rennie, possessed by the frightening knowledge that he could cause Zelda to become psychotic within minutes of 'well-planned conversation . . . I would only need to intimate that I was interested in some other woman and bring on her insanity again.'

As the erosion of their marriage continued Scott had to unburden himself to someone, anyone, and when he drank too much he would keep the cook or the nurse up all night telling her about himself and Zelda. His secretary says: 'The next day they'd be gone. He'd said too much. . . . He'd talked about her all the time. I told him, "No woman could live with you!" He'd laugh and look mischievously at me.' When he was sober, 'he was charming and polite and as attractive as any man I've ever met'.

Zelda seemed to her a much more private person. 'We had a formal relationship. ... Zelda was a very, very polite person; terribly kind and generous.' She was still athletic, and it was part of her regimen to swim and ride or play tennis for a period each day. She enjoyed high dives that terrified the secretary. When they went horseback riding and took a jump, it suddenly became clear that Zelda hadn't the slightest notion how to sit properly for jumping. Zelda wrote Maxwell Perkins: 'I have taken, somewhat eccentricly at my age, to horseback riding which I do as non-committally as possible so as not to annoy the horse. Also very apologeticly since we've had so much of communism lately that I'm not sure it's not the horse who should be riding me.'

She was not pretty any more, but there was something fresh and clean about her looks still. Scott's secretary remembers her as 'skinny, and her skirts were never straight – shirt-tail-out type. She moved fast. ... She looked like a harassed woman when I knew her.' She spent long periods in her room at the top of the house, dancing by herself, or writing or painting. She loved to take long walks within the grounds of La Paix, stopping by the flower garden to gather a bouquet.

In the spring of 1933 the Fitzgerald marriage incurred another lesion which would leave them both permanently scarred. Scott once wrote: 'Family quarrels are bitter things. They don't go according to any rules. They're not like aches or wounds; they're more like splits in the skin that won't heal because there's not enough material.' Fitzgerald was at the end of his tether and felt he had been driven there by Zelda. Together they were visiting Phipps once a week for conferences with Dr Meyer and Dr Rennie. This had been going on for about six months and the effectiveness of these meetings was, in Scott's opinion, negligible. Scott was drinking heavily and taking Luminal. Meyer kept trying to persuade him to get along without alcohol, and he told Fitzgerald flatly, 'It would mean much for the ease of Mrs Fitzgerald.' But Scott was at the point where he could not stand to see Zelda at the dinner table. 'I've never forgotten the novel. Its terrible resentment.' Unless he kept persistently at Zelda, she broke her schedule, and he had come to hate the constant nagging. 'Four days ago I told her I was trading my health for her sanity, and I was through. She could go to bed if she liked.'

A few days after he made that remark, Scott wrote Dr Meyer a long letter in which he said he could no longer stand up under the strain of living with Zelda. He said that when their 'conversations' at Phipps had begun they worked beautifully 'because she [Zelda] was still close to the threat of force and more acutely under the spell of your personality. ... And I know also that you were trying to consider as a whole the *millieu* in which she was immersed, including my contributions to it. ...' He had brooded about her case for years, 'arriving at the gate of such questions as to whether Zelda isn't more worth saving that I am. I compromised on the purely utilitarian standpoint that I was the wage-earner, that I took care of wife and child, financially and practically, and beyond that that I was integrated – integrated in spite of everything, in spite of the fact that I might have two counts against me to her one.' He realized that Zelda was talented, that she somehow presented a 'much more sympathetic and, superficially, more solid [picture of herself] than the vision of me making myself iller with drink as I finish up the work of four years'. He was, he knew, compromising himself in the eyes of the psychiatrists by his demonstrations of lack of self-control. 'I will probably be carried off eventually by four strong guards shrieking manicly that after all I was right and she was wrong, while Zelda is followed home by an adoring crowd in an automobile banked with flowers, and offered a vaudeville contract.'

Scott felt that he needed some strongly enforced authority over Zelda, for there was no longer 'a mutual bond between equals'. He wanted to be able to order her '*to pack her bag and spend a week under people who can take care of her*', at Phipps. He wrote that if Dr Meyer doubted his ability to judge when such a course of action was necessary, '*then hasn't the case reached such a point of confusion psychologically that I had better resort to legal means to save myself, my child and the three of us in toto*' (Fitzgerald's italics). He recognized two phases in Zelda's illness. The first was one of intense self-expression when she indulged in an exaggeration of her physical and mental powers; the second was a period of 'Conservatism, almost Victorianism, dread of any extremes or excess. . . .'

'One of her reasons for gravitating toward the first state is that her work is perhaps at its best in the passage from the conservative to the self-expressive phase, just before and just after it crosses the line – which, of course, could be the equivalent of the period of creative excitement in an integrated person.' But she was not able to keep herself within those bounds, except when she was hospitalized and submitted to the imposed discipline of the clinic. 'With much pushing and prodding she lived well, wrote well and painted well.' (He is referring to August and September of the previous year.) 'Possibly she would have been a genius if we had never met. In actuality she is now hurting me and through me hurting all of us.' Zelda, Scott wrote, had begun to believe 'that her work's success will give her some sort of divine irresponsibility backed by unlimited gold. It is still the idea of an Iowa high-school girl who would like to be an author with an author's beautiful carefree life.' She used Scott's sheltering (he called it 'a greenhouse which is my money and my name and my love') but at the same time felt no responsibility to him. He said it was her idea 'that because some of us in our generation with the effort and courage of youth battered a notch in an old wall, she can make the same kind of crashing approach to the literary life with the frail equipment of a sick mind and a berserk determination'. He wanted Dr Meyer to let Zelda feel the sting '*of being alone, of having exhausted everyone's patience*' (Fitzgerald's italics), and to know that Meyer was not just benevolently neutral, but would stand behind Scott's exercise of authority. 'Otherwise the Fitzgerald's seem to be going out in the storm, each one for himself, and I'm afraid Scotty and I will weather it better than she.'

Dr Meyer answered Fitzgerald the next week. He too had sensed the futility of their joint conversations, but he felt that what was involved was not simply a question of Zelda's *case*; it was Scott's life as well. Zelda, of course, was his patient, but Meyer saw Scott as someone who, though unwilling, also needed help. He didn't want Scott to function as a sort of boss to Zelda, nor as a psychiatrist-nurse. He wanted a closer understanding of both of the Fitzgeralds, but he was certain that could be achieved only if Scott gave up alcohol.

Scott thought that they were working together, bringing a collaboration of perspectives to bear on Zelda's illness. 'I felt that from the difference between my instinctive-emotional knowledge of Zelda, extending over 15 years, and your objective-clinical knowledge of her, and also from the difference between the Zelda that everyone who lives a hundred consecutive hours in this house sees and the Zelda who, as a consumate actress, shows herself to you – from these differences we might see where the true center of her should lie, around what point it's rallying ground should be.'

But Meyer had hit a nerve, and Scott had no intention of undergoing whatever kind of psychological care Meyer cautiously suggested. He also felt unable to relinquish liquor. He was ruffled by the suggestion that his abuse of alcohol might impede Zelda's recovery, or in some way diminish his ability to handle her. He said: 'I can only think of Lincoln's remark about a greater man and heavier drinker than I have ever been – that he wished he knew what sort of liquor Grant drank so he could send a barrel to all his other generals.' He added that if Meyer considered him on the same level as a schizophrenic, he was rather alarmed about his role in the whole business.

On 28 May 1933 Zelda and Scott sat down at La Paix, with a stenographer, and Dr Rennie as moderator, to discuss their troubles, or at least to air them again. The 114-page transcription of their talk provides another key to those 'splits in the skin' of their marriage at this juncture. It was 2.30 on Sunday when they began and the afternoon sunlight fell short of the interior of the darkening room in which they sat. Scott began by saying he was being destroyed by the present situation of his marriage. 'It is all unfair. It is all unfair. . . . I am paid those enormous prices, and not for nothing. I am paid for a continual fight and struggle that I can carry on. . . . the whole equipment of my life is to be a novelist. And that is attained with tremendous struggle; that is attained with a tremendous nervous struggle; that is attained with a tremendous sacrifice which you make to lead any profession. It was done because I was equipped for it. I was equipped for it as a little boy. I began at ten, when I wrote my first story. My whole life is a professional move towards that.

'Now the difference between the professional and the amateur is something that is awfully hard to analyze, it is awfully intangible. It just simply means the keen equipment; it means a scent, a smell of the future in one line.'

Zelda, Scott said, had written some 'nice, little sketches'; she had a satiric point of view toward her friends, and she had certain experiences to report, 'but she has nothing essentially to say. To have something to say is a question of sleepless nights and worry and endless motivation of a subject, and the endless trying to dig out the essential truth, the essential justice.'

As they talked one aspect of the problem became clear: Scott had not published a novel for eight years (in the transcript he said 'seven years – six years') and he blamed it on Zelda. 'Three of those years were directly because of a sickness of hers, and two years before that indirectly, for which she was partly responsible, in that she wanted to be a ballet dancer; I backed her in that.'

Finally Zelda interrupted him: 'You mean you were drinking constantly. . . . Well, that is the truth . . . it is just one of the reasons why I wanted to be a ballet dancer, because I had nothing else.'

Several pages later in the transcript Scott turned to Zelda and told her outright what he thought of her talents: 'It is a perfectly lonely struggle that I am making against other writers who are finely gifted and talented. You are a third rate writer and a third rate ballet dancer.'

'You have told me that before.'

. . . .

'I am a professional writer, with a huge following. I am the highest paid short story writer in the world. I have at various times dominated . . .'

Zelda again broke in: 'It seems to me you are making a rather violent attack on a third rate talent then.'

Repeatedly throughout the afternoon, they came back to this point: Scott was the professional writer and he was supporting Zelda; therefore, the entire fabric of their life was his material, none of it was Zelda's. He spelled it out: 'Everything we have done is my . . . I am the professional novelist, and I am supporting you. That is all my material. None of it is your material.' Zelda told him he was 'absolutely neurotic on the subject of your own work anyway. You are so full of self-reproach about not having written anything for that long period of time that you stoop to the device of accusing me.'

'One thousand dollars a month in Switzerland.'

'You did not do it for seven years.'

'Yes, seven years. Three years I took care of you. Three years I pulled up after *The Great Gatsby*, and two years we tried to be swell and live in a great mansion in Delaware.'

Scott had very fixed ideas of what a woman's place should be in a marriage: 'I would like you to think of my interests. That is your primary concern, because I am the one to steer the course, the pilot.'

'I tell you, my life has been so miserable that I would rather be in an asylum. Does that mean a thing to you?'

'It does not mean a blessed thing.'

What, then, Zelda asked him, did he want her to do.

'I want you to stop writing fiction.'

The novel that Zelda was working on, the one about psychiatry, touched too closely on Scott's material for *Tender Is the Night*; he could not tolerate another encroachment, such as *Save Me the Waltz* had been, on his literary territory. Zelda had put a double lock on the door to the room where she wrote, because Scott said he would destroy her book. He said to her now, 'I told you if I came in and found you writing on it, I would crumple it up.'

'I do not want you to tear it up. You know that some of it is awfully good prose; and you know it would break my heart to tear it up.'

'You know I would not do it.'

Zelda insisted that she did not want to be dependent on Scott. Dr Rennie asked her if she meant financially dependent, and Zelda said: 'Every way. I want to be, to say, when he says something that is not so, then I want to do something so good, that I can say, "That is a bad damned lie!" and have something to back it up, that I can say it.'

Scott said. 'Now, we have found rock bottom.'

Dr Rennie said he thought they had.

'And I think it is better to shut yourself up in an institution than to live this way', said Zelda.

Scott wanted her to be what he called a 'complementary intelligence'. That was not at all what she wanted to be.

Finally, Dr Rennie asked Zelda if being an oustanding woman writer would compensate for a life without Scott. Would being a creative artist mean enough to her if she were alone? 'Would that mean enough to you when you were sixty?'

After a lapse of about a minute, during which no one spoke, Zelda replied: 'Well, Dr Rennie, I think perhaps that is sort of a silly question. ... How can I tell what it would mean?' Even at this point in their lives, in the face of Scott's denunciations, Zelda would not directly say that she could live without him. A few moments later she turned to him and asked: 'What is our marriage anyway? It has been nothing but a long battle ever since I can remember.'

'I don't know about that. We were about the most envied couple in about 1921 in America.'

'I guess so. We were awfully good showmen.'

'We were awfully happy', Scott said.

The argument kept returning to the question of Zelda's writing. Finally, Scott gave her an ultimatum; she had to stop writing fiction. She asked, 'Of any kind?'

'If you write a play, it cannot be a play about psychiatry, and it cannot be a play laid on the Riviera, and it cannot be a play laid in Switzerland, and whatever the idea is, it will have to be submitted to me.'

Zelda said she was sick of being beaten down, of being bullied into accepting Scott's ideas of everything. She would not stand it any longer; she would rather be in an institution. Their talk ended with nothing settled and a great deal of salt rubbed in their wounds. Scott for the first time seriously considered divorcing Zelda, and consulted a lawyer about the possible conditions under which he could be free of her. He found that in the state of Nevada with only six weeks' residence he would have no trouble whatsoever accomplishing that end. He chose not to. They continued living together under the condition of strain and distrust that the transcript makes painfully clear.

Scott felt cornered, as indeed he had been for some time, and when he talked about his equipment as a novelist, it was without fully realizing that it was just that equipment, his very real sensitivity to people, his ability to throw himself completely into the mood of a moment and charge it with himself, that made so hazardous his current relationship with Zelda. In a few more years, by 1936, he would understand it more clearly and write: '... what can you do for meddling with a human heart? A writer's temperament is continually making him do things he can never repair.' The Fitzgeralds were no longer dazzling youngsters, charmingly self-promoting, with a cache of youth and stamina to rescue them. What Zelda needed was peace, calm, and reassurance of herself at every point of uncertainty. Scott could not give what he did not have. But it was asked of him again and again. He was asked to be – as the remarkably dedicated Leonard Woolf seems to have been so perfectly for his wife, Virginia – Zelda's bulwark, her ballast. Scott Fitzgerald was simply not equipped to play that sort of role for anyone; his courage was in trying so very hard against considerable odds to offer that kind of assistance to Zelda. In 1933 he was dangerously close to the end of his resources and he knew it. Always before this he had been able to recoup his losses, but his reserves were low. The Fitzgeralds were, in every sense, in the midst of a depression. Railing at Zelda would not help; it would in fact imperil the one thing Scott had believed in as a constant. But he seemed helpless against the potent tides of her illness: dragged into the quagmire of her puzzled existence, he fought for his very survival. If he fought dirty sometimes that does not diminish the fact that he refused to give up.

The spring before this one, sixty young students from the Baltimore area had formed a group called the Vagabond Junior Players. They were an offshoot of the Vagabonds, which was a smart and active little-theatre group in Baltimore. The Junior Vags, as they were soon called, planned to produce three plays in the summer of 1933. Each play would run six nights. For their second play they chose Zelda's *Scandalabra*, which would run from 26 June through 1 July. She designed and executed the sets and screens for the production. A young man who starred in the production, Zack Maccubbin, remembered his unusual introduction to the author early in the spring of 1933. He was walking down a lane toward the gates of the Sheppard and Enoch Pratt sanitarium. On his left was La Paix.

'Ahead of me, near the gate, was a woman going in the same direction that I was. However, I soon caught up with her and we said "Hello." ... She was a tall, slender blonde with a classic profile and other than a slight impediment in her speech, was obviously a "Southern Lady". As we approached the top of the hill she told me that she was from the Victorian house near the gate that I had so admired.' As they began to talk he found out that Zelda was having treatments at Sheppard-Pratt, and without much prodding he told her he was an actor. Zelda was delighted with her discovery and told the young man she had a play she wanted him to read and perhaps act in. 'Now we were at the top of the hill. The original buildings of the hospital were to our left. Great red brick Victorian buildings with towers, turrets and a look of having been there for years on end. ... As we stood there the lady asked me to dinner the following Sunday at La Paix. She charmed me. I accepted with great pleasure. ... She walked slowly away to her appointment.'

The next Sunday Mr Maccubbin came promptly at the right time and after several martinis dinner began, but it was interrupted when Scott learned that although the young man had gone to military school he had not learned to box. Scott decided 'to give me a lesson right then and there. Zelda tried to stop us, but he paid no attention. I did think it damn peculiar, but went along with it. You know he taught Scottie to box, too. I remember a circle of green lawn between the driveway and the front entrance of the house. It was just a little larger than a ring. He'd have Scottie put her fists up and they'd circle around each other.' When the boxing lesson was over, they returned to dinner. Afterward Maccubbin was left alone to read *Scandalabra*, and when he was finished he read several scenes from it aloud to Zelda. It was, he remembers, 'equally as strange as its title implies. However, I was too new in the theatre to be much of a critic and, at that time, a leading role impressed me more than the subject matter of the play. As I remember, it had dozens of scenes from the Riviera to New York City and back again. ... Scott had never read the play and saw no rehearsals. Zelda had wanted this to be her own project ... with no help from Scott or anyone else.'

The rehearsals began in June in a building that was a converted carriage house on Read Street. 'I don't think we ever got through the whole play in any one day prior to dress rehearsal. Mrs Penniman [the director] ... [was] a slow talker. Zelda's impediment that I had noticed that first day turned out to be the result of having bitten the inside of her lower lip during the first illness in Europe, so that she had gotten in the habit of extending her lower lip even though it was now healed.' Her speech sounded rhythmic and she hit the s's. Mrs Penniman tried to cut the play, but Zelda would not yield; she would insist, '"Mrs Penniman, that is a very important part of the play. It is cleared up completely in the third scene of the second act!"' They would then go into a huddle together and usually Zelda won her point and they stuck close to the original script.

Maccubbin recalls:

Zelda and Scott had a whole train load of guests down from New York City. They were personal friends, agents and the usual people interested in a play by a 'name' that was being tried out prior to a possible Broadway production. I remember the weather was that particular summer heat that Washington and Baltimore have of which there is nothing anywhere else to compare it to. Scott in a sack-suit, but with a Turkish towel looped over his belt to wipe off the perspiration, would walk up and down Read Street with a friend declaiming in a loud voice that he understood this was a great play, or that he heard it was very funny. Then he would go to the box office and buy two or three tickets, walk away and do the whole bit over again in hopes of impressing the passersby. As far as I remember we went up on time at 8:15, but the final curtain didn't come down until after one A.M.! It set a record for length if not quality. By the time Zelda came backstage she had realized from her friends, if not from Scott that something had to be done. She now turned to Scott for help and he was right there and ready.

The cast gathered with the Fitzgeralds in the theatre's Green Room. Scott took a thronelike chair with the rest of us in a circle around him. He was only drinking beer at that point, but there were several cases to his right. The rest of us had been told to order whatever we particularly liked and the first session got under way. He decided that he would read a speech and if the actor, whose line it was, or someone else, could not give a good reason for it being a part of the script, he would red pencil it within a given period of time. Under these conditions many lines tumbled! Even so by four A.M. we had only scratched the surface of Act One. So it came to pass that each night we continued cutting where we left off the night before and each night we gave a different performance! ... by the end of the week we had a play that at least ran within the normal bounds of modern drama.

If *Scandalabra* ran within the time limits of normal drama, it did not run within its guidelines. Granted that it was a farce, a 'farce-fantasy' at that, it was still woefully bad. The plot dealt with a nice young man from the farm (Andrew Messogony, played by Zack Maccubbin) suddenly willed millions *if* he will promise to live a life of utter dissipation and wickedness. It was like a funhouse mirror's reflection of the plot of *The Beautiful and Damned*. In that novel Anthony Patch's grandfather (of whom Patch is the namesake, as in *Scandalabra* Andrew Messogony is his uncle's), who is enormously wealthy, a teetotaller guarded by a manservant, refuses to will his millions to the Patches because of the extravagance of their lives. When Gloria and Anthony finally do win the old man's millions their marriage has been destroyed, Anthony is half-mad and Gloria is but a shadow of her former radiant self. In *Scandalabra* young Messogony (and here Zelda must be playing heavy-handedly on both misogamy and misogyny as sources for his name) marries a showgirl, for a start, only to find that she loves him truly. In a panic of ridiculous situations they try unsuccessfully to live up (or down) to the terms of the will. Finally, the young man renounces all of the tomfoolery, grabs his showgirl by the hand and announces that the estate can keep its money; he for one has had enough of debauchery; it's back to the out-of-doors. In what is one of the least clever turnabouts in the history of farce, it becomes clear that this outcome is what his uncle had intended. The young man was supposed to put his foot down against evil influences *after* he had tasted them. The characters' names and a sampling of a few lines are enough to convey an accurate idea of the play: Flower, the showgirl turned wifely; Anaconda Consequential (which is Zelda at her zany best, sort of Restoration-Depression drama), the wife of a young man to whom Flower pretends to be attached; a manservant called Baffles or Bounds, apparently at the whim of the person addressing him; and a leprechaun.

From the *Prologue*:

BAFFLES: The young people don't seem to know how to misbehave anymore – *except* by accident.

UNCLE: We must all have some possibilities for evil, if we can just look on the wrong side of things.

BAFFLES: Don't you think, sir, that life will correct the good in Mr. Andrew?

Act I, page 4:

BAFFLES: I don't want to criticize, Mr. Andrew, but don't you think Miss Flower's looking rather – well – *well* lately?

Act III, page 4:

BAFFLES: The trouble with birds is they imitate the vaudeville acts, and the vaudeville acts imitate the birds till we can't tell a real conception from a misconception any longer.

After a few hours of this banter the reviewers reeled out of the unbearably hot little theatre, staggered to their typewriters, and wrote comments such as these: 'There is probably nothing more embarrassing to any normally intelligent observer in the theater than to witness a fantasy that has gone haywire. ... But "gone haywire" is surely the only way of describing the progress, in a prologue and two acts, of Mrs Fitzgerald's play. ... Occasionally an observer with a sound memory will be reminded of a warped and mangled Oscar Wilde endlessly spouting epigrams that just won't click.' The night *Scandalabra* closed another reviewer who had gone back to give it the benefit of his considerable doubts said that 'there is no question of its being a fantasy', adding that it was 'mere persiflage'. Even Scott's revisions couldn't salvage it.

In the middle of July Zelda received word from Mrs Sayre that Zelda's brother, Anthony, had become ill in the South. He was suffering from what is called by that ominous euphemism 'nervous prostration'. Anthony was sent to Charleston, South Carolina, for a rest on the coast, but he did not improve, and it was recommended that he see a nerve specialist in Asheville. There the doctors said he needed absolute quiet and no visitors. On 6 August Anthony was taken by the Sayres' family doctor in Montgomery to another nerve specialist in Mobile; he asked to be taken to Johns Hopkins, where Zelda was, but his family wouldn't hear of it. They could not afford it and turned to Mrs Sayre for help. In Mobile the doctors tried to eliminate what they called 'toxic poisoning', due to a recurring case of malaria. Mrs Sayre warned the Fitzgeralds that this was what happened when her children kept something from her. The doctor said she was stronger than any of her children; Mrs Sayre said she should have taken Anthony in hand from the first.

Shortly after Anthony's hospitalization in Mobile he committed suicide by leaping from the window of his room. He had been depressed about the loss of his job and his inability to meet his expenses. Mrs Sayre had helped him frequently in the past, and he had begun to have terrible dreams that he would kill her. He told his doctor that he knew he should destroy himself instead. All but the most superficial details of his suicide were concealed from the Fitzgeralds.

17

. . . I play the radio and moon about . . . and dream of Utopias
where it is always July the 24th 1935, in the middle of summer
forever.

ZELDA, in an undated letter to Scott

The tensions within the Fitzgerald household mounted until
they became nearly palpable. Scott tinkered cautiously with
his final revisions for *Tender Is the Night* (which at this late
date was still called *Doctor Diver's Holiday*) and began preparing it for serialization in *Scribner's Magazine* which would
begin in January 1934. Zelda spent most of her time in her
studio painting. The Fitzgeralds seemed never to just sit down
and relax, together or apart. When Malcolm Cowley came
down to visit them he noticed Zelda's paintings and later wrote
that they were 'better than I expected; they had freshness,
imagination, rhythm, and a rather grotesque vigor, but they
were flawed, exactly as her writing had been, by the lack of
proportion and craftsmanship. Zelda herself dismayed me. . . .
Her face was emaciated and twitched as she talked. Her mouth,
with deep lines above it, fell into unhappy shapes. Her skin in
the lamplight looked brown and weather-beaten. . . .' Later in
the evening Scott stood in front of Cowley and told him:
'That girl had everything. . . . She was the belle of Montgomery, the daughter of the chief justice of the Alabama
Supreme Court. . . . Everybody in Alabama and Georgia knew
about her, everybody that counted. She had beauty, talent,
family, she could do anything she wanted to, and she's thrown
it all away.'

'That sounds like something from one of your own stories',
Cowley said.

'Sometimes I don't know whether Zelda isn't a character
that I created myself. And you know, she's cuckoo, she's crazy
as a loon. I'm madly in love with her.'

Madly in love with her or not, Scott was fuming about the direction Zelda's relationship to Dr Rennie seemed to be taking. Both of the Fitzgeralds were drawn to the doctor by his warmth and youth, but Zelda had been, according to Scott, duping him. Scott wrote Rennie saying she was selling the naïve young psychiatrist (as Scott liked to think of him)

the small accumulation of personal charm that she ought to be selling in the house. . . . Can't you imagine that every single judgment upon my drinking that could be made has been made, every struggle tried, won or lost, in detail and the fight continues and will continue? . . . Maybe I'm ruined and could never again pose as a cinema hero or a social success, but these have not recently figured among my ambitions. My line is to do a certain amount of straight thinking and observation, embody them in as perfect a technique as I can master.

Rennie, it seemed to Scott, was making judgements about his drinking as well as about Zelda,

conditioned on the charm of a very shrewd and canny woman, whose motives, both healthy and pathological, can stand a good examination. . . . You have indicated, merely from your interest, that you realize the importance of the factors with which you are dealing. Which, then, is more important? Responding to the mood of a psychopath or aiding someone to bring off what promises to be a work of art? (I hate like hell to make such a guess!) I couldn't think that there should be much choice on your part. . . . I am fighting my way through an old American tendency toward puritanism, not during the frequent insomnia involved wondering whether I will get through to the end, I worry sometimes whether you, Tom Rennie, or all your generation will laugh yourselves out of existence before you have begun to think. I *think* you think – but, I'm not absolutely convinced, because you, I am speaking of you personally, can be distracted by stray bits of color. . . . This lecture is worth a thousand dollars, but I don't regret it because you have sent in no bills. Why don't you? . . . I think we should split up. . . .

In closing Scott added that he had 'no more to be ashamed of than the average human being'.

Neither of the Fitzgeralds could bear living at La Paix any

longer, for the house had taken on for them the shapes and shadows of their troubles. In June Zelda had tried to burn some old clothes in an unused fireplace upstairs, inadvertently starting a fire, ruining several of the rooms on the upper floor, and leaving a permanent haze of sepulchral gloom over the rest of the house. The newspapers covered the fire and said it was due to defective wiring. Scott asked the Turnbulls to postpone having repairs made, for he was deep in his manuscript and did not want to be interrupted. But by November living at La Paix made them both jittery and they moved to a smaller place in town at 1307 Park Avenue, which was also less expensive. At the end of the month, at the suggestion of Dr Meyer, who insisted that a respite was necessary, the Fitzgeralds took a brief trip to Bermuda. Unfortunately, constant rain spoiled their holiday and after a week they returned unrested, with Scott suffering from pleurisy.

Scott had toyed for some time with the idea of exhibiting a selection of Zelda's paintings in New York. He would hire a gallery and test her work in a professional milieu. A friend of theirs, Cary Ross, talked Scott out of renting space for the show, for he felt that Zelda's work was good enough to interest a gallery without Scott's having to pay for the showing. Eventually Ross exhibited the paintings at his own gallery on East Eighty-sixth Street. At first Zelda was thrilled by the prospect of such an exhibition, but as the details of the arrangement were being worked out by Scott and the art dealer, she became irritated and refused to discuss anything with either of them. She said something about her paintings being too personal to her and went to bed. No one was quite certain what precipitated her relapse, but after this scene with Scott and Ross she was sent back to Phipps. She re-entered on 12 February 1934, exactly two years after her first entry. Zelda told her doctor, 'I don't think I could paint myself anyway if it weren't for – it's my way of communicating with someone.' The doctors realized that her relapse was a serious one, and Zelda was put under constant observation as a precaution against suicide, required to stay absolutely at rest in bed, and given sedatives each day. On her re-entry she was fifteen pounds underweight.

This time she did not make the slightest effort to cooperate with the doctors or the other patients. The only exception to her generally hostile behaviour was that in a dancing and exercise class she was later able to attend she would walk over to those patients in the group who were most ill and try to help them.

The serial version of *Tender Is the Night* was running in *Scribner's Magazine* throughout January, February, March, and April 1934. On Zelda's re-entry to Phipps she had probably read at least the first half of the novel, and it affected her profoundly. In a sense this was her most thorough confrontation with the Doctor Diver material Scott had been working on since 1932, for although she had seen and heard portions of the various drafts this was perhaps the first time she had seen it in its entirety.

Although the Divers were at the simplest level a composite of the Murphys and the Fitzgeralds, and the lyric opening of the novel drew on the spell the Murphys cast, Scott moved from that blending of sources until he was drawing deeply upon Zelda's and his life together. He mercilessly exposed Zelda in his characterization of Nicole Diver. He drew upon Zelda's most terrible and private letters to him, written in the anguish of the early months of her illness in Switzerland, snipped and pieced them together in Book II with very little regard for Zelda's reaction or for the precarious balance of her sanity. *Tender Is the Night* would not, of course, be recalled from Scribner's as *Save Me the Waltz* had been because of Scott's fictional exploitation of Zelda's mental illness in the novel. There was no one to act in Zelda's behalf, as Scott had once acted in his own. The letters written from Nicole to 'Mon Capitaine' and 'Captain Diver' were not simply echoes from Zelda's letters to Scott; there were whole phrases used exactly as he had received them. Among many examples are the following.

In *Tender Is the Night* Scott wrote:

Last year or whenever it was in Chicago when I got so I couldn't speak to servants or walk in the street I kept waiting for someone to tell me. It was the duty of someone who understood. The blind must be led. Only no one would tell me everything – they would just tell me half and I was already too muddled to put two and two together. One man was nice – he was a French officer and he understood. He gave me a flower and said it was 'plus petite et moins entendue'. We were friends. Then he took it away. I grew sicker and there was no one to explain to me.

In one of Zelda's letters from Prangins she had written Scott:

I could not walk in the streets unless I had been to my lesson. I could not manage the apartment because I could not speak to the servants ... and still I did not understand what I was doing. . . . You have given me a flower and said it was 'plus petit et moins entendue'. We were friends. Then you took it away and I grew sicker and there was nobody to teach me.

And there was this on the following page of the novel:

I write to you because there is no one else to whom I can turn and it seems to me if this farcicle situation is apparent to one as sick as me it should be apparent to you.

Compare with Zelda's letter, which read:

I would always be more than glad to see you, and will always be devoted to you – but the farcicle element of this situation is too apparent for even a person as hopeless and debilitated as I am.

The last sentence in the novel was lifted from another of Zelda's letters.

The mental trouble is all over and besides that I am completely broken and humiliated, if that was what they wanted.

Zelda had written Scott:

At any rate one thing has been achieved: I am thoroughly and completely humiliated and broken if that was what you wanted.

Scott wrote:

I would gladly welcome any alienist you might suggest.

And Zelda had written him:

I will more than gladly welcome any alienist you may suggest.

Fitzgerald even quoted directly in *Tender Is the Night* from Bleuler's diagnosis of Zelda's case.

Three days after Zelda went back to Phipps she admitted that she was 'a little upset about it [*Tender*]. . . . But a person has a right to interpret – But it really doesn't matter. What made me mad was that he made the girl so awful and kept on reiterating how she had ruined his life and I couldn't help identifying myself with her because she had so many of my experiences.

'It was a chronological distortion and I suppose one has a right to do that in an artistic creation. But on the whole I don't think it's true – I don't think it's really what happened.'

Suddenly she began to cry uncontrollably. 'I can't get on with my husband and I can't live away from him – materially impossible – so I think the only thing to do is to get my mind on something. . . . I'm so tired of compromises. Shaving off one part of oneself after another until there is nothing left. . . .'

Now Zelda did not show any signs of improvement. She began smiling to herself, she avoided answering questions put to her, and she laughed suddenly for no reason at all. In a coherent moment the sadness of her position in relation to Scottie came out. 'She [Scottie] is about as far away from me as anyone can be. She doesn't like any of the things I like although I've tried to interest her in them. She's just like her father, she's a cerebral type. She's crazy about history, French and English – and I don't know any so she rather looks down on me. Scott said he wanted to take her education in his hands so I've never interfered. I've kept out of it carefully because I realized that eventually Scott and I would have to separate and she is his child, she's so like him and he adores her. It would just be the undoing of him to take her away from him.'

Each day her condition grew worse; she was preoccupied, moody, and irritable. She began to insist that she be allowed to leave Phipps. (Zelda was never confined, in a legal sense, to any hospital. She went of her own volition and was not therefore 'committed'; if she asked to leave persistently enough, she had to be released.) She said she couldn't work in the clinic; she was restless and antagonistic toward the doctors. She began to write a study of Aristotle, which rambled on peculiarly about abstract emotions; she was grasping at straws, anything that would compensate for the breakdown in her relationship with Scott.

Meanwhile, Scott worked on the final revision of galley proof for *Tender Is the Night*. (Because the book was going to be published in April it had to be set from the magazine galleys. In February Scott was still reworking the last serial instalment; at some points because of the time pressure he was probably, as Matthew Bruccoli suggests in his textual study of the novel, working on magazine and book galleys at the same time.) It was cold, painstaking labour and he wrote Perkins:

After all, Max, I am a plodder. One time I had a talk with Ernest Hemingway, and I told him, against all the logic that was then current, that I was the tortoise and he was the hare, and that's the truth of the matter, that everything that I have ever attained has been through long and persistent struggle while it is Ernest who has a touch of genius which enables him to bring off extraordinary things with facility. I have no facility. I have a facility for being cheap, if I wanted to indulge that ... but when I decided to be a serious man, I tried to struggle over every point until I have made myself into a slow-moving behemoth (if that is the correct spelling), and so there I am for the rest of my life.

That Scott managed to pull the galleys into shape at all under the circumstances is astonishing. At the close of the same letter he told Perkins that *Tender Is the Night* was 'a woman's book' and that he had

lived so long within the circle of this book and with these characters that often it seems to me that the real world does not exist but that only these characters exist, and, however pretentious that remark sounds (and my God, that I should have to be pretentious about my work), it is an absolute fact – so much so that their glees and woes are just exactly as important to me as what happens in life. Zelda is better.

But she was not. There were days when Zelda refused to get out of bed in the morning, and once she ran to her nurse and said she had to call Scott. She needed two hundred dollars immediately in order to leave for Europe; she decided that she absolutely had to leave Phipps.

At just about this point Zelda must have been reading the March issue of *Scribner's Magazine,* for she wrote Scott:

Dear, Monsieur, D.O.;

The third installment is fine. I like immensely that retrospective part through Nicole's eyes – which I didn't like at first because of your distrust of polyphonic prose. It's a swell book. . . . I wish I could write stories. I wish I could write something sort of like the book of revelations: you know, about how everything would have come out if we'd only been able to supply the 3-letter word for the Egyptian god of dithryambics. Something all full of threats preferably and then a very gentle confession at the end admitting that I have enfeebled myself too much by my own vehemence to ever become very frightened again. . . .

D.O.:

You *don't* love me – But I am counting on Pavloff's dogs to make that kind of thing all right – and, in the mean-time, under the added emotional stress of the breek-up of our state, perhaps the old conventions will assume an added poignancy – . . . Besides, *anything* personal was never the objective of our generation – we were to have thought of ourselves heroicly; we agreed in the Plaza Grill the pact was confirmed by the shaking of Connie Bennets head and the sonority of Ludlow's premature gastritis –

A few days later, on 8 March 1934, after three and one-half weeks at Phipps, Zelda left. She was no better. In desperation Scott remembered Forel's recommendation of Craig House in Beacon, New York. From a descriptive letter sent to Scott in 1932, when he first investigated Craig House, it sounded like a very handsome establishment for the wealthier of the mentally ill. Located on 350 acres on the Hudson River, about two hours above New York City, it had cottages and private nurses for each patient. The treatment aimed (and all the brochures of mental hospitals seemed to stress this, probably to relieve the minds of the relatives of the patients) to provide as much freedom and personal liberty as was possible; there were no locks and keys. There were indoor and outdoor swimming pools, a golf course with its own clubhouse and golf pro, tennis courts, a masseuse and a hostess who organized bridge, backgammon, and ping-pong tournaments. The minimum rate without laundry or the use of the swimming pool was $175 a week. Scott took Zelda there quickly.

After he had left her she wrote to him.

Do-Do:

It was so sad to see your train pull out through the gold sheen of the winter afternoon. It is sad that you should have so many things to worry you and make you unhappy when your book is so good and ought to bring you so much satisfaction. I hope the house won't seem desolate and purposeless. . . . This is a beautiful place; there is everything on earth available and I have a little room to paint in with a window higher than my head the way I like windows to be. When they are that way, you can look out on the sky and feel like Faust in his den, or an alchemist or anybody you like who must have looked out of windows like that. And my own room is the nicest room I've ever had, any place – which is very unjust, considering the burden you are already struggling under.

Dear – I will see you soon. Why not bring Scotty up for Easter? . . . And I *promise* you absolutely that by then I will be much better – and as well as I can.

Dear:

PLEASE remember that you owe it to the fine things inside you to get the most out of them.

Work, and don't drink, and the accomplished effort will perhaps open unexpected sources of happiness, or contentment, or whatever it is you are looking for – certainly a sense of security – If I were you'd, I'd dramatize your book [Scott was considering giving it to a young man he knew in Baltimore to do] yourself. . . . a character play hinging on the two elements within the man [Dick Diver]: his worldly proclivities and his desire to be a distinguished person. I wish I could do it.

Love, dear –

She said she played tennis almost every day and took long walks, but that she was homesick for La Paix

– and even for those lonesome bicycle rides when I would come in to find 'the Baron' behind his rhodedendrons and his diamond-leaded windows [Scott's study at La Paix had a leaded-glass bow window.] You were so sad all year and I wanted so desperately for you to be happy. Will we be close again and will I feel the mossy feeling back of your head and will I share those little regulations by which you keep your life in order: the measured drinks, the neatly piled papers; to see you choose which shirt to please the day and hear you fuss about the fancy handkerchiefs.

Darling –

The initial opinion at Beacon about Zelda's condition was that she was suffering from fatigue. She was described as mildly confused and mentally retarded – with a degree of emotional instability.

Thirteen of Zelda's paintings and fifteen drawings were exhibited from 29 March through 30 April at Cary Ross's studio. (There was a much smaller supplementary exhibit in the lobby of the Algonquin Hotel.) At the top of the red, white, and blue brochure for the show was a swan with a banner bearing the legend 'Parfois la Folie est la Sagesse'. Zelda came down from Beacon for her exhibition accompanied by a nurse; she visited her show, saw an exhibition of Georgia O'Keeffe's paintings, and then attended a luncheon with Scott, Maxwell Perkins, and a few others from Scribner's before returning to Craig House. On the train journeying back to Beacon she became hysterical and was given medication to quiet her.

Gerald Murphy, who went to her exhibit, and who had painted himself, felt that Zelda's work was formed from a visual distortion. He talked about an oil painting he and Mrs Murphy bought for $200 called 'Chinese Theater'. 'Those monstrous, hideous men, all red with swollen intertwining legs. They were obscene – I don't mean sexually . . . and everyone who saw them recognized that quality of repellent human life; they were figures out of a nightmare, monstrous and morbid.'

Later when Zelda learned of the Murphys' purchase, she wrote Scott:

Dearest Do-Do: . . .
Cary wrote that Ernest was back in N.Y.; that he had been to see my pictures. Why don't you ask him down? . . . He also said the Murphys bought the acrobats. I am going to paint a picture for the

Murphy's and they can choose as those acrobats seem, somehow, singularly inappropriate to them and I would like them to have one they liked. Maybe they aren't like I think they are but I don't see why they would like that Buddhistic suspension of mass and form and I will try to paint some mood that their garden has conveyed.... And don't pay any attention to that initialled moth-hole in the Times. [Earlier in this letter she had referred to a review of *Tender* by J.A.D., which she thought obtuse.]

Apparently the Tribune man still believes that movie stars got there via the gutters of Les Miserables – But we can't buy him a ticket to Hollywood, and, on the whole, it was an intelligent and favorable review – and the liked the book even if he didn't know what it was about psychologicly. He will like it better when he reads it again.

I hope Ernest liked it....

Several of Zelda's drawings were sold, but not one to persons whom the Fitzgeralds did not know personally. Dorothy Parker bought one of the portraits of Scott called 'The Cornet Player'. She remembered that the drawings 'were pitifully inexpensive. There was the portrait of Scott wearing this piercing crown of thorns. They dug in; it did look like him; she had talent. I also bought something called 'Arabesque' which showed a dancer working out at the bar – it was a little vague, but with a striking resemblance to Zelda. I bought the portrait of Scott . . . because I thought it the best she did. But I couldn't have stood having them hang in the house. There was that blood red color she used and the painful, miserable quality of emotions behind the paintings.'

John Biggs came up for the showing and remembered seeing the portrait of Fitzgerald. 'Yes, it was good. The eyelashes were feathers; it was astoundingly really – looked like him, and then those mad, lovely, long feathery eyelashes.' Zelda had also caught perfectly the color of Scott's eyes, and Biggs said they were 'very cold blue eyes – almost green – they were as cold as the Irish Sea someone said. I can't remember if it was Gerald Murphy or Bunny Wilson – but . . . it was quite true.'

The New York *Post* ran an article on 3 April (ironically the Fitzgeralds' fourteenth anniversary) entitled 'Jazz Age Priestess

Brings Forth Paintings'. They said Zelda had 'confounded' them with her paintings and noted that they were not exactly 'jazzy', as indeed they were not.

When *Time* magazine covered her show they invoked Zelda's link to an era that had disappeared: 'There was a time', the article began, 'when Mrs Francis Scott Key Fitzgerald was a more fabulous character than her novel-writing husband. That was when she was Zelda Sayre...'

To Zelda's disappointment very little space was given in the press to the paintings themselves. Most, like *The New Yorker*, gave the exhibit a puff with a cutting edge: 'Paintings by the almost mythical Zelda Fitzgerald; with whatever emotional overtones or associations may remain from the so-called Jazz Age.' *Time* magazine did at least mention the paintings.

Last week ... Zelda Fitzgerald showed her pictures, made her latest bid for fame. The work of a brilliant introvert, they were vividly painted, intensely rhythmic. A pinkish reminiscence of her ballet days showed figures with enlarged legs and feet – a trick she may have learned from Picasso. An impression of a Dartmouth football game made the stadium look like portals of a theatre, the players like dancers. *Chinese Theatre* was a gnarled mass of acrobats with an indicated audience for background. There were two impressionistic portraits of her husband, a verdant *Spring in the Country* geometrically laced with telephone wires.

From the sanatorium last week which she temporarily left against doctors' orders to see a show of Georgia O'Keeffe's art, Zelda Fitzgerald was hoping her pictures would gratify her great ambition – to earn her own living.

The article read like an obituary.

Scott stayed on at the Algonquin after Zelda returned to Beacon because he wanted to be in New York for the publication of *Tender Is the Night* on 12 April.

Another writer spotted him ordering a drink at Tony's on Fifty-second Street at ten o'clock one night. 'The collar of his topcoat was turned up rakishly on one side and his hat, which he kept on, was pulled down jauntily over one eye. It was an almost studied effect, but it was oddly contradicted by Fitzgerald's curious air of self-disapproval.' The writer observing

Scott was James Thurber, and although they had never met before, the two men were to spend the next several hours together. Thurber remembered: 'He was . . . witty, forlorn, pathetic, romantic, worried, hopeful, and despondent, but the Scott Fitzgerald I met was quiet and pleasant, too, and not difficult. When two big guys, not unlike the Killers in Hemingway's story, walked past our table and, as luck would have it, one of them said something disparaging about Ernest, my companion rose dramatically to his feet and said to them, "I am Scott Fitzgerald." Before he could ask them to apologize, they muttered something and walked away.' That was as close to trouble as they came that night. Mostly they just talked. Thurber told Scott how much he admired *The Great Gatsby,* but Scott didn't want to hear about it. What he wanted to talk about was the book he called 'my Testament of Faith' – *Tender Is the Night.*

As Scott talked he kept drawing from his pockets brochures for Zelda's show. He had dozens of them about his person and by midnight so did Thurber. At three o'clock in the morning he asked Thurber if he knew any *good* girl he could call on. Somewhat apprehensively Thurber went off to the telephone to see whom he could round up at that hour. Finally, an actress he knew said they could come by, but to give her half an hour. Punctually the two tight flowers of American prose entered her apartment. Thurber went into another room, because, as he said, it was Scott who wanted to talk to a good girl and not he. But he noticed that as Scott and the girl sat next to each other talking until daybreak, Scott would occasionally, absentmindedly, pass some of Zelda's catalogues to the girl until she too was inundated with them.

Throughout the period of Zelda's stay at Craig House she corresponded regularly with Dr Rennie. Her letters were written in ink on large sheets of grey drawing paper. Also on the face of the letters were drawings in pencil. The effect of these letter drawings was eerie, with the written text dripping and winding through curling, swelling shapes that were anatomical and weirdly potent. None of the eight letters were dated. In one Zelda seemed to be writing to Rennie while she was listening to music. She said she was drawing him the flowers on her table. There were violets drawn to Strauss's *Salome* and roses drawn to Schubert. The interior parts of the flowers were carefully shaded, the stamens and pistils taking on shapes more phallic than floral, while the petals curled and ruptured like the breaking of eggs. The stems of the flowers were spiny, skeletal almost, and frondlike, as if the buds of the flowers were held to vertebral columns. The buds themselves were often shaped like foetuses. Macabrely, the flowers seemed to move as if in repulsion from their own interior parts.

After Zelda's trip to New York she wrote Dr Rennie:

My pictures looked very nice the way Cary had them hung. . . . I will send you the white flowers when the exhibit closes; they are the best and very like some way I've wanted to be, sometime – only, of course, being like that would necessitate being a stainless victim of some mighty and revolutionary circumstance. (Excuse my pompous comment.)

I went to see Georgia O'Keefe's pictures. They are so lonely and magnificent and heart-breaking, and they inspire a desire to communicate which is perhaps the highest function of anything creative.

Gradually her letters to Dr Rennie became more disconnected and incoherent; her handwriting was uneven and cramped and the content of the letters became grand and increasingly abstract: 'I wish I could write a beautiful book to break those hearts that are soon to cease to exist: a book of faith and small neat worlds and of people who live by the philosophies of popular songs. . . .'

When she wrote to Scott she nearly always asked him about *Tender Is the Night:* could he send her copies of the reviews; why had he neglected to send her the book itself; how were the sales going? But mostly she simply praised the novel. 'I have now got to the Rosemary-Rome episode. It makes me very sad – largely because of the beautiful, beautiful writing. Recapitulation of casual youth in the tenderer terms one learns to cling to later is always moving. You know I love your prose style: it is so fine and balanced and you know how to achieve

the emphasis you want so poignantly and economicly. It's a
fine book. . . .' Later in the same letter she tells him what she
is doing: hammering away, as she puts it, at golf balls. 'You
know my psychological attitude toward golf: it was just the
sort of thing they would have brought into England during
the reign of Chas. II. The French probably played it in high-
heels with stomachs full of wine and cheated a little.'

In another letter she described her bridge game:

You know how I play: I sit and wait for Divine Guidance to
show me the difference between a finesse and a (insert any technical
term you know here). Then when I've made the mistake I pretend
I was thinking of something else and utter as convincing lamenta-
tions as I can at my absent-mindedness.

It's so pretty here. . . . I suppose you wouldn't like to rest, but I
wish you could for a while in the cool apple-green of my room. . . .
Of cource, you can walk to where young men in bear-cat roadsters
are speeding to whatever Geneva Mitchells dominate the day – but
mostly we walk the other way. . . . *Please* send the book.

Scott did send her a batch of the first reviews of *Tender Is
the Night* and she immediately wrote, telling him: 'You have
the satisfaction of having written a tragic and poetic personal
drama against the background of an excellent presentation of
the times we matured in. You know that I have always felt
that the chief function of the artist was to inspire *feeling* and
certainly "Tender" did that.' Another time she wrote, 'Those
people are helpless before themselves and the prose is beautiful.
. . .' She said she was reading Book I again.

Scott cautioned her about projecting too much of themselves into the book, and she replied:

You seem afraid that it will make me recapitulate the past:
remember, that at that time, I was immersed in something else –
and I guess most of life is a re-hashing of the tragedies and happi-
nesses of which it consisted in days before we started to promul-
gate reasons for their being so. Of cource, it is a haunting book.
. . . Scott: this place is most probably hideously expensive. *I do not
want you to struggle* through another burden like the one in Switzerland for my sake. You write too well. Also, you know that I live

much within myself and would feel less strongly now than under normal circumstances about whatever you wanted to do. You have not got the right, for Scottie's sake, and for the sake of letters to make a drudge of yourself for me.

Scott continued to insist that she not have 'too much traffic with my book, which is a melancholy work and seems to have haunted most of the reviewers. *I feel very strongly about your re-reading it*. It represents certain phases of life that are over now.' He told her they were both on the upgrade now, and even if they did not know where it would take them, he did not want her to feel gloomy about their future:

... the only sadness is the living without you, without hearing the notes of your voice with its particular intimacies of inflection.

You and I have been happy; we haven't been happy just once, we've been happy a thousand times. The chances that the spring, that's for everyone, like in the popular songs, may belong to us too – the chances are pretty bright at this time because as usual, I can carry most of contemporary literary opinion, liquidated, in the hollow of my hand – and when I do, I see the swan floating on it and – I find it to be you and you only. But, Swan, float lightly because you are a swan, because by the exquisite curve of your neck the gods gave you some special favor, and even though you fractured it running against some man-made bridge, it healed and you sailed onward. Forget the past – what you can of it, and turn about and swim back home to me, to your haven for ever and ever – even though it may seem a dark cave at times and lit with torches of fury; it is the best refuge for you – turn gently in the waters through which you move and sail back.

This sounds allegorical but is *very* real, I want you here. The sadness of the past is with me always. The things that we have done together and the awful splits that have broken us into war survivals in the past stay like a sort of atmosphere around any house that I inhabit. The good things and the first years together, and the good months that we had two years ago in Montgomery will stay with me forever. I love you my darling, darling.

At the beginning of this letter Scott had apologized to Zelda for dictating it; he said she would understand if she could see the clutter of unanswered mail on his desk. But, as authentic as the emotion of the letter was for Scott, there is something distasteful about his having dictated it.

Zelda wanted to begin another novel. What, she asked, would Scott's attitude be towards her plans? She wanted to know before she began, for after all, she told him, *Tender Is the Night* was now published and she was free to make another stab at longer fiction. Actually, her doctors were against any such attempt, and so was Scott. Zelda seemed completely unaware of why they objected. Patiently she tried to explain to Scott: 'Dear: I am not trying to make myself into a great artist or a great anything. . . . Though you persist in thinking that an exaggerated ambition is the fundamental cause of my collapse . . . though, of course, the will-to-power may have played a part in the very beginning. However, five years have passed since then, and one matures.' Short fiction, she said, was 'a form demanding too concentrated an effort for me at present and I might try a play, if you are willing and don't approve of the novel. . . . *Please say what you want done,* as I really do not know. As you know, my work is mostly a pleasure for me, but if it is better for me to take up something quite foreign to my temperament, I will – Though I can't see what good it does to knit bags when you want to paint pansies, maybe it is necessary at times to do what you don't like.' Petulantly as a crossed child Zelda saw nothing disturbing in this latest flash of ambition and energy, and she pressed on. She wrote 'Show Mr and Mrs F. to Number —' and perhaps began 'Auction – Model 1934'. It is doubtful that she had time to begin the new novel, for on 19 May 1934, only nine weeks after she had entered Craig House, she was transferred to the Sheppard and Enoch Pratt Hospital just outside Baltimore in (as Scott noted in his Ledger) a 'catatonic state' – although there remains a real question as to whether or not she was catatonic. She was to remain there for the better part of the next two years. Just before this terrible relapse she had written Scott that Beacon was extremely expensive and

I do not feel as you do about state institutions. Dr. Meyer and,

I suppose, many excellent doctors did their early training there. You will have to conceal as much of this from Scottie as you can anyway. So in the words of Ernest Hemingway, *Save Yourself.* That is what I want you to do. . . . I am so glad your book is on the list of best sellers. Maybe now you will have some measure of that ease and security you have so long deserved. Anyway, I hope it sells and sells.

For the first two weeks of Zelda's hospitalization Scott was asked not to visit her. She was apathetic and remote, and wrote him dispiritedly:

Darling – I feel very disoriented and lonely. I love you, dear-heart. Please try to love me some in spite of these stultifying years of sickness – and I will compensate you some way for your love and faithfullness.

I'm sorry Scottie has had poison ivy. The other day when I kissed her good-bye the little school-child scent of her neck and her funny little hesitant smile broke my heart. Be good to her Do-Do. . . . I want so to see you. Maybe sometimes before very long I will be well enough to meet you under the gracious shadows of these trees and we can look out on the distant fields to-gether. And I will be getting better.

Fitzgerald accepted the doctors' decision, but reminded them that he had seen Zelda only twice during the previous two months, and that sometimes his effect on her was to raise her spirits. He also told them that he had been 'dogmatic' in the past about insisting that she not write serious fiction, and that he had perhaps been wrong. 'For it there is to be said that she grew better in the three months at Hopkins where it was al-lowed. . . .' It was his thinking along these lines, as well as his awareness of Zelda's listlessness, that prompted him to suggest to her that she bring together a collection of her short stories and articles for possible publication. And it must have been in yet another effort to stir her from apathy that he wrote to her the end of May that perhaps they could go to Europe together in late summer, 'even if only for six weeks. . . .'

During the last week of May Zelda seemed to be slipping into complete confusion. Her face was without expression. While talking to a doctor she would suddenly stop and ask him if he heard anything; he would assure her that he did not. But it was quite clear that Zelda was listening to hallucinated voices. Once she admitted that she was and said that she had heard them at Prangins too. Then they were her family's cries for help. Now it was Scott's voice she heard; it came to her out of walls, up from drain pipes, it seemed both near and far away. She said that she realized the voices were within herself, and hearing them alarmed her but was also a pleasant sensation. She said she was terrified of Scott; she said that he interpreted life for her. Sometimes his voice called her name over and over again, or repeated what she was saying, or said: 'Please, please, don't be in an insane asylum.' 'O, I have killed her!' 'I have lost the woman I put into my book.'

In a dream she saw herself asleep in the top room of a large, bright insane asylum, which was situated out in a broad field. It seemed to be a pleasant sort of place. But Scott was on the roof of the hospital and he was hunting for her, calling for her. In the dream she woke up and thought she recognized some nurses from the Phipps Clinic. The guards had left and all the patients of the asylum were together in a confused mob indulging in a sort of orgy. She watched but did not take part; she was amused and frightened. Zelda admitted to not being certain whether this was a dream or a hallucination. She said that she sometimes saw things – objects, her own face, distorted and discoloured – or double images of things. Abruptly she said she was not thinking of killing herself, but that death was the only way out.

Deeply moved by Zelda's feelings of helplessness, Scott was trying to find a refuge for her in work. His own morale had flagged, for *Tender Is the Night* was not doing as well as he had hoped; it was on the best-seller lists for several weeks, but its sales fell short of fourteen thousand copies. It was not only that he was disappointed by the failure of his novel to find a larger public, but that failure severely damaged his already wobbly self-esteem. Scott could understand Zelda's collapse of spirit – it was kindred to his own – but he fought against her resignation with plans that would stimulate her. About the collection of her short pieces, he wrote her, 'I want to do this if only for the salutary effect on you of keeping your hand in during this period of inaction.'

Fitzgerald outlined the form her book could take. He would write a five-hundred-word introduction to be followed by her stories. The book would be divided into three parts, the first to be called 'Eight Women'; this would include the sketches and stories Zelda had written between 1927 and 1932, primarily her *College Humor* pieces. Part II was to include three unpublished fables, and Part III, called 'Recapitulation', would be composed of Zelda's autobiographical articles for *Esquire* that Scott had helped her with earlier in the spring. (Those were 'Show Mr and Mrs F. to Number—', published in May 1934, and 'Auction – Model 1934', scheduled for July publication.) In Scott's opinion this sort of collection would nicely 'compete with such personal collections of miscellany as Dorothy Parker's etc. The very fact that the material is deeply personal rather than detached and professional make it expedient that it be presented in some way as this.' He did not think Scribner's should take it on, as a collection of his own stories, *Taps at Reveille*, was in the works for the same season, but he thought Perkins might suggest another publisher who would be interested.

Zelda responded with something of the zest Scott had counted on reviving in her; she was excited by the prospect of such a collection, and made plans to design the jacket. In good spirits she wrote him immediately:

(1) The Myers have gone to Antibes with the Murphys—

(2) Malcolm Cowley arrested for rioting in N.Y.

(3) I drink milk, one glass of which I consider equal to six banannas under water or two sword-swallowings – ... We have a great many activities of the kind one remembers pleasantly afterwards but which seem rather vague at the time like pea-shelling and singing.

She was afraid the title 'Eight Women' was 'too big a steal from Dreiser – I like, ironically, "My Friends" or "Girl Friends" better.'

The 'Recapitulation' articles are worth looking at more

closely, for they were both in a vein that Scott himself would mine deeply within the next eighteen months in his *Crack-Up* articles. He edited the first one, 'Show Mr and Mrs F to Number —', but there are few markings on 'Auction – Model 1934', and those are in Zelda's hand.

Together the pieces reviewed the Fitzgeralds' life from their marriage to 1934. 'Show Mr and Mrs F. to Number —' moves through the years 1920 to 1933 by reciting the hotel rooms the Fitzgeralds occupied in the various places where they lived and visited. In it there is a general air of nothing going right: there are fleas at the Grand Hotel in Rome; and in London, at Claridge's, there are strawberries in a golden dish, but the room is an inside room, and the weather is gloomy, as is their waiter. In a squib about the authors (the pieces were published under both Fitzgeralds' names) in 'Backstage with *Esquire*' the reader is invited to think of the Fitzgeralds in their familiar slick magazine role: classy models of American marrieds, with smart-alecky copy to back the role up: 'Anything you don't know about Scott and Zelda Fitzgerald, after reading this month's intimate addition to their joint journal, is certainly none of your business.' All that was missing was the sepia photograph from the twenties. But the tone was completely out of place. Zelda's entry for 1929 in 'Show Mr and Mrs F. to Number —' was more to the point. 'The night of the stock-market crash we stayed at the Beau Rivage in St Raphaël in the room Ring Lardner had occupied another year. We got out as soon as we could because we had been there so many times before – it is sadder to find the past again and find it inadequate to the present than it is to have it elude you and remain forever a harmonious conception of memory.'

Still, the tone of the past she evokes seems to contradict the content of the article; on the surface it is a rather flip and impersonal enumerating of the years. No one who is mentioned in the course of the article comes to life, the places the Fitzgeralds visited do not take on the glow of remembering, and the reader is not left with a sense that the author wishes to return to any of the scenes described. The motions of the Fitzgeralds' lives have been nicely recorded, dates are in their rightful places and so are the Fitzgeralds, but we are not permitted to enter into their lives. It is a cardboard telling. We sense great spaces of their lives left unmentioned, an urge toward revealing unfulfilled. It is only if we pay attention to the small words, the adjectives, that we sense the reality Zelda skirted. Cafés have a '*desperate* swashbuckling air', the moon falls over sand in a '*dead* white glow', fidelities are '*savage*', the pink of Arabian nougat and cakes is 'poisonous'. There is an interior meaning to the piece which lies in the slant of its style.

Scott's editing of the article was to Zelda's advantage, for he tightened and sharpened it. In a passage that is frequently quoted one can see how effectively he pared her prose into more striking shape. Her typescript read:

We walked at night towards a cafe blooming with Japanese lanterns and I followed your white shoes gleaming like radium in the damp darkness. Rising off the water, lights flickered an unimperative invitation far enough away to be interpreted as we liked; to shimmer glamourously behind the silhouette of retrospective good times when we still believed in summer hotels and the philosophies of popular songs. Another night, we learned to Wiener waltz, and once we regimented our dreams to the imperative commands of a nostalgic orchestra floating down the formal paths of the garden of a better hotel.

In Scott's revision:

We walked at night towards a café blooming with Japanese lanterns, white shoes gleaming like radium in the damp darkness. It was like the good gone times when we still believed in summer hotels and the philosophies of popular songs. Another night we danced a Wiener waltz and just simply swep' around.

But also he cut from it Zelda's use of *I*, which weakened the article by further depersonalizing it.

In the second essay, 'Auction – Model 1934', Zelda again reviews their shared past. This time her tone is more ironic. The Fitzgeralds are moving and the move gives her a chance to sort out their possessions. From them she will select only those objects worth keeping; the rest will be sold at auction. Among the souvenirs of their pasts were 'Twelve scrap books, telling us what wonderful or horrible or mediocre people we were.' The objects that she finds as she makes ready to pack them are used to refresh her memory and provide her with an opportunity to comment upon the circumstances in which they were acquired. Presumably it is through these objects that the reader is intended to be led into a rapport with the Fitzgeralds. But the tone of the piece is chill and mocking. In the second packing case are fifty photographs and drawings of the Fitzgeralds. 'In some of the pictures we are golfing and swimming and posing with other people's animals, or tilting borrowed surf-boards against the spray of younger summers. There are also many impressive photographs of old and very dear friends whose names we have forgotten.' Living always in houses that are rented and usually furnished, they have accumulated few permanent possessions; their china is broken, there are tops to jars, but no longer the jars themselves. Their treasures are chipped, worn, or moth-eaten, all flawed and unusable. In the end we realize that the article is not straight; it is a tease with the objects as bait. The narrator has no intention of selling anything. If their possessions are useless, they are nevertheless as good an example of their lives, as valuable, Zelda writes, 'as the Polish and Peruvian bonds of our thriftier friends'. They will keep them all, 'the tangible remnant of the four hundred thousand we made from hard words and spent with easy ones these fifteen years'.

Scott had early in his career consciously created an aura of legend about himself and Zelda. Articles like 'Echoes of the Jazz Age', published in November 1931, and 'My Lost City', which was sent to Harold Ober in July 1932, were efforts he made to come to terms with the heady glamour of his past. Emotions of loss, of time and feeling unrecapturable, infused his writing, as they did not Zelda's. Her lucid self-revelation was matchless in her private letters to Scott, but it was Scott who could, so to speak, use himself publicly. For the Christmas issue of *Esquire* he would write an essay about his own insomnia, called 'Sleeping and Waking', and it was yet another exercise in self-analysis and revelation touched by confession. Toward its end the essay comes close to the tone he will use effectively in *The Crack-Up*. He tries to put himself to sleep with his own dreams of glory, but he has used his dreams and they are as depleted as he is. When at last they work they

are of young and lovely people doing young, lovely things, the girls I knew once, with big brown eyes, real yellow hair.

> In the fall of '16 in the cool of the afternoon
> I met Caroline under a white moon
> There was an orchestra – Bingo-Bango
> Playing for us to dance the tango
> And the people all clapped as we arose
> For her sweet face and my new clothes –

Life *was* like that, after all. . . .

Neither of Zelda's articles has this sting of emotion, of nostalgia held close, as if the act of remembering were a restorative. It may have been that Zelda's dreams were never as potent as Scott's, but it is more likely that her gift of communicating feeling was simply less than his.

By the end of the summer it was clear to all concerned that Zelda's condition had taken another downward turn. As early as July the doctors were finding it futile to get her to discuss her illness, and her behaviour fluctuated wildly between violence and seclusiveness. She would have nothing to do with the other patients. There was no longer, even on Scott's part, any pretence about her ability to pull together a collection of her writings. In August he spent an hour and a half with her. 'She seemed in every way exactly like the girl I used to know. But, perhaps for that reason, it seemed to both of us very sad and she cried in my arms and we felt that the summer slipping by was typical of the way life is slipping by for both of us.' He wanted to believe that Zelda could be back with him on any basis for at least part of the time, and he was willing to have her living with him taking rest cures or visiting clinics when it was necessary to do so, rather 'than have her remain for long years of our lives in hospitals on the faint chance that when she came out she would suddenly become completely social'.

Scott visited Sheppard-Pratt frequently, and Dr William Elgin, Zelda's doctor, says it is Scott whom he remembers more clearly; he felt that it was really Scott whom he treated. While Fitzgerald said he came to discuss the cost of Zelda's treatment, he talked about himself. Eventually, he talked about everything. Zelda, on the other hand, was completely uncooperative and inaccessible. She left the impression of being colourless, a 'blob', with everything about her slowed down. Her face was expressionless. 'Once she condescended to tell me something about a painting. Usually her paintings were blobs – lines and squares. This one was simple – a streak of brown at the bottom, a blue streak in the middle and a little brown object up in the corner. I asked her what it was about. She said, "Oh, that's a table in Spain." I must have looked puzzled, for she then said, "Seen from the coast of the United States." ' Dr Elgin laughs. When asked if Zelda was perhaps putting him on or inviting his own response, he says that in those days he wouldn't have thought of that.

As usual Zelda spent Christmas with Scott and Scottie, but it was a sad reunion in the small row house in Baltimore, for they shared the knowledge that she must return to the hospital. Nineteen-thirty-five began with no reprieves for Zelda, no brighter future for the Fitzgeralds. Always now there was the pungent aroma of gin about Scott. The entries in his Ledger grew more despairing: '... work and worry ... Zelda seems less well. ... Debts terrible ... Zelda very bad on return. Terrible worry ... Zelda in hell.'

Zelda's letters to Scott were talismans of their past, lucid and touching. If her mind was broken, the spell it cast was not. Her life was now truly that of an invalid, and her mood was locked in elegy, confined to remembering. Her letters became her refuge, shared with Scott alone. 'Wouldn't you like to smell the pine woods of Alabama again? Remember there were 3 pines on one side and 4 on the other the night you gave me my birth-day party and you were a young lieutenant and I was a fragrant phantom, wasn't I? And it was a radiant night, a night of soft conspiracy and the trees agreed that it was all going to be for the best. Remember the faded gray romance.'

She read magazines and books to fill her time, and even people in advertisements looked enviable to her, for they were 'so young and soignées in the pictures'. Her letters were filled with wishing.

It seems rather Proustian to be rambling these deep shades again so close to La Paix. It makes me sad. . . . And I think of your book and it haunts me. So beautiful a book.

I wish we could spend July by the sea, browning ourselves and feeling water-weighted hair flow behind us from a dive. I wish our gravest troubles were the summer gnats. I wish we were hungry for hot-dogs and dopes and it would be nice to smell the starch of summer linens and the faint odor of talc in blistering bath-houses. . . . We could lie in long citroneuse beams of the five o'clock sun on the plage at Juan-les-Pins and hear the sound of the drum and piano being scooped out to sea by the waves.

Once when Scott came to visit her and she was desperate about the hopelessness of her condition, she ran from him toward railroad tracks that separated the grounds of Sheppard-Pratt from La Paix. Scott raced after her and caught her by the wrist moments before she would have thrown herself beneath the rushing train. It was not the only instance of attempted suicide.

Summer, another summer has gone – faded and wilted – and why can't we spend the fall to-gether? After all, we might as well be taking care of each other.

She signed this

For I am yours forever – whether you still want me or not –
and I love you

Finally she admitted to one of her doctors that she thought her condition was hopeless; she intended to take her life. He tried to tell her that as an agent of society he could not allow her to do so. Furious, Zelda asked how he justified taking such an attitude when he knew the pain of her existence. Throughout June, July, and August she persisted in whatever ways were open to her to try to harm herself. She refused to talk about herself to anyone on the staff – her letters to Scott were her only release.

It is summer time and past time – and I am very young when I didn't care. ... I wish I had been what I thought I was; and so debonnaire; and so debonnaire.

I think of boat houses in Atlanta with scaffolding and big dead moons and a drink behind the boats. I thought I was happy, or, at least, there was some pleasurable sense of things being in the world to conquer. ... You have been so good to me. My Do-Do. I wish I had not caused so much disaster. But I know you will be happy someday.

Over and over, endlessly repeating those tokens from a time irretrievable, Zelda tried to apologize for the destruction of their life together. She clung to the remnants of that life with what little hope she had to spare. Sometimes it ran out.

My dearest Sweetheart:

There is no way to ask you to forgive me for the misery and pain which I have caused you. I can only ask you to believe that I have done the best I could and that since we first met I have loved you with whatever I had to love you with. You are always my darling. I want you to be happy again with Scottie – someplace where it is bright and happy and you can have some of the things you have worked so hard for – always all your life faithfully. *You* are my dream; the only pleasant thing in my life.

Do-Do my darling! Please get well and love Scottie and find something to fill up your life – My love,
My love   My love

In February and again in May 1935, Scott had taken trips to North Carolina for his health and for his peace of mind. He wanted to be alone and he wanted to sleep. He spent part of the spring in Tryon and Hendersonville, and on 11 May back in Baltimore he wrote Perkins, 'Zelda is in very bad condition and my own mood always somehow reflects it.' He drank heavily in spurts and then laid off for a few weeks; he had always said that he drank to help him write, to stimulate himself, but he no longer even pretended that those were his reasons. That May an x-ray showed a spot of tuberculosis on one of his lungs and he returned to North Carolina to rest. What he suffered from was as much a collapse of his belief in himself as it was tuberculosis.

Zelda was not coherent during most of this period of Scott's absence, but once when she surfaced for a few days she wrote him: 'What *is* my business is that, under the circumstances, I do not see how you can reasonably expect me to go on unworriedly spending God-knows-how-much-a-day when we haven't got it to spend. You must realize that to one as ill as I am, one place is not very different from another and that I would appreciate your making whatever adjustments would rend your life less difficult.'

Scott must have understood that his life would be less difficult if he could detach himself somewhat from Zelda. He was no longer faithful to her, but his few affairs thus far had been desultory and even rather dull. Clearly the women did not interest him much or for long, and one suspects that he enjoyed the excitement of the game, the chase, more than the possession of the women themselves. As he once admitted to a friend, 'With a woman, I have to be emotionally in it up to the eyebrows, or it's nothing. With me it isn't an affair – it must be the real thing. ... Silly, isn't it? Look at all the fun we miss!' During the summer of 1935 he met Mrs Laura Guthrie Hearne in Asheville. Mrs Hearne was making her living telling fortunes at the elegant Grove Park Inn where Scott was staying. She remembers being dressed in a red gypsy costume with spangles across her forehead when they met: 'He was incognito and didn't mix with the other guests. He called himself, if I can remember correctly, Mr Johnston, and had just taken the cure at Tryon. I didn't know who he was and simply remember taking the hand of a shaky young man. Oh, there was such weakness in that hand of his. It was blotched and trembling.' She did such a convincing job of telling Fitzgerald's fortune that he revealed who he was. Writers and artists fascinated her and she told him that she was keeping a diary that she would like to show to him for his opinion. They became friends and when he could not find a secretary he hired Mrs Hearne.

She remembers his bouts with insomnia vividly. 'Scott never

wanted to sleep. He would think up any pretext to keep me with him.' He had begun to drink a lot again, first beer and later hard liquor. 'Thirty cans of beer a day; Scott smoked all the time, Sanos, I think. He said he drank to heighten his sensibilities. . . . He never wanted to be alone.

'He talked a lot about Zelda. She was his invalid. And he always asked himself if he had caused her breakdown. He was haunted – he could not sleep and he could not eat. All he would take was mashed potatoes or a little rice with gravy. He'd fall asleep suddenly, right at dinner or while he was talking to you. It was the strangest, most pitiful thing to see.

'He spoke of his tragedy; he made a fetish of their love and called it the mating of the age. She was the golden beauty of the South and he the brilliant success of the North.'

Mrs Hearne was certain that he used his attachment to Zelda 'to protect himself from permanent arrangements with other women'. She says: 'Scott Fitzgerald was beautiful; sober he was charming, but he was not faithful to Zelda. There would be this glint in his eye and he would tell me long lists of women he'd taken, but of course I never knew what to believe. He used to say to me, "Zelda can't understand that I'm a great writer." '

Staying at the inn at the same time was a pretty young Southern married woman who recognized Fitzgerald and pursued him. Soon they were involved. His emotional stamina was exhausted, and the last thing he wanted was to become embroiled in an ardent and lengthy affair. He made this quite clear to the girl. Mrs Hearne, privy to their affair, made copious notes on the romance. 'At first he didn't love her and then when the affair was no longer possible, her husband returned, he decided he did. They had unbelievable scenes together. She adored him and he tried to get rid of her.' Finally, somewhat callously, he apparently used a letter from Zelda to break off the affair. He enclosed it in a letter he had written to the young woman. 'The tough part of the letter is to send you this enclosure – which you should read now [a loving, dependent letter from Zelda]. . . . There are emotions just as important as ours running concurrently with them – and there is literally no standard in life other than a sense of duty. .... You once said, "Zelda is your *love!*" (only you said 'lu-uv'). And I gave her all the youth and freshness that was in me. And it's a sort of investment that is as tangible as my talent, my child, my money. That you had the same sort of appeal to me, deep down in the gut, doesn't change the other.'

Back in Baltimore in September he wrote Mrs Hearne that he had seen plenty of people hurt when they were thrown over, 'but I never saw a girl who *had so much* take it all so hard. She knew from the beginning there would be nothing more, so it could scarcely be classed even as a disappointment – merely one of those semi-tragic facts that must be faced.' To another friend he would admit quite candidly, '. . . it's done now and tied up in cellophane and – and maybe someday I'll get a chapter out of it'.

By the end of October he was able to see Zelda once or twice a week. He wrote Mrs Hearne that she was better. 'What she has been through troubles me – compared to her troubles mine seem like so much froth, except in so far as I have shared her suffering.' Slowly Zelda had given up trying to kill herself and as winter came and passed she retreated deeply into herself. She spoke to no one; she no longer wrote to Scott. In the spring of 1936 she began to say that she wanted to leave the hospital. She believed that she was under the control of God and was working with him to teach mankind certain things he had ordained to her. The end of the world was coming and she wanted to leave to preach this doctrine. The doctors had, she told them, destroyed her soul.

A member of her family came to visit her. Zelda was found dressed entirely in white, weighing less than a hundred pounds; she looked like a desperate angel. She had dropped to her knees by the side of her bed in prayer. When she noticed her visitor, she stood and faced her expressionlessly. Very quietly, in a singsong voice, she asked her visitor for two things. Would this person look after Scottie, and could she have a candy bar?

Clearly Zelda was not getting better. And therefore Scott, who had decided to make Asheville his home base and who wanted her near him, asked that she be released. Zelda left

Sheppard-Pratt on 7 April 1936. Scott took her to Highland Hospital in Asheville, North Carolina, the following day. He wrote in his Ledger, 'Me caring about no one and nothing.' He had written the Murphys about his decision the week before.

... Zelda now claims to be in direct contact with Christ, William the Conqueror, Mary Stuart, Apollo and all the stock paraphernalia of insane-asylum jokes. Of course it isn't a bit funny but after the awful strangulation episode of last spring I sometimes take refuge in an unsmiling irony about the present *exterior* phases of her illness. For what she has really suffered, there is never a sober night that I do not pay a stark tribute of an hour to in the darkness. In an odd way, perhaps incredible to you, she was always my child (it was not reciprocal as it often is in marriages), my child in a sense that Scottie isn't, because I've brought Scottie up hard as nails (perhaps that's fatuous, but I *think* I have). ... I was her great reality, often the only liason agent who could make the world tangible to her –

Scott put Zelda in the care of Dr Robert S. Carroll, stayed in Asheville less than two weeks and returned to Baltimore, apparently at the suggestion of Dr Carroll, who later explained to him, 'You are her [Zelda's] ideal; you are her emotional disorganizer. I recognize that while here your desire was to give her every possible assistance. We did not, however, organize her treatment until after you left.'

Highland Hospital, which was taken over by Duke University in 1945, is located just outside Asheville and is ringed by the splendid mountain ranges of the Blue Ridge, Smokies, and Balsams. Dr Carroll, the founder of the hospital, had chosen Asheville because of its temperate climate. Part of his routine in the curing of the mentally ill was exercise, and a five-mile daily hike was at the centre of his programme. Carroll believed that mental illness, or 'nervous disease' as it was called then, could be cured, or at any rate kept within the patient's control, by the help of strict diet as well as rigorous physical exercise. He took only sixty-five patients at a time and when he could he recruited staff members from the ranks of those who were cured. His staff was therefore unique: they were compassionate and highly aware of the needs of the unbalanced; they were also extraordinarily devoted to Dr Carroll. There was no question that Carroll was something of an original in American psychiatry, and was rather unorthodox. He had written a number of popular books on the treatment of 'nervousness' and a novel in 1922 called *The Grille Gate* (which appears to be a thinly disguised autobiography concerning the maturing of a devoted young doctor). In 1941 he would publish a book on alcoholics, with a preface by Dr Adolf Meyer. In it Dr Meyer said that Carroll had 'proved his hospital one of the most effective systematic agencies in the treatment of victims of alcohol, along lines that are also his methods and principles in the treatment of the rank and file of mental disorders as he sees them in the axiom: *mens sana in corpore sano* – a healthy person in and through a healthy body'.

An example of Carroll's system was his belief in the benefits of an exercise he had devised which involved climbing a hill. The patient was to climb a particular distance, up and down the hill, so many times each day. Each individual had a certain level of achievement, determined for him by the doctor. This was not hiking, nor was it supposed to be a particularly enjoyable exercise; it was to teach the disturbed to overcome obstacles by learning perseverance. A nurse who was at the hospital at that time said that the exercise 'was to accustom the patient to the reality of endeavour, endless and routine. The monotonous plodding along of everyday life might be a sound analogy.'

Carroll permitted no tobacco, drugs, alcohol, or rare meats, and he insisted on a minimum of sweets, plenty of milk, eggs, starch, natural juices, and vegetables. He forbade his female patients the use of mirrors, for he felt that primping in front of them, as well as the use of rouge and lipstick, were false modes of concentration on the self. Patients were expected to be up, breakfasted and out of doors by eight o'clock. There were calisthenics, medicine ball, and volleyball in the mornings and at 10.30 they took nourishment such as milk and whole-wheat bread with peanut butter. The hours from eleven to one were devoted to gardening. After lunch there was a rest period, followed by various treatments specially chosen according to the individual patient's needs and progress. On Sunday afternoons there were vespers led by Dr Carroll, who as the son and brother of ministers was zealous in his preaching. There were also guest lecturers and specially planned activities such as square dances and travel slides.

In July 1936 Scott gave up his house in Baltimore and moved

to the Grove Park Inn in Asheville. Scottie was sent to camp and Scott wrote her there that he had seen Zelda twice: 'Your mother looks five years younger and prettier and has stopped that silly praying in public and all that. Maybe she will come all the way back.' He and Zelda made plans to meet for lunch at Grove Park Inn for her thirty-sixth birthday, but Scott was forced to cancel the date when he fractured his shoulder diving (he had been showing off his prowess to a young woman at the inn). As a result of his injury, for the rest of the summer he was in an enormous plaster cast that ran from his navel out to the tip of his right hand.

Zelda and Scott did not see much of each other that summer. Scott told Perkins, 'I have been within a mile and half of my wife all summer and have seen her about half dozen times.' When they did meet it was usually at the inn. Grove Park Inn was a fashionable resort hotel surrounded by garden walks and clay tennis courts with the view of the mountains always in the distance. It looked like a stone fortress, for the central part of the inn was built of massive grey boulders and thick wooden beams, and the fireplace was as tall as two men and deep enough for a small automobile to park inside. There were spacious verandahs where dance bands played in the evening while the guests dined at their leisure.

When the Fitzgeralds met it was usually for lunch. They would sit in the dining room far away from the other guests. Scott did not introduce Zelda to anyone and frequently they would sit through an entire meal in silence. After lunch they walked down the terraced gardens into meadows rimmed with pines and sat on white wicker settees overlooking the mountains, Scott smoking constantly, Zelda lost in silence. A woman who worked at the inn remembered the Fitzgeralds. 'They never spoke to anybody. They would come for luncheon and, my, the way she looked. Long old clothes, long skirts and a face like a little girl's. She always liked cucumbers in sour cream. Sometimes she'd eat just that. . . . She was offish and refined; he was so elegant.'

The staff of Grove Park liked Scott; he tipped handsomely and was generally gracious to them. (But when he was drinking he had a habit of calling all Southerners 'farmers' and that didn't sit well.) A telephone operator remembers his long conversations with the Flynns in Tryon. He had met them when he first came to North Carolina in the spring of 1935. Nora Flynn was a vivacious, merry woman, who went to considerable lengths to rekindle the vitality Scott had once had. When he was dejected he would call her. 'He would cry over the phone, then call back and say he was all right, it was just that things were in such a damn mess, and start crying all over again. The other party would say, "Scott, now you stay right there and we'll come over and pick you up", and he'd say, "No, that's all right, I'm fine now", and begin bawling all over again.' Even Nora Flynn could no longer brighten his life.

When his shoulder mended Scott bought an old Packard for $80 and roamed the back roads of the mountains. He was a bad driver and insisted on driving more slowly than the speed limit required. He was not interested in the landscape and he said he didn't understand why people raved about it. A snapshot of him from this time shows him in an old but spruce checked sports jacket with plain trousers, collegiate saddle shoes with red rubber soles and a knit tie. He was a little thicker around the waist. The secretary he hired that summer remembered that when indoors he always wore a worn grey flannel robe. When he was feeling tops he would suddenly crouch into a boxer's pose, circling, feinting, and jabbing for a few seconds, telling her he had been pretty good once. He might dictate to her for a while only to break off and ask if she was cold; he always seemed to be, she said. Solicitous of her comfort, even if she protested, he would drape blankets about her shoulders. He was drinking very heavily during this period, and he assured his secretary that his problem with alcohol grew out of Zelda's illness and his own inability to write, and that he had always before been able to keep his drinking in hand.

In October Zelda showed the first signs of improvement and slowly she entered into the routine of hospital life. She still had grand plans about her spiritual mission to mankind, but she was not permitted to talk about them. Dr Carroll wrote Dr Rennie in Baltimore that Zelda was now able to go everywhere on the grounds of Highland.

At a New Year's costume ball Zelda danced a fragment from a ballet she had made up and seemed to the doctor 'the happiest thing in North Carolina'. She was an angel, Carroll said, 'wings a bit singed, otherwise a joy'. At the beginning of 1937 he was able to say that Zelda was at her 'veribist' and 'quite charming'.

A woman who worked closely with Dr Carroll and Zelda at that time says: 'We were careful with Zelda, we never stirred her up. She could be helped, but we never gave her deep psychotherapy. One doesn't do that with patients if they are too schizophrenic. We tried to get Zelda to see reality; tried to get her to distinguish between her fantasies, illusion and reality. That is not easy for a schizophrenic. The psychotherapy was very superficial. We let her talk out things which bothered her. Discussed her reading and what things meant to her. Explained the "why" of her orders and routine. She often rebelled against the authority, the discipline. ... She didn't like discipline, but she would fall into it.'

Badly in debt now and ill, Scott was in worse straits than he had ever been before. Zelda's expenses were staggering, and that fall he sent Scottie to Ethel Walker, a boarding school in Connecticut, which was costly. Once in a while he thought of changing his style of life. He wrote Perkins about 'Such stray ideas as sending my daughter to a public school, putting my wife in a public insane asylum ... but it would break something in me that would shatter the very delicate pencil-end of a point of view. I have got myself completely on the spot and what the next step is I don't know. ... My God, debt is an awful thing!' He had been considering writing an autobiographical book, but his *The Crack-Up* articles for *Esquire* seemed to have done him more harm professionally than good, and he felt that further work in that vein would damage his literary reputation, although he never truly understood how clearly he had revealed himself in those essays concerning his alcoholism. He wrote Perkins that he had a novel in mind, but neither the time, money, nor energy to write it. Finding a job in Hollywood was of course one solution and a contract with a major studio would set him up again, but the studios were wary of him. Ober wangled one offer, but Scott had to turn it down because it was made during the time his shoulder was injured. It was not until June of 1937 that Ober's dickering brought Fitzgerald a solid offer of $1,000 a week from M-G-M. It was for six months, renewable if they liked his work. It was an economic reprieve and he took it.

Scott was in New York when he was hired, and it was probably during this trip that Carl Van Vechten took the famous photographs that adorn the jacket of *The Far Side of Paradise*, appear in *Scott Fitzgerald*, and form the frontispiece of his collected *Letters*. Van Vechten remembered the scene clearly. 'I hadn't planned to meet Scott; I was to have lunch with Edmund Wilson, I think. We were to meet at the Algonquin. As I came into the room my eyes had to readjust to the darkness and I noticed a man with Wilson. I didn't recognize him and went forward to be introduced. It was a terrible moment; Scott was completely changed. He looked pale and haggard. I was awfully embarrassed. You see, I had known Scott for years. Well, he was shaken and we all tried to laugh it off. Wilson attempted to smooth things over, but we just sat there stunned. Afterwards I asked Scott outside for a few quick shots. I used to go everywhere with my camera. He posed for two or three and that was the last time I saw him.' Scott stood in his checked sports jacket in a white button-down-collared shirt with a collegiate striped knit tie blown apart, his fingertips touching nervously. His smile was wan and uncertain in the harsh sunshine. The fatigue, the disappointment, the sensitivity all showed.

Zelda, meanwhile, grew stronger. The athletic director of Highland, Landon Ray, remembers her standing in a brown tailored suit she liked, walking with her head thrown back, her hair no longer in a short bob, but almost to her shoulders and worn with bangs. 'She was rather reserved, but could warm up to you if she was interested. She was a good conversationalist about things which she enjoyed.' Zelda was, of course, still precariously subject to shifts of mood. If she was talking with Ray and the conversation turned to something that threatened her, he remembers, her eyes suddenly narrowed and became cold and cruel. It was then one knew there was something out of kilter beneath the pleasant exterior and felt the wrongness strike out. She could change for the slightest of reasons; if someone else came up and broke into their talk she would walk off and sulk. 'She felt the other person had intruded and that threatened her. Then she would change. She would darken.'

When Zelda learned that Scott would be leaving for Hollywood she wrote to him: 'Have fun – I envy you and everybody all over the world going and going – on no matter what nefarious errands.'

The first week Scott was in Hollywood he met Sheilah Graham, an attractive young Englishwoman who was writing a syndicated movie column. It was no more than a fleeting glance, but it took. Miss Graham has written movingly of their love for each other in her book *Beloved Infidel*: how, when she met Fitzgerald a second time, handsome but tired looking, as if he needed 'light and air and warmth', he had observed her for some time and then leaned forward toward her and said simply, 'I like you'; how attentively he had taken her in as she spoke and as they danced together, how cherished he had made her feel. She remembers: '. . . it seemed to me that dancing with him was like being with the American college boys I had seen in films – you know, either cheek to cheek, or held far out'.

Piece by piece she learned from others on the West Coast who had known Fitzgerald in the past about his extraordinary career and marriage, as well as something about Zelda's tragic insanity. But Fitzgerald, at this time, spoke very little about himself and said nothing about Zelda to her. Some who had known Zelda found a remarkable physical resemblance between the two women, but Sheilah Graham was more disciplined than Zelda had ever been, and more down to earth. In part it was her resemblance to Zelda, of which Scott was well aware (he stressed it in the manuscript of *The Last Tycoon*), as well as Miss Graham's vitality, her enthusiasm for life, her real spunk that attracted him. When Scottie visited her father in Hollywood that summer of 1937, Sheilah Graham saw another side of Fitzgerald: the fretful father, middle-aged and anxious, scolding his daughter unfairly at the slightest provocation. Although it astonished her, she fell even more deeply in love with him than before.

Although Scott was working very hard, he managed to visit Zelda in September and again during the Christmas holidays. She looked forward to these breaks from hospital life with a desperate nostalgia. 'I wish we were astride the tops of New York taxis and a little hilarious in parcs and public places, and younger than young people.' Scott's reaction to their first trip together was one of disappointment. 'Zelda is no better ... she held up well enough but there is always a gradual slipping. I've become hard there and don't feel the grief I did once – except sometimes at night or when I catch myself in some spiritual betrayal of the past.'

A letter to Scottie written after his return from his meeting with Zelda at Christmas-time was not much more enthusiastic. 'Your mother was better than ever I expected and our trip would have been fun except that I was tired. We went to Miami and Palm Beach, flew to Montgomery, all of which sounds very gay and glamorous but wasn't particularly.'

By this time Scott's involvement with Sheilah Graham must have affected his attitude toward Zelda, but it is remarkable how little it did when one realizes how deeply he cared for Miss Graham and what a renewed claim on life she was giving him, with very few counter demands of her own for a permanent attachment. There were suggestions in letters between Scott and Dr Carroll that Fitzgerald hoped he might one day be freed from Zelda. But his commitments were to Scottie, to Zelda, to himself, and then to Sheilah, in that order. For, much as Scott loved Sheilah Graham, there was precious little of him left to love with; his energies were low, his faith in himself just beginning to heal. There was always a puritanical streak in Fitzgerald, and there is no doubt that something of it came into play in his relationship to her. One learns from Miss Graham's book how nastily he treated her when he was drinking. He struck her; he reminded her of her origins (about which she was deeply sensitive, as Scott was well aware); he gave her a silver-fox jacket only to take it back after a quarrel and send it to his daughter; he flung the word 'paramour' at her as an epithet – although it was somewhat quaint for the late thirties.

For her part Zelda was maintaining what the doctors called the most comfortable level physically and nervously that she had achieved during the last few years. After she returned from her trip with Scott she joined in a masquerade ball at Highland Hospital to celebrate the beginning of 1938. The theme of the ball was Mother Goose and Zelda chose to be 'Mary, Mary, Quite Contrary'. According to a member of the staff she had little difficulty in fulfilling the role.

In March, Scott suggested to Dr Carroll that he and Zelda take a trip to Virginia Beach; he planned to take Scottie along and make it a family reunion of sorts. But he had no more illusions about his relationship with Zelda.

I have, of course, my eternal hope that a miracle will happen to Zelda, that in this new incarnation events may tend to stabilize her even more than you hope. With my shadow removed, perhaps she will find something in life to care for. ... Certainly the outworn pretense that we can ever come together again is better for being shed. There is simply too much of the past between us. When that mist falls – at a dinner table, or between two pillows – no knight errant can traverse its immense distance. The mainsprings are gone.

At the end of this letter he tipped his hand ever so slightly and one realizes how much the lifeline Sheilah Graham was giving him meant:

And if the aforesaid miracle should take place, I might again try to find a life of my own, as opposed to this casual existence of many rooms and many doors that are not mine. So long as she is helpless, I'd never leave her or ever let her have a sense that she was deserted. ... I know scarcely a beautiful woman of Zelda's generation who has come up to 1938 unscathed.

For myself, I work hard and take care of myself. ... If it ever comes to a point when a divorce should be in the picture, I think I would rather have you [than himself or members of Zelda's family] watch over Zelda's interests .

Zelda was allowed to join her family at Virginia Beach, but the trip from husband's and daughter's points of view was not a success. Zelda was irritable with both golf and tennis pros from whom she took lessons, and was patronizing with Scottie, to whom she constantly gave advice coated with a very thin and entirely forced sweetness. When Scottie chafed in reaction, Zelda grew red-faced with anger and reported her to Scott. Scott took about as much of this as he could stand and then got drunk. Zelda thereupon told everyone in the hotel that he was a dangerous man and had to be watched. The episode had its comic side, but not to those directly involved. Scott reported to Carroll that in their corridor of the hotel only himself and Scottie believed that he was not a lunatic: 'All this isn't pretty on my part, but if I had been left alone, [it] would have amounted to a two day bat. ...' In a huff he told Carroll that Zelda 'imagines herself as a sort of Red Scourge in golden heels, flitting East and West, back and forth across the ocean, munificently bicycling with Scottie through Provence. ... My part is to stay here and pay for this grandiose expedition with no control over it.' He insisted that his usefulness in Zelda's case was over. When he had lived like a vegetable in Tryon they had gotten along well enough, but now their relationship had dissolved, 'for I am unable to feel any of the pity which usually ameliorated whatever she did'.

Returning to Hollywood from this Easter trip he called Sheilah Graham from the airport and told her that they were going to be married. He was still drunk. When she saw Scott and heard the story of his dreadful trip, she begged him to stop drinking. She had no idea what she asked of him. Later in her life Miss Graham said that she did everything she could, always, to avoid having him become upset or strained, because it resulted in his drinking. She could not tell at first when he was drinking and would try to sniff his breath (which, she says, infuriated him), or count bottles.

Shortly after his return Fitzgerald put himself in the care of a doctor, and after three days of sweating it out and being fed intravenously got himself back into shape. He would never again, he swore to his daughter, stand 'any repetition of this Easter trip'.

From his previously quoted letter to Dr Carroll, written that April, to the end of May eight letters were exchanged by the two men in an attempt to come to an agreement over the terms of Zelda's treatment. Carrol's reaction to Scott's initial letter about the Virginia Beach fiasco was to assure him that Zelda's point of view had to be disregarded. Someone other than she had to manage her future, if she was to have one. He suggested that every three months she could have a two-week vacation or excursion in the company of a companion or the Carrolls. That would assure her of a break in her routine which she would look forward to. But he made no mention of Zelda's being able to be permanently out of the hospital. He suggested giving her $50 a month allowance in addition to the approximately $6,000 yearly expenses of the hospitalization itself.

Scott wrote a note at the top of his copy of Carroll's letter saying that it was the first he had received which showed they completely disagreed. Scott answered the doctor that his recommendations lacked only two things, 'provision for hope and for sex'. He said that he now knew there was, in a sense, no hope for Zelda, but everyone needed at least 'the illusion of hope to survive'. He remembered another time at Sheppard-Pratt when Zelda was in better shape than she had been for an entire year. Her morale suddenly plunged and she became melancholy. She tried to strangle herself. The action came, Scott told Carroll, utterly without warning, when her 'existence seemed to have settled into an appalling monotony'. He never again wanted her to feel that she was sinking into total invalidism. 'Hope meant a lot in the best part of our lives, the first eight years we lived together ... but I think in our case it was even exaggerated, because as a restless and ambitious man, I was never disposed to accept the present but always striving to change it, better it, or even sometimes destroy it.' He was certain that Zelda would come to realize how limited she was and not be able to bear it.

He told Carroll that although he could not sleep with Zelda any more – 'I cannot live in the ghost town which Zelda has become' – he nevertheless thought that Zelda needed someone. Someone who would be attracted to her and to whom she would feel attraction – 'and that by some miracle, such a relation might lead to something, some man whose personality might be a rock on which she might steady herself more permanently'. He could not betray her, that 'old bond of justice that existed between us', by just giving up hope: '. . . this may seem strange from one who has no desire ever again to personally undertake her supervision. That period has gone, and each time that I see her something happens to me that makes me the worst person for her rather than the best, but a part of me will always pity her with a sort of deep ache that is never absent from my mind for more than a few hours: an ache for the beautiful child that I loved and with whom I was happy as I shall never be again.'

Scott insisted that Dr Carroll at least allow her the illusion of larger horizons, and suggested that Carroll give her more freedom, two weeks out of every two months, or one month in three. That would give her the benefit of the hospital as the core of her existence, and yet permit her a life outside. Fitzgerald wanted to be freed from Zelda's complete dependence on him, but he also felt required to give her every chance. 'Supposing Zelda at best would be a lifelong eccentric, supposing that in two or three years there is certain to be a sinking, I am still haunted by the fact that if it were me, and Zelda were passing judgment, I would want her to give me a chance. . . .'

In an ordinary black looseleaf notebook Zelda began carefully to enter her ideas, written sketches, and drawings, as well as outlines for paintings and dances. During part of the period that she kept this notebook she was going through another spell of thinking of herself as a vehicle for God's pronouncements. Her handwriting was almost cautious in its clarity. She seemed to write down thoughts as they came to her, and the innocent surfaces of her prose were bulwarked by strange metaphors as they had been in *Save Me the Waltz*: 'I love the casual gallantry of a grey March day ominous of spring.'

When she was working out an idea for a painting – and her paintings at this time seemed always to be pale abstractions of ideas – she wrote about it. She equated colour with emotional qualities. For instance, aspiration might be pale orchid, 'anchored', she wrote, 'with passion (vermilion)'. She made up a ballet about Scott and one about herself, and she adorned the pages of her choreography with ballet terms and drawings of lighting effects and movements, punctuated by triangles and arcs of soft watercolour. She described 'men in oyster-white tulle dresses' and 'women in hyacinth with pointed capes like the sails of Greek boats'.

There were few personal notes, and when there were they were usually linked to a concept of beauty, God, gallantry, hope, or prayer: 'My lillies died; they just plain died and so I can only maybe paint the memory of white desirability of so much beauty. So perfect. I used to gather them in Alabama under the pines and from the ooze of a dried lake bed and they were always so spiritually splendid.' She pressed leaves between the lined pages and let them dry. She tried for a while to keep a calendar of the months and she saw them distinguished from each other in terms of flowers and heat: 'September a browner month. . . .' 'White violets like souls in flight.'

Of course this was a private notebook and Zelda did not bother to (or could not) make herself clear. These were the notes of a lonely woman who found loneliness around her in everything she saw. 'I take a sun bath and listen to the hours, formulating, and disintigrating under the pines, and smell the resin-y hardi-hood of the high noon hours. The world is lost in a blue haze of distances, and the immediate sleeps in a thin and finite sun.'

Scott had gone through a period in 1935–6 when he made lists of everything he could think of in an effort to give his life a semblance of order – lists of popular songs, of girls he had known, of the kings of England and of France. In Zelda's notebook it seemed as if she were trying to catalogue all that she felt or had felt, was afraid of, thought and dreamed. Sometimes the notebook was filled with extravagant gestures of religious belief, undercut for the reader by the incoherence of it all: 'We are grateful to God for the infinite beauty of the patterns of God's concept in which we are being evolved and which is the realm of human consciousness and which is the soul in accordance with our capacity to acknowledge.' And then among the mental meanderings a phrase would strike clear: 'Nothing is more indicatible of civilizations than the solaces that people seek.'

As Scott and Dr Carroll were trying to reach an agreement on the necessary extent and degree of Zelda's hospitalization, Mrs Sayre entered into the dispute. Zelda had visited her mother briefly that spring. She had followed the hospital routine to the letter, walking her five miles a day in the tropical heat, eating no meat, and shunning alcohol – although her mother would not have had any in the house. It was on the basis of Zelda's performance during that visit, as well as Mrs Sayre's own deep concern for her daughter's complete recovery, that Mrs Sayre renewed her efforts to have Zelda released. She sincerely believed that she could make a home for Zelda and that they could live in peace together. She realized that the climate was not good for Zelda and was willing to move elsewhere if it was for her daughter's benefit. She was not trying to combat the doctors' orders; she was trying to provide protection for Zelda, by having her in contact with her own family. At least they should try the arrangement. Mrs Sayre planned to spend two months of the coming summer near Asheville in Saluda (where the Sayres had spent their summers when Zelda was a child) and see Zelda as often as the hospital permitted. If Zelda could return to Montgomery in the fall that would be perfect. She felt, as did other members of the family, that Zelda was well enough to be released to her care. Neither Dr Carroll nor Scott, who were both in a better position to judge, agreed with her. But it was an unhappy situation. Her family wrote to Zelda, urging her to push for her release, assuring her that she was well enough to come home, and thereby forced the doctor's hand. Scott tried to inform Zelda's family, by sending them the correspondence between himself and Carroll, of Zelda's position as well as his own. But communication between them was too charged with accusation and mutual distrust to be fruitful. They wanted Zelda to be returned to them with an allowance from Scott. He was to let the Sayres manage as best they could. They were convinced that Scott had destroyed Zelda.

Finally Dr Carroll wrote Mrs Sayre. He told her that Zelda was fine physically, but mentally her condition was precarious. Certainly she did not need confusion of counsel. Zelda was being placed in the unfortunate position of receiving advice from all sides, and in reaction swung from one idea to another, each time in hope of a larger freedom for herself. Dr Carroll put it plainly to Mrs Sayre: Zelda was not prepared to live with any of the members of her family, and if they cared to do the best for her, they would treat her as they would someone with tuberculosis. She was permanently damaged mentally. Any letters to her about such plans as her eventual release should be directed to Dr Carroll, not to Zelda, if her family cared to preserve her peace of mind; this pressuring for Zelda's release was terribly unfair to her, for it gave her a false and premature notion that she would be able to leave.

Scottie was graduating from boarding school in Connecticut in June and Zelda wanted to go to her commencement. Dr Carroll said it would be feasible and Scott arranged for her to go with Rosalind, who was then living in New York. She would be accompanied as far as New York by a nurse. He wrote Scottie: 'Do try to make your mother happy for two days – excuse her enthusiasm. In her youth, she didn't know such schools existed.' It was a casual remark, but it underlined the complicity that had come to exist between father and daughter; theirs was 'a sense of partnership', Scott wrote Scottie, 'that sprang out of [Zelda's] illness'. But it was just that aspect of their relationship that must have hurt Zelda most, for it undermined what little closeness she had with Scottie. Nevertheless, her trip North was a success. She looked smart for Scottie's commencement at Ethel Walker, and was very proud of Scottie, who was voted the most popular girl in her class. It seemed to Zelda that Scottie and she might become closer, or at least there was the promise of a relationship they could enjoy and cultivate. Zelda wrote Scott: 'Scottie is the prettiest girl. . . . She wore white gardenias and white flannel and white hopes and the freedom and grace of the best and we are very proud and devoted. . . . Meanwhile – life is so nice, when one can have some. . . . Scottie is a very good thing to have. I'm so glad we've got her.'

After the graduation exercises and Zelda's return to Asheville, Scottie, who was studying for college boards at Ethel Walker, went off campus without permission and was asked to leave the school. Fitzgerald wrote her in cold fury:

When I was your age I lived with a great dream. The dream grew and I learned how to speak of it and make people listen. Then the dream divided one day when I decided to marry your mother after all, even though I knew she was spoiled and meant no good to me. I was sorry immediately I had married her but, being patient in those days, made the best of it and got to love her in another way. You came along and for a long time we made quite a lot of happiness out of our lives. But I was a man divided – she wanted me to work too much for *her* and not enough for my dream. She realized too late that work was dignity, and the only dignity, and tried to atone for it by working herself, but it was too late and she broke and is broken forever. . . . The mistake I made was in marrying her. We belonged to different worlds – she might have been happy with a kind simple man in a southern garden. She didn't have the strength for the big stage – sometimes she pretended, and pretended beautifully, but she didn't have it. She was soft when she should have been hard, and hard when she should have been yielding. She never knew how to use her energy – she's passed that failing on to you.

For a long time I hated *her* mother for giving her nothing in the line of good habit – nothing but 'getting by' and conceit. I never wanted to see again in this world women who were brought up as idlers.

Scott's bitterness toward Zelda was not only for what he felt she had forced him to do for her during the early years of their marriage, it was also stimulated by his feeling that Zelda had failed him, had used him financially. His letter to Scottie implied that she might do the same. The air was cleared considerably when Scott learned that Scottie did well on her boards and was accepted by Vassar for the coming fall. But the vehemence of his rancour towards Zelda was clear. It was she who had ruined him; she who had made him exhaust his talents. This was of course only one facet of his attitude toward Zelda, but it was definitely there in reserve to be drawn upon. He had been cheated of his dream by Zelda.

Scott had promised Scottie a trip to Europe that summer, and with things back on an even keel she left. Fitzgerald wrote her: '. . . quite possibly these are the last few years in which you will be able to see Europe as it was'. He wanted Scottie to have that opportunity. She sent him a postcard from the Brasserie Lipp in Paris, and later, after visiting a fortuneteller, she wrote him that the woman 'told me some amazing things – that my mother was sick and was going to get a little better but not completely well, and my father was "willful and nervous" (ha!) and we were going to have a few fights but always make up, and I was going to have an unstable career with hunks of money here and there'. When she returned in September Zelda was in New York to meet her boat.

Just being in New York buoyed Zelda's spirits. The city was for her 'bliss, again'. And Scottie was 'prettier than ever; Scottie is on the brink of being ravishing . . .' The only thing that was missing was Scott. 'I wish you had been able to come East – It would be fun to meet you here again.' She saw the Murphys for the first time in eight years and her reflections on them were tinged with resentment. She wrote Scott that they looked 'very engaging; age and the ages leaves them untroubled and, perhaps, as impervious as possible. That was, indeed, a remunerative relationship – If they knew how much of other peoples orientations that they had influenced, they would less resent any challenge to their own.'

Talking with Scottie about Europe tripped open Zelda's memories. 'It fill[s] me with dread to witness the passage of so much time: another summer is half gone, and maybe there'll never be anymore sun-burns and high hot moons. Do you suppose they still cook automobiles at Antibes, and still sip the twilight at Kaux, and I wonder if Paris is pink in the late sun and latent with happiness already had.'

She stayed with her nurse at the Hotel Irving on Gramercy Park, where Rosalind and her husband were living. Mrs Sayre,

who had gone to Saluda to be near Zelda, came North with
her, and to both of them New York was magical. With Clothilde
(who lived in Larchmont, New York), Rosalind, and Zelda in
New York it was a family reunion. Zelda roamed New York,
window shopping, remembering other times shared with Scott;
she tried to see some shows but nothing good was on, she said.
They ate at outdoor restaurants and drove along the new Henry
Hudson Parkway. They also saw Scott's film *Three Comrades*;
she wrote him, '. . . maybe we'll get some more money and
more prestige and more liberties and all sorts of other desirable
attributes. And meanwhile Mamma is here; and lovely and
eager as ever, but a year older than she was last year which
makes me sad –' Being with her sisters and mother reminded
Zelda of how much she was missing in the circumscribed life
she led at the hospital. She asked Scott for permission to go to
Montgomery for Thanksgiving, Christmas, 'and soon for ever?'

'I am so sick of the moralistic tone and repressive atmosphere
of that hospital that I don't know how to endure. At my most
desirable of attainments, they would have classified me at best
as *suspect*. . . .'

The longer Zelda stayed at Highland the more rigorously she
protested against its discipline. She felt imprisoned. Even if Dr
Carroll considered her ability to make decisions reduced to the
level of that of a bright child, she did not and resented being
treated as one. She pressed for release in her letters to Scott:
'Dear, I would be so deeply grateful if you would let me *try*
existing outside a hospital. I don't want to nag you. . . . I have
been for years, and years, and years tidying up my room and
not making noise in the halls.' She missed Scott, who was her
link with the life she had lived before her illness, her one contact out of the morass of illness, and whom she saw so infre-
quently. She would plead to him: 'D. O. *Won't* you let me go
home? Whats the use of wasting what short space of life remains in a routine . . . or anything else save a living death. . . . I
wonder if you will ever be East again? – You must be quite
a different fellow than when I.

'D. O. I'm so sorry about the hard luck that pursues us so
relentlessly –'

Sometimes she asked Scott for small presents; she called them her necessities. Her taste, always whimsical, now ran to the colourful. She wanted a cowboy belt studded with bright stones and brass nails, size 28 (although her waist she carefully told him was 27) and a pair of beaded leather moccasins, size 5, and a vial of perfume. On the back of her list she added, 'Don't give up anything to get these, but I'll be mighty happy when they *come*.' Scott dutifully made notes at the bottom of the letter indicating which Hollywood drugstore carried the perfume, and the address of a Western costume store for the belt and moccasins.

By the fall it was clear that Dr Carroll thought of Zelda's improvement in terms of a very limited ability to cope with reality. He wrote to Scott telling him that her life had to be arranged for her on simple terms, and on that reduced level she could maintain her equilibrium with ease. From Dr Carroll's point of view it was unfortunate that Scott and Zelda's family considered her current style of living unsatisfactory. Was it, he wondered, due to their imagining themselves having to live within it?

The letters that continued to pass between Dr Carroll and Scott were about preserving this balance. Arrangements were made for Zelda's brief trips – to Florida, a few days with Scottie, a holiday at home in Montgomery with her mother – but always with the members of Zelda's family pushing for more: for her to be able to travel without a companion or nurse, for her to be released from the hospital. Christmas 1938 she spent in Montgomery at home – but with a nurse who stayed at a nearby hotel. Zelda spent two hours with her each morning; they walked together and discussed the coming day; then she was free until the following morning. The nurse was a necessary ballast even if Zelda's family did not think she was. The family constantly urged that Zelda be released to them. Their urging made Scott furious, and Dr Carroll tried to assure them that what he was doing was in *Zelda*'s best interests. Zelda could not live alone. Scott wrote Rosalind: 'Imagine Zelda running amuk in Montgomery! . . . The next time Zelda runs off the track God knows what form it will take. . . . I keep up a continual pressure to get Zelda more liberty. Cure her I cannot and simply *saying* she's cured must make the Gods laugh.'

After Zelda's Christmas at home Scott tried to write Mrs Sayre a letter about Zelda that she could understand and accept. It must have cost him dear to keep remembering and trying to plan for Zelda, to maintain even the simplest level of hope on her behalf. Rosalind, he wrote Mrs Sayre, 'seems to feel that establishing Zelda in the world is a simple matter – like the issuing of a pass – not at all the problem that the best people in the profession have been working at for ten years. . . . There is no favorable prognosis for dementia praecox. In certain diseases the body builds new cells, drawing on its own inner vitality. When there has been destruction in the patterns of the mind only the very thinest shell can be formed over them – so to speak – so that Zelda is always living in a house of thinly spun glass.'

In February 1939 Zelda was off to Sarasota, Florida, for an entire month with the Carrolls. She took her first formal art courses in life drawing and costume design in the Ringling School of Art, and she baked on the beaches of Miami and Key West. Almost as soon as she returned to Asheville Scottie visited her there briefly. Scott was pleased with their visit: 'You have made a great impression on your mother. How different from a year ago at Virginia Beach when you seemed as far apart as the poles, during those dreary tennis games and golf lessons! Of course, the fact that she is so much better accounts for a good deal of it . . . write your mother, because I've been putting off a visit to her and may possibly have to be here three weeks longer on this damned picture and she probably feels that I'm never coming.'

Prior to Zelda's trip to Florida Dr Carroll had asked Scott if Zelda might travel to Cuba with a group from Highland. Scott agreed, but too late for arrangements to be made for Zelda's going. She wrote Scott: 'Havannah is probably a substantial sort of place and may be will stay there till next time. Anyway, its all very expensive, and we are so well adapted to spending money to-gether. When you come East there will be that much more justification for buying things. I am as grateful to you as if I were on board.' At the end of the letter she added a plea: 'Come on! Let me see you fly East! We can go to Cuba ourselves, as far as that goes.'

Somewhat surprisingly that was exactly what Scott did. According to Sheilah Graham's account in *Beloved Infidel*, Scott left for Asheville after a fierce quarrel with her. He had been drinking straight gin for several weeks and in a desperate effort to stop him Miss Graham, herself hysterical after a violent fight over a revolver he kept in his dresser, slapped him and swore she'd never see him again. The following morning, still drunk, he flew to North Carolina. He picked up Zelda and together they flew to Cuba. The trip was a disaster from beginning to end, and the end was in New York at the Algonquin, where Scott, who had been badly beaten in Cuba for trying to stop a cockfight, was so drunk and exhausted that he required hospitalization. Zelda tried to cope with him, but was in no condition herself to handle the situation. Finally she called her sister and brother-in-law in Larchmont for help and returned to Asheville alone. Scott was put in Doctors Hospital, where he remained under treatment for nearly two weeks. Zelda, afraid she had somehow provoked the situation and antagonized Scott, wrote to him just before she left.

It seems useless to wait any more; I know that you are better; and being taken care of; and I am of no assistance; so I'll go back to the hospital on the 2:30 train. ... Why don't you come to Tryon? ... we could keep a little house on the lake and let you get better. We might have a very happy summer in such circumstance – You like it there, and I am very clever at serving bird-song and summer clouds for breakfast.

Scottina could visit us; and we could find a better meaning to so many things ...

Please believe that I stayed over solely to the purpose of helping you if I could. I know from experience what a difference it makes in life where somebody cares about your troubles. ... I know that I have written you all this before but, as you know my letters are censored from the Hospital and I wont have another chance to communicate until we meet again.

To the Hospital, this version: We had a most enviable trip. And everything was according to the rules. This last refers to cigarettes and wine concerning which I will follow our agreement as to any irregularity of arrival. Your lungs are bad, and required attention, and I am capable of travelling alone so there wasnt any use in your adding another tiring journey to what you had before you.

D.O. please take care of yourself. So you will be well again and happier than these last times. There are so few people of our era who have made original contributions to the life about us, and not many who can be so charming, and almost not any with a greater capacity for enjoyment.

There are still a great many things which could give us pleasure
And there are such a lot of people fond of you. . . .

Back at Highland Zelda stuck to her story, although the staff was quite aware of the pattern most of the Fitzgeralds' trips together took. 'We were all afraid when she went off with him of what would happen – and it always did', one staff member recalls. 'They simply could not be in each other's company for more than a few days at a time. Dr Carroll would allow them to go together for a week or so, but they always came back a few days early and usually something terrible had occurred. It was awful, it really was, because you could see that he still loved her very much and did not want to abandon her. But they couldn't be together for any prolonged length of time.'

Zelda wrote Scott soon after her return. 'Don't feel bad. You were so sweet in the station. I wish things had been so that we were going on to-gether, somewhere. There are lots of happy places: it says so in the time tables, and before long we'll surely find one . . .

'Meantime: You know I'll be there waiting on that green hillside: and expecting you.'

Back in Hollywood after his stint in the hospital, Scott wrote her at once:

You were a peach throughout the whole trip and there isn't a minute of it when I don't think of you with all the old tenderness and with a consideration that I never understood that you had before. . . . You are the finest, loveliest, tenderest, most beautiful person I have ever known, but even that is an understatement because the length that you went to there at the end would have tried anybody beyond endurance. Everything that I said and that we talked about during that time stands –

Unknown to either of them, this was the last time they would see each other.

As devastating as their vacation together had been, the contact between them renewed Zelda's feelings for Scott; to some measure it must also have rekindled Scott's toward her, for in May he was seriously considering bringing Zelda to Hollywood for a month. He had not yet made up with Sheilah, but when he did Zelda remained in North Carolina. Scottie had an attack of appendicitis during her spring term at Vassar and her doctor recommended that she have an appendectomy. Scott decided that this would provide a perfect opportunity for Zelda and Scottie to come together. He arranged for Scottie to have her operation in Asheville and recuperate during the month of July in Zelda's company.

When Scottie came Zelda said she'd 'never seen her so pretty before. . . .' Their round-faced little girl had become a lively slim blonde. Scottie recovered quickly and spent most of the month swimming and taking long walks with her mother; she was also working on a novel she had just begun.

Scott, who was undergoing financial and health troubles on the West Coast, wrote Scottie that she was welcome to come and visit him for the rest of the summer, but he warned her that she might find him 'depressing, over-nervous about small things, and dogmatic. . . .' Above all he wanted to avoid any situations of excitement. Somewhat gruffly he told her that he'd rather not see her at all, 'than see you without loving you'. He felt it was imperative for her to realize that her home now was Vassar.

Scottie let her mother read this letter, and Zelda tried to explain to Scott what a burden he put on Scottie, who was, after all, not yet eighteen.

Dearest: I trust that you will not resent this. . . . [Scottie] bears the best morale a child could possibly have considerring the fact of that absence of the moral support that a conventionally established family conveys, and I think it's rather a needlessly painful punishment to remind her of the absence of material attributes which to a person of twenty-one every child has a right to the sense of safety. ... She is such a particularly brave and self-reliant child that it would be lamentable to allow a sense of the absence of stability to twist her mind with neuroses concerning the necessity to make a living. ...

I do not criticize your letter: but I believe that the only right of a parent to share his tragedies with children under age is of a most factual nature – how much money there is and the technical name of his illness is about the only fallibilities that debutantes are equipped to encompass ... and it doesn't do any good to let them know that one is harassed. Nobody is better aware than I am, and, I believe, so is Scottie, of your generosity, and the seriousness of your constant struggle to provide the best for us. I am most deeply grateful to you for the sustained and tragic effort that you have made to keep us going. ... I wasn't critical, only trying to remind you of the devastating ravages that a sense of insecurity usually manages to establish when theres nothing to do about it.

During Scottie's period of recovery with her mother she decided Zelda was well enough to live with Mrs Sayre and no longer needed to remain in the hospital. After all Scott had been through on this score he impatiently wrote Dr Suitt, who assisted Dr Carroll with Zelda at Highland Hospital, and suggested that he have a talk with Scottie. He wanted the doctor to mention to Scottie how adversely the menopause could affect Zelda's mental balance; he warned that Scottie's attitude toward Zelda could affect 'my whole future relation with my daughter'. He did not want her to swing over to the Sayres' side. It was one of the reasons he hesitated to have her come out to California. 'She is a dominant little girl in a polite way and to have her appear here as a sort of ambassador of what I call the Montgomery point of view – "throw Zelda on her own immediately" – would be much more than upsetting.'

Although Scottie and Zelda got on well enough that summer, the visit was really only a qualified success. For one thing Scottie was still too young to realize how deeply Zelda resented any advice from her, no matter how harmless it appeared to be on the surface. Zelda concealed her reactions from Scottie, but not from her doctors. For her part Zelda tried very hard, too hard, to quickly re-establish with Scottie a relationship which was largely non-existent, and which between any mother and seventeen-year-old daughter would have been difficult. Scottie was not, and had probably never been, dependent upon her mother for either direction or emotional sustenance. During Scottie's visit Zelda wanted to share, as well as oversee, Scottie's attentions from young men, and when Scottie left Asheville Zelda began referring to herself as 'the glamorous Mrs Fitzgerald'.

But to Scott she confided her aloneness: 'My tennis progresses – by which I mean that I can play about half as well as I can play – Its almost demoralizing to have attained the age where all ones attributes are visibly retrogressing; speed, volume . . . Ashville regales itself on 3 days of folk dance. . . . I wish I had a beau but I haven't got any beaux. . . .'

By late summer Zelda's letters to Scott were marked by a forlorn sadness. She wrote about the only things that happened to her, her walks, five miles each day, through fields of phlox and marguerites in the mountains. 'Roads lace the mountains to earth, far below and leading home and nowhere, and the people are tan and brown and wreathed in lonliness.' But it was her own loneliness that pierced these letters to Scott.

Writing to Scottie she tried to remind her of times they had shared in the past and of her dreams for her: 'Be brown and happy. . . . Buy yourself a white dress with a long and lovely sash, an ashes of roses sash or a sash as pale and chrystalline as a Greek ocean – and buy yourself a leghorn hat – and you will be as picturesque as a summer path over the meadows.' Zelda was saying – be me, my daughter, as I was.

Time passed slowly for Zelda and she grew more and more aware of its passing, not in any anxious way, but aware of it as a pastoral stream, with seasons changing, flowers to be watched and painted, flowers marking the changes of season, breaking time into rhythms. Scott once wrote Scottie, 'Think of the enormous pleasure amounting, almost, to the consolation for the tragedy of life that flowers have been to your mother and your grandmother.'

Again and again Zelda would appeal to him and let him know how much she missed him. 'If you flew East I'd be glad – and if I flew West so would I.' She wanted to meet him again, to try for something they had had which she remembered, but which they had lost. Perhaps she was trying to win him back, but only the disadvantages were on her side. She was truly alone now.

When you come won't you bring me another pair of mocassins because I'm a very good little Indian girl, sometimes, and I deserve them.

And don't let yourself get drowned in the perfect California climate – We got sunshine here – And springtime too, and weather that's mostly a raison d'etre –

May I go to France and Greece and Italy? At once, next week – Devotedly, Dear. I wish that I could see you –

Zelda

She also began, cautiously at first but with increasing fervour, to prod Scott on every occasion with what she considered to be constructive suggestions for leaving Highland. To a certain degree she was echoing her family's advice to her, but undoubtedly she shared their opinions: 'If Alabama should prove an unfortunate venture I can always come back; which I assure you I would do most gratefully rather than run the risk of any further debacles. Having accepted the concept of me as a precarious and dangerous experiment at best, am I to relegate, at considerable inconvenience to both yourself and myself to invalidism for the rest of my life?'

Dr Carroll had not heard from Scott for nearly two months. On 27 September 1939 he did. Scott had been ill and was without money. Harold Ober, who had always generously lent him whatever he needed, no longer felt that he could. Consequently, Fitzgerald broke with him, insisting that Ober no longer believed in him. Scott asked Dr Carroll to trust him for another month and not have Zelda deprived of anything she needed. 'As you know I tried to give Zelda every luxury permissible when I could afford it (the trip to Florida, etc.) but it is simply impossible to pay anything, even on installments when one drives a mortgaged Ford and tries to get over the habit of looking into a handkerchief for blood when talking to a producer.' Grimly he added that the hospital could reimburse itself out of his life insurance if things continued downhill.

October was worse than September and he wrote Zelda: 'I am almost penniless – I've done stories for *Esquire* because I've had no time for anything else with $100.00 bank balances.' Friends of theirs had helped him send Scottie back to Vassar.

After her, you are my next consideration; I was properly moved by your mother's attempt to send for you – but not enough to go overboard. ... I ask only this of you – leave me in peace with my hemorrhages and my hopes, and what eventually will fight through as the *right* to save you, the *permission* to give you a chance.

Your life has been a disappointment, as mine has been too. But we haven't gone through this sweat for nothing. Scottie has got to survive and this is the most important year of her life.

In the following letter, which is undated, Zelda answered Scott.

Needless to say, your letter somewhat hurt me. Very possibly you do not give thought to the fact that this hospital regimentation, while most excellent for whipping into shape, is very gruelling over long periods of time. ... I am now well able to make a social in the bigger sense effort: Mamma would be happy to have me: if any trouble arose I could and would return here – and short of your possible paranoiacal self-defensive reflex I cant see any legitimization of keeping me under hospitalization much longer. ... There is every reason to believe that I am more able to observe the social dictats than yourself – on the evidence of our 'vacations' from the hospital – which have been to date a dread affair of doctors and drink and confirmation of the impossibility of an equitable reunion. Although you know this – and that the probabilities are much against our ever having any life together again – you are persistent in not letting me have a chance to exist alone – at least in comfort – in Alabama and make my own orientation. Or even in Ashville. I *might* be able to get a job: ... Won't you, in fairness, please consider this letter from some other basis than that I am your possible enemy and that your first obligation is self-defensive ...

It was in October 1939, under enormous duress, that Scott began in earnest to write his novel *The Last Tycoon*. It would be about Hollywood, which he would view with a basilisk eye. He wrote Scottie:

Look! I have begun to write something that is maybe great, and I'm going to be absorbed in it four or six months. It may not *make* us a cent but it will pay expences and it is the first labor of love I've undertaken since the first part of *Infidelity* [a movie starring Joan Crawford]. ... Anyhow I am alive again ... with all its strains and necessities and humiliations and struggles. I don't drink. I am not a great man, but sometimes I think the impersonal and objective quality of my talent and the sacrifices of it, in pieces, to preserve its essential value has some sort of epic grandeur.

Dr Carroll had answered Scott's pleas by trusting him and waiting. He assured Fitzgerald that he would not let the Sayres talk him into releasing Zelda to their care. Scott thanked him and wrote explaining that his first allegiance (and therefore what little money he had or could raise) was to Scottie; he could not back down on her education. 'For better or worse Scottie and I form a structure. ... For me, life goes on without very much cheer, except my novel, but I think if there is any way to stop this continual nagging through Zelda it will be a help.' Scott sent *Collier's* magazine the first section of *The Last Tycoon* and a synopsis; if they liked it they might back him. (As it turned out they wanted to see more before they paid him.) He also sent it to Scribner's, and as soon as Perkins read the first part of the manuscript he committed himself: he told Scott it was wonderful writing, and he sent him $250 out of his own pocket. Although Scott's finances were still tight, under these improved circumstances some of his old feeling for Zelda crept back into his next letter to Dr Carroll. 'She doesn't complain . . . in fact her last letter is awfully sweet, and not restless and demanding, which I know indicates that you have talked with her and which I *hope* indicates that the Sayres have found some other mischief with which to occupy their idle hands. My God, how I detest "good people". I mean people that are good and think it is quite sufficient as a career.' Zelda wrote him: 'I'm sorry about our present estate. So many years ago when we were first married and making Holiday about the Biltmore corridors, money was one of the things one simply stated the necessity for, went through the requisite ritual and waited.'

She truly had very little idea how difficult life was for Scott; she lived in isolation, insulated by her illness. But she let him know that she tried to understand, that she was not fighting against him. 'Dearest: I am always grateful for all the loyalties you gave me, and I am always loyal to the concepts that held us together so long: the belief that life is tragic, that a mans spiritual reward is the keeping of his faith: that we shouldn't hurt each other. And I love, always your fine writing talent, your tolerance and generosity; and all your happy endowments. Nothing could have survived our life.'

Late in November Mrs Laura Guthrie Hearne at last met Zelda, about whom she had heard so much from Scott during the summer she was his secretary. There was a tea party in Asheville to which they were both invited. In her diary she described her impressions of Zelda.

Zelda does not wear a bit of make up, which she needs. Her eyes have a sad and haunted look. She wears a straight bang and the rest of her dark hair falls just to her shoulders where it ends in a little curl. She wore a very simple black thin suit and white blouse with a black felt hat turned up all around. She had no overcoat though the rest of us wore our fur coats and did not feel too warm. Zelda began to talk brilliantly when I got her started on her greatest love, the ballet, and told how she studied with the Russians in Paris long ago. She has a brilliant mind and as we ate we all listened to her and watched her use her graceful arms and hands to illustrate what she was saying. She believes that all is rhythm, and that the ballet is the best exponent of life, also that we only need four hours of sleep a night, which is all they [dancers] get. The rest of the time we should work or practise and get more and more tense – or rather, full of the vibration of living.

The other women listened respectfully, but, privately they considered Zelda's opinions somewhat bizarre.

At Highland she was considered well enough now to go into

Asheville alone shopping or visiting; and she was also asked to assist in directing the morning gym classes. This reduced her expenses and made her feel that she was contributing something of value. Staff members remember Zelda at her best as an appealing person who could exercise considerable influence on other patients. It was amazing how well and patiently she worked with those patients who were mentally retarded or extremely ill, but she was not so good with those less ill than herself.

That winter Dr Carroll asked Zelda to paint large floral screens for the windows of the new assembly building at Highland. He would furnish the necessary materials and pay her something for her work. Zelda was extremely pleased, the more so when she learned that Duke University would eventually take over Highland Hospital and thereby ensure her work a larger audience. But she was edgy about being taken advantage of. She wrote Scott: 'I sent word that I ultimately would not subscribe to the commandeering of a professional talent. The fact that an artist is temporarily incapacitated ought not to make him fair game to anybody who is able. My talent has cost a lot in heart-ache and paint-bills; and I don't want to compromise myself on such a major project that will make it difficult to get away, should such opportunity arise.' Still, the idea intrigued as well as flattered her, and she began preliminary sketches for the design. Within a few weeks she found out that the screens would not be used in the assembly building, but instead in the patients' bedrooms. She protested bitterly to Scott: 'To waste a professional talent, the cumulative result of years of effort, aspiration and heartbreak on a venture which will never see the light of day but most probably will be maltreated by every manifestation of psychosis is, to me, an abuse of the soul, human faith, and metier that is almost beyond my capacity to envisage.'

Of course she was still to be paid for her work, but even that irritated her, for what 'the authorities' promised to pay her would be applied to her bill. Frustrated and hurt by what she considered to be the real motive behind asking for her work, to contribute to payment of hospital fees, she told Scott: 'I feel that this is your obligation, as I myself have vent every resource towards getting out of here and have, to my honest estimate been well able leave for a year. I don't want to pay these bills, because I do not need what they buy.' But what could she do? she asked him; she was afraid that if she flatly refused to paint the screens her refusal might 'come under one of their heads of psychosis'.

That Christmas of 1939 Zelda was well enough to travel alone to Montgomery for the first time since her hospitalization. When she returned she renewed to Scott her pleas for release. 'There isn't forever left to either of us; and now, for the immediate instance I have a home to turn to while I organize an existence – which will not always be the case . . . I now have no resources left; can't go to the movies because there isn't any money. Under such circumstances, wouldn't it be wiser and more economical that I should be at home. . . . I ask you to acknowledge not only on the basis of your obligation to me – as your wife – but also on the terms of your social obligation: . . . Meantime; it's good to be able to receive uncensored mail – I do believe I'm growing up.'

Fitzgerald tried to soothe her, tried to suggest that she make friends within the hospital. But she wrote him: '. . . a person *could,* as long as they followed the hospitals somewhat bigoted stipulations – I want to leave there. It's a hospital for those who want to be absorbed into Dr Carrolls, feudal, picturesque, and most restrictive formulas. Not that I am not grateful for all that he's done for me:

'because I am most deeply grateful of even the possibility of entering the world again –'

Once after Scott had called her she told him: 'Darling, you were sweet to 'phone me. I am learning a speech to say when telephoned to. It is to be very formal and will include many invitations to parties which will never be given and balls that are long since over. And the response will be yes, yes, yes –'

On Valentine's Day she sent Scott a plain card, neglecting to sign it. A week later she sent him another, perhaps having forgotten about the first one, underlining a line in the text that read, '*Here is my heart.*' Beside it Zelda wrote, 'The last thing you said to me before you left for the port of embarkation –'

At Highland she and Dr Carroll reached a compromise over the screens; they were to be in tempera and decorative only, 'which is a less distressing entertainment than having to think of my best and most exacting talents being buried within the confines of psychotic morass'. She told Scott she had a hunch Carroll was going to let her out soon.

On 4 March 1940 Dr Carroll tentatively suggested to Scott that Zelda might be ready to fend for herself; he said she had spent a week on her own in Montgomery at Christmas and had held to her routine admirably. Mrs Sayre wrote the doctor that Zelda might be able to find a part-time job in Montgomery if she continued to improve, adding as always that Zelda could live with her if everyone concerned was amenable. Dr Carroll wondered what Scott's attitude toward this arrangement might be – if a letter was sent to Mrs Sayre outlining the danger signals of an approaching breakdown, so that it could be recognized and avoided.

Scott replied, 'Your letter was a complete surprise, but of course I am delighted. . . . The news that she had been home alone in December was a complete surprise to me though as you know I would have been in agreement if you had ever thought before that a journey without a nurse was desirable.' Inevitably he worried about Zelda's ability to maintain her present level of sanity, 'but since I am utterly unprepared to take on the job again I suppose it is lucky that there is any sort of home where she will at least be loved and cherished. The possibility of dissipation frightens me more than anything else – which I suppose is poetic justice.'

Scott wired Zelda immediately about Carroll's recommendation. Zelda's reaction was that of a prisoner who had been punished and is now relieved beyond belief at her pardon. 'I will be very, very happy to escape the spiritual confines of medical jurisdiction. Also, I will be very meticulous in my social conduct and promise not to cause any trouble: I will be able to have vacation with Scottie, maybe and do all sorts of half-forgotten pleasant things from such a long time ago. . . .

This has been an awful time for you; and maybe, at last, we begin to emerge.'

She then began to make plans for her life outside the hospital. It took no l'tle courage to form these plans, for she was not completely unaware of the obstacles she would have to face. 'As soon as I have renewed associations and found all the trees where I used to make play-house again, I will try to find a job. Needless to say I am conversant with the difficulties which will probably confront me: Middle aged, untrained, graduate of half-a-dozen mental Institutes. However, there may be something blow[n] in on a box-car or one of those things like that.'

Four years and one week after Zelda's admission to Highland Hospital she was released. Dr Carroll wrote the letter concerning her case that he had mentioned to Scott. One copy was sent to Mrs Sayre in Montgomery and another to Scott for safekeeping. The final paragraph stated the precariousness of Zelda's mental condition: her history showed a tendency to repeat itself in cycles. She could be irresponsible and suicidal. Zelda might well be unable to face what was ahead of her in Montgomery. At present she was gentle and reasonable; her capacity for making mature judgements was, however, permanently reduced.

4. Going Home

19

.... Scott, the bright hotels turn bleak;
The pace limps or stamps; the wines are weak;
The horns and violins come faint tonight.

EDMUND WILSON, 'Dedication'

Carefully Scott explained to Zelda the terms of their limited finances: '. . . you will be a poor girl for awhile and there is nothing much to do about it'. He would send her $30 a week, half of which was to go to Mrs Sayre for Zelda's board. The other half he would give her in amounts of $10 or $20 in alternating weeks; she would therefore receive $25 one week and $35 the next. He said it was a way of saving for her so that in alternate weeks she'd have a larger sum for pocket money. He knew that she would be cramped, but he owed the government a considerable amount and he was deeply committed to having Scottie complete her education. He wrote Zelda that if Scottie were forced to leave Vassar, 'I should feel like quitting all work and going to the free Veterans Hospital where I probably belong.'

Alone at dawn Zelda boarded a bus for Montgomery. She believed that this was her chance for another beginning, and balancing a sheet of paper on her lap she wrote Scott: 'I think of you and the many mornings that we have left believing in new places to-gether. This country is so nostalgic with its imperative possibilities of escape from the doom of the mountains. . . .' She did not know that she had been released with a letter which paroled her to her mother; she rode toward Montgomery completely unaware that it was the cul-de-sac of her life, that for her there were to be no more fresh starts.

Zelda was nearly forty and she was largely alone. Friends stopped by to see her the first few days, but not many, and Zelda felt she had little in common with those who did. She was grateful for her mother's company. Almost at once a tone of bewildered disappointment marked her letters to Scott, whom she had not seen for a year. She wrote him regularly each Monday and usually her letters began by thanking him for his cheque. She said there wasn't much to do; she was not invited to parties and no one seemed particularly interested in her. 'To this sort of town a beau is almost indispensible; but there don't seem to be any left.' Soon the swimming pools would open, which she looked forward to, and she considered buying a bicycle. She told Scott she prayed for him, 'for the just reward of your talent; and for a more proportionate acknowledgment of your contribution to American letters'. But she no longer addressed him as Dearest Do Do, or Goofo; from now on it was plain 'Dear Scott'. Her letters were not signed 'Love', but 'Devotedly'. It must have been clear to her that their estrangement was all but complete.

With Zelda out of Highland, Scott's expenses were considerably reduced. He tried to think of things for her to do; he suggested renting a cool room as a studio for painting; he hoped she was happy. 'I wish you read books (you know those things that look like blocks but come apart on one side) – I mean loads of books and not just early Hebrew metaphysics.' He even suggested that she try to write again, telling her that although she was completely unable to plot a story she might try something along the line of Chekhov's 'The Darling'. She did not answer that letter and Scott quickly apologized for having been snappish. He said he really did want to know about her life, and he questioned her relentlessly. How did she like her old friends; how was her mother's health; did she have any plans for the hottest part of the summer? 'I should have said in my letter that if you want to read those stories upon which I think you might make a new approach to writing some of your own, order *Best Russian Stories,* Modern Library, from Scribners and they will charge it to me.'

He had no idea how difficult it was for Zelda to readjust herself to life outside a clinic. She put it plainly. 'I don't write; and I don't paint: largely because it requires most of my resources to keep out of the hospital. I've had such a difficult struggle over the last ten years that making the social adjustment is more difficult that I had supposed. . . .'

But she did garden and she had learned something about patience, if not equanimity, during these long years of illness. She could be amused at planting a garden 'full of 25c worth of 15c worth of mustard', and refer to herself as a failed truck farmer. She did not mind when the weeds turned out to be hardier than the plants. What disturbed her were the unavoidable things she faced every day reminding her of her own past: The young girls in their sheer summer dresses; the deep green alleys that made her think of Cannes. The landmarks of her youth were as altered as she was, some beyond recognition. She walked out to the spot where Camp Sheridan had been and found in its place a cotton mill. She continued to walk five miles a day as part of her physical regimen, as she had promised Dr Carroll. (She did, however, ask Scott if he thought Dr Carroll would live forever holding her to that promise.) When friends saw her on the street they would stop their cars and offer her a ride, which she always refused. But they did not know why she refused and considered her walking a peculiarity. If they tried to engage her in conversation she would often seem uninterested, and although her eyes watched them as they spoke, they were left with the uncomfortable feeling that she did not quite take in what they said. Eventually they began to avoid her.

Scott toyed with the idea of sending Scottie to relatives in Virginia for part of the summer and of letting her visit Zelda in Alabama for the latter half. But Scottie wanted to go to summer school at Harvard and that struck him as a better idea. He wrote Zelda: 'You remember your old idea that people ought to be born on the shores of the North Sea and only in later life drift south toward the Mediterranean in softness? . . . I want Scottie to be hardy and keen and able to fight her own battles and Virginia didn't seem to be the right note – however charming.' Later on the same day, 7 June, Scott wrote Scottie telling her he had just received a very depressed letter from Zelda, as well as one from Mrs Sayre: 'the second told me in cautious language that your mother had had a "toxic attack". I know what this means, only I expected her to hold out at least two months.' Although Zelda seemed to have recovered, Scott could not be sure what was about to happen and he insisted that Scottie spend at least ten days with Zelda. He told her, 'this may be the last time you have a chance to see your mother in a sane period. . . .'

Much as he had fretted over Scottie's development in the past – that she was not tough enough, that she was prone to exhaust herself, over-extend herself as he had at Princeton – he was now pleased with her. For it seemed to him that she was at last proving herself to be, his highest accolade, 'a worker. . . .' Perhaps she would not turn out like Zelda, which was really his deepest fear. He wrote Scottie:

Your mother's utterly endless mulling and brooding over insolubles paved the way to her ruin. She has no education – not from lack of opportunity because she could have learned with me – but from some inner stubbornness. She was a great original in her way, with perhaps a more intense flame at its highest than I ever had, but she tried and is still trying to solve all ethical and moral problems on her own, without benefit of the thousands dead. Also she had nothing 'kinetic', which, in physics, means internal driving force – she had to be led or driven.

By the fourteenth it was settled that Scottie would visit Zelda briefly in Montgomery before summer school. Then in August, the worst part of the hot Alabama summer, if a movie script Scott had written from 'Babylon Revisited' was produced, he might have enough money to send Zelda to the shore. In his letter to Zelda he explained the revised plans, then facing his own memories he wrote:

Twenty years ago *This Side of Paradise* was a best seller and we were settled in Westport. Ten years ago Paris was having almost its last great American season but we had quit the gay parade and you were gone to Switzerland. Five years ago I had my first bad stroke of illness and went to Asheville. Cards began falling badly for us much too early.

At the last minute just before Scottie was to leave for Alabama, Scott received a wire from Zelda: 'I WONT BE ABLE TO STICK

THIS OUT. WILL YOU WIRE MONEY IMMEDIATELY THAT I MAY RETURN FRIDAY TO ASHVILLE. WILL SEE SCOTTIE THERE. DEVOTEDLY REGRETFULLY GRATEFULLY ZELDA.' In the afternoon of the same day Zelda wired again: 'DIS-REGARD TELEGRAM AM FINE AGAIN. HAPPY TO SEE SCOTTIE. DEVOTEDLY. ZELDA.'

Immediately he notified Scottie that the situation looked black. If it was, she should talk it over with the doctor in Montgomery herself and leave. 'There's a point beyond which families can do nothing.' But by the twentieth when Scottie arrived everything seemed fine. Relieved, Fitzgerald wrote that all he wanted was to think of the two of them together, swimming, 'diving from great heights and being very trim and graceful in the water'.

When Scottie left for Cambridge Zelda felt that although she hadn't been able to 'open any deep chanels of "maternal advice" I somehow seemed to have made a *little* headway as to ingratiating myself'. Zelda told Scott that Scottie seemed sorry to leave, and clearly she was pleased by that. Scottie discussed with Zelda the possibility of leaving Vassar, and Zelda told her Scott would never permit it, and would be deeply hurt by the suggestion. Still, Scottie turned the idea over in her mind; she could not help being keenly aware of the financial burden her education was to her father. And besides she half wanted to fend for herself. A sketch she wrote was published by *The New Yorker* that summer, and *College Bazaar* had taken a story, which was a promising start for an eighteen-year-old. She considered trying to find a job on the Baltimore *Sun* and she also thought of working in publishing in New York. Scott's reaction was a predictable and succinct negative.

As July and August passed, Scott complained that Zelda never wrote him what she was doing; had she begun to paint or write? 'I do wish you were sketching a little if only to keep your hand in. You've never done any drawing at all in Alabama and it's so very different in flora and general atmosphere than North Carolina that I think it would be worthwhile to record your moods while down there.' He thought he could arrange an exhibition for her again. His letters to her were always alive with plans and questions. He realized that Zelda's life had slowed to a tempo that was as unacceptable to him as it once would have been to her. Her existence was now largely a matter of taking her five-mile daily walk, working her garden, and spending two days a week at the local Red Cross, where she folded bandages. Other than that, she sat with her mother on their front porch fanning herself and drinking crushed ice with fruit.

On her fortieth birthday Scott sent a large box of dahlias and gladiolas. Her letter thanking him was to 'Dearest Scott' and she said one of the hardest things about being in Montgomery again was that it reminded her of their early days together. She promised to paint 'as soon as I attain the vitality to both live, *and* aspire'. But for once she did not mind playing casino with her mother, or lingering over dishes of peaches and fresh figs, or falling asleep in the rocker with only the thoughts of the tail end of the summer on her mind. She asked if Scottie could visit her again before fall term began at Vassar. Contact with Scottie was invigorating to her and she badly wanted another opportunity to strengthen their rapport.

Scott, sympathizing with Zelda's sense of isolation, wrote Scottie reminding her of her obligation to her mother. 'I know it will be dull going into that hot little town early in September – but you are helping me. Even invalids like your mother have to have mileposts – things to look forward to and back upon. .... Only think how empty her life is and you will see the importance of your going there.' Dutifully Scottie spent four days with Zelda in Montgomery at the end of the summer; to Zelda these days were filled with moments she clung to. She wanted a chance to be a parent and to show off her lovely and talented daughter. She could not help remembering herself when she was Scottie's age. 'Things are so different than when I was young when girls sat an hour on the curbing waiting for a ride in one of the few extant automobiles; nowadays nobody seems to know what a script-dance was, and the jelly bean lingo is indeed obsolete.'

But for all Zelda's goodwill there were still problems in her relationship to Scottie. Zelda was troubled when Scottie did not report her whereabouts to her and Scottie chafed at being continually checked up on like a child. In a letter to her father Scottie revealed how she felt about her visits.

I have been as an Angel with Halo with Mama and we have really gotten along rather well. ... I even went so far as to discuss marriage with her so's she'd feel she had some ideas to contribute. She is really not unhappy ... I always forget how people can dull their desire for an energetic life. She is nevertheless like a fish out of water. Her ideas are too elaborately worded to be even faintly comprehensible to anyone in the town, and yet too basically wrong to be of real interest to people who really know anything (I don't mean me!). ... I wonder what is ever to become of her when Grandma dies.

It was Scott who had guided his daughter's life; he and not Zelda who made lists of books for her to read, who wanted to be kept posted about life at Vassar. 'What proms and games? Let me at least renew my youth! As a papa ... what do you do? and how?' It was he who now offered her advice about men. She would have the best range of choice for marriage between 'nineteen years, 6 months, to 20 years, 6 months – or so I figure', he wrote seriously. Businessmen and their wives developed into bores, he advised, unless the women were extraordinary and of great natural charm like Sara Murphy. He wanted Scottie to find someone with whom she could share a larger life. He asked her to question herself about any specific man, 'is he his own man? Has he any force of character? Or imagination and generosity? Does he read books?' All he really cared about, he told her, 'is that you should marry someone who is not too much a part of the crowd'. Scott, at the same time he advised Scottie, was making plans for Zelda, and forming what Sheilah Graham has called their 'College of One', setting out to give Miss Graham a liberal education based upon carefully drawn lists of recordings, books, and paintings. In this Scott revealed a penchant for making Galateas of his women, simultaneously undertaking to stimulate and direct the lives of his daughter, his wife and his mistress. It took valuable time from his novel, but it was as if by educating his women he formed a buffer against his personal bogies of alcohol, debt, and sickness.

What few suggestions Zelda made to Scott were along the lines of their old terms of success. Why, for instance, she asked, couldn't he write for the *Saturday Evening Post* again? Patiently, Scott tried to explain to her that it was not only that magazine writing was a 'very definite trick' and that editors had changed. The special touches he brought to his early short stories were no longer within his grasp. 'It was partly that times changed ... but part of it was tied up somehow with you and me – the happy ending. ... essentially I got my public with stories of young love. I must have had a powerful imagination to project is so far and so often into the past.'

On 28 September 1940 Scott wrote to Zelda: 'Autumn comes – I am forty-four – nothing changes.' He noted that Hemingway's novel *For Whom the Bell Tolls* had been taken by the Book-of-the-Month Club and asked Zelda if she remembered 'how superior he used to be about mere sales?' He told her about a tea that was being given at Dorothy Parker's to which he thought he'd go. Zelda had forgotten his birthday and when she remembered she wired him immediately saying she was sorry, but she had lost her sense of time 'due to being segregated from life and its problems', and added a note of hurt at his no longer being with her. He had, she wrote, her 'deepest impersonal gratitude for the many happy times we spent together – though it was long ago'.

In his next weekly letter Scott told her he'd felt 'passé' at the tea party among a younger generation, and decided to buy himself a new suit. He still complained of a fever and cough, but was improving; 'the constitution is an amazing thing and nothing quite kills it until the heart has run its entire race'. He told her he'd really try to come East at Christmas. He said his room looked like the study at La Paix, covered with notes and charts for his new novel. It was going to be shorter than *Tender*, more like *Gatsby*, closely patterned and tight. He aimed at completion the middle of December. 'I am deep in the novel, living in it, and it makes me happy.' Other than working on it, he did little but listen to the Princeton football games on the radio and follow the war reports from Europe.

In the nostalgic mood which now aften imbued Zelda's letters she wrote: 'Mamma's little house is so sunshine-y and so full of grace; the moated mornings remind me of twenty-five years ago when life was as full of promise as it now is of memory. There were wars then, and now ... but the race had more gallantry at that time and the more romantic terms in which we took life helped us through.'

Scott's life with Sheilah Graham was a quiet one; she remembers him working in a faded blue dressing gown with lots of pencils around, one always behind his ear, a tuft of hair sticking up corkscrew-like, for he pulled at it as he wrote. But when he prepared to go out he dressed very carefully in an old Brooks jacket and pink shirt. He liked bow ties and he often wore sweaters. Buff Cobb used to say he looked like a cross between Lucius Beebe and Baudelaire. He was entirely unathletic and fretted about his health. Miss Graham remembers with amusement how he would order the swimming pool on an estate where they had rented a cottage filled for her, and then stand on the shady side of the pool giving her instructions. 'The only thing we did together that was at all athletic was to play ping-pong. We always had a ping-pong table set up. Scott would be very funny, cross his eyes when he served, do pirouettes, that sort of thing and it was just killing. He was a very gay man when he felt well and it was an infectious gaiety – he would literally choke with laughter. Strange words amused him. We used to go to a delicatessen, a Jewish delicatessen, and he would ask the names of things. I think "knish" just floored him. He would ask again and again for it just to hear it pronounced.'

Sometimes they talked about Zelda, with Scott showing Miss Graham some of her letters. She said he told her so much about the South that she could taste it – about the heat and the girls putting their make-up on first and then getting in the bath to cool off until their dates arrived, and then dressing. He said he had once fought a duel for Zelda's honour with her French aviator and that he had never loved her as well as when he had to fight for her. The duel, he said, was exactly as he had written it in *Tender Is the Night*.

On a grey Thursday afternoon in late November 1940 Scott

left Sheilah Graham for twenty minutes to get a pack of cigarettes at Schwab's drugstore. He returned ashen and shaky. He
told her he had almost fainted at the drugstore. The following
morning he went to the doctor for a check-up and found that
he had experienced a cardiac spasm. On 6 December 1940 he
wrote Zelda that he was lucky he had not suffered a major heart
attack and if he was careful not to overtire himself he would
recover. He told her Scottie planned to visit her at Christmas
and he envied their being together. 'Everything is my novel now
– it has become of absorbing interest.' But he realized that it
would take him until February to complete. One week later he
was writing her that another cardiogram showed that slowly his
heart was repairing itself. 'It is odd that the heart is one of the
organs that does repair itself.'

In order to avoid the strain of climbing stairs he moved into
Sheilah Graham's apartment on the first floor; his had been
on the third. He made her promise not to discuss his case with
the doctor when he was not present, and she did not. They set
up a writing board which could be moved into place over his
bed or arm chair. He was completely engrossed in his book. He
cancelled a doctor's appointment on Friday 20 December in
order to work out a problem in his writing. That night, having
solved the quandary, he and Sheilah decided to celebrate and
go to a press preview at the Pantages Theatre of *This Thing
Called Love*. Standing before a mirror as he dressed to leave,
he gave a last straightening touch to his bow tie and told her
teasingly that he'd always wanted to be a dandy.

When the movie was over and they began to leave the theatre,
Scott suddenly lurched forward, grabbing the armrest of his
seat to steady himself. As Sheilah came to his side he told her
he felt everything begin to go as it had that earlier afternoon at
Schwab's. But the air outside made him feel better and they
went home. The next morning Scott, dressed in slacks, shirt, and
a pullover, dictated a letter to Scottie. He talked a lot about his
daughter that morning, about how pleased he was with her and
how well she was doing at school. He said the one thing he
wanted was to see her finish Vassar. After lunch while waiting
for the doctor to arrive, he settled into an armchair before the

fireplace and began making notes in the *Princeton Alumni Weekly* on an article about the football team. He was eating a chocolate bar. Suddenly he stood up, reached for the mantel and then collapsed to the floor. In a moment he was dead.

Harold Ober called Zelda and told her of Scott's death. At first she could not believe it. On Christmas Day she wrote Ober:

> In retrospect it seems as if he was always planning happinesses for Scottie and for me. Books to read – places to go. Life seemed so promisory always when he was around: and I always believed that he could take care of anything.
>
> It seems so useless and purposeless that I won't be able to tell him about all this. Although we were not close anymore, Scott was the best friend a person could have been to me. . . .

Zelda was not able to attend Scott's funeral in Rockville, Maryland, on 27 December and asked her brother-in-law, Newman Smith, to go in her stead. It was a raw wintry day and only a handful of Scott's friends were there: Judge Biggs, Gerald and Sara Murphy, the Perkinses and Obers, Ludlow Fowler, the Turnbulls and Scottie with some of her friends. The Protestant service was simple and brief. Scott was denied the Catholic burial he had wanted because he had not died within the church. His books were proscribed. Therefore, he was not buried in the old tiny Catholic cemetery among the Scotts, the Keys, and the Fitzgeralds, but close by in the Rockville Union Cemetery. Afterward Scottie went to Montgomery to spend a few days with Zelda.

On the day of Scott's funeral Edmund Wilson wrote Zelda from his home in Stamford, Connecticut:

> I have been so terribly shocked by Scott's death. I had had two letters from him lately, in which he had sounded as if he were getting along well with his book. – Though I hadn't seen much of him of recent years, we had a sort of permanent relationship, due to our having known one another at college & having started in writing at the same time. It has brought so many things back – the days when you & he arrived in New York together – & I have been thinking about you a lot these last few days. I know how you must feel,

because I feel myself as if I had been suddenly robbed of some part of my own personality – since there must have been some aspect of myself that had been developed in relation to him.

Zelda was touched by his letter and told him of her grief. She had known Scott was ill, but she could not believe that he would never come East again for her. Never again 'with his pockets full of promise and his heart full of new refurbished hopes'. She mentioned to Wilson that Maxwell Perkins told her he wanted to publish the manuscript Scott left. She very much wanted this done, 'as I have always felt that a genius has a right to live as long as the scene which evoked him (or he evoked). I thought that the bitter haunted stories in Esquire were very compelling and might warrant publication –

'Posthumous works seem to gain favour of late.'

In a letter to Rosalind she expressed herself more personally. She said Scott would be remembered, for he had 'kept too many midnight vigils for others', younger or less fortunate writers than he, not to be. 'I am proud of his literary achievements, and of his faithful courage. All the long months he spent by my side in Switzerland, and the reams of hospital bills and diagnoses he bore so uncomplainingly are more poignant in retrospect than they were adequately appreciated at the time.' There was a certain pride in these statements to her sister, for they emphasized her unity with Scott, rather than their hard times. She told her sister she knew Scott was quick-tempered, but she balanced that by talking about his good looks, his talent, and his considerable charm, which won them friends wherever they went. 'I miss him – that he isn't somewhere, pursuing the policies that sustained him . . . is going to be a grievous loss.'

Zelda was more alone now than she had ever been. It was true that she had not seen Scott for over a year and a half, but he had written her every week. On Fitzgerald's part these letters were to his invalid, but there was something more of himself invested in them than that word suggests. She was the person who had shared his life when it was most worth sharing. Only to her could he admit how forgotten he had become, because only Zelda knew fully how well known he had been. Their shared pasts did not give them grounds for the future, both had admitted that, but it gave them an intimacy that was immune to further alteration. With Scott gone Zelda retreated more and more deeply into their past, where things had been the best she'd known. Young men would now and then come to her as Scott's widow and she was kind to them, talking about Paris and writing and Hemingway and Scott, telling them things they were eager to hear, and then making them promise before they left never to smoke or drink.

She had her mother and she had Scottie. But certainly she could not hope to share Scottie's life in any real sense of that word. For years now she had been forced to accept reduced circumstances, not only in the sense of diminished finances, but of diminshed relations with people. With Scott dead her life would become largely a matter of recollecting, and when it was not, of a courageous effort to face her recurring illness and live with it.

Maxwell Perkins showed Edmund Wilson the manuscript of *The Last Tycoon*, asking him if he thought it was worth publishing. Wilson said that it was and agreed to edit it for nothing, Perkins's terms. Scott's death had been unsettling to Wilson and going through his notes for the novel must have been even more so, for in the process of editing *The Last Tycoon*, Wilson came to realize Scott's splendid literary gifts with greater intensity and admiration than ever before. When he was finished he placed Fitzgerald among the best of his generation.

Among the copious notes for the novel that Scott had been making since at least 1937 was a working title, *The Love of the Last Tycoon*, subtitled 'A Western'. It was published in October 1941 in a volume with *The Great Gatsby*, 'May Day', 'The Diamond As Big As the Ritz', 'The Rich Boy', 'Absolution', and 'Crazy Sunday'. Shortly after its publication (which was ten months after Fitzgerald's death), Stephen Vincent Benét reviewed the novel. In the review he struck a note that has reverberated through nearly three decades: '. . . the evidence is in. You can take off your hats now, gentlemen, and I think perhaps you had better. This is not a legend, this is a reputation – and, seen in perspective, it may well be one of the most secure reputations of our time.' He would have agreed with a note Scott made to himself while working on *The Last Tycoon*: 'I'm the last of the novelists for a long time now.'

After Zelda read the novel she wrote Wilson her own assessment of Scott's reputation: 'Surely when future generations look for an indicative measure of the tragic and ominous imperatives which have been life to this one, Scott's work will have become a source. . . .' She thought that there was an American temperament grounded in belief in oneself and 'will-to-survive' that Scott's contemporaries had relinquished. Scott, she insisted, had not. His work possessed a vitality and stamina because of his indefatigable faith in himself.

She did not like the heroine, and in the same letter to Wilson she told him Kathleen was 'undesirable: the sort of person who knows how to turn the ice-man's advances to profitable account.' A week later she wrote Mrs Turnbull in the same vein except that her jealousy of the heroine was more transparent. She may not have known of the specific existence of Sheilah Graham before Scott's death, but she certainly sensed and resented the intrusion of another feminine model in Fitzgerald's prose: 'I confess that I don't like the heroine, she seems the sort of person who knows too well how to capitalize the unwelcome advances of the ice-man and who smells a little of the rubber-shields in her dress. However, I see how Stahr might have found her redolent of the intimacies of forgotten homely glamours, and his imagination have endowed her with the magical properties of his early authorities.'

20

'He talked a lot about the past, and I gathered that he wanted to recover something, some idea of himself perhaps, that had gone into loving Daisy. His life had been confused and disordered since then, but if he could once return to a certain starting place and go over it all slowly, he could find out what that thing was. . . .'

FITZGERALD, *The Great Gatsby*

After the publication of *The Last Tycoon*, probably in 1942, Zelda began writing a novel called *Caesar's Things*. She never finished the book, but she worked on it throughout the rest of her life. When she died she left a typed manuscript of 135 pages which were divided into seven chapters (the last in rough draft), as well as several fragments involving the same cast of characters, which were presumably to be worked into the novel.

As early as 1940, in a letter to Scott about a short story she was sending to him, Zelda stated an attitude that had begun to mark all her writing. 'Although you may not like it, and may find it moralistic, it conveys a message that I would be most grateful to put across: that the story of life is of far deeper implication in religious terms.' By the summer of 1942 she was writing Mrs Turnbull: 'I am trying to write a novel with the thematic intent of inducting the Biblical pattern of life into its everyday manifestations.' Taken together these two statements suggest a possible key to *Caesar's Things*. The problem is that Zelda's religious fervour seems to have been closely linked to the most delusional aspects of her illness, and therefore what might have been the central thematic device of the novel is instead the most forced and peculiar portion of her book. Its subject was once again the story of Zelda's life. Only this time the reader confronts the rigidity of Zelda's psychosis head on, and the novel moves at a strained pace, swinging in and out of fantasies whose meanings are known only to the author. It is a sort of collage of autobiographical writing, fantasy, and religiosity. There is no sum of the parts of this novel, but only the parts themselves, truncated and wildly incoherent.

The novel seems to have originally been written in the first person, but haphazardly throughout the manuscript the *I* was changed to *she*, or Janno, the narrator's name. (All of the main characters' names begin with the letter *J*: Janno's husband's name is Jacob, her French aviator's name is Jacques, as it was in *Save Me the Waltz*. There is a confusion of names for Jacob. He is introduced as 'Harold', but that name is dropped almost immediately to be replaced by either 'Jacob' or 'Jacques'; most often he is 'Jacob'. Fitzgerald had used a number of names beginning with *J*, Jay Gatsby, Judy Jones, and Jordan Baker among them, but whatever Zelda's intentions may have been on this score they remain impenetrable.)

More than half of the book, the first four chapters, deals with Janno's youth in a small town in the South, and although the town is not named, it is Montgomery. Chapters 5 and 6 and the incomplete Chapter 7 are about Janno's marriage to Jacob (who is a painter as David was in *Save Me the Waltz*) and the gradual dissolution of their marriage as they move from New York to Paris and the Riviera.

Janno is the youngest girl in a large family. Her father is a judge. She has an older brother whom she adores and follows. He is called 'Monsieur', which was one of Zelda's nicknames for Scott. (Within the Sayre family, 'Mister' had been Anthony Sayre's nickname.) One day the family moves into a small house across from which a hospital is being built. The Judge warns Janno and her brother to stay away from the building site. He gives them no reason, but he suggests that trouble is expected there that afternoon. (Later in the manuscript the Judge says a new wing is being added for 'psychiatrists to practice in'.) Both children are intrigued by the building and the brother, disobeying his father and leaving Janno behind, runs off to play there. Janno walks down to the end of her street and begins to tell herself a story; she wants to follow her brother, but is uneasy about his disobedience.

Suddenly Janno starts to run toward the hospital. She falls. 'The child was dead from strain, and effort, and excitement. She clung across the dried grass with the stubble sticking into her mouth, "if you will only let me get there – let me get there lest such obscenity should be –"' Janno picks herself up and begins to run again. She hears the sound of violent whacking 'and cries of a spectral ballgame reverberated through the lone air'. Perhaps her brother is playing ball, perhaps not; she wants to make sure. She is terrified as she approaches the spot where she thinks her brother is playing. She sees him astride something that looks like a scarecrow; the ground around him is in considerable disorder. Janno yells at him to stop whatever he is doing. The language of the little girl becomes stilted and oddly formal as if, within a scene that is becoming increasingly violent and surreal, Janno's is the voice of balance, reason, and justice. She makes moralistic pronouncements on the action.

'What right have you to stop me?' The boy was angry at his rights being contested. He had found the thing. It was his – or more his than hers anyway.

Maybe she didn't have a right.

'There are lots of other more felicitous things to do – a little further on in the parc,' she proffered fairly.

'Don't you want to see me make a poppa?' This unidentified operation held possibilities of interest; her curiosity wavered.

'What's that?' It had an interesting sound anyway, like the de-capping of a bottle of soda-watter.

Mysterious voices begin to advise Janno to stop her brother, but she is afraid to.

Before she could say anything, her brother had his thumb in the eye-sockets and the child died of horror as the eye-ball came out in a film of white plasm. It was a pale blue eye; and that was the first indication that the thing he was playing with was a corpse.

Janno screams in horror as her brother tries to remove the remaining eye. 'That God would let this happen had broken her heart forever and that was the way she would live.' She runs from the scene 'because she didn't want to cause any trouble' and lies down beneath a big oak tree. While lying there Janno is visited by God in a splendour of piercing white light: 'The light was Charity, the Justice of Cause and Effect and INFINITE MAJESTY.'

The action of the novel continues as if it were a natural

order of events. Two men, apparently interns from the hospital, carry Janno home; she has a fever and is about to die. ('Janno was dead, and dying. . . .') Her brother is already at home when they bring her in and is lying on a couch with his face to the wall. Janno tries to apologize to him, but he only snarls at her. Her father's voice reaches her as if from far away. Abruptly the novel has again shifted gears and the reader realizes that they are no longer in the home, but in a hospital where Janno has been taken for the night. The Judge is saying, ' "You've ruined her, now you can keep her." ' Shortly thereafter the story line totally disintegrates. Then the author steps in to provide another strangely formal commentary:

> A successful life is able to summon to memory few episodes of the past save the contributing factors to success, but a soul fallen into the hands of psychiatrists find the seeds of nervous disorder and even abberation scattered plentifully over the past. . . . She forgot all about this year of her life until she was grown, and married and tragedy had revivified its traces – as she then saw, carved from the beginning.

Zelda's implication is that there was a biographical equivalent in her own life for the action that has taken place in Janno's. If there was, it is unrecorded. All we can know is that Janno's fantasy (never admitted as fantasy within the text), alive with images of mutilation and death, seems to be grounded on the simplest level in the fear of the consequences of disobeying her father's authority. No one from her family comes to her rescue or assistance, and uncertain even whether she is alive, dying, or dead, Janno is completely at the mercy of those in the hospital (which need not be taken literally as a hospital at all, but could stand for any sort of institution – family, marriage, school). By the end of this scene Janno is totally rejected by her father, as well as by her brother. And, in a pattern that becomes central to the novel, there are revelations, a vision of God, strange and provocative 'voices' which warn and direct Janno, which do nothing to alleviate the terror of the child, and lead her instead only deeper into the nightmare of her existence. Her voices become part of the natural order of the novel. She is moved by them; she is defenceless against them.

The third chapter begins with the death of Janno's grand-mother and the throwing away of her things. Janno is sent to school for the first time, but she doesn't like it and runs away. It is decided that she may remain at home another year (as Zelda had in Montgomery). Janno wanders down to the spring-house where butter and fresh milk were kept; in an adjacent trough of water Negresses wash clothes. Janno decides to wash her doll's clothes. A voice speaks to her from the well, telling her that she's washing in an 'antiquated method'. Janno ignores the advice. Then there are more voices and they turn grim; they suggest that Janno jump into the well, and their 'authority was dark and ominous'. They offer her a golden kingdom which has been awaiting her. But she doesn't want to jump; she's afraid she won't be able to get back out. The voices prom-ise her food; she can become a Lorelei. The well goes through to China, the voices tell her, to a 'golden kingdom asleep – a fat old China king and rich courts, sleeping forever, forever counting his money'. Still Janno refuses to leap in and goes home.

Another day she returns to the well. Its voices question her: has she learned Latin, can she play the piano? She regrets that she has neither of these accomplishments. Suddenly the well and the countryside around it begin to change before her eyes. It becomes a theatre curtain, the curtain 'melts' and in its place 'was the green room, and oak-panelled corridor and people in heated argument'. They are talking light-heartedly about scenes of violence: 'seduction, theft, kid-napping and murder'. Janno wants to know what happened. She says it doesn't make sense; the voices reply, 'Far more sense than you do.' She says she tries to make sense and leaves the room. There is blood in the hallway; Janno waits and the scene changes again.

Two men and a woman sit at a long table, large enough for twelve. One of the men is in uniform, 'at least a colonel'; he carries a sword 'which rested in challenge with its tip on the floor'. The other man is pale, 'chestnut-haired and fragile; he seemed to be on some other than the conventional relationship with the woman'. The military man says he does not accuse the pale man, but he cannot accept treason, and he intends to defend the honour of the house. The woman is wan. The men accuse her of looking 'dissolute, but she was tired from self-abnegatory spiritual effort: the keeping of many rigorous and more materialistic obligations than a person was able'. A 'Nubian' pours her something to drink from a gold cup. She realizes that it will kill her if she drinks; she can see a powder dissolving to 'mucus' in the cup; 'she leaned back in tragic defiance'.

Janno, who is not part of the scene, but only observing it, knows that if the woman does not drink from the cup her head will be cut off by the Nubian; Janno is, however, too exhausted to worry about how it comes out. The scene is summarized: 'The weak dark man who seemed to have other things on his mind was evaluating. He acknowledged to no relationship with the woman other than as a good friend of the husband. After [a] while, when the colonel had challenged him and withdrawn, the pale man said, "I wanted the jewels as much as the woman. The pearls were my family heritage".'

Suppose that the uniformed colonel, the 'weak dark man' is Jozan. He challenges 'the pale man', who may or may not be the woman's husband, i.e., Scott. But whatever the colonel's relationship to the woman has been, he now abandons her and withdraws from the scene. The pale man is no more interested in the woman than he is in 'the jewels . . . The pearls', and in essence both men have abandoned her. They turn on her and accuse her of being debauched. Her reply is similar to the language Zelda uses when discussing her mental illness, and seems to have nothing to do with the situation at hand. But nothing can be taken literally. What is the cup, and why is it gold? Why mucus? What jewels? The scene could be a distorted mirroring of Zelda's self at various stages of life. The little girl, Janno-Zelda, views the young woman, who may represent an older Zelda, as foredoomed in her dilemma, and is incapable of doing anything to change the course of her life. But like symbols in a dream, or in a poem, there is no one meaning.

Following this scene is a series of fragmented fantasies which are completely impenetrable. At one point Janno is sitting on a throne in a bright light and doctors are conferring about 'the case and they decided that in case of death they would proceed with the regular medical routine'. It is this sense of being handled or manipulated, of being a 'case', of being unable to alter or control what is happening to her, even of being moved helplessly toward her death, while being a witness of it, that gives the novel its terrifying air of nightmare.

In an abrupt time switch Janno begins to grow out of childhood; Zelda stresses her faulty upbringing, which makes her unsure of herself. She worries about her popularity with boys, and even more about her own standards of behaviour. 'Janno . . . wished that her mother had told her not to go like that with the boys; she wished that there had been rules and prescriptions for right. But there wasn't.' In a passage punctuated by strange warnings about Christ's right and the ways of the Lord, Zelda writes about Janno's feelings of social inferiority.

Then something happened: they had better clothes than she did, and better manners, and she had better accept their standards of conduct. It was clearly a threat. . . . Then the boys assumed the air of authorized committee 'You won't have any friends – nobody else will come to see you. That I promise you.' . . . They went up to the haunted school-yard so deep in shadows and creaking with felicities of murder to the splintery old swing and she was so miserable and trusting that her heart broke and for many years after she didn't want to live. . . .

Whatever happened to Janno in the schoolyard is suggested but left unsaid. Later in the manuscript Zelda writes that what happened to Janno was 'the kind of thing one forgets. . . . until years later. . . . [when] this sort of thing looms up in a different light. It is then no longer a departure from an habitual rectitude, but a presage of the disasters which finally came; a monstrous weakness pervading life until finally it has prevailed, and declared that to corrupt and to degrade had always been its intent.' The manuscript is immersed in this sense of doom. Nothing is what is seems. The past holds only the seeds of future decay and corruption.

Janno's romance with Jacob begins on a different footing. To her he is from the first a romantic figure and she imagines him living in a world totally different from her own. She makes up stories about him. 'In some of the dreams he lived in a dark mahogany-haunted house with ferns and red-coated ancestors and sometimes he lived at various Country-clubs.' He is a young lieutenant stationed in Janno's Southern town during World War I; he comes in with the army and he leaves with Janno. She has been equivocal about marrying him for a while, but she thinks (as Zelda had) that you can marry or you can be a stenographer, and 'life was gayer and the things of marriage were more familiar to a young girl than the disciplines of offices'. In passages clotted with images of violence and destruction the author establishes what will become the dominant tone of the marriage. She forecasts disaster and moves towards it relentlessly.

'So they were desperately in love and being desperately in love involves a desperate existence.' Zelda uses the word 'desperate' in its most literal sense, thereby extending the slang phrase into a darker area of meaning. Janno and Jacob drink, shoot good golf, and (as Zelda becomes apocalyptic again) survive on the 'possibility, and hope, of sin'. Zelda calls this phase of Janno's life 'Nemesis incubating', adding that she tried to adopt Jacob's taste, failing miserably.

And Janno, who is not content to become Jacob's 'evocateur' ('to him women were agents – evocateurs of his own grace'), begins to examine Jacob's relationship with other women in his life. She concentrates on the women in his family, for it was toward them (or in reaction against them) that she believes his attitudes were formed.

He hated his sister. ... largely because he never could find out what it was about her that he so heartily resented. He hated his mother because ... he blamed her for the failure of his life. He hated Janno for the same reason but this did not come to light until many years later when it really had become difficult to make money and some of his portraits were – O well, over the garage in case they were ever wanted again.

The same cool, even cold, observation is given to Jacob's person and mannerisms.

Jacob went on doing whatever it was that Jacob did; he was always doing something with pencils or pieces of string or note-books or things which he found in his wallet; this made him absent-minded and preoccupied and also gave savour of material purpose. He was more important than Janno; she always felt as if she should be helpful about his tinkerings; they were intricate enough to need an assistant.

Their marriage begins to fall apart: Jacob drinks too much, but when Janno asks him to stop he tells her to mind her own business. Janno is not able to cope with Jacob's increasing success as a portrait painter. She envies New York, where they are living; its 'wondrous chic . . . the nail-polish and orchids, the hushed florescence of the gilded restaurants, the subdued arrogance of people who really had much to lose, the disciplined pomp of winter hotels, the swish of leisure' intimidate her.

Jacob has a flirtation with a nineteen-year-old girl he has been commissioned to paint. Janno thinks the girl 'vulgar' and feels strangled by her own inability to do anything other than watch. Suddenly Jacob decides to go to Europe; Janno does not want to go, but her husband 'never tolerated any policies of inertia'. And then the about-face. Tacked on this description of the early days of their marriage is Janno's comment that Jacob is really a 'sweet man', sweet because he gives her presents on holidays. 'She was grateful and devoted; promising gratitude and devotion to God for having sent him. She was a lucky girl. . . .'

At the opening of the sixth chapter, entitled 'Over here, over there . . . Flight', they arrive in Paris and once again enter the world of sophisticated wisecracking and general discontent. Janno is busy 'redecorating the gilded cage'. Their time is spent at the Ritz bar, to which they are described as superior. But the entire opening is weighted with bitterness and irony. They run into chic people to whom Janno is 'socially deferential'. She must pretend to admire them, all the while abhorring their taste and pretentiousness. 'Everybody liked them as standard millionaires the same way a good hotel or a crack train is appreciated. They were able.'

At the parties among the rich Janno feels the restlessness, she and Jacob and the others must move on to other parties, driven by the idea 'that somewhere else might be nearer the center'. Jacob's flirtatiousness makes her unhappy.

Janno had always been jealous. Situations which had to be faced with dishonesty and endured for the sake of a code to which she did not subscribe made her sick. She couldn't say to Jacob, 'I don't want you to go, you're obligated to me. Anyway she's not as nice as I am.' She sat being tragically poignantly courageous and saying to herself that after all, such was all in the game. This sophistry disoriented her momentarily and by the time she had organized an adequate humility to meet the humiliation the two people had got away and the table settled to another rhythm. The party went somewhere else and rattled negligibly along where the night was padded in red leather cushions.

'Now listen,' the baron kept saying, 'you ought to be making something out of a promising girl like you.'

It was gratifying to feel that one might be a financial asset. However, she was making something of herself: the best she was able, under the circumstances. All these bedraggled wan spectres seemingly so immersed in the pattern of tragic futility were very much engaged in turning accident into memoir. They imagined things about themselves, then forgot the thread of the current romance and disintegrated through the fumes of the night in search of the story of their lives.

Couples begin to pair off, but Janno is excluded; she does not want to be left out, but she cannot participate in affairs such as those taking place right under her nose. 'During the first shock of infidelities the realization that the ties in which one has invested are nevertheless perishable gives poignancy.' Janno realizes that she can't force Jacob 'to feel fidelity', therefore she 'trooped her colours and accepted this, the custom of the country, with tragedy, regret and compensation'.

Eventually, however, Janno leaves one of the parties with a Mr Fish, and they drive out to St Cloud, kissing and drinking wine until the morning. At the end of the scene in St Cloud

Janno makes a moral pronouncement, 'This is wrong', and she and Fish leave.

Jacob disapproves of Janno's staying out all night, but he is in no position to protest. Finally he decides to forget it and presents her with a golden necktie. Janno calls it 'a gala emblem'. Jacob replies, 'I'll let you wear it sometime – next time you want to hang yourself for instance.' And the conversation is left at that, as if it were a clever *bon mot*.

Janno and Jacob meet the Cornings, a rich couple who own a house in St Cloud set in a magnificent pebbled garden. The description of the couple and their house, with its black glass tables and gilded ceilings, recalls the Murphys; what is unexpected is the undertone of irony and dislike in Zelda's description of them: 'He and Charity put much effort into human relationships; having friends made such a difference.' Their house is filled with hundreds of dollars' worth of the most recent magazines from America. Corning insists upon two Bacardi cocktails before meals; it is only one of the minor details in his plan for a correct evening. The Cornings give wonderful dinners 'to the stars and to migratory Americans and to French people of consequence; not on the same evening'. But there is a tradition, Zelda writes, 'amongst the rich and famous that they have earned the right to know the people they want. . . .'

All of the Cornings' parties have the air of having been rehearsed. The only thing Zelda says Corning worries about is never having lost his temper: he is afraid it is a defect of temperament. He perfects 'his garden, his gadgets, his graces, his retainers, his dependents, his children', each with the same attention to detail. He misses only one thing according to the narrator, 'love'. He is charming and impersonal; the love he says he gives is, in the narrator's estimation, 'parental solicitude'.

'Corning said, "I want all these people to love one another because I love all of them –" . . . The guests obediently loved him: everything was so good and so new and so well-dramatized; he gave them some more.'

'Now this was paradise', begins Zelda's last chapter, echoing

David's reaction to the Riviera in *Save Me the Waltz*. 'We are now in Paradise – as nearly as we'll ever get. . . .' Janno and Jacob are on the Riviera and Zelda tells of the young wife's romance with a French aviator, Jacques. It is related in greater detail than in *Save Me the Waltz*. Janno and Jacob have met the son of an advocate 'and several young flying officers from the depot at Frejus. . . . The flying officer who looked like a Greek God was aloof.'

They meet at a pavilion set back from the sea, facing the ring of bright lights strung in a crescent around the perimeter of the shore. Jacob insists that Janno begin a conversation with the officer, but she is reluctant.

> Janno was vaguely baffled by the pleasurable expectancy which she felt concerning the French lieutenant. . . . life suddenly offered possibilities to a reckless extravagance which she didn't like. She had premonitions of wanton adventure.

Jacob is rather bored; he

> didn't really like the sitting around in a wet bathing-suit and he hated the taste of sand. He liked expatiating about values and origins and was exhaustive in his way of making the stories of people fit into his impetuous pre-conclusions about them. He kept nagging and asking and third-degreeing his acquaintances till it all made acceptable continuity with what he thought it ought to be dramaticly. He said people had to have friends. She didn't have to have anything save the baby and him and a pint of wine with meals.

The setting is permeated with a sense of furtiveness, concealment, and utter confusion. The villa on the Mediterranean becomes a place of seclusion, a 'secret house', hidden by the lushness of the landscape, a 'design of escape', a place 'for the heart to die or the world be hid. . . .'

When Janno again meets Jacques he immediately invites her to his apartment. 'She said she would; she was horrified. She could not possibly not do so.' Apparently Janno's idea of herself forces her to go to Jacques; she is driven into a tryst not because she is dominated by love, but because she is afraid of it. To succumb to her fear would be a weakness, a violation of her code, and therefore she must confront it. But there is at no point in the chapter a clarification of the romance and only by ominous reactions to it can we feel the author's point of view.

Unable to reconcile or resolve the conflicts between her heroine's feelings, her behaviour, and convention, Zelda allows Janno to escape all responsibility for her actions by blaming destiny.

She could not bring herself to deny her love its right of hearing, of clarification. She could go and see what in this destiny was ultimately inalienable; let issues declare themselves so that they might be faced and mastered. It was confused because she so hardly spoke the language and she was never quite sure about what she was saying. ... One night the lights went out in the brine-blown pavillion. She danced with Jacques while the others drank the really good champagne on the porch. ... Janno forgot to think. The lightning played about mysteriously and the night swayed black with arbitrary might outside. She kissed Jacques on the neck. It doesn't matter now. The storm raged; this might be the end of the world. One was afraid; it might be God's mal-diction. The kiss lasted a long time and there were two of them. She did not mean to do this; and when the dance was over and she joined the others, and put the matter aside. The young French officer treated her preciously and she knew that no matter what it was it would be tragedy and death: ruin is a relative matter.

If she loved him anyway she could not possibly hurt her husband and her child. ... If she loved him, she could not possibly love him and live with another: she wouldn't be able. If she loved him, there wasn't any answer.

The trouble was she should never have kissed him. First, she should never have kissed Jacques; then she shouldn't have kissed her husband; then after the kissing had become a spiritual vivi-section and half-massochistic there should not have been any more. Life in those darkened days behind the blinds with unidentified purposes humming outside and poitesses [?] hanging abeyant and reproachful over the inside, was venemous and poisoned. There wasn't much in calling the doctor; though she did. He prescribed champagne.

Janno considers her relationship to Jacques almost exclusively in terms of ruination, and Zelda's writing is made uncertain by her circling around the situation. Jacob seems completely unaware of what is happening. 'Jacob littered his fire-place with duplicates from his files and receipts for his insurance and cigarette-butts and pencil stubs and wine bottles. Then he shoved the screen across the disarray and tipped the maid a little extra and was absolved.' Eventually, Janno asks herself, 'How was she going to live if she did run off; if he [Jacob] did acknowledge the situation? What was he supposed to do?' Janno daydreams 'that she would come back over the red clay where the sharp pines shed the blood of summer some day and die. This was probably the influence of Byron. It was a sad love affair holding no promise and too impassioned to be dignified.' Then suddenly Jacob acts: ' "I'll get out of here as soon as I can. In the meantime, you are not to leave these premises – You understand?"'

'Of course she understood, a locked door is not difficult of comprehension. So she told her husband that she loved the French officer and her husband locked her up in the villa.' She reads books and no longer goes to the beach. She desperately wants to see Jacques. But she makes no attempt to; Janno remains essentially passive, both in her love and in her thinking about it. The scene never closes, and the manuscript dwindles away after a discourse on adultery. There are a few more pages, but the life and love that Zelda has been trying to describe, which are beyond Janno's control, are also beyond hers. Beyond even making an effort toward control. It is that failure that mars the entire novel and gives it its floating, directionless quality.

The writing of *Caesar's Things* occupied the last six years of Zelda's life, years without Scott, years of quiet balance punctuated by spells of relapse. It is a difficult novel to read and to understand not only because it is fragmentary and at times incoherent, but because of the peculiarity of Zelda's grammar, her piling of image upon image, her displacement of conventional syntax.

There are a number of fragments that accompany the novel and there is a characteristic that they share: each hovers on the edge of something about to happen. There is always a portentous ambience, a precarious situation which remains unfulfilled. Nothing is resolved. And a word Zelda uses again and again is *exigency*. The novel itself seems to be in this state: situations press, but the characters are held immobile. Zelda reveals a confused anguish as she reviews her life. *Caesar's Things* ends where it does by no accident, for Zelda is up against a decisive incident from her sane life and she cannot cope with it in conventional terms. She dodges the implications of Janno's affair with Jacques and its effects upon her marriage to Jacob, just as it seems Zelda had done in her romance with Jozan. The covertness of her setting on the Riviera underlines the mood of the affair itself, and Zelda's artistry lies in her being able to convey as much as she does. But in the end we blunder against the locks of her own vision, if not of her madness, and she veers from us.

Among the fragments of fiction left in Zelda's papers is one entitled 'The Big Top'. In this, Zelda again uses the names Janno and Jacob, but it has nothing to do with the novel as it stands. In it Zelda describes Janno's feelings upon the death of her husband.

> He was gone ... they had been much in love. He had been gone all summer and all winter for about a hundred years. Everything he did had been important.
> She wasn't going to have him anymore; not to promise her things nor to comfort her, nor just be there as general compensation. ... She was too old to make any more plans – the rest would have to be the best compromise.
> She remembered the ragged edges of his cuffs, and the neatness of his worn possessions, and the pleasure he always had from his pile of sheer linen handkerchiefs. When she had been away, or sick or something, Jacob never forgot the flowers, or big expensive books full of compensatory ideas about life. He never forgot to make life seem useful and promising, or forgot the grace of good friendship, or the use of making an effort.

This is not Janno, but Zelda, who in remembering Scott has registered his death. She ends by writing about herself.

Nobody has ever measured, even the poets, how much a heart can hold. ... When one really can't stand anymore, the limits are transgressed, and one thing has become another; poetry registers itself on the hospital charts, and heart-break has to be taken care of. ... But heart-break perishes in public institutions.

21

All these were excellent people; personable companions.
Morally, they were, perhaps, the last romantics, and it may
be that the worst enemy the romantic has to fear is time. Or it
may be that, like the earlier Romantics, they did not know
enough. But at least they knew their own predicament.

JOHN PEALE BISHOP

Throughout 1943 and into the beginning of 1944 Scott's will
was in probate. Under California law Zelda received half of
Fitzgerald's estate; she could count on roughly $15,000. Judge
Biggs, who was Scott's literary executor, advised the purchase
of an annuity for Zelda, which would yield her about $50 a
month for the rest of her life. There was also a small bank
account established for her, to be used only in an emergency.

Zelda and her mother had lived since 1940 in a white frame
bungalow at 322 Sayre Street, which was nicknamed 'Rabbit
Run' because of the compact arrangement of its small rooms.
Its tiny front porch was trimmed with green paint, and an
array of potted plants and climbing roses gave the exterior of
the house a cozy air. The inside of the cottage was simply
furnished: the front room contained an old upright piano, a
chintz-covered sofa and rockers, and a handsome cherry secretary from the Machen home. A visitor there recalls that the top
of the piano as well as the walls and end tables were covered
with family mementos and photographs, primarily of Zelda,
Scottie, and Scott, and that the general impression of the cottage was one of comfort without much style or flair. Two bedrooms, a kitchen with an outdoor patio behind it, and a dining
room made up the rest of the house. Zelda's eldest sister, Marjorie Brinson, and her family lived next door.

Sayre Street, which had once been in the most fashionable
part of Montgomery, was in a declining neighbourhood by the
1940s. Rooming houses had sprung up on the street during
the war, and there was constant noise from children running
on the street, taxis honking, screen doors slamming shut. Mrs

Sayre used to say 'Bottom Rail's getting on top!' Zelda took refuge in the quiet of the patio, where she painted.

In May and again in December of 1942, Zelda's paintings and sketches were put on exhibition at the Museum of Fine Arts and at the Woman's Club in Montgomery. In both exhibits there were a large number of pencil sketches of flowers. These were executed with exacting attention to detail; Zelda said they were drawn 'after the Chinese'. Among the twenty-one water colours and pencil drawings in the December show was a self-portrait and a painting of Scott. The portrait of Fitzgerald has been lost, but the one of Zelda survives. She glares full face out of the painting, her eyes dominating the portrait. Her mouth is pale and tight, her high cheekbones wide and accented by a flush of rose colour, which gives the face a curious flatness. The colours are muted and chalky. It is the intensity of the entire face that is jarring and memorable. There is something strained about the face; it has a stiffness, a quality of being visually tense that suffuses much of Zelda's work. The painting looks rigid on the paper.

Since Scott's death a change had slowly come over Zelda's letters to Scottie. In her earlier letters to her daughter she had often seemed to be straining for an effort of cleverness, an amusing touch, a phrase in French, as if to add sparkle to the monotonous surfaces of her messages. The change of tone must have reflected what Zelda felt her new role to be: she offered advice, somewhat gingerly, and she tried hard to be a conscientious and sensible parent. She worried about her daughter; she wanted Scottie to say her prayers and to pray for her as well.

I trust that life will use you far less inexorably than it has used me, but should it prove harder to master in later years than at present seems probable – you will be most grateful that your past does not present any profound cause of regret. ... If I seem querulous, and severe – such is not the case. I simply must (from desire to communicate from my heart from parental obligation and devotion) offer you whatever my tragic experience has mercifully indicated to be the best way of life. ... It isnt just a frustrate inhibited desire to assert myself, but my deepest love that makes me want you to love God and pray.

In February 1943 Scottie married Lieutenant (j.g.) Samuel Jackson Lanahan in New York. Lanahan was a Princeton man from Baltimore whom she had begun to date before Fitzgerald's death while she was at Vassar. It was a quick wartime wedding, with the handsome young groom in his dress blues and Scottie in a long white gown which Mrs Harold Ober (who had been a sort of foster mother to Scottie for years) bought for her the day before the ceremony. Shortly after their marriage Lanahan left Scottie for overseas duty.

Zelda did not go to her daughter's wedding. On 22 February she wrote Harold Ober: 'Giving Scottie away must have brought back the excitement of those days twenty-years ago when there was so much of everything adrift on the micaed spring time and so many aspirations afloat on the lethal twilights that one's greatest concern was which taxi to take and which magazine to sell to.' New York was, she said, 'a honeymoon mecca', a perfect place to begin. To Anne Ober, who made all of the wedding arrangements, Zelda wrote that she was disappointed that she 'couldn't be of any service'. She added that she received the wedding cake and shared it with John Dos Passos, who was passing through Montgomery on his way to Mobile to observe the war construction there.

Zelda wrote that she wanted Scottie to have whatever was left of her and Scott's housekeeping equipment. 'Do not consider these mine; your life contributed the greater solace and deepest pleasure of our domestic ventures and I wish that there were more adequate testimony of our happiness to give you – because, despite the brawls and the despairing, we had long periods of a felicity such as one does not often encounter when all we wanted was our family and to be together.' She said that after her mother died (quickly adding that she saw no reason why Mrs Sayre wouldn't continue for another decade) she might buy a cottage in North Carolina and just waste away under the pine trees.

Scottie decided that she would spend her 1943 summer vacation with Zelda in New York. The two-week trip in July was a delight for Zelda and a trial for Scottie, who could not help being edgy about her mother. Andrew Turnbull, who had just become a naval officer remembers going to see *Oklahoma!* with them both. He felt that Zelda, who extravagantly admired his handsomeness in his fresh white ducks, was 'acting the flirtatious *jeune fille*'. Scottie, sensitive to the warning signals of her mother's illness, was right to be uneasy about her behaviour. In August 1943 Zelda was back at Highland Hospital for the first time since she left in 1940. She wrote Anne Ober: 'Asheville is haunted by unhappy, uncharted remembrance for me.'

A staff member who worked closely with Zelda during her second stay at Highland remarked that when Zelda was ready to go home 'she looked almost pretty again, and cheerful. But, you see, it just wasn't permanent'. Her doctors knew perfectly well that Zelda's situation with her mother would not last for very long. There was, however, no other place for her to live, and in February 1944 Zelda returned to Montgomery.

Lucy Goldthwaite remembers seeing Zelda at a garden party that spring in Montgomery. Miss Goldthwaite had gone to high school with Zelda and had left Montgomery in the twenties for New York, where she eventually became an editor for *McCall's* magazine. When she was first in New York people who knew she was from Alabama would come up to her at cocktail parties and ask her if she knew Zelda and Scott Fitzgerald. 'You must remember how attractive they both were. They were so much of their time. I don't know if they would be considered beautiful today, but Scott really did look like the man in the Arrow collar ad!' She did not recognize the haggard woman who came up to her in the Southern garden in 1944 and said, 'Lucy, I'm Zelda Sayre.' Zelda's hair was dark and her permanent badly styled; her dress was long and shapeless. While Miss Goldthwaite assured Zelda that she had recognized her, Zelda explained that she had just returned from Asheville, where she had been recuperating from an illness. Looking directly at Lucy for a moment, Zelda said, 'We play parlor games from *The Ladies Home Journal*.' And in Miss Goldthwaite's startled silence Zelda quickly moved away from her. Later, Miss Goldthwaite remembers that Zelda spoke to her about Scottie, saying that she wanted Lucy to talk to her daughter in New York and tell her about herself when she was young and life was before her.

Zelda became intensely religious again in 1944 and, evangelical in her zeal, she mimeographed tracts that she wrote to save the souls of her friends. Because her friends included Gertrude Stein, Edmund Wilson, and Carl Van Vechten, her little religious essays were saved. She believed that she was in direct communication with God and she envisioned her friends as hellbound. In February she wrote Wilson: 'You should redeem yourself; pray and repent. Believing as I do that no matter what the floral catalogues may designate as rose, the odor remains funereal.' She later said that she did not like to think of his burning. 'You are much to be respected and handsome and have a genius for interesting people. You must look to your salvation.'

She also wrote Scottie such directives as this:

Right things are the best things to pursue and to do, by the nature of their being. A thing is right to do because it contributes the most constructive possibility; is right because the concensus of the best authorities have endorsed it; and is the *right* course because it is the most spiritually remunerative of any possibility – Knowing the right there isn't any alternative – because right is that which is most spiritually advantageous and all souls seek betterment. The purpose of life on earth is that the soul shall grow –

So grow – by doing what is right.

Zelda began to live more and more exclusively within these circles of rightness, altered only by remembering. Within a few months she was writing Scottie: 'Time passes: the japonica still blooms and the garden has been expectantly promisory with jonquils and the peach trees bud. . . . These rainy twilights are glamorous and sorrowful and make me wish that I weren't too old to remember tragic love-affairs.' Her life was peopled with memories. The editors of *The American Mercury* wrote to her asking permission to reprint 'Crazy Sunday' in a collection of their best work. They offered her $50. She told Scottie: 'Scott would have been so pleased; it is good that he is still remembered. I wish that my reams of epic literature would spin themselves out to a felicitous end. I write and write and have, in fact, progressed. The book [*Caesar's Things*] still makes little sense but makes it very beautifully and may find a reader or two eventually.'

Sometimes she got tired of making the best of everything, of having to be a financial wizard to keep herself off the rocks on $50 a month, and at those times she would admit to Scottie that her family in the South was 'oppressive and I am sick to death of hypochrondia and the simplicities of the poor. Maybe a few months in the mountains will give me a more sociable attitude.' It was during such periods as these that she would think back on her life with Scott.

I always feel that Daddy was the key-note and prophet of his generation and deserves remembrance as such since he dramatized the last post-war era & gave the real signifigance to those gala and so-tragicly fated days. He tabulated and greatly envied foot-ball players & famous atheletes and liked girls from the popular songs; he loved gorging on canned voluptés at curious hours and, as you have had many controversial run-ins with, was the longest & most exhaustive conversationalist I *ever* met. He loved people but was given to quick judgments and venomous enmities: I had few friends but I *never* quarreled with any; save once with a friend in the Paris Opera whom I loved. Daddy loved glamour & so I also had a great respect for popular acclame. I wish that I had been able to do better one thing & not so give[n] to running into cul-de-sac with so many.

Her moods did not lift easily, and when her life seemed to her useless, only faith gave her respite. She wrote Mrs Ober:

I used to feel desperately sad in the hospital when I thought of time going by and my being unable to turn it to any account, then I reconciled myself and had to accept with grace the implacable exigences of life. I would not exchange my experience for any other because it has brought me the knowledge of God. Revelations of His Divine presence are a greater honor than any which the world could give; a greater beauty and a more compelling inspiration.

She bought two doves and sat before the cage listening to their sounds, 'wishing that somebody would send me a Valentine'.

When Zelda learned that Scottie's husband was returning from active service she offered advice about decorating a home. She told Scottie to avoid 'imitation decorator's items'. Pewter pots, earthenware jugs, calico curtains, gingham table cloths and plain white Fiesta-ware dishes were more 'engaging' and cheaper. 'There isn't any real reason why sheets should be white: pink sheets would be most entertaining and one could sew the strips together with narrow embroidery. . . . *Don't* buy all the spoons and sauce-pans which one always seems to need. . . . They breed under the kitchen sink if left to themselves. . . .' She suggested 'croissants for breakfast' to make the meal more interesting for a man, 'unless they're like Daddy who not only wanted an egg every day but the *same* egg every day'.

At the beginning of 1946 she returned to Highland. Landon Ray, the athletic director, remembers one of their hikes together there, when they walked up and across Sunset Mountain near the Grove Park Inn. As they walked it began to rain, a light spring rain, 'but she had no complaints about her own discomfort. She seemed to enjoy just being there. Once we made camp the first thing we did was to build a fire. Zelda went for wood and I remember stopping while I was talking to one of the other people and just watching her going through the deep laurel and wet briar selecting the best pieces for kindling. The hike was a sort of test of mettle.' That vignette formed his final memory of Zelda – a dishevelled and middle-aged woman bending in the dim light and rain, alone and searching for wood.

While Zelda was at Highland, on 26 April 1946, Scottie's first child was born. Zelda had been certain Scottie would have a son and couldn't resist crowing with pleasure when it turned out she was right. Immediately after the birth of Timothy Lanahan, she wrote Scottie: 'Aren't you wonderful! What a good idea to have a 7½ lb boy! I don't feel any older, but I suppose I should put strings on my bonnets.' Five days after Timothy's birth Zelda sent Scottie another letter telling her she had been to see a movie of George White's *Scandals*. She felt dated; 'it brought back our honey-moon in New York. They sang "Bowl of Cherries" & I remembered our peregrinations through the lights of Broadway with Geo Nathan so many years ago.' It was wonderful to be a grandmother: 'I haven't been so beaming in years and I can't wait to hold him and see how he works. . . . Continue to be good and eat your ice-cream and you will be well and at home in no time. . . .'

To Ludlow Fowler she wrote: 'It is completely incredible to me that one of my generation should be a grandmother; Time is no respector of convention anymore and goes on as if behaving in a rational manner. . . . Down here the little garden blows remotely poetic under the voluptes of late spring skies. I have a cage of doves who sing and woo the elements and die. . . .'

At the end of the summer Zelda went East to see her grandson for herself. She went on from New York to visit the Biggses in Wilmington. Mrs Biggs recalls that she had picked some berries for the centre of her table because she thought Zelda might like them. As Zelda passed through the dining room she stopped by the table and said, 'There are berries on your table!' Mrs Biggs didn't know what to say and waited. 'They have thorns. The crown of thorns. Christ wore a crown of thorns. You must get rid of them immediately!' Not wanting to disturb her, Mrs Biggs threw the berries out quickly, but for a moment she was afraid of Zelda.

On Zelda's last evening at the Biggses' they were all sitting on a porch waiting to leave. Mrs Biggs remembers: 'John mentioned that it was time to catch the train back to Montgomery. Zelda didn't seem to pay any attention and we stressed it a little more obviously. It was late. Perhaps we'd better get into the car, and so forth. Zelda said we didn't need to worry, the train would not be on time anyway. We laughed and said, perhaps, but it was a risk we didn't intend to take. "Oh, no", she said, "it will be all right. Scott has told me. Can't you see him sitting here beside me?"' The Biggses were speechless, neither knowing what to say or do. At last Judge Biggs insisted that they leave. 'When we got to the station we had a half hour wait. The train *was* going to be late.' It was in an uneasy silence that they waited together until it came.

Mrs Ober was on the train, since Zelda had persuaded her to

visit Montgomery. She remembers the trip with mixed feelings; she had gone for Scottie's sake, not for Zelda's. She liked Mrs Sayre enormously. 'She was a marvelous woman, big and comfortable. She was very protective about Zelda; she was her baby, after all. I remember asking her about the South during the Civil War, and she answered me, "Darling, just read *Gone With the Wind*." ' Zelda would not always get up in the mornings; when she did finally make her appearance they would all have their 'meat' breakfast, which consisted of ham and sausages and bacon and grits and delicious hot cakes. They would eat again at midday for the last time, because the maid went home after that. 'Zelda', Mrs Ober thinks, 'played her mother's protectiveness for all it was worth, played on it all the time. I don't think Mrs Sayre ever understood Zelda.' When they all talked together Zelda would reminisce about being a girl in Montgomery, and about her life with Scott.

By October 1946 Zelda, who had caught cold in New York, was on the edge of another collapse. She wrote Anne Ober that she would despair were it not for the knowledge 'that God can help me if He so wills – thus I live; hoping to find grace and knowing that no agency of man can be of any assistance'. In November her asthma returned. It kept her from sleeping half the night, and 'evil spirits plague the other half. I beseech the Lord until I do not see how God could in justice ignore my plaints – still I do not progress.' She felt herself growing old 'enveloped in dreams and lost in yearnings' and she fretted about her greying hair and her increased weight. Still, she held on. She painted bowls for Scottie depicting the various places they had lived during her childhood; Zelda said they would form 'a real saga of your life'. She asked for a photograph of Scottie's first house, or of the church she had been married in, for the salad bowl. She etched trays for the Biggses and the Obers. And when she could she received those few visitors who came to see her.

Paul McLendon met Zelda for the first time in 1941, when he was in high school in Montgomery. He was a friend of Livye Hart Ridgeway's son, and Livye Hart and Zelda had been friends since girlhood. In his freshman year at the University of

Alabama his room-mate was crazy about F. Scott Fitzgerald and was trying, according to Paul, to run himself out as Fitzgerald had. When he learned that Paul had met Zelda he pressed him for details. A little embarrassed that he could remember none, Paul decided he would call on her the next weekend he was home. He did, and thereafter became a frequent visitor. Paul wanted to be a writer, and brought his stories to Zelda for criticism. After one such afternoon's talk, Zelda wrote him, 'I am not au-courrant with the affairs & morals of our day and live, indeed an anachronism. ...' But she was deeply troubled by a story he had written and she wanted to know: 'What happened to you? Young men once believed in the Sunday school picnic & the Constitution of the United States. I grievously lament that so much of contemporary literature should present such bitterness and misgiving. ...' Still, whatever her doubts were, she gave him good direct advice about his story. She said it could use more atmosphere and she suggested he write it twice more, then send it off to *Harper's Magazine*. At the end of her letter she asked him to 'Be good'.

A few months later, when Paul told her about a novel he wanted to write and about his fears that it might draw too deeply upon the lives of people close to him, Zelda, who understood such problems all too well, told him that 'the world is fair game to the greedy themes of the literary-minded. It is difficult to make one's close associates realize that all things are meat to a writer's imagination and that interpretation & transpositions are the biggest part of his game and are not always transgressions of devotion. ... I'd just go on & write & explain to my friends later, you'll probably have to apologize anyway.' She also said she wasn't looking forward to winter that year and she asked him if it was not too late for a picnic in the park together: '– The woods are a romantic idyll at this time of year over which I dream & reminisce.'

Paul realized that Zelda enjoyed his company partly because he brought her into contact with a younger world than the one in which she lived with her mother. Mrs Sayre, who suffered from rheumatism, rarely left her house any more. Her snow-white hair was worn in braids about her head and she was always seen sitting in a rocker on her front porch wearing long cotton housedresses and solid Aunt Pittypat shoes. She was, however, an alert old woman with a tart wit and she enjoyed nothing better than talking with the cronies who gathered around her in the afternoon. But it was a restricted world for Zelda, who often spent long hours indoors listening to her record player. Once after Paul had invited her for a day at Tuscaloosa she replied: '... please forgive and ask me later again and I will be so happy to share with you the idyll of youth ....' She said she was ill and harassed by 'evil spirits' from the 'spirit world (which really do not deserve a trip to a university.) ... – Please let me come some other time.'

Usually when Paul came to visit, Mrs Sayre would stay chatting for a few minutes with them both as if to make sure that everything was all right and then leave him and Zelda to their long conversations. But one afternoon Mrs Sayre told him Zelda couldn't talk to him that day, and she asked him to keep her company on the porch. They were talking when suddenly a cry came from inside the house. It was a low wail, like that of a wounded animal, rather than a human cry. In an instant the cry stopped and then a door slammed shut violently. Mrs Sayre and McLendon were silent. Then Mrs Sayre said, 'You know I've had that door facing replaced three times.' McLendon left shortly afterward.

On good days Zelda and he would sit for hours talking about the times she had shared with Scott in Paris in the twenties. He noticed that it was in recollection and reverie that her conversation flowed most easily. But she seemed to him plagued with a sense of repentance. Again and again she would speak or write to him about Divine Purpose, atonement, and forgiveness of sins. McLendon would listen and try to remember. In the winter they sat in front of the fire, in summertime out on the patio at the rear of the cottage. On its walls Zelda had painted colourful murals from scenes of her life with Scott.

McLendon remembers one of the last times he saw Zelda.

The time was early, early spring. Flowers were beginning to bloom, though the air was still nippy and the wind brisk. It was a Saturday, and I was home from Tuscaloosa for the weekend. I went by to see Zelda, and while there, I told her of a pair of Alfred von Munchausen prints I had seen in a store window downtown, and of how much I liked them. Zelda said that we should walk to town so that I could point the pictures out to her, and then she would paint a similar picture for me.

Zelda went to her room for a moment, and returned wearing a rather strange collage of attire – a dress length coat of deep blue wool, with gray caracul fur about the collar & cuffs – & on her head, a very dark green felt cloche-type hat – from the crown of which were long streamers of green felt, end-tipped at the shoulders with white felt dogwood blossoms.

We began our walk to town, and her spirits were soaring – as were my own – the day was beautiful & we were off on a lark. After only a block & a half, or so, there were three children walking toward us on the sidewalk, two girls & a boy – ages about 9, 11, 12. As they approached, Zelda & I were talking, but when we were 3 or 4 yards from them we both saw one of the girls punch the other & say, 'You see there, there's that crazy woman mamma's been telling us about!' and they passed us by.

They continued walking in absolute silence. Zelda had heard the girl and turning to Paul she quietly told him she didn't feel too well. They could go to town another day. Together they walked back to her little house.

On 10 March 1947 Zelda wrote to Paul and told him that she was ill, and although she suffered, 'He sends His angels to help. ...' She said she could see a lone jonquil blooming in her garden. And she was painting to make 'pin money with trays & trays & trays'.

Henry Dan Piper was discharged from the Army at Anniston, Alabama, that same March. He'd gone to Princeton as an undergraduate and while there became greatly intrigued by Scott Fitzgerald's writing. He decided to take advantage of his proximity to Scott's widow and to try to visit her in Montgomery. He had only a weekend, 13 and 14 March, in which to see Zelda and he wasn't sure she would want to talk to him. But he telephoned and Zelda immediately invited him to come by at four o'clock that same afternoon for tea. She met him at the door to the cottage and began by apologizing, 'I don't have much to tell you'.

As Piper took off an old camel's hair polo coat he had bought from Finchley's in New York while at Princeton, Zelda reached out to touch it and said, delightedly, 'Oh, it looks just like Scott's!'

Piper was moved by the winsomeness of her gesture and remembers feeling that there was something not only spontaneous about her reaction but very feminine. Watching her as she began to speak, Piper noticed that her hair was darker than he had expected, and greying. She wore black, a plain voile dress with girlish lace trimmings at the sleeves and throat. Her nose was sharp and pointed and she wore a little too much powder. Her mouth was thin-lipped. He says: 'Every once in a while her face would grow strained, and the mouth fall away and be lost in a hundred deep lines that decomposed all her lower face and gave her an aged ugliness. She had a strange mannerism of now and then screwing up her eyes into many wrinkles and looking away into space, working her mouth and lips.' As his glance strayed over her he noticed that her legs and hands and fingers were older looking than his first impression of them. Her hands particularly looked gnarled from strain.

Mrs Sayre was with them at the beginning of their conversation, but soon retired to the kitchen. Zelda followed her and began bringing out an abundance of cakes and pastries she said she had made herself. There were custards with meringue, small frosted cakes, honey biscuits with curls of sweet butter – much more than they could possibly eat.

Piper began by assuring Zelda of his interest in Scott's writing. He let her know he had read everything Fitzgerald had written and he was considering writing a biography. Then he tried to draw her out about their life together. He says: 'Zelda was amazed and touched, I think, by my interest. She several times said to me, "Oh, how flattered Scott would be to think that people still remember him." '

Then she began to discuss her own writing. She told Piper she had been working on a novel which would be called *Caesar's Things*, for she had learned to separate, she said,

Caesar's things from God's. Their conversation moved quickly from one subject to another. On the whole it tended to be a theoretical and energetic, but abstract discussion, with neither of them, according to Piper, paying much attention to the other's opinions. She asked him at one point if he didn't believe in revelations, saying, 'I know! I've had them! I have been dead and seen another world and come back again alive to this one.' Zelda was taken with the idea of Fascism as a way of holding everything together, of ordering the masses. She told Piper she joined every organization she could 'to keep things from falling apart and to keep the finer things from being lost or extinguished.'

Relaxing with him at last she said: 'Well, now, tell me about your work. I think it's a fine idea, by all means. Surely a biography – He was so fine a person and had a really interesting life.

'Nora Flynn – he loved her I think – not clandestinely, but she was one of several women he always needed around him to stimulate him and to turn to when he got low and needed a lift. Sara Murphy was that way, too.'

Piper then told her about the collection of Scott's personal and literary papers he had seen five years earlier at Judge Biggs's. Shortly after he mentioned this Zelda seemed shaken and told him she had to lie down. She said that her mother would take care of him, and that although she regretted leaving him, when she was tired she had to rest. She invited him to return for lunch the following day. They went back and forth about the time, finally settling on twelve-thirty, and Zelda left the room.

Piper wrote this down about the last few moments of that first day:

In our brief talk of Scott, I had emphasized the disparity between his good and bad stories – some were full of poetry, others of forced writing and a concocted plot. But she didn't get my point.

[Zelda said] 'I always felt a story in the Post was tops; a goal worth seeking. It really meant something, you know – they only took stories of real craftsmanship. But Scott couldn't stand to write them. He was completely cerebral, you know. All mind.' ... Only when I mentioned the marvelous passages at the opening of Gatsby, with the wind rippling coolly and setting everything in motion was she really alert – listening to me with more than half an ear. At this delightful reference her eyes lighted up and smiled charmingly. She has suffered much around the eyes, but they are still grey and very alert.

The next day Piper came promptly at twelve-thirty only to find Zelda wringing her hands and quite distressed, insisting that they had set the time for twelve. She and Mrs Sayre had already eaten. But they had saved dinner for him and out of the kitchen came delicious fried chicken, rice, candied yams, tomatoes and lettuce, with cake and plums for dessert.

It was during their second meeting that Zelda showed Dan Piper her portfolio of paintings, as well as some illustrations she was painting for her eleven-month-old grandson based on the Book of Genesis and Grimm's fairy tales. A great many were paintings of flowers. All were in motion, it seemed to him. Zelda said to him about her art: 'What I want to do is to paint the basic, fundamental principle so that everyone will be forced to realize and experience it – I want to paint a ballet step so all will know what it is – to get the fundamental essence into the painting.'

After lunch they walked to Montgomery's art museum to look at Zelda's paintings. Walking back she told him Scottie and her family were coming for a visit in June and that she knew she would be tired out afterward and have to return to Asheville to rest. She said it was good to know that she could go there to rest, that it reassured her.

Piper remembers the energy that radiated from her, her quick tenseness. She walked rapidly and gestured jerkily. Afterward they stopped at a small bar in town. He had heard that she must absolutely have no liquor, but she insisted on going into the bar. Piper ordered a beer, and Zelda to his relief ordered a vanilla soda, which had to be brought in from a drugstore. He remembers sitting opposite her, making small talk, wondering if the alcohol was a temptation for her, wondering if the entire two days had been a charade, but deciding that they couldn't have been. For a moment he just enjoyed having her opposite him, the legendary and forgotten Zelda as his companion.

When they were finished they returned to her little house and she gave him the portrait of herself.

At the beginning of June 1947 Scottie, her husband, and their baby did come South and Zelda gave a party for them at the Blue Moon restaurant. There were twenty at the table and the food was delicious, ample Southern fare. However, one of the women who was there commented about the guests: 'If Charles Dickens had been present he would have written a sequel to *Pickwick Papers*. There was the oddest assortment of animals.' Nevertheless, neither Scottie nor Jack behaved as if that were the case. Jack stood and made a beautiful toast to his mother-in-law, which very much pleased Zelda.

But it was clear to everyone that Zelda was not well. By the end of the hot summer she was close to collapse, she grew weak and furtive, and she refused to see a doctor. Finally, Mrs Sayre called Scottie. On 2 November 1947 Zelda returned to Highland Hospital for treatment and rest. A taxi was called to take her to the train. Mrs Sayre, Marjorie, and Livye Hart stood on the sidewalk by the porch, having said their good-byes. Suddenly, just as Zelda was about to enter the taxi, she turned and ran back up to her mother. She said, 'Momma, don't worry. I'm not afraid to die.' Then she left them.

At the beginning of 1948 Zelda was given a series of insulin treatments and was moved to the top floor of the main building at Highland, where patients stayed while recovering from them. In early March in a letter to her mother she wrote that in Asheville the jasmine was in full flower and crocuses dotted the lawns. She wanted to get home, she said, to see 'our lillies and larkspur bloom in the garden and I'd like to be there to watch the fires die down'. She thought her bridge game was getting better and she played twice a week; she sewed and took long walks; she thanked her mother for her constant devotion.

On 9 March she wrote Scottie that the snow had fallen once again just as she thought winter was finally over. She had been at Highland four months and during that period Scottie's second child, a daughter, was born. Zelda told her she had gained twenty pounds owing to the insulin treatments, 'making a grand total of 130 lbs at which I shudder in the privacy of my boudoir'. Scottie's maternity clothes would probably fit her perfectly, she said, and she would need something to travel home in when she would at last be released.

'Anyhow: to-day there is promise of spring in the air and an aura of sunshine over the mountains; the mountains seem to hold more weather than elsewhere and time and retrospect flood roseate down the long hill-sides. . . . I long to see the new baby, Tim must be phenomenal by this time.'

At midnight the following night, 10 March, a fire broke out in the diet kitchen of the main building where Zelda was sleeping. The flames shot up a small dumbwaiter shaft to the roof and leaped out onto each of the floors. The stairways and corridors were filled with smoke. A pair of stockings pinned to a line on a porch on the top floor could be seen dancing wildly in the wind created by the heat of the fire. There was no automatic fire-alarm system in the old stone-and-frame building and no sprinkler system. The fire escapes were external, but they were made of wood and quickly caught fire. Firemen and staff members struggled valiantly to bring the patients to safety, but they were hampered by locked doors, and by heavy windows shackled with chains. Nine women were killed, six of them trapped on the top floor. Zelda died with them.

Her body was identified by a charred slipper lying beneath it. She was taken to Maryland for burial. It was St Patrick's Day, 17 March 1948, and the day was warm and sunny, in striking contrast to the cold, raw afternoon when Scott was buried. The service was simple and a small group of friends stayed until her grave was filled in. Her death seemed a relief and they felt bound together by their memories of the Fitzgeralds; they shared a haunting intimacy in witnessing the last and mortal death of Zelda. Clusters of bright spring flowers were placed upon the raw turf of her grave, and Mrs Turnbull brought two wreaths of pansies from La Paix and placed them over Scott and Zelda, who were at last in peace together.

NOTES AND SOURCES

The following abbreviations are used. My pagination is usually to the most available edition, which is indicated in parentheses.

B&D *The Beautiful and Damned*, Charles Scribner's Sons, New York, 1922. (The Scribner Library paperback.)

CT *Caesar's Things*, an unpublished novel by Zelda Fitzgerald.

CU *The Crack-Up*, edited by Edmund Wilson, New Directions, New York, 1945. (New Directions Paperbook, 4th printing, 1959.)

FSF F. Scott Fitzgerald.

Gatsby *The Great Gatsby*, Charles Scribner's Sons, New York, 1925. (The Scribner Library paperback.)

Ledger Fitzgerald's 189-page record book from which some pages have been torn and others are missing. It contains 'Record of Published Fiction; Novels, Plays, Stories (Not including Unpaid for Juvenilia)', his 'Earnings by years', 'Zelda's Earnings', and a 39-page 'Autobiographical Chart', or 'Outline of My Life'.

Letters *The Letters of F. Scott Fitzgerald*, edited by Andrew Turnbull, Charles Scribner's Sons, New York, 1963.

NM Nancy Milford

Scottie Frances Scott Fitzgerald Lanahan Smith

SMTW *Save Me the Waltz*, Zelda Fitzgerald, Charles Scribner's Sons, New York, 1932. (Southern Illinois University Press, 1967. Hardcover.)

Tender *Tender Is the Night*, Charles Scribner's Sons, New York, 1934. (The Scribner Library paperback of the original text.)

Cowley – *Tender* *Three Novels of F. Scott Fitzgerald*; *Tender Is the Night*, 'The Author's Final Version,' edited by Malcolm Cowley, Charles Scribner's Sons, New York, 1953.

TSOP *This Side of Paradise*, Charles Scribner's Sons, New York, 1920. (The Scribner Library paperback.)

ZSF Zelda Sayre Fitzgerald

It is difficult to imagine having had to work without the benefit of the two biographies of F. Scott Fitzgerald – the excellent *The Far*

Side of Paradise by Arthur Mizener, and the deeply moving *Scott Fitzgerald* by the late Andrew Turnbull. I am grateful for them both. Among the many books and articles that I read while preparing to write this book, the following were especially helpful: *The Composition of Tender Is the Night* by Matthew J. Bruccoli; *That Summer in Paris* by Morley Callaghan; *The Mind of the South* by W. J. Cash; *Beloved Infidel* and *College of One* by Sheilah Graham; *I Never Promised You a Rose Garden* by Hannah Green; *A Moveable Feast* by Ernest Hemingway; *The Apprentice Fiction of F. Scott Fitzgerald, 1909–1917*, edited by John Kuehl; *The Divided Self, The Politics of Experience* and *The Bird of Paradise* by R. D. Laing; *The Genain Quadruplets*, edited by David Rosenthal; *Schizophrenia as a Human Process* by Harry Stack Sullivan; 'Living Well Is the Best Revenge', Calvin Tomkins' *New Yorker* profile of Gerald and Sara Murphy; *Patriotic Gore* and *The Shores of Light* by Edmund Wilson.

Prologue

page

xiii I remember Gerald Murphy . . . : Gerald Murphy to NM, interview, 26 April 1963.

xiii Sara Murphy caught something of it . . . : Sara Murphy to FSF, 20 August [no year].

xiv I remember talking to two old men . . . : Colonel Jesse Traywick to NM, interview, 31 May 1968.

xiv How curious that the same woman . . . : *Letters*, p. 173.

xvi Once Zelda asked the lady . . . : Mrs Nash Read to NM, interview, 27 July 1963.

xvi. Writing about Montgomery . . . : 'Southern Girl', *College Humor*, October 1929. p. 27.

Chapter 1

3 If there was a confederate . . . : Sara Mayfield to NM, interview, 16 March 1965.

3 Willis B. Machen . . . : *Cyclopaedia of American Biography*, edited by James Grant Wilson and John Fiske, Vol. IV, D. Appleton & Co., New York, 1888.

Lamb's *Biographical Dictionary of the United States*, edited by John Howard Brown, Vol. V, Federal Book Company of Boston, 1903.

W. H. Perrin, *et al.*, *Kentucky, A History of the State*, 5th ed., Batten, Louisville, 1887.

5 Anthony's mother, Musidora Morgan, was the sister of . . . : Senator Morgan became something of a national figure when he urged annexation of Cuba and the Philippines. He was an expansionist who envisioned an Isthmian canal as a gateway of Southern trade with the Pacific.

See the *Dictionary of American Biography*, edited by Dumas Malone, Vol. XIII, Charles Scribner's Sons, New York, 1943, pp. 180–81. Zelda was also related through her paternal grandmother to the flamboyant and wily Confederate brigadier general 'Raider' John Hunt Morgan. See Edmund Wilson, *Patriotic Gore: Studies in the Literature of the American Civil War*, Oxford University Press, New York, 1962.

6 The first years of the Sayres' marriage ... : Helen F. Blackshear, 'Mama Sayre, Scott Fitzgerald's Mother-in-Law', *The Georgia Review*, Winter, 1965, Vol. XIX, # 4, Athens, Georgia.

7 He worked relentlessly and well ... : *Who Was Who in America*, Vol. I, The A. N. Marquis Company, New York, 1942.

8 When Zelda was asked later ... : The following quoted material is excerpted from records kept during Zelda's stay at Les Rives de Prangins, 5 June 1930, to 15 September 1931, and was prepared and translated for the author by Mme Claude Amiel at the direction of Doctor Oscar Forel, who first diagnosed Zelda Fitzgerald a schizophrenic. Hereafter this material will be referred to as Prangins.

10 The Pleasant Avenue house ... : Mrs Everet Addison to NM, 8 December 1965.

11 A younger friend of hers ... : Sara Mayfield to NM, interview, 16 March 1965.

11 In 1909 Zelda's father was appointed ... : Elizabeth S. Fritz to NM, 2 November 1965.

12 Her schoolmates noticed ... : Mrs H. L. Weatherby to NM, 12 August 1963.

13 She read whatever she found ... : Prangins.

14 Whether she was stylish ... : Mrs E. Addison to NM, 15 September 1965.

14 At fifteen Zelda was striking ... : Mrs E. Addison to NM, 29 September 1965.

Chapter 2

15 To make sure that all went smoothly ... : Leon Ruth to NM, interview, 30 July 1963.

16 That summer a story appeared ... : ZSF's scrapbook. This is a personal scrapbook kept by ZSF which includes mementos from childhood through 1924.

17 One of her beaus remembers her ... : Fred Ball to NM, interview, 30 July 1963.

17 There is a snapshot of her ... : ibid.

18 Later in her life she wrote about Alabama Beggs ... : *SMTW*, p. 29.

19 For even as her father's position ... : *SMTW*, p. 26.

20 Mrs Sayre remembered ... : Mike Fitzgerald, ' "So You'd Like to Hear About Scott ..." ', The San Diego *Union*, 10 November 1963, p. e6.

20 The men came from every imaginable ... : *SMTW*, pp. 34–5.

22 On their way they passed ... : Mrs Virginia Breslin to NM, 2 November 1965.

22 Key-Ice had as its central ritual . . . : Carl Carmer, *Stars Fell on Alabama*, The Literary Guild, New York, 1934, p. 15.
23 The tensions inherent in that charade of Southern womanhood . . . : *SMTW*, p. 56.
23 School wasn't going well . . . : Montgomery Public Schools, to NM, 13 October 1965.
23 She remarked later . . . : Prangins.
23 On April Fool's Day . . . : Mrs E. Addison to NM, 25 June 1965.
24 There had been a lot of discussion about what the girls should wear . . . : Lucy Goldthwaite to NM, interview, 20 May 1965.
25 At the last moment Zelda sat in the audience . . . : Irby Jones to NM, interview, 30 July 1963.

Chapter 3

26 It was a hot Saturday night . . . : Mike Fitzgerald, ' "So You'd Like to Hear About Scott . . ." ', the San Diego *Union*, 10 November 1963, p. e6.
26 Later in her life Zelda remembered . . . : *SMTW*, p. 35.
26 Once having met . . . : Edmund Wilson to NM, 19 July 1965.
27 Scott once wrote . . . : *The Romantic Egotist*, FSF unpublished novel, p. 2.
27 'He . . . came from another America . . .': 'The Death of My Father', *The Apprentice Fiction of F. Scott Fitzgerald, 1909–1917*, edited by John Kuehl, Rutgers University Press, New Brunswick, 1965, pp. 178–80.
27 And it was from his father . . . : *The Romantic Egotist*, p. 4.
28 It is not surprising, then, to discover . . .: 'Princeton', *Afternoon of an Author*, Charles Scribner's Sons, New York, p. 72.
28 As Scott's biographer Arthur Mizener . . . : Arthur Mizener, *The Far Side of Paradise* (2nd ed.), Houghton Mifflin Company, Boston, p. 14.
28 He once wrote his daughter . . . : *Letters*, p. 5.
28 He not only cared deeply about what others thought . . . : *Thoughtbook of Francis Scott Key Fitzgerald*, Princeton University Library, Princeton, 1965, p. xvi, xxiii.
29 'I saw a musical comedy . . .': 'Who's Who – and Why', *Afternoon of an Author*, p. 83.
29 Mizener observes that . . . : *The Far Side of Paradise*, p. 29.
29 He decided to become . . . : *TSOP*, p. 43.
30 As a classmate of Scott's said . . . : Professor Gregg Dougherty to NM, interview, July 1966.
30 He wrote the lyrics for *Fie! Fie! Fi-Fi!* . . . : 'Princeton', *Afternoon of an Author*, p. 75.
30 He later wrote that he would never forget . . . : *CU*, p. 24.
31 The young man who would write of the hero . . . : *TSOP*, pp. 17–18.
31 'But I had lost certain offices . . .': *CU*, p. 76.
31 As he wrote later, 'A man does not recover . . .' : ibid.
31 In 'A Luckless Santa Claus' . . . : *Apprentice Fiction*, p. 48.
32 She says of herself . . . : ibid., pp. 97–8.
32 In 'Babes in the Woods' . . . : ibid., p. 136.

32 She has 'beauty and the most direct . . .': ibid. pp. 168–9.
33 'I wandered around . . .': ibid., p. 170.
33 'He knew what was wrong . . . .' : ibid., p. 151.
34 Fitzgerald spent the summer of 1917 . . . : *Letters*, p. 318.
34 He had also begun a novel . . . : ibid., p. 323.
35 Shane Leslie, an Irish novelist and critic . . . : Shane Leslie to Charles Scribner, n.d.
35 Scott sent a chapter of it to Zelda . . . : FSF to ZSF, n.d. ZSF's scrapbook.
36 Scott never forgot his first invitation . . . : Gerald Murphy to NM, interview, 26 April 1963. It is altogether possible that Scott or even Zelda made up this incident to add pungency to the story of their courtship, for it does not seem in keeping with Judge Sayre's sense of decorum. On the other hand, the Judge was seriously ill for nine months in 1918 with 'nervous prostration', according to Mrs Sayre, who nursed him.
36 Describing her attraction to him . . . : *SMTW*, p. 37.
37 Many years later she wrote: 'He was almost certainly falling in love . . .' : *CT*, Chapter IV, p. 30.
37 She teased him . . . : ibid., p. 32.
38 He wrote a letter to an old friend . . . : *Letters*, p. 454.
38 He was to call it 'The most important . . .' : Ledger, p. 173.
38 Cautious as she had been in the late autumn . . . : Notebooks, G., 'Descriptions of Girls'.
39 All of the dances on Zelda's card . . . : ZSF's scrapbook.
39 'She, she told herself . . .' : *SMTW*, p. 29.
39 In a gesture of consummate confidence . . . : ZSF's scrapbook.

Chapter 4

41 But Scott did keep Zelda's . . . : *TSOP*, p. 198.
41 He showed it to at least one friend . . . : Stephen Parrott to FSF, 27 April 1919.
42 At the end of February Zelda told him . . . : ZSF to FSF, n.d. (ca. February 1919).
    All of Zelda's letters to Scott in the text of this chapter were written during their February–June 1919 courtship and undated.
42 At the bottom of his invitation to Auburn . . . : ZSF's scrapbook.
42 Today he remembers Zelda as . . . : Francis Stubbs to NM, 28 December 1965.
43 He had arrived in the city . . . : 'Who's Who – and Why', *Afternoon of an Author*, p. 85.
46 On 22 March he wired her . . . : FSF to ZSF, 22 March 1919, ZSF's scrapbook.
47 Scott again wired her . . . : FSF to ZSF, n.d. ZSF's scrapbook.
49 He put her letter almost verbatim . . . : *TSOP*, p. 170.
50 After the trip he wrote in his Ledger . . . : Ledger, p. 173.
54 His story 'Babes in the Woods' . . . : *CU*, pp. 59, 86.
54 Adding, with that touch of self-perception . . . : See *TSOP*, p. 170.
56 The society columns and rotogravure sections . . . : ZSF's scrapbook.

57 Edgy and fatigued, knowing full well . . . : *CU*, p. 86.
57 They sat together in the familiar front room . . . : See FSF short
   story, 'The Sensible Thing'. In *Letters*, p. 189, he wrote Maxwell
   Perkins that it was 'about Zelda and me, all true . . .'
58 He believed, as he would soon write . . . : *TSOP*, p. 216.

Chapter 5

59 In a story Zelda wrote later . . . : 'Southern Girl', *College Humor*,
   October 1929, p. 27.
59 'The drug stores are bright at night . . .' : ibid.
60 He had decided to rewrite his novel . . . : *CU*, p. 85.
60 He wrote Edmund Wilson . . . : *Letters*, pp. 324–5.
60 As soon as he received word of its acceptance . . . : ibid., p. 139.
61 In a section of the novel called 'The Débutante' . . . : FSF to Shane
   Leslie, 6 August 1920 (*Letters*, p. 376). 'I married the Rosalind of the
   novel, the southern girl I was so attached to, after a grand reconciliation.'
61 'Rosalind', he wrote 'is – utterly . . .': *TSOP*, pp. 170–72.
61 'I'm mighty glad you're coming – . . .' : ZSF to FSF, n.d. (ca. fall
   1919).
61 After he heard from Zelda, he wrote to Ludlow Fowler . . . : FSF
   to Ludlow Fowler, n.d. (ca. fall 1919).
62 Before he left again wrote Fowler . . . : FSF to Ludlow Fowler, postmarked 10 November 1919.
62 In a story called 'The Sensible Thing' . . . : *The Stories of F. Scott
   Fitzgerald*, edited by Malcolm Cowley, Scribner's, New York, 1951,
   pp. 156, 158.
62 Nonetheless, before he left . . . : *Letters*, p. 144.
62 And she added: 'Somehow . . .' : ZSF to FSF, n.d.
63 The cheeky young man who wrote . . . : *Letters*, p. 456.
63 'all the iridescence . . .' : *CU*, p. 25.
63 After she had read it she wrote . . . : ZSF to FSF, n.d.
63 Scott had already begun to make plans . . . : ZSF to FSF, n.d.
64 'THE SATURDAY EVENING POST . . .' : Both of these telegrams are
   in ZSF's scrapbook.
65 In his Ledger he wrote . . . : Ledger, p. 174.
65 'Yesterday I almost wrote a book or story . . .' : ZSF to FSF, n.d.
66 Mamma came in with the package . . .' : ZSF to FSF, n.d. (ca.
   January 1920).
66 During Scott's trips up from New Orleans . . . : ZSF to FSF, n.d.
   Scott, who nearly always drew deeply on his own life in his fiction, had
   begun a new novel called *Darling Heart*, 'which turned completely on
   the seduction of the girl . . .' (*Letters*, p. 143.) By February he had given
   it up. Just how deeply the experience of sex with Zelda before their
   marriage marked him can only be guessed at. Certainly he felt ambi-
   valent about it. Later in his life he was to embarrass Hemingway,
   Gerald Murphy and several other men by asking them if they had
   slept with their wives before marriage. Seduction of Daisy by Gatsby
   and the affair of Anthony Patch and Dorothy Raycroft in *The Beau-*

tiful and Damned are examples of ways in which he cast his feelings about himself and Zelda.

66 On 26 February, while staying at Cottage . . . : Mrs Isabel Amorous Palmer to N M, 26 February 1968.

67 'No personality as strong as Zelda's . . .' : FSF to Isabel Amorous, 26 February 1920.

67 He then wired Zelda . . . : ZSF's scrapbook.

67 He had in his hand a colour-illustrated . . .: C. Lawton Campbell memoir, 'The Fitzgeralds Were My Friends', unpublished. Hereafter this fascinating account of Mr Campbell's relationship to the Fitzgeralds will be referred to as Campbell Memoir..

68 'Darling Heart, our fairy tale is almost ended . . .' : ZSF to FSF, n.d. (ca. March 1920).

69 At last they decided to marry on .'. . : FSF to ZSF, 30 March 1920. ZSF's scrapbook.

Chapter 6

73 Zelda and Scott put their first . . . : *C U*, p. 60.

73 Somewhat painfully Scott saw Zelda for the first time . . . : FSF, 'Does a Moment of Revolt Come Sometime to Every Married Man?' *McCall's*, March 1924, p. 21.

73 Zelda had organdy dresses with great flounces . . . : Mrs Marie Hersey Hamm to NM, 1 September 1965.

73 She wrote later: 'It was the first garment . . .': *C U*, p. 60.

74 'Vincent Youmans wrote the music . . .': *S M T W*, p. 45–6.

74 Scott undressed at the *Scandals* . . . : *C U*, pp. 27, 28, 41.

74 As she wrote in *Save Me* . . . : *S M T W*, p. 42.

74 Dorothy Parker never forgot meeting Zelda . . . : Dorothy Parker to NM, interview, 26 August 1964.

75 Scott was suddenly 'the arch type . . .': *C U*, pp. 26–7.

75 He kept a diary in which he made frequent entries . . . : Alexander McKaig Diary, 1919–1921. All quotations from McKaig are excerpted from this diary.

76 Dorothy Parker's impressions of Zelda . . . : Dorothy Parker to NM, interview, 26 August 1964.

76 'When I entered, the room was bedlam . . .' : Campbell Memoir.

76 Their own conversation ran playfully . . . : *S M T W*, pp. 46–8.

77 'We watched him wave his cigarette . . .': 'Re Gossip Shop', *The Bookman*, April 1921, p. 190.

77 Still he and Zelda were safe . . . : *C U*, p. 28.

77 For a part of Scott was aware . . . : ibid., p. 25.

77 Ruth recalled: 'Neither of them could drive . . .' : Leon Ruth to NM, interview, 30 July 1963.

78 Zelda wrote Ludlow Fowler . . . : ZSF to Ludlow Fowler, 19 May 1920.

78 It would be about Anthony Patch . . . : *Letters*, p. 145. *The Flight of the Rocket* was later retitled *The Beautiful and Damned*.

79 Soon each of Nathan's letters to Westport . . . : George Jean Nathan to ZSF, n.d.

79 During one of his weekends in Westport he had discovered . . . : George Jean Nathan, 'Memories of Fitzgerald, Lewis and Dreiser', *Esquire*, October 1958, pp. 148–9.

81 'Zelda was up. This was obvious . . .': 'The Cruise of the Rolling Junk', *Motor*, February 1924, p. 24.

81 'HURRY BACK TO MONTGOMERY . . .' : Telegram to ZSF, 17 May 1920. ZSF's scrapbook.

82 When Zelda's mother was an old woman . . . : Mike Fitzgerald, 'So You'd Like to Hear About Scott . . .'', the San Diego *Union*, 10 November 1963, p. e6.

82 'We've been in Alabama for two weeks . . .' : ZSF to Ludlow Fowler, 16 August 1920.

83 At the end of August Zelda and Scott reappear . . . : McKaig Diary.

85 Shortly after the incident McKaig refers to, Zelda wrote . . . : ZSF to FSF, n.d.

87 Scott summarized his impression of the year's . . . : Ledger, p. 175.

87 'She would stretch out on the long sofa . . .': Campbell Memoir, C. Lawton Campbell to NM, interview, 19 September 1965.

91 Zelda and Scott had spent a lonely Christmas . . . : *CU*, p. 27.

91 This time a Hawaiian pageant was put on . . . : Campbell Memoir.

91 'I was sitting one evening at a table . . .' : Campbell Memoir.

92 He had written in the manuscript of his new novel . . . : *B&D*, p. 157.

93 But the most exciting event of their visit . . . : Sir Shane Leslie to NM, 6 July 1965.

93 From London they travelled to Windsor and . . . : The snapshots, as well as the misquotation from Rupert Brooke, are in Zelda's scrapbook.

93 Scott wrote Edmund Wilson . . . : *Letters*, p. 326.

94 After much discussion about where their baby . . . : *CU*, p. 29.

94 At the end of August . . . : ibid.

94 In his Ledger Scott described the year . . . : Ledger p. 176.

94 Zelda wrote: 'In the fall . . .' : *CU*, p. 42.

94 'Oh, God, goofo I'm drunk . . . ' : Ledger, p. 176.

95 They named their daughter Patricia . . . : ZSF's scrapbook.

95 As soon as Zelda was on her feet . . . : ZSF to Ludlow Fowler, 22 December 1921.

Chapter 7

96 The Fitzgeralds were behind the spoof . . . : ZSF's scrapbook. Mrs C. O. Kalman was also kind enough to send me her copy of *The Daily Dirge*.

97 But the changes he did make were not substantial . . . : *Letters*, p. 152.

97 The jacket sketch irritated him . . . : *Letters*, p. 153.

97 'The baby is well . . .' : *Letters*, p. 329.

97 In Scott's Ledger during March . . . : Ledger, p. 176.

98 Even then Scott commented . . . : *Letters*, p. 331.

99 'I think if you could view it . . .': Burton Rascoe to ZSF, 27 March 1922. ZSF's scrapbook.

99 The tone of the review was self-conscious . . . : The New York *Tribune*, 2 April 1922. The clipping of Zelda's review is in her scrapbook.

99 'It also seems to me that on one page . . .': ibid.

99 One such portion from the novel . . . : *B&D*, pp. 146–7.

100 'I think the heroine is most amusing . . .': The New York *Tribune*, 2 April 1922.

100 John Peale Bishop was keenly aware . . . : Bishop, 'Three Brilliant Young Novelists', *The Collected Essays of John Peale Bishop*, pp. 229–30.

101 'Even with his famous flapper . . . : ibid., p. 230.

101 In June the *Metropolitan Magazine* did publish . . . : 'Eulogy on the Flapper', *Metropolitan Magazine*, June 1922. ZSF's scrapbook.

102 'How can a girl say again . . .': ibid.

103 In the summertime of 1922 the Fitzgeralds . . . : Mrs Robert D. Clark to NM, 21 July 1965.

103 'She was very athletic and wanted to be out . . .': Mrs C. O. Kalman to NM, interview, September 1964.

103 It was in New York, while they were temporarily living at the Plaza . . . : John Dos Passos to NM, interview, 17 October 1963.

104 'I met them together for the first time . . .': ibid.

105 At the time *The Beautiful and Damned* was published . . . : Arthur Mizener, *The Far Side of Paradise*, p. 157.

105 Scott published a selection of short stories . . . : *Letters*, p. 158.

105 As Zelda was to write . . . : *SMTW*, p. 57.

105 In October the Fitzgeralds found the house . . . : *Afternoon of an Author*, pp. 89–90.

105 'our nifty little Babbitt-home . . .': ZSF to C. O. Kalman, 13 October 1922.

106 He made the Fitzgeralds Cinderella and the Prince . . . : ZSF's scrapbook.

106 At Christmas Lardner sent her a poem . . . : ibid.

107 When Scott came to make his summary of 1922 . . . : Ledger, p. 177.

107 In the Sunday section of the *Morning Telegraph* . . . : Roy L. McCardell, 'F. Scott Fitzgerald – Juvenile Juvenal of the Jeunesse Jazz', New York *Morning Telegraph*, 12 November 1922, p. 3.

108 There were parties where the Fitzgeralds did not arrive . . . : Newspaper clipping in ZSF's scrapbook.

108 Gilbert Seldes, who was then editor of *The Dial* . . . : Gilbert Seldes to NM, interview, 27 May 1965.

109 'Fitzgerald blew into New York last week . . .': *Between Friends, Letters of James Branch Cabell and Others*, edited by Padraic Colum and Margaret Freeman Cabell, Harcourt, Brace & World, New York, 1962, p. 254.

109 In his Ledger at the beginning of 1923 . . . : Ledger, p. 177.

109 What he had written in *The Beautiful and Damned* . . . : B&D, p. 226.

110 'You know, I was famous . . .': Carl Van Vechten to NM, interview, 17 April 1963.

110 'She was an original . . .': ibid.

110 Rebecca West's impressions of the Fitzgeralds . . . : Dame Rebecca West to NM, 10 August 1963.

111 'I am running wild in sack cloth . . .': ZSF to Ludlow Fowler, n.d. (ca. 2 November 1923).

112 'I like to write . . .': 'What a "Flapper Novelist" Thinks of His Wife', the Baltimore *Evening Sun*, 7 October 1923, sec. 5, p. 2.

113 During 1922–1923 she sold two short stories . . . : Ledger, pp. 7, 54, 55, 143.

114 He once commented that he had to stop . . . : *Letters*, p. 163.

114 'Zelda and I have concocted a wonderful idea . . .': *Letters*, p. 337.

114 In November the play opened in Atlantic City . . . : Newspaper clippings in ZSF's scrapbook.

114 'It was,' he wrote later . . . : *Afternoon of an Author*, pp. 93–4.

115 When he summarized the year . . . : Ledger, p. 178.

115 Zelda wrote in her unpublished novel . . . : *CT*, Chapter V, p. 32.

115 Lardner said goodbye in a poem . . . : ZSF's scrapbook.

Chapter 8

116 Lawton Campbell spotted them strolling . . . : C. Lawton Campbell to NM, interview, 19 September 1965.

116 During the several days they spent in Paris . . . : *CU*, p. 43.

117 He said they had left America because . . . : Gerald Murphy to NM, interview, 26 April 1963.

117 Paris was, as Sara said . . . : Calvin Tomkins, 'Living Well Is the Best Revenge,' *The New Yorker*, 28 July 1962, p. 50.

117 Sara Murphy said . . . : Sara Murphy to NM, interview, 26 April 1963.

118 'The train bore them down through the pink . . .': *SMTW*, p. 72.

118 In June they came to St Raphaël . . . : *Afternoon of an Author*, p. 111.

118 'Zelda must have spent days . . .': Gerald Murphy to NM, interview, 2 March 1964.

119 That summer the air of the Riviera . . . : Mrs Robert Benchley to NM, interview, 3 March 1965.

119 She wrote, 'Oh, we are going to be so happy . . .': *SMTW*, p. 79.

119 'After all, Scott had his writing . . .': Gerald Murphy to NM, interview, 2 March 1964.

119 Yet the days were monotonous for her . . . : *SMTW*, p. 80.

119 Zelda wrote Edmund Wilson: . . . : ZSF to Edmund Wilson ca. summer 1924.

120 Casually at first, Zelda and one of the young aviators . . . : Admiral Édouard Jozan to NM, 11 January 1967. *CU*, p. 44.

120 Édouard Jozan cannot remember any longer how he first met . . . : Admiral Édouard Jozan to NM, 11 January 1967.

121 In 1940 he commanded a naval . . . : M Georges Poull to NM, 3 December 1966. It is M Poull who suggested to me that the name 'Josanne' (the name mentioned in Fitzgerald's Ledger) was perhaps a misspelling of Jozan – as indeed my subsequent correspondence with Admiral Jozan proved.

122 When Zelda described him in *Save Me* . . . : *SMTW*, p. 83.
122 Sara Murphy thought that Zelda . . . : Sara Murphy to ZSF, interview, 2 March 1964.
122 Then, abruptly, Zelda and Jozan were no longer . . . : Gerald Murphy to NM, interview, 2 March 1964. Ledger, p. 178.
123 There was not a hint of discord . . . : Gilbert Seldes to NM, interview, 27 May 1965.
123 Joseph Conrad had died in England . . . : *Gatsby*, The Modern Library, New York, 1934, p. viii.
123 'The road from their villa . . .': Gilbert Seldes to NM, interview, 27 May 1965.
123 In August Scott wrote . . . : Ledger, p. 178.
124 At about three or four one morning . . . : Calvin Tomkins to NM, 4 January 1966.
124 It was not until much later in his life . . . : Notebooks, I, 'Ideas'.
124 In September he wrote . . . : Ledger, p. 179.
125 'But they both had a need of drama . . .': Admiral Édouard Jozan to NM, 17 February 1967.
125 In *Save Me the Waltz*, Alabama says . . .: *SMTW*, p. 98.
125 He told Maxwell Perkins . . . : *Letters*, pp. 165, 166.
125 In November Scott entered in his Ledger . . . : Ledger, p. 179.
125 He worried about the title . . . : *Letters*, p. 169.
126 She read aloud to him . . . : *Letters*, pp. 170, 173.
126 Scott wrote, . . . : *Letters*, p. 357.
126 That spring in Paris was composed . . . : Ledger, p. 179.
126 The previous fall, Fitzgerald, upon reading . . . : *Letters*, p. 167.
127 Hemingway's first wife, Hadley . . . : Mrs. Paul Scott Mowrer to NM, interview, 25 July 1964.
128 Hemingway perceptively noticed two kinds of jealousy . . . : Ernest Hemingway, *A Moveable Feast*, pp. 180–81.
128 Hadley feels that Zelda 'was . . .': Mrs Paul Scott Mowrer to NM, interview, 25 July 1964.
128 When Scott had finished it he had written . . . : *Letters*, p. 357.
128 He told Perkins . . . : *Letters*, pp. 180–81.
129 Then Gilbert Seldes reviewed it . . . : Gilbert Seldes, 'Spring Flight', *The Dial*, No. 79, August 1925, p. 162.
129 In May Gertrude Stein wrote . . . : *CU*, p. 308 (Gertrude Stein to FSF, 22 May 1925).
129 Eliot wrote him . . . : *CU*, p. 310 (T. S. Eliot to FSF, 31 December 1925).
129 Neither Zelda nor Hadley was included . . . : Mrs Paul Scott Mowrer to NM, interview, 25 July 1964.
130 In an anecdote which has become a part of the Fitzgerald-Hemingway canon . . . : Gerald Murphy to NM, interview, 26 April 1963.
130 'At that time', . . . : ibid.
130 She said: 'The portrait of Zelda . . .': Mrs Paul Scott Mowrer to NM, interview, 25 July 1964.
130 They returned to the South of France . . . : *CU*, p. 19.
130 The Fitzgeralds joined the Murphys one evening for dinner . . . : Gerald Murphy to NM, interview, 26 April 1963.
131 Several years later, writing about the scene . . . : *CU*, p. 58.

131 'You see,' Gerald Murphy commented . . . : Gerald Murphy to NM, interview, 2 March 1964.

131 In September Scott summarized the year . . . : Ledger, p. 180.

132 She wrote: 'We had a play on . . .': *CU*, p. 46.

132 'That the Fitzgerald's are the best looking . . .': John Chapin Mosher, 'That Sad Young Man', *The New Yorker*, 17 April 1926, pp. 20–21.

132 'Any place that Sara touched . . .': Mrs Paul Scott Mowrer to NM, interview, 25 July 1964.

133 Scott wrote: 'The mistral is raging . . .': *Letters*, pp. 203–4.

133 Zelda was not seen during the day . . . : Mrs Archibald MacLeish to NM, interview, 11 March 1965.

133 In a film taken during the summer . . . : I would like to thank Gwinn Owens for arranging for me to see a special screening in Baltimore of his film about Scott Fitzgerald called *Marked for Glory*. Let me also thank John Q. of Station WJZ-TV 13 in Baltimore.

134 One evening the Murphys and the Fitzgeralds were sitting . . . : Gerald Murphy to NM, interview, 26 April 1963.

134 Mrs MacLeish remembers . . . : Mrs Archibald MacLeish to NM, interview, 11 March 1965.

135 Gerald Murphy described the way Scott and Zelda seemed to work together . . . : Gerald Murphy to NM, interview, 2 March 1964.

135 Prior to the operation, however, Zelda had suffered . . . : In Rome, the year before, Zelda had had a minor operation to enable her to become pregnant. An infection set in and she was ill throughout the following year. Her doctor in Paris did an abdominal operation but no gynecological condition was found and her appendix was removed. Later in her life she would refer to her illness as peritonitis.

135 She was having drinks one afternoon . . . : Sara Mayfield, 'The Fitzgeralds: Exiles from Paradise', *Comment*, The University of Alabama Review, Vol. IV, Winter 1965, p. 45.

136 Miss Mayfield remembers a specific conversation . . . : ibid.

137 'I think that was the time I told him . . .': Gerald Murphy to NM, interview, 26 April 1963.

137 Sara added: 'She never, never spoke personally –' . . . : Sara Murphy to NM, interview, 2 March 1964.

138 Still, she was absolutely loyal . . . : ibid.

139 Zelda had been ill throughout the year . . . : Ledger, pp. 179–81.

139 'God,' he wrote Perkins . . . : *Letters*, p. 207.

140 Zelda was quoted in a newspaper . . . : This clipping is in her scrapbook.

140 Years later Zelda realized that for herself . . . : *CT*, Chapter V, p. 39.

Chapter 9

141 'It is so hot we can't wear coats . . .': ZSF to Scottie, n.d.

All of the letters from Zelda to her daughter quoted in this chapter were undated and were written during the eight weeks Zelda and Scott were in Hollywood. Most of them were written on the letterhead of the Ambassador Hotel.

142 The seventeen-year-old screen star was . . . : George Jean Nathan,

'Memorie of Fitzgerald, Lewis and Dreiser', *Esquire*, October 1958, pp. 148–9.

143 In the story the girl's youth is seen as a shield . . . : 'Jacob's Ladder', *Saturday Evening Post*, August 1927, p. 5.

143 'Silently, as the night hours went by . . .': ibid., p. 63.

144 Samuel Goldwyn gave a costume party . . . : Colleen Moore, *Silent Star*, Doubleday, New York, 1968.

154 It was through the assistance of Scott's old friend . . . : Judge John Biggs, Jr, to NM, interview, 9 June 1963.

145 Before Scott left Europe . . . : *Letters*, p. 207.

145 Zelda later evoked the archaic charm . . . : *C U*, p. 47.

145 Zelda cleverly had outsized furniture . . . : Mrs Anna Biggs to NM, interview, 9 June 1963.

146 Zelda must have concealed . . . : Mrs Clarence M. Young to NM, 14 May 1965.

146 The first, 'The Changing Beauty . . .' 'The Changing Beauty of Park Avenue', *Harper's Bazaar*, January 1928, p. 60. See the Ledger. ZSF received $300 for this story, $300 for 'Looking Back Eight Years', which was sold to *College Humor*, and $180 for 'Who Can Fall in Love After Thirty?' *College Humor*, October, 1928. 'Editorial Photoplay', was apparently sold for $500, but it appears to have been unpublished and I have not been able to locate the manuscript.

146 Zelda's second article was called . . . : 'Looking Back Eight Years', *College Humor*, June 1928, pp. 36–7.

147 '. . . surely some of this irony . . .': ibid.

147 Soon Scott and Zelda were throwing . . . : John Dos Passos to NM, interview, 17 October 1963.

147 Edmund Wilson once remarked . . . : Edmund Wilson, 'Weekend at Ellerslie', *The Shores of Light, A Literary Chronicle of the Twenties and Thirties*, Farrar, Strauss and Young, New York, 1952, p. 382.

148 During those first several months at Ellerslie . . . : ZSF to Carl Van Vechten, 27 May, 29 May, 9 June, 14 June, 24 June, 6 September, 14 October, 1927.

149 At the beginning of summer Sara Murphy wrote . . . : Sara Murphy to ZSF, 28 June 1927.

150 'One of the objects that caught her fancy . . .': Mrs Anna Biggs to NM, interview, 9 June 1963.

151 Her husband added that he had heard . . . : Judge John Biggs, Jr, to NM, interview, 9 June 1963.

151 Scott met her train, explaining that Zelda . . . : Mrs John Hume Taylor to NM, 10 August 1965.

151 'Scott seemed to be the moving spirit . . .': ibid.

152 'She talked intensely when she was interested . . .': Mrs John Hume Taylor to NM, 29 September 1965.

152 After the party Scott and Zelda and Cecilia . . . : ibid.

153 Angoff remembers that Scott had been drinking . . . : Charles Angoff, *H. L. Mencken: A Portrait from Memory*, Thomas Yoseloff, Inc., New York, 1956, pp. 98–9.

154 'Have got nervous as hell . . .': *Letters*, p. 301.

154 Scott wrote: 'The book is fine . . .': ibid., pp. 300–301.

ccording to Matthew Bruccoli . . . : Bruccoli, *The Composi-*
^, Tender Is the Night, University of Pittsburgh Press, 1963, p.
18.

155 'They were on their way . . .': *SMTW*, p. 98.

155 Zelda wrote to Eleanor Browder, who had recently married . . . :
ZSF to Mrs E. E. Addison, postmarked 29 May 1928.

155 Gerald Murphy introduced Zelda to Madame Lubov Egorova . . . :
Gerald Murphy to NM, interview, 2 March 1964.

156 'It seemed to Alabama that, reaching . . .': *SMTW*, p. 124.

156 'Zelda wanted immediate success . . .': Gerald Murphy to NM, interview, 2 March 1964.

157 'Each time someone was brought to be introduced . . .'; Sara Murphy
told me this anecdote in the spring of 1963; she had also passed it on
to Calvin Tomkins, who quoted her in his perceptive *New Yorker*
profile of the Murphys. Although I interviewed many of Zelda's
childhood friends, I was never able to discover the meaning of 'the
marble ring'.

157 Zelda later recalled 'long conversations . . .': *CU*, pp. 48–9.

157 His entry for July in the Ledger read . . . : Ledger, p. 182.

158 When they returned to America . . . : ibid.

158 She practised in front of the great ornate . . . : Judge John Biggs, Jr.,
to NM, interview, 9 June 1963.

158 'And there was the lone and lovely child . . .' ZSF, 'Autobiographical
Sketch', 16 March 1932.

159 Scott wrote Maxwell Perkins . . . : *Letters*, p. 213.

Chapter 10

163 Zelda said: 'I worked constantly . . .': ZSF, 'Autobiographical
Sketch', 16 March 1932.

164 Morley Callaghan, a young Canadian writer . . . : Morley Callaghan,
That Summer in Paris, Coward-McCann, New York, 1963. See Chapters XI, and XVIII.

164 At their first meeting . . . : Callaghan, ibid., p. 152.

165 The next time they met, Callaghan remembers, Zelda . . . : ibid., pp.
160–63.

165 In the winter of 1928–1929 Zelda began writing the first in a series of
short stories* . . . : These stories are: 'The Original Follies Girl'
(sold March 1929), *College Humor*, July 1929, $400; 'The Poor Work-
ing Girl' (sold April 1929), *College Humor*, January 1931, $500 (from
the date of sale it seems pretty clear that this was the second story to
be written, but it was the last to be published in the series. A note in
Scott's Ledger says, erroneously, that it was unpublished), 'Southern
Girl', *College Humor*, October 1929, $500; 'The Girl the Prince Liked'
(sold September 1929), *College Humor*, February 1930, $500; 'The
Girl with Talent' (sold October 1929), *College Humor*, April 1930,
$800; 'A Millionaire's Girl' (sold March 1930), *Saturday Evening
Post*, 17 May 1930, $4,000.

*Dates of sales are given in order to approximate when the stories were
written.

166 Most of the stories, he told Ober . . . : FSF to Harold Ober, n.d.

166 A wire from New York assured him . . . : 'MILLIONAIRES GIRL CAN SELL POST FOUR THOUSAND WITHOUT ZELDAS NAME CABLE CONFIRMATION', 12 March 1930.

166 Scott later wrote that the story . . . : FSF to ZSF, 13 June 1934.

166 Zelda had written them . . . : *Letters*, p. 223.

167 As she says of one of them . . . : 'The Original Follies Girl', *College Humor*, 29 July, p. 41.

168 'You know how sweethearts have a song . . .': H. N. Swanson, 'The Last Word', *College Humor*, October 1929, p. 134.

169 She and Scott attended few parties . . . : See Callaghan, *That Summer in Paris*, pp. 152, 162–3, 193. There is also a lot of this in Hemingway, *A Moveable Feast*.

169 He has Dick say . . . : *Tender*, p. 301.

169 Zelda wrote, 'Nobody knew whose party . . .': *SMTW*, p. 99.

169 'To be a tall rich American girl . . .'; Cowley – *Tender*, p. 341. See Hemingway, *A Moveable Feast*, p. 181.

170 Hemingway must have relayed the accusation . . . : *Letters*, p. 216.

170 Then they came back out and began to cross . . . : Callaghan, *That Summer in Paris*, p. 207.

171 He said: 'The laughter was her own . . .': Gerald Murphy to NM, interview, 26 April 1963.

171 'There were all sorts and varieties . . .': ibid.

172 Sara Murphy said, 'I don't think he knew . . .': Sara Murphy to NM, interview, 26 April 1963.

172 'She once wrote Scott . . .'; Sara Murphy to FSF, n.d.

172 'My latest tendency is to collapse . . .': *Letters*, p. 306.

172 It was on the automobile trip back to Paris . . . : ZSF, 'Autobiographical Sketch', 16 March 1932.

173 Zelda wrote, 'There were Americans . . .': *SMTW*, p. 102.

173 On 23 September 1929, Zelda was invited . . . : Madame Julia Sedova to ZSF, 23 September 1929.

173 As late as 1936 he was writing . . . : *Letters*, p. 402.

173 'It was a trying winter' . . . : *CU*, p. 51.

174 'We immediately sensed something wrong . . .': Gerald Murphy to NM, interview, 2 March 1964.

174 During a luncheon party in April . . . : Mrs C. O. Kalman to NM, interview, September 1964.

175 Madame Egorova, too, had begun to notice . . . : Princess Lubov Troubetskoy-Egorova to NM, 31 October 1968.

175 Scott wrote Perkins at the time . . . : *Letters*, p. 222.

177 Later she was to write of that journey . . . : ZSF, 'Autobiographical Sketch', 16 March 1932.

Chapter 11

178 She was diagnosed . . . : Dr Oscar Forel to NM, 9 March 1966.
      In the many years that have passed since Dr Forel first diagnosed Zelda he has 'put aside' that original diagnosis of schizophrenia. '. . . apart from the clinical and classical forms . . . certain symptoms and

behaviours or activities, are called *schizoid* and this does not mean
that the person is schizophrenic.' (Dr Forel to NM, 18 May 1966.)

178 James Joyce's daughter . . . : Richard Ellmann, *James Joyce*, Oxford
University Press, New York, 1959, pp. 677, 687–8.
179 Dr Forel noted . . . : Prangins.
179 Scott wrote to Dr Forel on the same day . . . : FSF to Dr Oscar
Forel, 8 June 1930.
180 '. . . as she would have it understood . . .': ibid.
180 'When I saw the sadness . . .'; FSF to ZSF, n.d. (ca. summer 1930).
181 She wrote Scott . . . : Mrs A. D. Sayre to FSF, 14 July 1930.
181 She had gone through similar periods . . . : Mrs A. D. Sayre to FSF,
16 July 1930.
181 'Just at the point in my life . . .': ZSF to FSF, n.d. (ca. June
1930).
   All of the following letters quoted in this chapter from Zelda to
Scott were written during the fifteen months Zelda was in Prangins and
none of them were dated. When there is internal evidence from which
to hazard a fairly close guess of the date, I do so. For example, in this
letter Zelda asks Scott to write to Egorova. He wrote to her on 22
June 1930.
183 Dr Forel was absolutely certain . . . : Dr Forel to FSF, 23 June 1930.
183 She wrote that Zelda . . . : Princess Lubov Troubetskoy-Egorova to
FSF, 9 July 1930.
184 'Every day it seems to me . . .': ZSF to FSF, n.d.
185 'There is no use my trying . . .': ZSF to FSF, n.d.
185 'To recapitulate : . . .': ZSF to FSF, n.d.
186 Knowing how defeated . . . : FSF to Dr Oscar Forel, 14 July
1930.
186 By mid-June Zelda . . . : Prangins.
187 'On her admittance she had been . . .': *Tender*, p. 183.
187 'Please, out of charity . . .': ZSF to FSF, ca. June 1930.
187 'The panic seems to have settled . . .': ZSF to FSF, n.d.
188 In early fall Scott wrote Maxwell Perkins . . . : *Letters*, p. 224.
188 'When I last saw you . . .': FSF to Dr Oscar Forel, n.d. (ca.
summer 1930).
190 He had begun to work on a sixth draft . . . : See Matthew J.
Bruccoli, The *Composition of Tender Is the Night*, pp. 67, 69. See
also 'One Trip Abroad', *Afternoon of an Author*, pp. 147, 164.
Although the Fitzgeralds' connection to the Kellys is clear enough,
it is worth noticing that it was Gerald Murphy, and not Scott, who
was funded by a private income, just as it was he who painted a
12′ × 18′ picture of a smokestack from an ocean liner ('Boatdeck:
Cunarder') – which achieved something of a *succès scandale* in Paris
at the Salon des Indépendents in 1923.
191 'I hope it will be nice at Caux . . .': ZSF to FSF, n.d. (ca. August
1930).
191 'I wish I could see you . . .': ZSF to FSF, n.d. (ca. August/
September 1930).
192 Once when things seemed very black . . . : Prangins, Summer 1930.
194 'I have read Zelda's manuscripts . . .': Maxwell Perkins to FSF, 5
August 1930.

195 Scott replied that he . . . : *Letters*, p. 224.
195 She wrote Scott: . . . *'Please . . .'*: ZSF to FSF, n.d. (ca. end of August 1930).
195 'I seem awfully queer . . .': ZSF to FSF, n.d.
196 He hypnotized Zelda . . . : Dr Oscar Forel to NM, 6 May 1966.
196 'Goofy, my darling . . .': ZSF to FSF, n.d.
197 Although by the end of October . . . : Prangins.
198 Dr Forel says . . . : Dr Oscar Forel to NM, 6 May 1966.
198 Dr Forel wrote . . . : Prangins, 15 October 1930.
198 Scott wrote Judge and Mrs Sayre . . . : FSF to Judge and Mrs Sayre, 1 December 1930.
198 Zelda's personal reaction . . . : Dr Oscar Forel to FSF, 1 December 1930. ('. . . *que votre femme traite de grand imbécile.*')
198 Bleuler told Scott . . . : FSF to Judge and Mrs Sayre, 1 December 1930.
199 'It is excellent . . .': ZSF to Scottie, ca. winter 1930.
200 'I know this then – . . .': FSF, 'Written with Zelda Gone to the Clinique', n.d.
203 (*fn*) According to his biographer . . . : Arthur Mizener, *The Far Side of Paradise*, p. 56.
203 'Your letter is not . . .': ZSF to FSF, n.d. (ca. summer 1930).
204 'I am tired of rummaging my head . . .': ZSF to FSF, n.d.
205 He said that, although a first-year medical . . . : FSF to Dr Oscar Forel, 29 January 1931.
205 'In brief my idea is this . . .': ibid.
206 'Then she went into the other personality . . .': ibid.
206 She ate her meals at the table . . . : Prangins.
206 'I keep thinking of Provence . . .': ZSF to FSF, n.d. (ca. spring 1931).
207 'I can't write . . .': ZSF to FSF, n.d. (ca. spring 1931).
208 Gerald Murphy, who was living with his family . . . : Gerald Murphy to NM, interview, 2 March 1964.
209 'I went to Geneva all by myself . . .': ZSF to FSF, n.d. (ca. spring 1931).
210 They said they would never . . . : *CU*, pp. 52–3.
210 'My dearest and most precious . . .': ZSF to FSF, n.d. (ca. end of July 1931).
210 'At first we were petrified . . .': Gerald Murphy to NM, interview, 2 March 1964.
211 'Well, it's all written . . .': ibid. See *Tender*, pp. 261–5.
211 'Please don't be depressed . . .': ZSF to FSF, n.d. (ca. summer 1931).
211 Her case was summarized . . . : Prangins.
212 Earlier that year . . . : ZSF to FSF, n.d.

Chapter 12

213 Zelda wrote, 'In Alabama . . .': *CU*, p. 54.
213 By October Scott was bored . . . : Ledger, p. 186.
214 He wrote at the top . . . : ibid.

214 'You know the kind: women of fifty . . .': ZSF to FSF, n.d.
    All of Zelda's letters to Scott which are quoted in this chapter
    were written between the end of October and 20 December, while he
    was in Hollywood. None were dated.
214–215 . . . She finished at least seven stories . . . : 'All About the
    Down's Case' (the revised story), 'Cotton Belt', 'Sweet Chariot',
    'Getting Away From It All', 'The Story Thus Far', 'A Myth in A
    Moral', and 'A Couple of Nuts'.
215 '*Please* tell me your *frank* opinion . . .': ZSF to Harold Ober, 21
    December 1931.
215 The story is about a young American couple . . . : 'A Couple of
    Nuts', *Scribner's Magazine*, August 1932, pp. 80, 82, 84.
216 The story was reviewed in St Paul . . . : James Gray, 'St Paul's
    Family of Writers Have Almost Scribner's Monopoly'. The St Paul
    Dispatch. This newspaper clipping is in one of Zelda's clipping
    albums.
218 In an obituary in the Montgomery newspaper . . . : The *Mont-
    gomery Advertiser*, 19 November 1931.
223 In late November Scott wrote Dr Forel . . . : FSF to Dr Forel,
    November 1931.
224 In the December issue of *Scribner's* . . . : 'Miss Ella', *Scribner's
    Magazine*, December 1931, pp. 661–5.
225 Miss Ella's life seems as orderly . . . : ibid., p. 663.
226 'Even her moments of relaxation were . . .': ibid., p. 661.
227 Their plans for a life together were . . . : ibid., pp. 663–4.
230 Buoyed by their holiday, Scott wrote . . . : *Letters*, p. 226.
230 Without warning a spot of eczema . . . : FSF to Dr Oscar Forel,
    1 February 1932.
231 'She had been working all day . . .': ibid.
231 Scott was worried and told Forel: 'For the first time . . .': ibid.
231 'My haste,' Scott later wrote . . . : FSF to Dr Oscar Forel, 18 April
    1932.

Chapter 13

235 The end of February Zelda wrote . . . : ZSF to Scottie, n.d. (post-
    marked 29 February 1932).
236 In his Ledger he wrote, 'Scotty . . .': Ledger, p. 186.
236 Zelda seemed to understand how deeply . . . : ZSF to FSF, n.d.
236 A friend of theirs remembers Fitzgerald gently . . . : John Tilley to
    NM, interview, 27 July 1963.
237 'We always have such fun pricking . . .': ZSF to FSF, n.d. (ca.
    February 1932).
237 'I am reading Ian Gordon's . . .': ibid.
238 'I am proud of my novel . . .': ZSF to FSF, n.d. (ca. end of Feb-
    ruary/early March 1932).
238 'The lack of continuity in her novel . . .': FSF to Dr Mildred T.
    Squires, 8 March 1932.
238 Zelda sent it immediately to Maxwell Perkins . . . : ZSF to Maxwell
    Perkins, n.d. (postmarked 12 March 1932).

238 For four years, he wrote, he had been forced . . . : FSF to Dr
 Mildred T. Squires, 14 March 1932.
239 'It is getting more and more difficult . . .': ibid.
239 His anger did not subside and two days later he wired . . . : FSF to
 Maxwell Perkins, 16 March 1932.
239 In January 1932, he proceeded to sketch out a longer novel . . . :
 Letters, p. 226.
240 In early spring Scott drew up his 'General Plan' . . . : This material
 as well as the 'Further Sketch' and the chart paralleling Zelda's case
 with Nicole Diver's – reproduced for the first time – is drawn from
 the Fitzgerald Collection at Princeton University Library.
242 His income in 1931 was at its apex . . . : Ledger, p. 67.
242 'Dr Squires tells me you are hurt . . .': ZSF to FSF, n.d. (ca. March
 1932).
244 She answered: 'Dear – You Know . . .': ZSF to FSF, n.d. (ca.
 March 1932).
244 'Of cource, I glad[ly] submit to anything . . .': ZSF to FSF, n.d.
 (ca. March 1932).
245 Yet at the end of March just before he left Alabama . . . : FSF to
 Dr Mildred T. Squires (ca. March 1932).
245 On the other hand, he could not 'stand always . . .': ibid.

Chapter 14

248 *Save Me the Waltz* is not a defence . . . : *SMTW*, p. 57.
248 'Zelda's novel is now good . . .': *Letters*, pp. 226–7.
248 Then he asked Perkins to keep whatever praise . . . : ibid., p. 227.
249 '. . . I'm not certain enough of Zelda's present . . .': ibid.
249 He wrote: 'Here is Zelda's novel . . .'. ibid., p. 228.
249 Somewhat cavalierly Fitzgerald added that he would withdraw his
 restraint on praise . . . : ibid., pp. 228–9.
250 Alabama has overheard David telling Miss Gibbs . . . : *SMTW*,
 pp. 109–11.
250 The following morning . . . : ibid., p. 117.
251 'I can't stand this any longer . . .': ibid.
251 When David tells her that he understands . . . : ibid., p. 118.
251 But she has also turned to the dance . . . : ibid., p. 116.
251 Alabama says, 'Can't you understand that . . .': ibid., p. 141.
253 She establishes the Judge's importance at the beginning . . . : ibid.,
 p. 3.
253 He is 'entrenched . . . in his integrity . . .': ibid.
253 'By the time the Beggs children had learned . . .': ibid., p. 4.
253 It is to her that the girls turn for relief . . . : ibid., p. 5.
254 'Millie, who had never had a very strong sense of reality . . .': ibid.,
 pp. 4–5.
254 'The wide and lawless generosity . . .': ibid., p. 11.
255 'Tell me about myself when I was little . . .': ibid., pp. 5–6.
255 'And did I cry at night and raise Hell . . .': ibid., p. 6.
256 'White things gleam in the dark . . .': ibid., p. 7.
256 'She grows older sleeping . . .': ibid., p. 8.

257 When the war comes Alabama plans 'to escape . . .': ibid., p. 29.
257 She falls in love with the romantic figure . . . : ibid., p. 37.
257 'Say, "dear",' he said . . . : ibid., p. 38.
257 'So much she loved the man . . .': ibid.
257 (*fn*) 'His whole life has been torn . . .': R. D. Laing, *The Divided Self, An Existential Study in Sanity and Madness*, Penguin Books, Baltimore, 1965, p. 37.
258 Alabama, then, in a fantasy, enters David's head . . . : ibid.
258 ' "The tops of buildings shine like crowns . . ." ': ibid., p. 40.
259 Alabama turns to memories of her father for sustenance: 'She thought . . .': ibid., p. 129.
259 'Alabama's peculiar genius lay . . .': ibid., p. 227.
259 The first sentence was altered to read . . . : ibid., p. 48.
260 'From the sense that she had nothing . . .': ibid., p. 51.
260 'Alabama had a way of abnegating . . .': ibid., p. 220.
260 'Alabama had known this would be their attitude . . .': ibid., p. 55.
261 'Understand,' the Judge was saying . . . : ibid., pp. 55–6.
261 'Wouldn't you mind?' she said . . . : ibid., p. 226.
261 No one but Alabama has dressed for dinner . . . : ibid., pp. 229–30.
262 Alabama thinks, 'If they hadn't been so completely impervious . . . : ibid., p. 231.
262 Alabama reflects, ' "Another tie broken . . ." ': ibid., p. 233.
262 'The top of New York twinkled like a golden canopy . . .': ibid., pp. 46–7.
263 Then David says: 'I'll have to do lots of work . . .': ibid., p. 47.
263 '. . . she hadn't been absolutely sure . . .': ibid., p. 50.
263 'Vincent Youmans wrote a new tune . . .': ibid., p. 56.
264 'The New York rivers dangled lights along the banks . . .': ibid., pp. 56–7.
264 'It costs more to ride on the tops of taxis . . .': ibid., pp. 57, 60.
264 The foliage is 'black', . . . : ibid., p. 72
265 'Pastel cupids frolicked amidst the morning-glories . . .': ibid., p. 79.
265 ' "It's a man's world . . ." ': ibid., p. 80.
265 'When she was a child and the days . . .': ibid., p. 90.
265 She says, 'Yes – I don't know . . ." ': ibid., p. 93.
265 'I'll have to tell him . . .': ibid.
266 She rips up the letter, and 'Though it broke her heart . . .': ibid., p. 98.
266 This is an almost exact repetition . . . : ibid., p. 29.
266 He wrote one of Zelda's doctors . . . : FSF to Dr Thomas Rennie, 28 May 1933.
266 It is only when the Knights leave the Riviera . . . : *SMTW*, p. 99.
266 In Paris the flowers are artificial . . . : ibid., p. 102.
267 In that Parisian world of parties . . . : ibid., p. 106.
267 'I think . . . that it would be the very thing . . .': ibid., p. 113.
267 'Life has become practically intolerable . . .': ZSF to FSF, n.d.
268 Alabama pushes her body beyond the pain . . . : *SMTW*, p. 127.
268 'Why will you never come out . . .': ibid., p. 126
268 'Yellow roses she bought with her money like Empire . . .': ibid., pp. 138–9.
269 ' "You're so thin," said David . . .': ibid., p. 147.

269 'The bones had begun to come up in her nose . . .': ibid., p. 174.
269 There is no car, but 'a flea-bitten . . .': ibid., pp. 175–6.
270 'We should have taken the train-de-luxe . . .': ibid., p. 180.
270 As Bonnie looks about her she notices 'Ladies .'. .': ibid., p. 181.
271 'Riding home through the flickering night . . .': ibid., p. 187.
271 'Oh, my father, there are so many things . . .': ibid., p. 199.
272 'Her father!' she had written before Alabama . . . : ibid., p. 195.
272 ' "He must have forgot," Alabama said . . .': ibid., pp. 203, 204.
273 Alabama says: ' "We grew up founding our dreams . . ." ': ibid., p. 110.
273 'We've talked you to death . . .': ibid.
273 'Always . . . we will have to seek some perspective . . .': ibid., p. 211.
273 She tells David it is 'very expressive . . .': ibid., p. 212.

Chapter 15

274 'The eyes of the psychiatrist moved . . .': ZSF, 'Autobiographical Sketch', 16 March 1932. Dr Mildred T. Squires, to whom Zelda dedicated *Save Me the Waltz*, is the psychiatrist referred to at the opening.
280 'Darling, Sweet D.O. – . . .': ZSF to FSF, n.d. (ca. end of March 1932).
280 'It all went back to Zelda . . .': This untitled sketch which exists in typescript and is six pages long was attached to a letter written by Fitzgerald to Dr Squires, 4 April 1932.
282 'Honey, when you come out into the world . . .': FSF to ZSF, n.d. (ca. late spring 1932).
282 'We have been so close this last year . . .': ZSF to FSF, n.d.
283 'Analogy' . . . : 'Analogy', by FSF, unpublished.
283 Scott gave an interview to the Baltimore . . . : The Baltimore *Evening Sun*, 'He tells of Her Novel', 8 May 1932.
284 A colleague of Dr Meyer . . . : Dr Eleanor Pavenstedt to NM, 15 January 1969. Dr Pavenstedt cared for Zelda during her second period at Phipps, 12 February 1934 – 8 March 1934.
284 Dr Forel had suggested that if Zelda . . . : Dr Forel to FSF, 8 March 1932. Dr Forel to FSF, 11 May 1932.
285 Scott wrote Dr Squires that he wanted Zelda to take the move . . . : FSF to Dr Mildred T. Squires, 20 May 1932.
285 'We live in a nice Mozartian . . .': ZSF to John Peale Bishop, n.d. (ca. summer 1932).
286 The Turnbull's son Andrew, who was eleven . . . : Andrew Turnbull to NM, interview, 6 August 1964.
286 'When things were going well for them . . .': ibid.
286 Mrs Turnbull found him a charming . . . : Mrs Bayard Turnbull to NM, interview, 12 October 1963.
287 A woman who worked as Fitzgerald's secretary . . . : Mrs Isabel Owens to NM, interview, 12 October 1963.
288 'Dearest: I'm writing because I don't want . . .': FSF to ZSF, n.d. (ca. late summer 1932).

288 Maxwell Perkins visited him and described . . . : Maxwell Perkins to Ernest Hemingway, 22 July 1932, in *Editor to Author, The Letters of Maxwell E. Perkins*, edited by John Hall Wheelock, Charles Scribner's Sons, New York, 1950, p. 79.

289 He entered in the Ledger . . . : Ledger, p. 186.

290 'We are delighted with the book . . .': ZSF to Maxwell Perkins, n.d. (ca. 6 October 1932).

291 Zelda wrote Perkins unhappily after publication . . . : ZSF to Maxwell Perkins, n.d.

291 Zelda liked a review written by William McFee . . . : ibid.

291 '. . . here is a peculiar talent . . .': William McFee, 'During the Jazz Age', the New York *Sun*, 8 October 1932, p. 12.

291 'In the desperate attempt to be contrary . . .': ibid.

292 'It is not only that her publishers . . .': 'Of the Jazz Age', the *New York Times*, 16 October 1932.

292 'There is a warm, intelligent . . .': Dorothea Brand, 'Seven Novels of the Month', *The Bookman*, October 1932, p. 735.

292 Zelda told the woman . . . : Newspaper clipping in Zelda's clipping album.

293 *Save Me the Waltz* sold 1,392 copies . . . : Burroughs Mitchell to NM, 16 February 1968.

293 Zelda earned $120.73 . . . : Maxwell Perkins to ZSF, 2 August 1933.

293 'Maybe I ought to have warned you . . .': ibid.

293 'It moves me a lot . . .': Malcolm Cowley to FSF, 22 May 1933.

294 'But in her subconscious there is . . .': FSF to Dr Thomas Rennie, n.d. (ca. October 1932).

Chapter 16

295 She also wrote Perkins, saying . . . : ZSF to Maxwell Perkins, n.d. (ca. 6 October 1932).

295 'He just wasn't a stationary man . . .': Mrs Isabel Owens to NM, interview, 12 October 1963.

296 In an article written during this period . . . : 'One Hundred False Starts', *Afternoon of An Author*, pp. 131–6.

296 But the crowd no longer seemed to him . . . : Ledger, p. 68.

296 First he blamed his mother, then Zelda . . . : Mrs Isabel Owens to NM, interview, 12 October 1963.

297 His secretary remembered them talking to each other . . . : ibid.

297 His secretary says: 'The next day . . .': ibid.

298 'We had a formal relationship . . .': ibid.

298 Zelda wrote Maxwell Perkins . . . : ZSF to Maxwell Perkins, n.d. (ca. 22 October 1932).

298 Scott's secretary remembers her as 'skinny . . .': Mrs Isabel Owens to NM, interview, 12 October 1963.

298 Scott once wrote: 'Family quarrels . . .': *CU*, p. 198.

299 He said that when their 'conversations' . . . : FSF to Dr Adolf Meyer, 10 April 1933.

299 Scott felt that he needed some strongly enforced authority . . . : ibid.

300 'One of her reasons for gravitating . . .': ibid.

301 Dr Meyer answered Fitzgerald . . . : Dr Adolf Meyer to FSF, 18 April 1933.

301 'I felt that from the difference between my . . .': FSF to Dr Adolf Meyer, n.d. This letter exists in a pencil draft and may never have been sent to Dr Meyer. It is, however, clearly a response to Meyer's letter of 18 April.

301 He said: 'I can only think of Lincoln's . . .': ibid.

305 In a few more years, by 1936, he would understand it more clearly . . . : 'Author's House', *Afternoon of An Author*, p. 188.

306 The spring before this one, sixty young students from the Baltimore area . . . : I am indebted to Don Swann, to Mrs Rita Swann, and to Jack Day (who played Uncle Messogony) for their reminiscences about the Vagabonds.

306 'Ahead of me, near the gate . . .': The description of Zack Maccubbin's meeting with Zelda, his Sunday dinner with the Fitzgeralds, as well as of the rehearsals for *Scandalabra*, are drawn from an unpublished sketch Mr Maccubbin, now Mr Zack Waters, wrote 10 October 1963. Some of this material is also drawn from our interview, 12 May 1965.

308 If *Scandalabra* ran within the time limits . . . : *Scandalabra* exists only in a sixty-one page typescript. This must be Fitzgerald's revision of the farce, for it has a prologue and three acts. In the programme for the original performance, *Scandalabra* is said to have a prologue and two acts.

310 'There is probably nothing more embarrassing . . .': H. B. S., The Baltimore *Evening Sun*, 27 June 1933.

310 The night *Scandalabra* closed another reviewer . . . : J. P. C., 'Final Performance of Scandalabra Given', The Baltimore *Evening Sun*, 2 July 1933.

Chapter 17

311 When Malcolm Cowley came down to visit . . . : Malcolm Cowley, 'A Ghost Story of the Jazz Age', *Saturday Review*, XLVII, 25 January 1964, pp. 20–21.

312 Scott wrote Rennie saying she was selling the naïve young psychiatrist . . . : FSF to Dr Thomas Rennie, 6 October 1933.

312 '. . . conditioned on the charm of a very shrewd . . .': ibid.

314 'Last year or whenever it was in Chicago . . .': *Tender*, p. 122.

315 'I could not walk in the streets . . .': ZSF to FSF, n.d.

315 'I write to you because there is no one else . . .': *Tender*, p. 123.

315 'I would always be more than glad to see you . . .': ZSF to FSF, n.d.

315 'The mental trouble is all over and besides . . .': *Tender*, p. 123.

315 'At any rate one thing has been achieved . . .': ZSF to FSF, n.d. See Chapter 11, p. 168, where this particular letter is quoted in full.

316 'I would gladly welcome any alienist . . .': *Tender*, p. 124.

316 'I will more than gladly welcome any alienist . . .': ZSF to FSF, n.d.

316 Fitzgerald even quoted directly in *Tender* . . . : *Tender*, p. 128. According to Dr Bleuler's 22 November 1930 report on Zelda, fear

for one's own sexual identity is a classic element of schizophrenic disintegration. Her accusation about Fitzgerald was a 'typical counter-effect'. Dr Forel to NM, 6 May 1966.

317 'After all, Max, I am a plodder . . .': *Letters*, p. 247.

317 At the close of the same letter . . . : ibid., pp. 247–8.

318 'Dear, Monsieur, D.O., The third installment . . .'; ZSF to FSF, n.d.

318 'You *don't* love me . . .': ibid.

319 'Do-Do: It was so sad to see your train pull out . . .': ZSF to FSF, n.d. (ca. March 1934).

319 '– and even for those lonesome bicycle . . .': ZSF to FSF, n.d.

320 'Those monstrous, hideous men . . .': Gerald Murphy to NM, interview, 2 March 1964.

320 'Dearest Do-Do: . . . Cary wrote that Ernest was back . . .': ZSF to FSF, n.d. (ca. April 1932).

321 She remembered that the drawings . . . : Dorothy Parker to NM, interview, 26 August 1964. This portrait of Fitzgerald was later given by Mrs Parker to Rosser Evans in Hollywood. Some years after the gift Mr Evans took it with him to Mexico where it was destroyed in a fire. In 1947 Zelda would tell H. Dan Piper that she had painted a portrait of Scott as a companion piece to her self-portrait (see second section of illustrations), and that Condé Nast had it. Neither Mr Piper nor I have been able to locate that portrait. A third portrait of Fitzgerald was destroyed after Zelda's death in a fire in a small shed behind the house Zelda had lived in with her mother in Montgomery.

321 'Yes, it was good. The eyelashes . . .': Judge John Biggs, Jr, to NM, interview, 9 June 1963.

321 The New York *Post* ran an article . . . : 'Jazz Age Priestess Brings Forth Paintings', the New York *Post*, 3 April 1934.

322 'There was a time . . .': 'Work of A Wife', *Time* magazine, 9 April 1934, p. 42.

322 'Last week . . . Zelda Fitzgerald showed . . .': ibid.

322 'The collar of his topcoat was turned up rakishly . . .': James Thurber, 'Scott in Thorns', *Credos & Curios*, New York, Harper & Row, 1962, pp. 157–60.

323 Throughout the period of Zelda's stay at Craig House . . . : In the one which begins 'My pictures looked very nice . . .' Zelda mentions that it is Easter, and it is clear that she is writing after her return from the New York exhibit (ca. April 1934).

324 'I have now got to the Rosemary-Rome episode . . .': ZSF to FSF, n.d. (ca. April 1934).

325 'You know how I play . . .': ZSF to FSF, n.d.

325 'You have the satisfaction . . .': ZSF to FSF, n.d.

325 Another time she wrote, 'Those people . . .': ZSF to FSF, n.d. (ca. late April 1934).

325 'You seem afraid that it will make me recapitulate . . .': ZSF to FSF, n.d.

326 Scott continued to insist that she not have 'too much traffic . . .': FSF to ZSF, 26 April 1934.

326 '. . . the only sadness is the living without you . . .': ibid.

327 Patiently she tried to explain to Scott . . . : ZSF to FSF, n.d. (ca. early May 1934).

327 It is doubtful that she had time to begin the new novel . . . : Ledger, p. 188.

327 'I do not feel as you do about state . . .': ZSF to FSF, n.d.

328 'Darling I feel very disoriented and lonely . . .': ZSF to FSF, n.d. (ca. end of May 1934).

328 Fitzgerald accepted the doctors' decision . . . : FSF to Dr William Elgin, 21 May 1934.

328 'For it there is to be said . . .': ibid.

328 And it must have been in yet another effort to stir her from apathy . . . : FSF to ZSF, 31 May 1934.

329 About the collection of her short pieces . . . : FSF to ZSF, 13 June 1934.

330 He would write a five-hundred-word introduction . . . : ibid.

330 In Scott's opinion this sort of collection would nicely 'compete with such personal collections . . .': ibid.

330 (Those were 'Show Mr and Mrs F to Number —' . . . : *Esquire*, May and June 1934. 'Auction – Model 1934', *Esquire*, July 1934. These articles are reprinted in *The Crack-Up*.

330 The Myers have gone to Antibes . . . : ZSF to FSF, n.d. (ca. mid-June 1934).

330 She was afraid the title 'Eight Women' . . . : ibid.

331 He edited the first one, 'Show Mr and Mrs F. . . .': On 26 June 1934, Fitzgerald wrote Perkins that he had 'fixed up and sold some of Zelda's little articles', which probably refers to these pieces. *Letters*, p. 249. By the beginning of November he was again writing Perkins that he had, since finishing the proofs of *Tender* in March 1934, 'rewritten three articles of Zelda's for *Esquire* . . .' *Letters*, p. 254.

331 'The night of the stock market crash . . .': *CU*, p. 50.

332 Cafés have a '*desperate* swashbuckling . . .': ibid., pp. 51–2.

332 In Scott's revision . . . : ibid., p. 53.

332 Among the souvenirs of their pasts . . . : ibid., p. 61.

333 'In some of the pictures we are golfing . . .': ibid., p. 57.

333 They will keep them all, 'the tangible . . .': ibid., p. 62.

333 When at last they work they 'are of young . . .': ibid., p. 68.

334 'She seemed in every way exactly . . .': FSF to Dr Harry Murdock, 28 August 1934.

335 'Once she condescended to tell me something . . .': Dr William Elgin to NM, interview, 8 March 1969.

335 The entries in his Ledger grew more despairing . . . : Ledger, pp. 188–9.

335 'Wouldn't you like to smell the pine woods . . .': ZSF to FSF, n.d.

336 'It seems rather Proustian to be rambling . . .': ZSF to FSF, n.d.

336 'Summer, another summer has gone . . .': ZSF to FSF, n.d.

337 'It is summer time and past time . . .': ZSF to FSF, n.d.

337 'My dearest Sweetheart: There is no way to ask . . .': ZSF to FSF, n.d.

337 He spent part of the spring in Tryon . . . : *Letters*, p. 264.

338 Zelda was not coherent during most . . . : ZSF to FSF, n.d.

338 As he once admitted to a friend ... : James Drawbell, *The Sun Within Us*, p. 177.
338 She remembers being dressed in a red gypsy ... : Mrs Laura Guthrie Hearne to NM, interview, 24 July 1963.
338 'Scott never wanted to sleep.': ibid.
339 Mrs Hearne was certain that he used ... : ibid.
339 'At first he didn't love her ...': ibid.
339 'The tough part of the letter is to ...': *Letters*, p. 530. There is some question as to whether or not Fitzgerald sent this letter. But even if he did not, the manner in which he expressed himself is a clear enough indication of his strategy.
340 Back in Baltimore in September ... : ibid., p. 531.
340 To another friend he would admit ... : ibid., pp. 528–9.
340 'What she has been through ...': FSF to Mrs Laura Guthrie Hearne, 25 October 1935.
341 He wrote in his Ledger, 'Me caring ...': Ledger, April 1936. This page is inserted into the Ledger and is not numbered.
341 '... Zelda now claims to be ...': *Letters*, pp. 425–6.

Chapter 18

342 'You are her [Zelda's] ideal ...': Dr Robert S. Carroll to FSF, 25 June 1936.
343 In it Dr Meyer said that Carroll had ... : Dr Robert S. Carroll, *What Price Alcohol?*, Macmillan, New York, 1941, p. ix.
343 A nurse who was at the hospital ...: Miss Gertrude Sykes to NM, 26 July 1963.
344 Scottie was sent to camp and Scott wrote her there ... : FSF to Scottie, 16 July 1936.
344 He and Zelda made plans to meet for lunch ... : FSF to ZSF, 27 July 1936: They sent for a bone specialist and he said it would have to be set immediately or else I would never be able to raise my arm as high as my shoulder again so they gave me gas ... and I fell asleep thinking you were in the room and saying, "Yes, I *am* going to stay; after all it's my husband." I woke up with a plaster cast that begins below my navel, extends upward and goes west out an arm.'
344 Scott told Perkins, 'I have been ...': *Letters*, p. 266.
344 A woman who worked at the inn remembered ... : Mrs Julia Lytle to NM, interview, 25 July 1963.
345 'He would cry over the phone ...': ibid.
345 The secretary he hired that summer ... : I am indebted to Myra Champion of the Pack Memorial Public Library in Asheville, North Carolina, for this information regarding the late Martha Marie Shank's reminiscences about Fitzgerald.
346 At a New Year's costume ball ... : Dr Robert S. Carroll to Dr Thomas Rennie, 6 January and 28 May 1937.
346 'We were careful with Zelda ...': Miss Mary Porter to NM, interview, 1 August 1963.
346 He wrote Perkins about 'Such stray ...': *Letters*, p. 269.

347 'I hadn't planned to meet Scott . . .': Carl Van Vechten to NM, interview, 17 April 1963.

347 'She was rather reserved . . .': Landon Ray to NM, interview, 25 July 1963.

348 'Have fun – I envy you and everybody . . .': ZSF to FSF, n.d.

348 Miss Graham has written movingly of their love . . . : Sheilah Graham and Gerold Frank, *Beloved Infidel*, Henry Holt and Company, New York, 1958, pp. 174–5.

348 She remembers: '. . . it seemed to me . . .': Sheilah Graham to NM, interview, 13 September 1968.

349 'I wish we were astride the tope of New York taxis . . .': ZSF to FSF, n.d.

349 'Zelda is no better . . .': FSF to Beatrice Dance, 27 November 1937.

349 'Your mother was better . . .': *Letters*, p. 22.

349 There was always a puritanical streak . . . : Graham, *Beloved Infidel*, p. 248.

350 'I have, of course, my eternal hope that a miracle . . .': FSF to Dr Robert S. Carroll, 4 March 1938.

350 'And if the aforesaid miracle . . .': ibid.

351 Zelda was irritable with both the golf . . . : FSF to Dr Robert S. Carroll, 7 April 1938.

351 'All this isn't pretty on my part . . .': ibid.

351 When he had lived like a vegetable in Tryon . . . : ibid.

351 Later in her life Miss Graham said . . . : Sheilah Graham to NM, interview, 13 September 1968.

351 He would never again, he swore . . . : *Letters*, p. 28.

352 Scott answered the doctor that his recommendations lacked . . . : FSF to Dr Robert S. Carroll, 19 April 1938.

353 'Supposing Zelda at best would be a lifelong . . .': FSF to Dr Robert S. Carroll, 19 May 1938.

353 'I love the casual gallantry of a gray March . . .': ZSF, Black Notebook. In September 1939, one of Zelda's doctors reported to Dr Rennie that she was writing unintelligible notes for a 'philosophical book'.

355 Mrs Sayre entered into the dispute . . . : Mrs A. D. Sayre to FSF, 26 April 1938.

356 He wrote Scottie: 'Do try . . .': *Letters*, p. 31.

356 It was a casual remark, but it underlined the complicity . . . : ibid., p. 40.

356 'a sense of partnership, . . .': *Letters*, p. 31.

356 Zelda wrote Scott: 'Scottie is the prettiest . . .': ZSF to FSF, n.d. (ca. June 1938).

357 'When I was your age I lived . . .': *Letters*, pp. 32–3.

358 Fitzgerald wrote her: '. . . quite possibly . . .': ibid., p. 26.

358 She sent him a postcard from the Brasserie . . . : Scottie to FSF, 7 August 1938.

358 The city was for her 'bliss . . .': ZSF to FSF, n.d. (ca. September 1938).

358 'It fill[s] me with dread to witness . . .': ZSF to FSF, n.d. (ca. fall 1938).

359 They also saw Scott's film *Three Comrades* . . . : ZSF to FSF, n.d. (ca. fall 1938).

359 'I am so sick of the moralistic tone . . .': ZSF to FSF, n.d. (ca. fall 1938).

359 She pressed for release in her letters to Scott . . . : ZSF to FSF, n.d. This terrible reduction of life – the essential submission to routine that happens to people who are hospitalized for lengthy periods of time – is caught perfectly in Frederick Exley's *A Fan's Notes*. However, for what I take to be the essence of the special fury, terror and revenge of the insane see Blaise Cendrar, *Moravagine*.

359 She would plead to him: 'D.O. *Won't* . . .': ZSF to FSF, n.d.

360 'Don't give up anything to get these . . .': ZSF to FSF, n.d.

360 Christmas 1938 she spent in Montgomery . . . : FSF to Rosalind Smith, 21 December 1938.

360 Scott wrote Rosalind: 'Imagine Zelda running amuk . . .': ibid.

361 Rosalind, he wrote Mrs Sayre, 'seems to feel . . .': FSF to Mrs A. D. Sayre, 3 January 1939.

361 'You made a great impression . . .': *Letters*, pp. 54–5.

361 She wrote Scott: 'Havannah is probably . . .': ZSF to FSF, n.d. (ca. end of January 1939).

362 'It seems useless to wait any more . . .': ZSF to FSF, n.d. (ca. end of April 1939).

363 'We were all afraid when she went off . . .': Miss Mary Porter to NM, interview, 1 August 1963.

363 'Don't feel bad. You were so sweet . . .': ZSF to FSF, n.d. (ca. end of April 1939).

363 'You were a peach throughout the whole trip . . .': *Letters*, p. 105.

364 Scott, who was undergoing financial and health . . . : ibid., pp. 57–8.

364 'Dearest: I trust that you will not resent this . . .': ZSF to FSF, n.d. (ca. summer 1939).

365 After all Scott had been through . . . : FSF to Dr R. Burke Suitt, 5 July 1939.

365 'She is a dominant little girl . . .': FSF to Dr Suitt, 27 July 1939.

366 But to Scott she confided her aloneness: 'My tennis progresses . . .': ZSF to FSF, n.d. (ca. summer 1939).

366 'Roads lace the mountains to earth . . .': ZSF to FSF, n.d. (ca. late summer 1939).

366 'Be brown and happy . . .': ZSF to Scottie, n.d.

366 Scott once wrote Scottie, 'Think of the enormous . . .': *Letters*, p. 51.

367 'If you flew East I'd be glad . . .': ZSF to FSF, n.d.

367 'When you come won't you bring me another pair . . .': ZSF to FSF, n.d.

367 'If Alabama should prove an unfortunate . . .': ZSF to FSF, n.d.

367 'As you know I tried to give Zelda . . .': FSF to Dr Robert S. Carroll, 27 September 1939.

368 'I am almost penniless . . .': *Letters*, p. 110.

368 'After her, you are my next consideration . . .': ibid.

368 'Needless to say, your letter somewhat hurt me . . .': ZSF to FSF, n.d.

369 He wrote Scottie: 'Look! I have begun to write something . . .': *Letters*, pp. 61–2.

369 'For better or worse Scottie and I form . . .': FSF to Dr Robert S. Carroll, 20 October 1939.

369 Scott sent *Collier's* magazine . . . : Andrew Turnbull, *Scott Fitzgerald*, Charles Scribner's Sons, New York, 1962, p. 303.

369 'She doesn't complain . . .': FSF to Dr Robert S. Carroll, n.d. (ca. 31 October 1939).

369 Zelda wrote him: 'I'm sorry . . .': ZSF to FSF, n.d.

370 'Dearest: I am always grateful for all the loyalties . . .': ZSF to FSF, n.d.

370 'Zelda does not wear a bit of make up . . .': I am grateful to Mrs Laura Guthrie Hearne for permitting me to quote this entry, 25 November 1939, from her diary.

370 At Highland she was considered well enough . . . : Dr Robert S. Carroll to FSF, 3 November 1939. Miss Mary Porter to NM, interview, 1 August 1963.

371 She wrote Scott: 'I sent word that I ultimately . . .': ZSF to FSF, n.d. (ca. winter 1939).

371 She protested bitterly to Scott: 'To waste . . .': ZSF to FSF, n.d. ca. winter 1939).

371–2 'I feel that this is your obligation . . .': ibid.

372 'There isn't forever left to either of us . . .': ZSF to FSF, n.d. (ca. winter 1939–1940).

372 But she wrote him: '. . . a person *could* . . .': ZSF to FSF, n.d. (ca. winter 1939–1940).

372 'Darling: you were sweet to 'phone me . . .': ZSF to FSF, n.d.

372 A week later she sent him another . . . : ZSF to FSF, n.d. (postmarked 13 February 1940).

373 At Highland she and Dr Carroll reached a compromise . . . : ZSF to FSF, n.d. (ca. end of February 1940).

373 Scott replied, 'Your letter was a complete surprise . . .': FSF to Dr Robert S. Carroll, 8 March 1940.

373 'I will be very, very happy . . .': ZSF to FSF, n.d. (ca. March 1940).

374 'As soon as I have renewed associations . . .': ZSF to FSF, n.d. (ca. March 1940).

374 Dr Robert S. Carroll to FSF, 6 April 1940.

Chapter 19

377 Carefully Scott explained to Zelda the terms . . . : *Letters*, p. 114.

377 'I think of you and the many mornings . . .': ZSF to FSF, n.d.

378 'To this sort of town a beau . . .': ZSF to FSF, n.d.

378 She told Scott she prayed for him . . . : ibid.

378 'I wish you read books . . .': *Letters*, p. 115.

378 'I should have said in my letter . . .': ibid., p. 117.

378 'I don't write; and I don't paint . . .': ZSF to FSF, n.d.

379 He wrote Zelda: 'You remember your old idea . . .': ibid., pp. 118–19.

379 Later on the same day, 7 June, Scott wrote Scottie . . . : ibid., p. 77.

380 For it seemed to him that she was at last proving . . . : ibid., p. 78.

380 'Your mother's utterly endless mulling . . .': ibid., pp. 78–9.

380 'Twenty years ago *This Side of Paradise* . . .': ibid., p. 119.

380–81 'I WON'T BE ABLE TO STICK THIS . . .': ZSF to FSF, 18 June 1940 (11.50 a.m.).

381 'DISREGARD TELEGRAM AM FINE . . .': ZSF to FSF, 18 June 1940 (2.46 p.m.).

381 'There's a point beyond which families . . .': FSF to Scottie, 19 June 1940.

381 Relieved, Fitzgerald wrote them . . . : *Letters*, p. 83.

381 When Scottie left for Cambridge Zelda felt . . . : ZSF to FSF, n.d. (ca. end of June 1940).

381 'I do wish you were sketching . . .': *Letters*, p. 121.

382 'I know it will be dull going . . .': ibid., p. 89.

382 'Things are so different than when I was young . . .': ZSF to FSF, n.d. (ca. summer 1940).

383 'I have been as an Angel with Halo . . .': Scottie to FSF, n.d. (ca. summer 1940).

383 'What proms and games? . . .': *Letters*, p. 62.

383 He asked her to question herself . . . : ibid., p. 91.

383 All he really cared about . . . : ibid., p. 98.

384 'It was partly that times changed . . .': *Letters*, p. 128.

384 On 28 September 1940, Scott wrote . . . : ibid., p. 125.

384 Zelda had forgotten his birthday . . . : ZSF to FSF, n.d. (ca. end September 1940).

384 In his next weekly letter Scott . . . : *Letters*, p. 126.

384 He still complained of a fever . . . : ibid.

384 'I am deep in the novel, living in it . . .': *Letters*, p. 128.

384 In the nostalgic mood which now often imbued . . . : ZSF to FSF, n.d.

385 Scott's life with Sheilah Graham was a quiet one . . . : Sheilah Graham to NM, interview, 13 September 1968.

385 Sometimes they talked about Zelda . . . : ibid.

386 'Everything is my novel now . . .': *Letters*, p. 131.

386 'It is odd that the heart is . . .': ibid., p. 132.

386 In order to avoid the strain of climbing . . . : The description of Scott's death is based on *Beloved Infidel*, pp. 322–30.

387 Harold Ober called Zelda . . . : Mrs Ober to NM, interview, 3 March 1964.

387 'In retrospect it seems as if he . . .': ZSF to Harold Ober, 24 December 1940.

387 'I have been so terribly shocked by Scott's death . . .': Edmund Wilson to ZSF, 27 December 1940.

388 Never again 'with his pockets full of promise . . .': ZSF to Edmund Wilson, 1 January 1941.

388 She said Scott would be remembered . . . : ZSF to Rosalind Smith n.d.

389 Maxwell Perkins showed Edmund Wilson the manuscript of *The Last Tycoon* . . . : Edmund Wilson to NM, 19 January 1968.

389 When he was finished he placed Fitzgerald . . . : See Mr Wilson's Foreword to *The Last Tycoon*, p. xi.

389 In the review he struck a note that has reverberated ... : Stephen Vincent Benét, 'The Last Tycoon' (*The Saturday Review*, 1941) in *F. Scott Fitzgerald: The Man and His Work*, edited by Alfred Kazin, pp. 131–2.

390 He would have agreed completely with a note Scott ... : General notes for *The Last Tycoon*.

390 After Zelda read the novel she wrote Wilson ... : ZSF to Edmund Wilson, 5 November 1941.

390 'I confess I don't like the heroine ...': ZSF to Mrs Bayard Turnbull, 13 November 1941.

Chapter 20

391 'Although you may not like it ...': ZSF to FSF, n.d.

391 By the summer of 1942 she was writing Mrs Turnbull ... : ZSF to Mrs Bayard Turnbull, n.d.

392 Later in the manuscript the Judge says a new wing ... : *CT*, Chapter I, p. 18. The pagination of *Caesar's Things* is not at all orderly. For example, the title page of the manuscript is preceded by a torn page of typescript. The title page reads (and this is handwritten in pencil):

Caesar's Things –
Chapter I
by
Zelda Fitzgerald
child –
clarify the Epic

There are then five handwritten pages, a quarter-page of typescript followed by twenty-one pages of typscript of varying size. There are three page ones. Chapter IV begins on page 18. Rather than this stew of pages, I will give chapter and pagination as Zelda has it.

392 'The child was dead from strain and effort ...': *CT*, Chapter I, p. 20.

393 'What right have you to stop me? ...': ibid.

393 'Before she could say anything ...': ibid., p. 21.

393 'That God would let this happen ...': ibid.

394 'Janno was dead, and dying ...': *CT*, Chapter I. There is no page number given to this brief slip of typescript. It falls between pp. 22 and 23.

394 The Judge is saying, 'You've ruined her ...' ibid., p. 22.

394 'A successful life is able to summon ...': ibid., p. 23.

395 A voice speaks to her from the well ... : *CT*, Chapter III, p. 7.

395 Then there are more voices and they turn grim ... : ibid., p. 8.

395 ... to a 'golden kingdom asleep ...': ibid.

395 It becomes a theatre curtain, the curtain 'melts ...': ibid., p. 9.

395 'Seduction, theft, kid-napping ...': ibid., p. 10.

395 One of the men is in uniform ... : ibid.

396 The men accuse her of looking 'dissolute ...': ibid., p. 11.

396 The scene is summarized: 'The weak dark men ...': ibid.

397 At one point Janno is sitting on a throne . . . : ibid., p. 12. It is entirely possible, I believe, to read a good deal of this novel as a fantasized memoir, a sort of parable about madness itself. In order to read it at all you have to float – I can think of no other way to express it – on the surfaces of Zelda's prose.

397 'Janno . . . wished that her mother had told her ₄₄₂': *CT*, Chapter IV, p. 22.

397 'Then something happened . . .': ibid.

397 Later in the manuscript Zelda writes that what happened to Janno . . . : ibid., p. 23.

398 'In some of the dreams he lived in a dark . . .': ibid., p. 29.

398 She has been equivocal about marrying . . . : ibid., p. 32.

398 'So they were desperately in love . . .': *CT*, Chapter V, p. 44.

398 Zelda calls this phase of Janno's life . . . : ibid., p. 32.

398 And Janno, who is not content to become Jacob's 'evocateur ₄₄₄': ibid., p. 33.

398 'He hated his sister . . . largely because . . .': ibid.

399 'Jacob went on doing whatever it was . . .': ibid., first page is not numbered.

399 She envies New York, where they are living . . . : ibid., p. 37₄

399 Suddenly Jacob decides to go to Europe . . . : ibid., p. 45.

399 'She was grateful and devoted . . .': ibid., p. 47.

399 Janno is busy 're-decorating . . .': *CT*, Chapter VI, p. 46.

399 'Everybody liked them as standard millionaires . . .': ibid., p. 48₄

400 At the parties among the rich . . . : ibid., p. 49.

400 'Janno had always been jealous . . .': ibid., p. 50.

400 'During the first shock of infidelities . . .': ibid., p. 51.

401 Janno calls it 'a gala emblem . . .': ibid., no page number given₄

401 'He and Charity put much effort into human . . .': ibid., p. 53₄

401 The Cornings give wonderful dinners . . . : ibid.

401 He perfects 'his garden, his gadgets . . .': ibid., p. 58.

401 'Corning said, "I want all these people to love . . ." ': ibid., no page number given. It falls between pp. 58 and 55.

401 'Now this was paradise . . .': *CT*., Chapter VII, p. 1.

402 Janno and Jacob have met the son of an advocate ₄₂ : ibid.

402 'Janno was vaguely baffled . . .': ibid., p. 2.

402 Jacob is rather bored; he 'didn't really like sitting . . .': ibid.

402 The villa on the Mediterranean becomes . . . : ibid., p. 3.

402 'She said she would; she was horrified . . . : ibid., p. 4₄

403 'She could not bring herself to deny . . .': ibid.

404 'Jacob littered his fire-place . . .': ibid., p. 5.

404 'How was she going to live . . .': ibid.

404 Then suddenly Jacob acts: ' "I'll get out of here . . ." ': ibid.

405 'He was gone . . . they had been much in love . . .': 'The Big Top', consists of seven typewritten pages, but the pagination begins at page 10. This quotation is from pp. 13–14.

406 'Nobody has ever measured, even the poets ₄₄₄': ibid., p. 15₄

Chapter 21

407 The inside of the cottage was simply furnished . . . : I am grateful to Dan Piper, Paul McLendon and Sayre Noble Godwin for their impressions of the inside of the house on Sayre Street.

408 In May and again in December of 1942 . . . : Newspaper clippings as well as a typed programme for both shows are in ZSF's clipping album.

408 She glares full face out of the painting . . . : See second section of illustrations. The painting is watercolour over a pencil sketch.

408 'I trust that life will use you far less . . .': ZSF to Scottie, n.d.

409 In February 1943, Scottie married . . . : Mrs Harold Ober to NM, interview, 3 March 1964.

409 'Giving Scottie away must have brought . . .': ZSF to Harold Ober, 22 February 1943.

409 To Anne Ober, who made all of the wedding . . . : ZSF to Mrs Harold Ober, postmarked 22 February 1943.

409 'Do not consider these mine; your life . . .': ZSF to Scottie, n.d. (ca. spring 1943).

410 Andrew Turnbull, who had just become . . . : Andrew Turnbull to NM, interview, 6 August 1964.

410 She wrote Anne Ober . . . : ZSF to Mrs Harold Ober, 11 August 1943.

410 Lucy Goldthwaite remembers seeing Zelda at a garden . . . : Miss Lucy Goldthwaite to NM, interview, 20 May 1965.

411 In February she wrote Wilson: 'You should redeem . . .': ZSF to Edmund Wilson, 1 February 1944.

411 'You are much to be respected . . .': ZSF to Edmund Wilson, 6 March 1944.

411 Within a few months she was writing Scottie . . . : ZSF to Scottie, n.d.

411 She told Scottie: 'Scott would have been so pleased . . .': ZSF to Scottie, n.d. (ca. spring 1944).

412 Sometimes she got tired of making the best . . . : ZSF to Scottie, n.d.

412 'I always feel that Daddy was the key-note . . .': ZSF to Scottie, n.d.

412 She wrote Mrs Ober: 'I used to feel desperately sad . . .': ZSF to Mrs Harold Ober, 26 June 1945.

413 She told Scottie to avoid . . . : ZSF to Scottie, n.d. (ca. summer? 1945).

413 At the beginning of 1946 she returned to Highland . . . : Landon Ray to NM, interview, 25 July 1963.

413 Immediately after the birth of Timothy . . . : ZSF to Scottie, n.d. (ca. late April 1946).

413 She felt dated; 'it brought back our honey-moon . . .': ZSF to Scottie, n.d. (ca. 1 May 1946).

414 'It is completely incredible to me . . .': ZSF to Ludlow Fowler, n.d.

414 Mrs Biggs recalls that she had picked some berries . . . : Mrs Anna Biggs to NM, interview, 9 June 1963.

414 Mrs Biggs remembers: 'John mentioned that it was time . . .': ibid.

415 'She was a marvellous woman, big . . .': Mrs Harold Ober to NM, interview, 3 March 1964.

415 She wrote Anne Ober that she would despair . . . : ZSF to Mrs Harold Ober, 29 October 1946.

415 It kept her from sleeping half the night . . . : ZSF to Mrs Harold Ober, 5 November 1946.

415 Paul McLendon met Zelda for the first time . . . : Paul McLendon to NM, 6 November 1965.

416 'I am not au-courrant with the affairs & . . .': ZSF to Paul McLendon, 24 May 1946.

416 '. . . the world is fair game to the greedy . . .': ZSF to Paul McLendon, 16 October 1946.

416 Paul realized that Zelda enjoyed his company . . . : Paul McLendon to NM, 6 and 27 November 1965.

417 Once after Paul had invited her for a day at Tuscaloosa . . . : ZSF to Paul McLendon, 5 November 1946.

417 But one afternoon Mrs Sayre told him Zelda couldn't . . . : Paul McLendon to NM, 27 November 1965.

417 'The time was early, early spring . . .': ibid.

418 'He sends His angels to help . . .': ZSF to Paul McLendon, 10 March 1947.

418 Henry Dan Piper was discharged from the Army . . . : I am especially indebted to Mr Piper for his generosity in allowing me to draw freely from his own interview with Zelda on 13 and 14 March 1947. I interviewed Mr Piper on 17 November 1965.

422 When they were finished they returned to her little house . . . : It was at this point, Mr Piper recalls, that Zelda told him about the companion portrait of Scott which she said Condé Nast had. Before giving him the self-portrait she had showed him a number of her paintings, then she said something to this effect: 'Maybe you'd like something really big. Would you like a self-portrait?' Mr Piper says that she then unrolled it. 'I told her I thought it ought to be at Princeton, and she seemed quite flattered by my interest.'

422 Mrs Sayer, Marjorie, and Livye Hart . . . : Mrs Harry Ridgeway to NM, interview, 1 June 1968.

422 She wanted to get home, she said, to see 'our lillies . . .': ZSF to Mrs A. D. Sayre, n.d. (ca. March 1948).

422 Zelda told her she had gained twenty pounds . . . : ZSF to Scottie, n.d. (postmarked 9 March 1948).

423 'Anyhow: to-day there is promise of spring . . .': ibid.

423 Zelda died with them . . . : The nurse who first discovered the fire said in a newspaper report that 'on the night of the fire she had personally given sedatives to . . . Mrs F. Scott Fitzgerald.' The Asheville *Times*, 27 March 1948, p. 11.

423 Her body was identified by a charred slipper . . . : It was further identified by recent dental work.

423 It was St Patrick's Day, 17 March 1948 . . . : Mrs Bayard Turnbull to NM, 30 September 1965.

INDEX

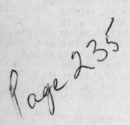